Scribal Culture and the Making of the Hebrew Bible

Scribal Culture

and the Making of the Hebrew Bible

KAREL VAN DER TOORN

HARVARD UNIVERSITY PRESS

Cambridge, Massachusetts, and London, England

Designed by Gwen Nefsky Frankfeldt

First Harvard University Press paperback edition, 2009.

Library of Congress Cataloging-in-Publication Data:
Toorn, K. van der.
  Scribal culture and the making of the Hebrew Bible / Karel van der Toorn.
    p. cm.
  Includes bibliographical references and index.
  ISBN 978-0-674-02437-3 (cloth : alk. paper)
  ISBN 978-0-674-03254-5 (pbk.)
  1. Bible. O.T.—History.   I. Title.
BS1130.T66 2007
221.6′6—dc22   2006049603

Contents

Acknowledgments

I owe the opportunity to write this book to the board of the Universiteit van Amsterdam, which granted me a generous sabbatical leave after my service as dean of the Faculty of Humanities. The leave allowed me to pursue an interest that had been with me since the completion of my book *Family Religion in Babylonia, Syria, and Israel,* which appeared in 1996. I had decided at that time to turn my attention to the scribes and scholars of the ancient Near East in an attempt to understand the social context of the religious writings they had produced. The Hebrew Bible presented itself as a natural focus for my research.

As my own thinking on the matter developed, it became obvious that I was working on an introduction to the Bible. Such introductions are familiar to teachers and students, but the one I saw emerging from my studies was unlike other representatives of the genre. I was exploring the scribal culture of the Near East as a means to understanding the making of the Hebrew Bible. The individual books of the Bible were of less interest to me than the social and intellectual background of the scribes behind them. The focus on the scribal milieu opened up new avenues of approach to the books of the Bible.

I did my research and writing at the Netherlands Institute of Advanced Studies in Wassenaar and at the Netherlands Institute for the Near East in Leiden. The pleasant and scholarly environment of these institutes has been a source of inspiration and encouragement. Several colleagues, some from places other than Wassenaar and Leiden, read parts of the manuscript; Joris Borghouts, Christopher Rollston, Mark S. Smith, and Marten Stol saved me from some serious errors, offered useful suggestions, and supplied me with a score of references.

Writing is usually a solitary pursuit; thinking often is too. Thus I feel all the more fortunate to have a few people whom I consider friends as well as intellectual sparring partners. My discussions with Peter van Rooden, Mark Smith, and Liz Bloch-Smith were so absorbing at times that it is difficult to say who came up with certain ideas that I eventually considered mine. Though I remain responsible for everything that is in this book, some of the better ideas are likely to go back to them.

Literature appearing after the completion of the manuscript at the end of 2005 has not been included in the Bibliography.

Amsterdam, December 2006

Abbreviations

ABD	*Anchor Bible Dictionary*, ed. David Noel Freedman, 6 vols. New York: Doubleday, 1992.
AfO	*Archiv für Orientforschung*
AOAT	Alter Orient und Altes Testament
CM	Cuneiform Monographs
COS	*The Context of Scripture*, ed. William W. Hallo and K. Lawson Younger, 3 vols. Leiden: Brill, 1997–.
DN	Divine name
JAOS	*Journal of the American Oriental Society*
JBL	*Journal of Biblical Literature*
JCS	*Journal of Cuneiform Studies*
JNES	*Journal of Near Eastern Studies*
JSOT	*Journal for the Study of the Old Testament*
K.	Tablets from Kuyunjik, as numbered in the British Museum
LÄ	*Lexikon der Ägyptologie*, ed. W. Helck, E. Otto, and W. Westendorf, 7 vols. Wiesbaden: Harrassowitz, 1972–1992.
LXX	Septuagint
MT	Masoretic text
NJPS	*Tanakh: The Holy Scriptures: The New Jewish Publication Society Translation according to the Traditional Hebrew Text*
OBO	Orbis Biblicus et Orientalis
RA	*Revue d'Assyriologie*

RIA	*Reallexikon der Assyriologie,* ed. Erich Ebeling et al. Berlin: W. de Gruyter, 1928–.
SAA	State Archives of Assyria
SBL	Society of Biblical Literature
VT	*Vetus Testamentum*
ZA	*Zeitschrift für Assyriologie*
ZAW	*Zeitschrift für die alttestamentliche Wissenschaft*

Scribal Culture and the Making of the Hebrew Bible

INTRODUCTION

Who wrote the Bible? The question is nearly as old as the Bible it-self. Jewish sages, quoted in the Talmud (*Baba Bathra,* 15a), were al-ready asking it, and it still echoes today in the minds of scholars and in the titles of textbooks.[1] For as long as the Bible has had the status of sa-cred book, people have been intrigued by its origins.

The Bible that this book is concerned with is the Hebrew Bible, adopted by the Christian church as the Old Testament. Its origins go back to early Israel. It is something of a paradox that the Israelites, steeped as they were in an oral culture, should leave a book as their leg-acy to the world. Their own world was one without books. Reading and writing were restricted to a professional elite; the majority of the population was nonliterate. Even if this observation seems perfunctory, it needs to be made, since modern readers of the Bible are prone to project their own book culture on the people of the Bible. Though Ju-daism has been defined as a "religion of the book," the book in ques-tion stems from a culture of the spoken word.

If we are to understand the making of the Hebrew Bible, we must fa-miliarize ourselves with the scribal culture that produced it. That cul-ture was the culture of a literate elite. The scribes who manufactured the Bible were professional writers affiliated to the temple of Jerusalem.

They practiced their craft in a time in which there was neither a trade in books nor a reading public of any substance. Scribes wrote for scribes. To the public at large, the books of the Bible were icons of a body of knowledge accessible only through the oral instruction presented by religious experts. The text of the Hebrew Bible was not part of the popular culture. The Bible was born and studied in the scribal workshop of the temple. In its fundamental essence, it was a book of the clergy.

Most of those involved in the making of the Bible left neither a name nor a biography. We do not know them individually. We can identify their milieu as that of the scribal elite, and it is that milieu that holds the key to the origins of the Bible. It can be circumscribed more narrowly as that of the scribal workshop of the Second Temple, active in the period between 500 and 200 B.C.E. The propagation of the books that were to constitute the Bible originates with the same institution. The scribes we will be looking at were scholars and teachers: they wrote, edited, copied, gave public readings, and interpreted. If the Bible became the Word of God, it was due to their presentation. Both the production and the promotion of the Hebrew Bible were the work of the scribes. The story of the making of the Bible is the story of the scribes behind the Bible.

Evidence: Internal, External, Comparative

The evidence on which the case for the Bible as a product of the scribal workshop must be built is of three kinds: some of it is internal, in the Bible itself; some external, illuminating the Bible from outside; and some comparative. It is essential to take these three types of evidence together. No one piece is by itself conclusive; in combination, their witness is compelling.

The *internal* evidence consists primarily in the unintentional traces of scribal involvement exhibited in the text of the Bible. Such evidence is to be sharply distinguished from the explicit references to authorship, textual fixation, and transmission. While the latter testimony deserves a careful assessment, it is intentional and therefore subject to caution.

Witnesses frame the truth as they see fit, and the same is true of superscriptions, colophons, and other text-related observations. Thus the
data provided in superscriptions to the prophetic books are quite misleading if they are interpreted in terms of actual authorship; Isaiah,
Jeremiah, and the other prophets did not write the books that the
superscriptions attribute to them. The clues we must look for are those
traditionally associated with the redaction criticism of the Bible: editorial expansions, scribal annotations, seams and incongruities in the
text, and the like.

When I speak of *external* evidence, I refer to extrabiblical material
from the time of the Bible that has the potential to shed light on its
making. This material is not comparative but has a direct bearing on
the people of the Bible, their history and institutions, and the development of the biblical text. Oftentimes the information provided by
epigraphic discoveries, such as the Samaria papyri or the texts from the
Jewish colony in Elephantine (Egypt), illuminates the background of
the Bible. At times the accounts of later writers, such as Josephus, add
pertinent data to the picture. In some cases, most notably that of the
scrolls from the caves near Qumran, the extrabiblical evidence throws
into relief the history of the very text of the Bible. In the latter respect,
the Greek translation of the Bible, traditionally known as the Septuagint, must also be taken into account. Parabiblical writings, known as
the Apocrypha, are an important source of information as well.

If the present study distinguishes itself from most other contributions
on the subject, it is mainly because of the extensive use it makes of the
available *comparative* evidence. The Bible is not the only collection of
writings from the ancient Near East. Babylonians, Egyptians, and Syri-
ans produced a wealth of written texts as well, canonized by virtue of
their secular transmission through schools and libraries. These texts
are comparable to the Hebrew Bible in more than one respect. Many of
them had the status of revelation transmitted by a god or a famous ancestor. They commanded the respect that written texts often command
in oral cultures. The very notions of books and authorship were very
different from what they are today. The writings of the ancient Near

East were created in a world in which there were neither books nor authors in the modern sense of those terms. Instead of books, there was the stream of tradition; instead of authors, there were scribes.

Once it is recognized that the Hebrew Bible is a product of the scribal workshop, the written evidence from the rest of the Near East becomes particularly significant on account of the vast amount of data on the scribal culture of the times. Two centuries of archaeology and deciphering have given us unprecedented access to the world of the Babylonian and Egyptian scribes. Their recruitment, training, career possibilities, social standing, professional identity, and the like can now be reconstructed in detail on the basis of reliable evidence. Such evidence is especially welcome in view of the dearth of data on the scribes of the Hebrew Bible. By good fortune, the scribal culture of the ancient Near East was anything but parochial: texts and traditions circulated internationally, scribes moved around; the scribal spirit was cosmopolitan. Evidence on scribal culture in Mesopotamia and Egypt, then, is often pertinent to scribal culture in Judah as well.

Taken by itself, each type of evidence is lopsided and might give rise to biased reconstructions. When not informed by external data, the internal evidence may easily get caught up in the circular reasoning by which a given theory frames or even creates the evidence. External evidence, on the other hand, is by definition circumstantial. We cannot use data that are not available; the risk of general inferences from particular data that happen to be extant is real. And comparative evidence may be overrated and lead to a kind of blueprint thinking or "patternism" that does not respect the unique features of the scribal culture behind the Bible. It is necessary to be aware of the potential dangers of using one type of evidence in isolation from the others. If the reconstruction defended in this book is to stand, it needs to be based on the combined witness of the three different types of evidence.

Plan of the Book

My investigation in this volume will follow a trajectory of four successive stages. Starting with a reconnaissance of the role of writing and authorship in antiquity, each stage builds on the outcome of the previous one, ending with an analysis of the historical process by which the books of the Bible were canonized as the Word of God.

Phase one of the investigation explores the place and function of written texts in the ancient Near East, and more specifically in Israel. Chapter 1 is devoted to the notion of books in antiquity, and Chapter 2 deals with the concept of authorship. An analysis of the available data leads me to conclude that the modern concept of books is unsuited to describe the written production from the ancient Near East. Prior to the Hellenistic era—that is, before ca. 300 B.C.E.—there were no books. There were documents, literary compilations, myths, collections of prayers, ritual prescriptions, chronicles, and the like, but no books, no trade in books, and no reading public of any substance. Written texts were the province of professionals. Insofar as literature reached a larger audience, it was by way of oral performance. To define the Bible as a collection of books, as implied in the Greek designation *biblia,* is an anachronism. The Bible is a repository of tradition, accumulated over time, that was preserved and studied by a small body of specialists.

Nor is the modern notion of authorship adequate to describe the realities of literary creation in antiquity. Books have authors, but the writers of texts of the ancient Near East are, as a rule, anonymous. That fact need not imply that there were no authors, simply that those who wrote the texts were not authors in our sense of the word. The authors of antiquity were artisans rather than artists. Our preoccupation with originality would have been foreign to them, nor did they care about intellectual property. What they admired was skill, technical mastery. The texts they produced were often coproductions—if not by a collective of scribes, then by means of a series of scribal redactions. In most cases, then, the quest for an individual author is pointless. The making of the Hebrew Bible is owed to the scribal class rather than a limited number of individuals. We should not be looking for authors but seeking to penetrate the mind-set of the scribal elite.

Phase two of the investigation takes its cue from the fact that all written records are scribal products. To discover the origins of the Bible, we must therefore study the scribal milieu and its modes of text production. Three chapters deal with these matters. Two of them explore the world of the scribes: one on the basis of texts from Mesopotamia and Egypt, the other on the basis of the biblical material. The comparative evidence presented in Chapter 3 provides a quite detailed reconstruction of the scribal milieu. Recruited from the social upper class, scribes went through years of training before they exercised their profession. Those who followed an advanced training became the scholars of antiquity. They were responsible for the creation, preservation, and interpretation of the classic texts of their time. Their professional center, materially as well as spiritually, was the workshop of the temple.

Chapter 4, on the scribes behind the Bible, locates them primarily among the clergy of the time. This identification is important for various reasons. It connects the scribes responsible for the Bible with the temple, and indicates a specialization within the priesthood focusing on writing and scholarship. The flourishing of scribal culture that produced the Hebrew Bible occurred in Judah in the Second Temple period, more specifically in the Persian and the Hellenistic eras (ca. 500–200 B.C.E.). There was an intimate link between the scribal profession as it took shape in the Persian era and the application and interpretation of the written Law (the Torah). Scribes were more than lawyers, however. Their training familiarized them with the works known as the Prophets and with the Writings as well. The Jewish scribes developed into the scholars of the nation and the guardians of its literary heritage.

Scribes were craftsmen. In their dealings with texts, they applied the methods and techniques of their craft. Chapter 5 looks at the scribal modes of text production. Once again the comparative evidence is crucial for the recovery of scribal practices in Judah. The Hebrew Bible as we know it is the result of a series of scribal interventions; previous textual stages have not been preserved, with a few exceptions known mainly through the discoveries from Qumran. Matters present themselves differently for cuneiform literature. The textual history of the *Epic of Gilgamesh,* for example, can be traced through copies from successive periods spanning altogether more than two millennia. Editorial techniques such as expansion, conflation, substitution, resumption, and harmonization are all illustrated in the Mesopotamian texts. The inventory based on this evidence facilitates the understanding of similar procedures reflected in the text of the Hebrew Bible.

In phase three of the investigation, the insights gained in phase two are applied to the Hebrew Bible. Two case studies illuminate the way in which the books of the Hebrew Bible took shape: Chapter 6 is devoted to Deuteronomy, Chapter 7 to an analysis of the textual history of Jeremiah. Since these two textual bodies stand for the Law and the Prophets, respectively, they are well suited to illustrate the making of the Hebrew Bible as a whole. Both Deuteronomy and Jeremiah exhibit successive layers of scribal intervention. The final compositions reflect the involvement of generations of scribes. While displaying great respect for the text as they had received it, they added their interpretations, framework, and other textual expansions. Deuteronomy was one of the first books of the Hebrew Bible to reach its final editorial shape, in the early Persian period. The Jeremiah tradition, on the other hand, was still in a state of flux in the Hellenistic era.

Phase four turns from the production process of the Hebrew Bible toward the factors that might explain its impact. Two concepts are of paramount importance in this connection: revelation and canon. Each is the subject of a separate chapter. In Chapter 8 the concept of revelation is shown to be as old as the Bible itself, harking back to the practices of divination and prophecy. What is new is the application of the concept to a collection of written texts. There are precedents for the phenomenon in Mesopotamia and Egypt, where the concept of revelation was invoked to buttress the authority of received texts. The Jewish scribes, too, used the concept as a means of persuasion, but it was not their only strategy. Texts might also be presented as a legacy from famous ancestors from a venerable past, to enhance their authority with an audience that might otherwise be reluctant to accept them.

The clinching factor in the transformation of the writings of the Hebrew scribes into the Word of God was the canonization of the biblical literature, described in Chapter 9. Canonization is an act of authority by which a limited number of texts are imposed upon a particular community as binding for all members, for all times. The biblical canon is typically a list of works, as their combination into one volume (the one Bible) does not occur until the birth of the codex. This list is closed. It is comparable to the catalogue of a library or the curriculum of a school but is nonetheless a category in its own right.

Scribal Culture and the Bible

The impact of the Hebrew Bible in the history of Western civilization is a triumph of scribal culture. Scribal culture did not create the religious appetite, but it did find a way to cater to that appetite with the invention of a book. The successful promotion of the Bible as the Word of God changed the nature of religious devotion. Pilgrimage, fasting, and sacrifice were not abandoned but took their place alongside the chanting and studying of texts, as a major means of personal edification and of pleasing God. Reading became an act of devotion.

If the origins of the Bible cannot be solved in terms of authors, the story behind the Bible is not for that reason any less fascinating. The Bible is an exceptional book, not because of some exceptional minds that wrote it but because of the exceptional way in which it came into being. Being a product of the scribal workshop, the Bible owes its existence to generations of scribes, each new one continuing the work of previous ones. This study is dedicated to investigating the universe of those scribes: their social role and status, their training, the arts of their craft, their ways of thinking; in brief, scribal culture. Whereas the individual scribes made themselves invisible in the texts they wrote, the Hebrew Bible is both a witness and a monument to their collective work.

chapter one

BOOKS THAT ARE NOT BOOKS

Writing in the World of the Bible

We commonly think of the Bible as a book or a collection of books—and naturally so, one might argue: the very name of the Bible goes back to the Greek word *biblia,* for "books."[1] Jewish writers referred to the Hebrew scriptures as "the books" (Dan 9:2) or "the holy books" (1 Macc 12:9) from the second century B.C.E. onward.[2] This has since become the accepted view of the Bible. It informs rabbinical discussions on the order and the authors of the biblical books, and explains our custom of speaking of the "Book of Genesis," the "Book of Isaiah," and the "Book of Job."

However old and widespread the notion of the Bible as a series of books may be, though, it is a misleading concept. The books of the Bible are not books in the modern sense of the word; to see them as such distorts the historical reality. There were no books in ancient Israel. Books are a Hellenistic invention, born in a time of increasing literacy as schools and libraries spread around the Mediterranean and in the Near East. Since the bulk of the Bible predates the Hellenistic era, calling it a collection of books is an anachronism.

If the books of the Bible are not books in the modern sense of the term, then what are they? To answer that question we must investigate the role of writing in early Israel and its Near Eastern context.[3] In this chapter, I propose to do just that. I will compare the practices of literary production in pre-Hellenistic Palestine with those that were current in ancient Mesopotamia. Historically, two factors have had a decisive impact on the nature of written documents in the ancient Near East: first, the fact that the civilizations of the time were at their core oral cultures, literacy being the prerogative of an elite; and second, the material conditions of writing in antiquity, meaning the writing materials that were used and the labor that was involved in the physical production of texts. We will see that neither the cultural nor the material conditions for writing were conducive to the development of a book culture, and that the first Jewish books date from the Hellenistic era.

Literacy in the Ancient Near East

The great civilizations of antiquity were oral cultures. Though the figures differ depending on place and period, literacy was always restricted to a small segment of society. The Mesopotamians were the first humans to write, but less than 5 percent of the population was actually literate.[4] In Egypt the rate of literacy was slightly higher than in Mesopotamia, but even the most generous estimates put it at no more than 7 percent of the population.[5] In the classical world the situation was not much different. Greece had an overall literacy rate of about 10 percent, yet it was still predominantly an oral culture, rhetoric being the foundation and eloquence the aim of education.[6]

Determining the level of literacy in the ancient Near East is not a matter of merely accumulating percentages and figures.[7] In the absence of incontrovertible evidence, estimated literacy rates fluctuate according to the motives, bias, and personal assumptions of modern scholars. Some authors exaggerate the presumed level of literacy whereas others tend to underrate it. Partly out of a reaction to the minimizing tendencies of earlier scholars, there is a modest trend toward higher estimates of literacy in antiquity.[8] However, even if basic reading skills were more common in certain places and periods than generally assumed, it is doubtful whether this constituted widespread literacy. The ability to decipher a letter, for instance, does not amount to an active command of the written tradition of a culture. "High literacy" was confined to a small group. For the majority of the population, word of mouth remained the principal channel of communication.

Whether the rate of literacy was higher in Israel than it was in Mesopotamia or Egypt is a matter of debate. While some authors are confident that writing was common practice in the lives of the Israelites,[9] others suggest that literacy was confined to a minority of scribes and priests.[10] The ideological overtones of the debate are hard to ignore.[11] However, the evidence suggests that the role of writing in Israel was about the same as elsewhere in the ancient Near East; the literacy rate was presumably similar to that in surrounding civilizations as well.

Some authors hold that the literacy rate in Palestine was higher than elsewhere because the Israelites used the alphabet. While it is true that the alphabetic script is considerably easier to learn than cuneiform or hieroglyphs, modern studies show that there is not an absolute correlation between the simplicity of the script and the level of literacy. If reading requires the mastery of some 3,000 signs, as in some logographic systems, the script is indeed an obstacle to popular literacy; but phonetic scripts, as once used in Mesopotamia and now in Japan, are not per se a greater deterrent to literacy than the alphabet.[12] The level of literacy depends on cultural values, social customs, and access to schooling more than on the ease with which a script can be mastered. The culture of the Israelites was predominantly oral. The ability to write down a name (Judg 8:14) or to read a letter (Lachish Letter 3) may have been quite common, but that does not mean Israel was a literate society. The transmission of cultural lore—stories of origins, legends of ancestors and heroes, dos and don'ts, professional skills and wisdom—was nearly always accomplished by word of mouth.

Written Texts for Oral Performance

The fact that the civilizations of antiquity were oral cultures had an impact on the texts that were committed to writing. In Babylonia and Israel, writing was mostly used to support an oral performance.[13] The native verbs for "reading" literally mean "to cry, to speak out loud" (Hebrew *qārā'*, Akkadian *šasû* and its by-form *šitassû*).[14] These verbs reflect the way texts were used. Written documents were read aloud, either to an audience or to oneself. Silent reading was highly unusual. Even the student who read in solitude "muttered" his text (Ps 1:2; compare Acts 8:30). So when someone was urged to read something assiduously, the phrase was that he should not allow the text "to depart from his mouth" (Josh 1:8).[15] Reading, in other words, was an oral activity.

Writing is a means of communication. In order for the message to reach its destination, however, the written text needed a voice. Texts were for the ears rather than the eyes; Isa 29:18 predicts a time in which also "the deaf will hear the words of a scroll [*sēper*]." Even such a mundane form of written communication as the letter usually required the intervention of someone who read its contents to the addressee. A messenger did not deliver the letter like a mailman; he announced its message, and the written letter served as aide-mémoire and means of verification. That is why Babylonian letters open with a formula addressed to the messenger: "To So-and-so speak as follows." For the few nonprofessionals who were able to read, the effort would be such that they would memorize a letter. As a military commander from Lachish observes, not without some pride, "Also, when I get a letter, once I have read it, then I can recite it back in its entirety."[16]

Other forms of communication in writing also needed the voice of a reader. For instance, in Mesopotamia and Egypt royal laws and decrees were promulgated through written texts. The reference to "those who write out evil decrees and compose iniquitous writings" in Isa 10:1 reflects this practice for Israel. Decrees were produced in numerous copies to be displayed in public places throughout the land, at city gates and temple gates, so as to inform the population. However, this alone would not have reached the general public. Dissemination was achieved through formal oral proclamation of these texts by appointed readers.[17] Thus, in Israel, the royal decision to prohibit sacrifice in local temples in order to centralize worship in Jerusalem was communicated to the population through copies of the decree that were posted at the gates and read out loud by public readers.[18]

The examples show that the invention of writing and the emergence of a written literature did not transform an oral culture overnight into a literate one. Writing has a profound impact on the intellectual development of a civilization, but so long as there is no industrial production of written texts, the spoken word remains the main channel of communication. Even the classic texts from Mesopotamia, familiar from the scribal curriculum, were designed for oral performance. The Old Babylonian tale of the Flood known as *Atraḫasis* is not a book or an essay but a "song" *(zamāru)*.

> This my song is for your [i.e., the god Ea's] praise.
> May the Igigi-gods hear [it] and extol your greatness to one another.
> I have sung of the Flood to all peoples: Hear![19]

Almost a thousand years later, myths newly written still referred to themselves as "songs." The epilogue to the *Song of Erra* specifies the rewards for those who promote the new composition:

> In the sanctuary of the god who honors this song,
> Abundance shall accumulate . . .
> The singer who chants it shall not die from pestilence,
> But his performance will be pleasing to king and prince.[20]

Atraḫasis and *Erra* illustrate that in Babylonia the products of creative writing could reach an audience only if a singer was willing to include them in his repertoire. Who but a few would have read the *Gilgamesh Epic?* The common people knew this work because they had heard it from the mouths of bards and singers.[21]

In Israel, written compositions were not produced for private reading either. Written texts reached their audience through oral delivery by a speaker. If prophets wrote—or had a secretary write—their message reached its audience through public readings. Habakkuk was ordered to write his prophecy down so that a herald might broadcast his message.

> Write down the prophecy,
> And inscribe it clearly on the tablets,
> So that a [town] crier may run with it.
>
> Hab 2:2[22]

Other instances of written prophecy had a similar goal. According to a narrative designed to authenticate the scroll of Jeremiah, Baruch the scribe wrote down the collected oracles of Jeremiah on a scroll. On a fast day, Baruch went to the temple and read these prophecies to the crowd of worshippers (Jer 36:1–10). Whether the narrative is historically accurate or not is beside the point; what matters is that it describes the custom of writing down texts with the intention of using them to give an oral performance.

Literary Style in Oral Cultures

Written for individual consumption by a solitary reader, books do not have to be read in one go. Their style and form allow the reader to take a break and then continue or to turn back and reread a few pages if he loses track. A book of this kind is not suitable for an oral performance. A story, a philosophical argument, or even a set of agricultural guidelines—any text with a linear plot and few redundancies—requires the kind of sustained attention an audience in an oral setting is unlikely to muster. Oral cultures dictate a particular style in written texts.[23]

In Israel and Babylonia, texts were an extension, so to speak, of the oral performers.[24] This is not to say that all texts were in origin oral artifacts, but that the oral delivery of the texts determined their style, even if they had originated in writing. The traditional texts from Israel and Mesopotamia are full of the stylistic devices of oral performance such as rhythm, repetition, stock epithets, standard phrases, and plots consisting of interrelated but relatively independent episodes. This holds true for narrative texts as well as exhortatory texts. The patriarchal stories in Genesis, just as the *Epic of Gilgamesh* in Babylonian literature, consist of a string of episodes owing their unity to the principal protagonists of the various stories. Their disposition is paratactic rather than hypotactic; the style is "additive rather than subordinative."[25]

Exhortatory texts are similar. Both in the Bible and in Babylonia, moral instruction preserved the oral form of proverbs or succinct observations, collected into larger literary units on the basis of catchwords or subject matter. The style is "aggregative rather than analytic."[26] Even Ben Sira, living in the second century B.C.E., continued to write like this. More philosophical works, such as Job and the *Babylonian Theodicy*, are not linear either; they progress by examining one issue from different angles.[27] Modern readers of these works, accustomed to the narrative structures of contemporary novels or the argumentative patterns of philosophical essays, are often left with the impression that no progress is being made at all.

Oral performance was not the only function of written texts in Israel and Babylonia. Writing also developed an archival function. Being first an aide-mémoire for messengers, heralds, and bards, texts came to be used secondarily as an extension or even a substitute for memory. Written texts could be used "for consultation," to quote an expression frequently found in Babylonian colophons.[28] What you do not remember, you can look up in your text. The use of writing for reference is especially prominent in texts that have an encyclopedic character, as is the case with law codes and handbooks. Thus the epilogue to the *Laws of Hammurabi* describes the wronged citizen coming to Hammurabi's stele to hear—from the mouth of a professional reader, presumably—his lawsuit and to examine his case.[29] In the reign of Esarhaddon, the exorcist Adadšumuşur consulted his house library before communicating the significance of a particular omen to the king.[30]

Law codes and handbooks have a common characteristic in that they are both compilations: the former of legal cases, the latter of omens, symptoms, formulas, and the like. Such biblical books as Leviticus, Psalms, and Proverbs have a similar structure: they are compilations, respectively, of rules and rituals, hymns and prayers, and pithy sayings. The separate literary units are strung together like beads on the single thread of genre, purpose, protagonist, or presumed author. The historical books are collections of episodes, while the prophetic books are collections of oracles and supporting narratives. They are less obviously anthological than Proverbs, Psalms, or the books of laws and ritual prescriptions, yet they are as composite as those latter genres.

These observations challenge the assumption that each book of the Bible should be considered a carefully crafted whole with a plan that is reflected in all its parts. The books of the Bible were not designed to be read as unities. They rather compare to archives. A biblical book is often like a box containing heterogeneous materials brought together on the assumption of common authorship, subject matter, or chronology. Whatever literary unity these books possess was imposed by the editors and is, to some extent, artificial. The editors could rearrange, expand, or conflate the separate units at their disposal in such a way as to achieve the illusion of a single book with a single message.[31]

The Cost of Written Texts

The question this chapter seeks to answer is whether the early Israelites, and more generally the inhabitants of the Near East in pre-Hellenistic times, were familiar with books as we know them. Addressing the issue from a cultural perspective, we have to conclude that this cannot have been the case. So long as oral transmission dominated communication, there was no place for books.

It is also interesting to explore this issue by looking at the material aspects of text production. To most modern-day readers, a book is a physical object that you buy in a bookstore, carry home in a bag, read, and put on a bookshelf together with your other books. A book can cost less than a good meal and be manageable enough to hold in one hand, even if it is 500 pages long. The differences between books nowadays and writing in antiquity are important to identify because they affect our idea of the Bible as a book. Two differences are particularly important: the first concerns the labor involved in text production; the second pertains to the nature of the writing materials.

The origins of the modern book culture go back to the advent of the printing press. Until then, books were made by hand; the process was labor intensive, so the production costs were high. Since writing materials were expensive too, books were beyond the reach of an ordinary individual reader. Only when books came to be mass produced did they become a relatively cheap commodity. Affordable, available books created demand and triggered the development of a new reading culture. So long as written texts were relatively rare, there was little incentive for literacy.

On the situation before the invention of the printing press, the production circumstances of medieval books are quite instructive.[32] A copyist in Paris needed, as a rule, one day for every two pages (or four columns) he wrote, which meant it took about four months to copy a substantial book.[33] Book prices varied widely, depending on the manuscript in question: the richly illuminated luxury books were at the one end of the continuum; excerpts for the use of students at the other. By modern standards, however, prices were often prohibitive; a book was indeed a treasure. While the costs of books did not prevent the existence of a robust and flourishing trade, it was confined to the upper classes. The possession of manuscripts was a sign of affluence and learning.

Compared with the prices of medieval books, the cuneiform tablets from Mesopotamia were relatively cheap. The clay the scribes wrote on was free; the production costs for works like *Gilgamesh* were simply labor costs. In the ancient Near East there were no books as we know them today, but scribes did produce book-length texts. The standard version of the *Epic of Gilgamesh* is about 3,000 lines long. Modern experiments by Assyriologists who have tried writing cuneiform themselves suggest that the ancient scribes would have needed less than a minute per line. This means that writing out the whole of *Gilgamesh* would have taken no more than fifty working hours—probably less.

An actual indication of the time involved in writing cuneiform tablets can be gleaned from the colophons of the Old Babylonian copies of *Atraḫasis* from Sippar. One Nūr-Aya copied the tablets while he was a junior scribe: tablet two on Shebat 28 in the eleventh year of Ammiṣaduqa; tablet one on Nisan 21, the next year; and tablet three in the month Iyyar of that same year.[34] He probably wrote the copies in his spare time, since the twenty-first and the twenty-eighth were holidays.[35] This demonstrates that a single day was all that was needed to produce a tablet of more than 400 lines.[36] Based on this evidence, a copy of *Gilgamesh* would require less than two weeks of work.

Since colophons often indicate the total number of lines on a tablet, it has been speculated that copyists were paid by the line.[37] However, there is no attendant evidence to support this assumption. In the third millennium, scribes received the same monthly wages as other male workers. By the first millennium their social status had risen and their remuneration was above average. Assuming a scribe was paid about twice as much as those in most other professions, a complete copy of *Gilgamesh* would cost a month's wages for an average worker. The fact that scribes sometimes donated a copy of a work to the temple library as a votive gift indicates that these tablets were regarded as valuable. However, these tablets were apparently not beyond the means of a well-to-do citizen.

It may come as somewhat of a surprise, therefore, to find that the Babylonians were unfamiliar with the phenomenon of a trade in books—or a trade in written tablets, if we want to avoid anachronistic terms. Some scribes did have their private libraries, but they acquired their texts by copying them from mother copies in the temple library. Such copying was traditionally left to the younger members of scribal families. Tablet collectors did not purchase texts for money. The case of Nūr-Aya, patiently copying *Atraḫasis* tablets in his spare time, is exemplary. Even Assurbanipal, to whom we owe the largest cuneiform library of the past, did not accumulate his tablets by purely commercial means. He had his servants confiscate tablets and ordered copies from his scribes.[38] The latter acquisition method might be called a form of buying—after all, scribes were entitled to an income—but the tablet production was on command. A free market in cuneiform tablets did not exist.

The earliest references to the buying and selling of Hebrew scrolls are from the Roman period.[39] Price is rarely mentioned. However, one rabbinic tractate from the late Second Temple period states that the price of a Torah scroll was 100 mineh, which equals 10,000 pieces of silver.[40] Considering the fact that the average laborer earned one piece of silver a day, this price is exorbitant.[41] This could just be an exaggeration, as in the Book of Acts where the author values the books of the magicians at Ephesus at 50,000 pieces of silver (Acts 19:19).

Reference to a more reasonable price for a written scroll is found in the Talmud story about a widow whose only possessions were "a woolen blanket, one Psalms scroll, and a tattered scroll with Job and Proverbs" (*b. Git.* 35a). Estimated value: 5 mineh, which equals 500 pieces of silver. Judging by this anecdote, a brand-new scroll of Isaiah would have cost about 200 pieces of silver—more than six months' income. Another Talmudic tale tells about a thief selling a stolen Torah (referred to in the story as "the book," *spr'*) for 80 pieces of silver; the receiver sells it to a third party for 120 pieces, thus pocketing a profit of more than 30 percent (*b. B. Qam.* 115a). This price seems realistic.

If the rabbinic references are of limited value in determining the price of written scrolls, they do show that there was a modest trade in written texts by the beginning of the Common Era. Because Jewish scribes used leather, papyrus, or parchment as writing material, those scrolls were liable to be more costly than cuneiform tablets. Papyrus was the least expensive material, although the practice of recycling written scrolls indicates that none of the writing materials was cheap.[42] The cost of a papyrus scroll in antiquity is estimated to have been equivalent to one to two weeks' wages for an ordinary worker.[43] This means that the costs of the writing materials were higher than the costs of writing.[44] In Roman times, the price of papyrus fell after the state monopoly on papyrus ended and Palestine was able to control its own papyrus production.[45] On the other hand, the Qumran scrolls show that, for the classic texts, scribes would use the more expensive parchment.

The income of a Jewish copyist was above average. In *Ecclesiastes Rabbah* (*Midr.Qoh.* 2.17), Rabbi Meir states that a good scribe could earn two pieces of silver a day, which was twice the average wage of an ordinary worker. Add to this the cost of the writing material, previously estimated at two weeks' wages, and the production costs of an Isaiah scroll would have been about a month's wages (30 pieces of silver)—assuming a trained scribe would need one week to copy the text. Thirty pieces is considerably less than the 200 pieces of silver estimated on the basis of the Talmud passage, as discussed earlier. Is the difference to be explained by the use of a more costly writing material? We know nothing of the margins of profit, but it may have constituted a considerable part of the price. The eunuch reading Isaiah on his way back to Ethiopia probably purchased the scroll during his visit to Jerusalem (Acts 8:26–40); what he paid, we do not know.

It seems highly improbable that there should have been a trade in scrolls before the Hellenistic era. The evidence at our disposal documents a book trade only from the Roman period onward. Even then, though, written scrolls were not cheap. The duty for each Jewish man to own a Torah copy was a stimulus to the process of copying, but it did not lead to the widespread acquisition of texts; it was not until the third century C.E. that private possession of a Torah became common among Jews. For most of them, a Torah scroll was the only written text they possessed—and it was acquired at considerable cost. The trade in texts other than the Torah was confined to scribal circles and to the upper strata of society in which literacy had become a matter of course.[46]

The Codex and the Scroll

There is another aspect of writing in ancient Israel that illustrates that the books of the Bible cannot be seen as books in the modern sense of the word. The format of the modern book goes back to the codex. A codex consists of a group of papyrus or parchment sheets, folded in the middle, and stitched together at the back. It was invented in late antiquity; the first example is from the late first century c.e.[47] By 300 c.e. the codex had become as common as the scroll, and then the format took over as the use of scrolls rapidly diminished.[48]

Modern editions of the Hebrew Bible are in the form of a book and thus display the format of a codex. In fact, the success of the codex was due in large part to its use in recording the sacred scriptures of Christianity.[49] In the period of the Second Temple, however, the Bible was still a collection of scrolls—not a codex. One might conceivably argue that the difference is merely one of physical format. Although the Bible started as a series of scrolls it could still be considered a single book with regard to its content. But was it? This immediately raises the problem of the order of the books of the Bible. If the books were originally scrolls, their order in the codex is arbitrary to some degree. Unless their sequence was indicated by the use of catch-lines, in conformity with Mesopotamian practice, the decision to put Lamentations right after Jeremiah or to relegate it to the Writings pertains to the editors of a particular codex.[50]

More important perhaps than the sequence of the scrolls are the constraints imposed by the use of papyrus and scrolls on writers, editors, and readers. Three observations are in order; the first concerns the writers of the time; the second, the editors; and the third, the readers and users of the text.

First, among modern writers we can distinguish those who conceive their text while writing from those who write only once they have their text in mind. The former category has increased since the introduction of the electronic word processor. In antiquity, authors normally composed their text before they wrote it down. There is evidence of the use by Hebrew scribes of potsherds for making notes and rough drafts.[51] Mesopotamian scribes used clay tablets and wax-covered boards for a similar purpose.[52] On the whole, scribes were trained to produce stock phrases from memory and to compose their text before they committed it to papyrus. The scroll served as the repository of a completed text. The composition of a text normally preceded its fixation in writing.[53]

Second, the use of papyrus scrolls as writing material has yet another consequence for its written content. If the codex corresponds to a book, the scroll corresponds to a storage room. In the first case, the length of the composition determines the size of the book; in the second, the volume of the scroll sets limits on the amount of text that can be accommodated. The standard scroll had twenty sheets of papyrus, which meant an average length of 340 centimeters. A longer scroll required forty, sixty, or even more sheets, but the gain in volume went to the detriment of user-friendliness. A scroll of 10 meters (sixty sheets) was at the limit of practicability.[54] A scroll of that size was not long enough for Samuel, Kings, or Chronicles, however. The reason that we now have a first and second book of Samuel, Kings, and Chronicles, respectively, is because those texts were too long for a single scroll. Conceptually, Samuel and Kings belong together as one work—or a single collection. Their division into four scrolls—or four "books" in our Bible—is directly related to the constraints of the writing material. The same is true for Chronicles, Ezra, and Nehemiah.[55]

While the division of a larger work over two or more scrolls is one consequence of the size of a scroll, the reverse also applies. Scribes used to write down a number of smaller compositions on one scroll for purposes of economy. A case in point is the scroll of the Twelve Minor Prophets; in the rabbinic tradition the twelve compositions came to be known as one book rather than as twelve (although they kept being referred to as "the Twelve"). These examples of division and combination illustrate scribal procedures that may lie behind other books of the Bible as well. Thus the conjunction of the First and the Second Isaiah (conventionally referred to as "Deutero-Isaiah"), could be inspired by reasons of economy more than by putative authorship. The boundaries of the literary composition are not by definition coterminous with the boundaries of the scroll. A scroll is not a book.

Third, the scroll differs from the book in yet another sense. To us, books are not only works of entertainment, instruction, and meditation, but also works of reference. We are accustomed to quotations that are precise—with reference to author, title, and page. Scrolls do not easily lend themselves to such references. Unwinding a whole scroll to find a single passage is cumbersome and accelerates the process of deterioration. That is why quotations in biblical literature, as among Greek and Roman authors, are often from memory. Inaccuracies are not uncommon, and the reference to the author or the scroll—assuming the two are distinguished—is very general.[56] The scroll served as a deposit box for the text; for daily use, people consulted their memory.

To speak about the books of the Bible is misleading on more than one account. Historically, the Hebrew Bible is a collection of scrolls, and scrolls cannot be simply equated with books. The difference between the two is not merely a matter of form; it affects the mode of writing, editorial strategies, and the way in which readers use the text.

Hellenistic Culture and the First Jewish Books

The first Jewish books in Hebrew, Aramaic, or Greek were written in the Hellenistic era. All books written before that time were not books in the modern sense of the term. The Jewish books that began to appear after 300 B.C.E. differ from earlier texts inasmuch as they do seem to resemble the concept of a book as a single work by a single author, aimed at a particular audience. Hellenism created the conditions under which this new phenomenon could occur. Among the many aspects of this new cultural climate, three have a special bearing on the birth of the Jewish book: the emergence of schools, the foundation of libraries, and the growth of a reading public.

The presence of schools in pre-Hellenistic Palestine has been as vigorously asserted as it has been contested. It is, in some measure, a matter of definition. Nobody doubts that in the time of the monarchy both the palace and the temple employed scribes. Since there can be no scribes without education, some form of scribal training must have existed at the time. The Hellenistic period, however, saw the emergence of schools for purposes other than training scribes or copyists. The first mention of a school *(bêt midrāš)* is in Ben Sira, ca. 180 B.C.E. (Sir 51:23). According to Talmudic tradition, there were 480 schools in Jerusalem (*j. Meg.* 73b), though that figure is exaggerated even for a much later date. Nevertheless, we can assume that the school of Ben Sira was one of many. These Jewish schools arose in part in response to the Hellenistic policy of establishing Greek schools in conquered territories.[57] As the tuition fee for schools was substantial (Sir 51:28), formal education was restricted to the well-to-do. Under the guidance of their teachers, students could familiarize themselves with the classics—Homer in the Greek schools; the Law and the Prophets in Ben Sira's *bêt midrāš* (Sir 39:1–3).

In conjunction with the spread of schools, libraries began to develop.[58] In a letter to the Jewish author Aristobulus from Alexandria, a Judean official boasts of the well-stocked library in the temple in Jerusalem. Allegedly founded by Nehemiah, this library owed its prestigious collection to Judas the Maccabee. He had accumulated this collection of previously "scattered" books (2 Macc 2:13–14).[59] The collection in Jerusalem was not the only library in Judah. The Dead Sea Scrolls can also be viewed as a library.[60] At least some of the manuscripts are known not to have been written at Qumran, since they have been dated, on paleographic grounds, to 250 B.C.E., which is more than half a century earlier than Qumran.[61] Text acquisition, conceivably by purchase, was instrumental in creating the collection.

Through the education they offered, the schools created a growing public of readers, and the libraries are testimony to this. In the oral culture of pre-Hellenistic times, readers used to be speakers who read texts out loud to others. Now a new type of reader was emerging. The new reader read alone. Perhaps he was a scholar consulting sacred texts (Dan 9:2) in order to penetrate their subtleties and hidden meanings (Sir 39:1–3); he may also have been an educated layman who read for his personal edification (Acts 8:26–40). Individuals began to buy their own private copy of the Torah (1 Macc 1:56–57). As the reading public grew in size, a book market of sorts developed. The Mishnah explicitly permits the purchase of a Torah scroll from a non-Jew "at its market value" (*m. Git.* 4:6). Scrolls began to circulate in increasing numbers. Local papyrus plantations were developed to meet the attendant demand for writing material.[62]

The Jewish texts produced in the Hellenistic period attest to the presence of a public for books. New genres developed in response to a growing number of people who wanted to read these texts for themselves. Scholars such as Qohelet and Ben Sira put their teachings into writing as a kind of spiritual testament. Their texts reflect a personal approach not seen before in Hebrew literature. Ben Sira even signs his book with his own name (Sir 50:27).

Another genre that emerged was the adventure story, although it always remained within the scope of historical fiction. It was written for entertainment as well as for educational purposes. The books of Ruth, Esther, Judith, and Tobit, as well as chapters one through six of Daniel, are examples in point.

Apocalyptic literature, written under the name of a famous sage from antiquity, such as Daniel or Enoch, abounds in the Hellenistic era. Its style supports the idea that it was composed while writing, unlike the way scribes transcribed collections of the prophets' oracles.

All of the new genres can be traced back to earlier genres: Qohelet and Ben Sira to Proverbs; the adventure stories to the historical narratives of Genesis, Samuel, and Kings; the apocalyptic literature to the scrolls of the prophets. Yet there can be no mistaking that these works from the Hellenistic era represent something distinctively new. The content and style define them as the first real Jewish books.

The Stream of Tradition

In his *Introduction to the Greek Tragedy*, Ulrich von Wilamowitz defines a book as a text published by its author through the medium of an organized book trade for the benefit of an expectant public.[63] By this definition, the term *book* is an anachronism when applied to the written documents from the ancient Near East.

Prior to the advent of Hellenism, the only text that was disseminated by means of "an organized book trade" was the Egyptian *Book of the Dead*. This text, however, was not written by a single author. Moreover, to speak of "an expectant public" is something of a euphemism. A copy of the *Book of the Dead* was purchased to be placed in a tomb alongside the mummified deceased, so that the latter might be protected from harm and reach the hereafter unscathed. This so-called book was not meant for reading. In other words, the only ancient Near Eastern "book" for which there was a real market, in fact served as an amulet.[64] In this respect it compares to the *Song of Erra*, which served a somewhat similar purpose in warding off pestilence. No other text from Mesopotamia was copied as often as the *Song of Erra*. Not because it was in demand by a reading public, but because a carefully positioned copy would keep all sorts of evil at bay.[65]

Aside from the *Book of the Dead*, then, there was no book trade per se in the ancient Near East; nor was there a reading public of any substance; nor were there books as we know them. One might, for the sake of argument, qualify *Gilgamesh* and Isaiah as the books of antiquity, but they are books only in a manner of speaking. Not only are the tablets of *Gilgamesh* and the scroll of Isaiah dissimilar to a book in form, but the text they contain does not conform to the concept of literature that is implied by the modern notion of a book. These book-length texts come from an oral culture and retain the characteristics of that culture. No one wrote books the way people write books in the modern age. The first books did not appear until the Hellenistic era.[66]

To avoid the misleading association of the term *books,* it is preferable to speak instead of the "stream of tradition." When A. Leo Oppenheim coined the phrase, he was referring to the cuneiform literature of Mesopotamia as it was studied and transmitted in the scribal schools.[67] By analogy, the Hebrew Bible is the collection of texts written, studied, and copied over the centuries by scribes in the Jewish centers of scholarship. They are the collective property of the scribal community; the Hebrew Bible is their legacy. To appreciate that legacy at its proper value, it is necessary to understand the scribal culture in which the stream of tradition found its bedding.

AUTHORSHIP IN ANTIQUITY

Practice and Perception

Modern concepts of the book usually entail a particular concept of the author, on the assumption that there are no books without authors. In perceiving the Bible as a book we therefore assume there must have been an author—or, when the Bible is viewed as a collection of books, a number of authors.

If one sees the book as a product of the author's mind, understanding the author is arguably the key to the interpretation of the book. This explains the fascination with writers' biographies and illustrates why many people presume that knowing about the author's life—particularly his or her psychology—will illuminate the literary product. What we tend to overlook in our eagerness for biographical detail, however, is that such an interest in the author is a relatively recent phenomenon.

Up until the end of the Middle Ages, readers were more concerned with the authority of books than their authenticity. The author was deemed relevant mainly as a source of authority. Our modern emphasis on the author as an individual artist is a legacy from the romantic movement. So pervasive is this idea in the modern imagination that few of us realize that the concept is not the only one possible. Yet if the books of the Bible are not books in the modern sense of the term, our notion of their authorship might have to be adjusted as well. We must be careful not to impose modern concepts of authorship on works that stem from a culture that entertained very different notions.

The present chapter is an attempt to delineate the practice and perception of authorship in the world of the Bible. After sketching the historical background of the modern idea of the author, I will compare this with the way in which the ancient texts from the world of the Bible address the issue of authorship. Most of these ancient texts are anonymous, a fact that in itself is significant and needs to be accounted for. Many other works were signed, but not by their real author. Texts were often attributed to great figures from the past as a way to impress their authority on the audience. The real author remained anonymous. These practices require that we first investigate ancient concepts of authorship.

A review of the textual evidence, both biblical and cuneiform, leads me to conclude that anonymity was the rule in the literary production of the ancient Near East. This anonymity was not merely an omission of names; it is evidence of a particular notion of authorship. The practice of pseudonymous authorship and the logic informing the ancient lists of works and authors betray a particular interest in textual authority. The author was seen as a source of authority. But how did the authors of antiquity see themselves? To answer this question I propose to use a model that can integrate the disparate data garnered from the texts in order to reconstruct the practice of authorship in antiquity. This model will open up new avenues in investigating the Hebrew Bible and the history of its making.

Rise and Demise of the Author

If we treat the Bible as a collection of books—standard procedure in introductions to the Bible—we implicitly subscribe to a notion of authorship that is characteristic of modern book production. Whether that notion is the proper way to address the making of the Hebrew Bible is highly questionable. The modern notion of the author as an independent writer of works of art, entertainment, or scholarship is the outcome of a long historical process. It is useful to remind ourselves of the dangers of taking a cultural construct for an empirical truth.

Generations of Bible students have been raised on the notion that the books of the Bible should be read and interpreted *e mente auctoris*. The Latin expression means that we must put ourselves in the mind of the author when reading the text—the author being the human author. In the sense of being a precaution against reading modern concerns into ancient texts, this advice is appropriate, but taken literally, it presupposes a concept of authorship that is distinctly modern—certainly one that was not held by the ancient authors themselves. A phrase in Latin carries the halo of antiquity, but the *e mente auctoris* maxim was first formulated in the seventeenth century.[1] In other words, this instruction for readers is an invention of the early modern era, as is the notion of the author that it implies.

Until the dawn of modernity, neither theologians nor lay people had any great interest in the individual authors who wrote down the Bible texts. The Bible was the Word of God; whichever humans had been involved in its making were looked upon as mere channels for a heavenly voice. Human authorship was of no interest in comparison to the issue of authority. This lasted until the Enlightenment, when the dogma of the literal inspiration of the Bible was eroded. Only when the Bible was no longer literally the Word of God did its human authors gain in importance.

The romantic movement reinforced the new interest in the human authors of the Bible. The romantics saw the author as an artist, the artist being an exceptional individual with access to a reality beyond ordinary reality. These sentiments are still with us today, as the following quote illustrates: "The awe we feel before artistic originality and creativity places art on the border of the numinous."[2] The view of the author as a creative genius, on the one hand, and the demythologization of the Bible, on the other, reinforced each other, and eventually the human author superseded God.

In the field of biblical scholarship, the shift of focus toward the human author gave birth to the genre of spiritual biography. Instead of commentaries, scholars wrote studies of the "life and times" of the men of the Bible. *Jeremiah: His Life and Times, Isaiah: His Life and Times* (both published in 1888), and *Mose und seine Zeit* (1913) are just three titles characteristic of those published in the late nineteenth and the early twentieth centuries.[3] These titles may make it look as though the genre is a revival of the Lives of the Prophets, a first century C.E. collection of popular lore on the prophets.[4] The similarity in terminology is misleading, however. The Lives of the Prophets establishes the place of birth of the prophets and the location of their graves, whereas the "life and times" publications focus on the spiritual trajectory of the prophets in the context of their time. They are closer to what we would now call psychological studies.

The romantic approach embodied in the life and times monographs is now largely out of favor, even if it still appeals to some sections of the general public. Paradoxically, the reason for its rise is the same as for its fall. The historical-critical study of the Bible highlighted the role of the human authors at the expense of the dogma of divine inspiration. But the names traditionally associated with the Bible as its authors—such as Moses, David, and Isaiah—were relegated to the realm of legend when historical criticism showed that the books these men allegedly wrote were not actually by them at all. Source criticism and redaction criticism made it impossible to maintain that the historical Isaiah wrote the Book of Isaiah. If not a single word in all the five books of Moses was written by Moses himself, a biography based on these texts is likely to be a piece of fiction. In the Bible, the sources cannot be traced to identifiable individuals and the editors are nameless; so the biographer and the psychologist have nothing to go on.

The disappearance of the spiritual biography from biblical studies does not mean that biblical scholars have changed their views on authorship altogether. Yet the traditional concept of authorship many scholars implicitly endorse stands in sharp contrast to ideas on authorship in contemporary literary theory. Since Roland Barthes announced "the death of the Author" in 1967, the role of the author has been under critical scrutiny.[5] Critics question the existence of the author as an autonomous creative agent, based on two points. First is the question of whether the author is the ultimate authority with regard to the meaning of the text; in other words, is the reader's personal interpretation less valid than that of the author? The second is the claim that the author can never be an independent agent because he or she is always a "function" of society. The first point goes against the *e mente auctoris* principle; the second strikes at the heart of the romantic notion of the author as the bearer of special insight, which still informs so much of biblical scholarship today.

The above considerations illustrate that the notion of the author as an autonomous agent of creative genius is a historical construct. It is not a fixed truth but was born in early modern times and may not make it through postmodernity. It is clear that such a disputed concept should not be uncritically applied to the literature from the ancient world. Before we posit the principle that the Bible should be read and interpreted *e mente auctoris,* we must first investigate the role of the author in antiquity. What do the texts themselves imply about authorship? I shall try to answer this question by looking both at the written texts of Mesopotamia and at biblical literature.

Anonymity

In the ancient Near East, it was uncommon for an author to sign his or her work. Ben Sira was one of the earliest Jewish authors to put his name to his book (Sir 50:27).[6] Until the Hellenistic era, anonymity prevailed. I shall look at the practice of anonymity—its occurrence and its motives—by focusing on literary production in Mesopotamia and Israel. A study of scribal notices—colophons, superscriptions, postscripts—provides a suitable entry into the matter.

In modern books the title, name of the author, publisher, and year of publication are separated from the main body of the text by a title page. The cuneiform equivalent of our title page is the colophon. The colophon is a scribal note at the end of a text, separated from its main body by a single or double marking. It generally includes the title of the work, an indication of the total number of lines on the tablet, and a reference to the master copy that was used. The only personal names that appear in the Babylonian and Assyrian colophons are those of the copyist ("by the hand of So-and-so") and the owner ("belonging to So-and-so"). What is conspicuously lacking is the name of the author.[7]

The consistent absence of any reference to the author suggests that anonymity was the rule in Mesopotamian literature.[8] This impression is confirmed, it would seem, by most Mesopotamian literary texts, such as the *Epic of Gilgamesh,* the *Myth of Adapa,* the *Epic of Creation,* and the *Descent of Ishtar*—none of which identifies the poet who might claim to be its author. When it comes to mythological works, there is only one text that is signed, called the *Song of Erra.* But this is a unique case that merits discussion in its own right, and to which I shall return later in the chapter. It is an exception to the rule, and that rule is anonymity.

Also works that we would classify as nonliterary but that nevertheless belong to the stream of tradition, such as astrological series and medical handbooks, did not name the author. Any names mentioned in connection with them are those of the editors. A postscript to a widely used medical compendium from Babylonia mentions Esagil-kīn-apli, a famous scholar of the late second millennium B.C.E., as the one who, on the basis of disparate sources, produced the standard version of the series.[9] Even though, in antiquity, it is hard to distinguish between author and editor, it is imperative, at this point, to be clear about the difference. To speak of "authorship" when discussing editorial supervision is misleading.[10] The author, if there was one, goes unmentioned.

The biblical counterpart to the cuneiform colophon is extant in the superscriptions ("rubrics") and subscripts ("colophons") of the Hebrew scrolls. These are now to be found at the beginning and the end of the various "books" of the Bible. They show that the Mesopotamian custom of anonymous authorship was current in Israel as well. The bulk of the biblical literature does not carry the name of its author. None of the so-called historical books (Joshua, Judges, 1–2 Samuel, 1–2 Kings, 1–2 Chronicles) contains superscriptions or any other reference to the author in the text. The same is true for four of the five books traditionally ascribed to Moses: Genesis, Exodus, Leviticus, and Numbers; none contains superscripts or any mention of an author.

The practice of anonymous authorship is related to ancient concepts of literature. In the previous chapter I argued that the books of the Bible are not books in the modern sense. To this I now add that they also depart from our concept of books in that they carry neither a title nor the name of an author. Instead of by a title, they were customarily referred to by the opening words or the main protagonists. It was not until about 400 B.C.E. that scribes began to refer to 1–2 Samuel and 1–2 Kings together as "the Book of the Kings of Israel and Judah" (2 Chron 35:27). The collection we now know as Lamentations received that title, plus the attendant ascription to the prophet Jeremiah, in the same period (2 Chron 35:25). The late Persian era heralded the beginning of a "book awareness" hitherto unknown in Palestine.

Under Another Name

In ancient times, authors might also remain anonymous by writing under a name other than their own. When a work had been commissioned, the author often would ascribe it to the patron. In other instances, an author would pretend to be a famous figure from the past. The former is a case of "honorary" authorship; the second, one of pseudonymity.

In several of the Mesopotamian law collections, a king is stated as being the author. Famous examples are the *Laws of Hammurabi* and the *Laws of Lipit-Ishtar.* The prologue and the epilogue of these collections purport them to be the work of Hammurabi and Lipit-Ishtar, respectively. These kings are thus honorary authors, while the scribes who actually wrote the texts remain anonymous. Honorary authorship was often used for purposes of political propaganda. The laws were designed to demonstrate the wisdom of the king.[11] The same can be said about royal inscriptions extolling the virtues of the monarch and the quality of his rule, and of royal letter-prayers, and hymns and prayers allegedly composed by kings but in fact the work of their scribes.[12] These texts attest to an ideology of kingship that holds that the monarch should excel in every field of human activity including that of scribe and scholar.

Honorary authorship is to be distinguished from pseudepigraphy. In pseudepigraphical texts, scribes attribute their work to a (fictive) author from remote times in order to present their work as a legacy from the venerable past. Antiquity implies authority. Pseudepigraphy is common in the literary genre of fictional autobiography. A prime example is the *Epic of Gilgamesh*. The introduction to the standard version presents the epic as an autobiographical account by Gilgamesh himself.[13] When the editor added this introduction, he turned Gilgamesh into an author, though he knew full well that the epic had been composed by earlier scribes. Other texts, such as the *Cuthean Legend of Naram-Sin* and the *Sargon Birth Legend,* adopt a similar ploy.[14] The scribes portrayed these legendary kings as authors to enhance the effect of their own text. They borrowed the voice of an ancient king to convey wisdom, as in *Gilgamesh* and *Naram-Sin,* or to legitimize temple claims to land and offerings, as in the Cruciform Monument of Manishtushu and the Agum-kakrime Inscription.[15] One pseudepigraphical text promotes a political program.[16] In all of these cases the prestige of the alleged author is used to confer authority on the text.

The Bible contains its fair share of pseudonymous texts as well. The earliest example is the Book of Deuteronomy, which purports to be a valedictory address by Moses spoken just before his death. The fictitious authorship harmonizes with the setting of the book (the period preceding the entry into the Holy Land, which puts the message in a time of origins) and provides the text with authority. The anonymous authors of Deuteronomy needed the authority of Moses to legitimize a cultic reform that was carried out in 622 by King Josiah. Precisely because the reform was a break with traditional practice, the propaganda presented it as the will of God as revealed to Moses, the prophet of prophets. The fraud may have been pious, but a fraud it was.

A straightforward case of pseudepigraphy in the Bible is the Book of

Daniel—or at least the second part (Dan 7–12). Ezekiel the prophet mentions Daniel along with Noah and Job as models of virtue and wisdom (Ezek 14:14). The name Daniel was later given to the main character of a number of entertaining and edifying tales about Jews in the Babylonian Diaspora (Dan 1–6). An author active in the early second century B.C.E. used the identity of this legendary sage to lend authority to his own work. Chapters 7 to 12 of the Book of Daniel are presented as Daniel's visions committed to writing by Daniel in person (Dan 7:1).

Modern scholars are divided over the meaning and the function of pseudepigraphy in antiquity.[17] Were the real authors deliberately trying to mislead their readers or were they simply following the literary conventions of their time? The controversy provoked by the alleged discovery of Deuteronomy demonstrates that fictive antiquity and pseudonymity were not simply conventions of the literary genre. Deuteronomy contains the text of the ancient "Book of the Torah," whose discovery served to legitimize a cult reform by King Josiah in 622 (2 Kings 22–23).[18] The prophet Jeremiah did not accept the claim of antiquity and denounced the book as a fraud manufactured by "the deceitful pen of the scribes" (Jer 8:8–9).[19] He was not the only one to have doubts; shortly after the book had been found, the officials in charge consulted the prophetess Huldah to check whether or not the document was authentic (2 Kings 22:11–20). The criticism of Jeremiah and the consultation of Huldah reflect a critical attitude toward the claim of antiquity.

The issue gets more problematic in the Hellenistic era. Considering the sheer number of texts attributed to Enoch, Noah, Moses, Solomon, Baruch, and others, it is hard to believe that the intended readers gave, or were indeed expected to give, credence to the fiction. Yet our amazement at the credulity of the public may be due to the global perspective we have on the matter. While it is implausible that every reader accepted the authorship of Enoch, Daniel, and others, many of them apparently did. In most cases, acceptance of the pseudonymous authorship was essential for the authority of the work. The authors of the apocalyptic works of Daniel and Enoch may have identified with their heroes, but they were actually using a famous alias to increase their credit with the readers.

Attributed Authorship

Pseudonymity is the strategy of an author who wishes to optimize the chances of a favorable reception of his work. It is to be distinguished from attributed authorship. Pseudepigraphy is the doing of the author; attributed authorship is the work of the editor. Often the text the editor works with has already established itself in some way. If the editor attributes it to a presumed author, it is to explain rather than to gain its reception by the public. Before I analyze the reasoning that informs this practice, however, let me give some biblical examples.

Traditional collections attributed to famous kings are Psalms and Proverbs. By the evidence of these books themselves, the attributions to David and Solomon are in fact simplifications. Bracketed by an editorial frame (Pss 1–2, 150), the Psalms are a compilation of five separate collections (Pss 3–41, 42–72, 73–89, 90–106, 107–149). Collection Two is defined as "the prayers of David son of Jesse" (Ps 72:20), and many psalms of this and other collections mention David in their superscriptions.[20] Yet the scribal editors have also attributed psalms to Solomon (Pss 72, 127) and Moses (Ps 90). Other alleged authors are Asaph (Pss 50, 73–83), Ethan (Ps 89), Heman (Ps 88), Jeduthun (Pss 39, 62, 77), and the Korahites (Pss 42–49, 84–85, 87–88). At the time the various collections originated, the Davidic authorship was not a doctrine yet. David was believed to have written a number of psalms, but other famous men of the past, including Moses, were credited with religious poetry as well.

Nevertheless, from the Hellenistic period onward the name "David" was the standard designation of the entire Psalter.[21] Such was David's reputation as pious king, skilled musician, and organizer of the temple liturgy (compare 1 Chron 16), that he absorbed paternity of all the Psalms.[22] The later tradition draws a parallel with Moses:

> Moses gave the five books of the Torah to Israel, and corresponding to
> them, David gave the five books of the Psalms to Israel.
>
> *Mid. Ps* 1:2

The Jewish sages sought to harmonize the doctrine of the Davidic authorship of the Psalms with the reality of other names in the superscriptions by saying that David had written the Psalms "at the instruction of" (*'al-yĕdê*, for the meaning of which compare 1 Chron 25:2) the
Ten Elders: "Adam, Melchizedek, Abraham, Moses, Heman, Yeduthun,
Asaph, and the three sons of Korah" (*b. B. Bat.* 15a). It is implied that
these "Elders" had preceded David, which means he had acted both as
an editor and as an author—much like the Hebrew scribes often acted
in this double capacity.

The case of Proverbs may seem more straightforward, since it carries
a superscription that mentions Solomon as author of the book as a
whole (Prov 1:1). Upon closer inspection, however, Proverbs consists
of four separate collections (1–9, 10:1–22:16, 22:17–24:22, 25–29)
that each has its own title. Proverbs contains "the Words of the Wise"
(Prov 1:6, 22:17, 24:23); "Proverbs of Solomon" (Prov 10:1); "Proverbs of Solomon which the men of King Hezekiah of Judah committed to writing" (Prov 25:1); and, in appendices, "the Words of Agur"
(30:1) and "the Words of Lemuel" (31:1). Here too, then, the attribution of the entire collection to Solomon is a simplification due to the
reputation of the king as a paragon of wisdom (1 Kings 3:4–28, 5:9–14).

The attribution of Song of Songs to Solomon and of Lamentations to
the prophet Jeremiah has no particular ground in these compositions
themselves except for the reputation of Solomon as a lover of women
(1 Kings 11:1–5) and of Jeremiah as a prophet and witness of Jerusalem's doom. The editors of Song of Songs attributed the book to Solomon in its superscription (Cant 1:1). The Hebrew version of Lamentations does not mention Jeremiah, but 2 Chron 35:25 presents the
prophet as the author of Lamentations, and the Septuagint makes the
connection explicit by its presentation of Lamentations as the words

that Jeremiah spoke "as he sat weeping and uttering this lament over Jerusalem."[23]

Attribution to a named author is standard for the books of the prophets. Later tradition, as reflected in Chronicles and in the superscription to the prophetic books, takes the prophets as the actual writers of their books—and of other biblical materials as well (2 Chron 26:22; 35:25). Not one of the prophetic scrolls is anonymous. In fact, it was a rule that prophetic books should have an identifiable prophet as their author. Anonymous prophecies were either accommodated in another collection of which the presumed author was known, as in Deutero-Isaiah; or the editors manufactured a name for the author, as in Malachi, whose name is derived from the reference to "my messenger" *(mal'ākî)* in Mal 3:1. Yet authorship of biblical prophecies is by definition attributed authorship. The rare prophets who actually wrote, as Deutero-Isaiah presumably did, never signed their texts. The names of the prophets are found in the superscriptions, and the superscriptions are the work of editors.

Pseudonymous authorship implies a concept of the author as a source of authority, whereas attributed authorship illuminates the nature of that authority. So why did David and Solomon qualify as the authors of collections that did not really need their authority to be accepted as Scripture? One reason could be their standing as the great kings of Jerusalem. But what was probably more important was the fact that they had been blessed with divine charisma. It was the Spirit of the Lord that touched David and gave him the right to speak the message of God (2 Sam 23:2; cf. 1 Sam 16:13). Likewise, Solomon owed his unparalleled wisdom to a special gift from God (1 Kings 3:12). Later tradition regarded David and Solomon as "prophets."[24] In all the examples of attributed authorship discussed above, the author is viewed as a privileged individual in direct contact with the divine.

In view of the simplification often implied in attributed authorship in the Bible, we may legitimately ask whether the editors who attributed the Psalms to David meant to say that David was really the author of the Psalms (and Isaiah of the Book of Isaiah, and so on and so forth). It has been asserted that among the Jews "attribution is primarily a claim to authoritative tradition, not a statement of literary origins."[25] This, however, is a false opposition. It is true that attribution implies a claim to authority, but that authority is intimately tied to the issue of authorship. Even if the attributions are in glaring contradiction with the results of modern critical analysis, it does not follow that the editors did not seriously believe that Moses wrote the Pentateuch and David the Book of Psalms. They most likely believed in the authorship of David; and from their perspective they had good reason to do so.

Signed by the Author

It is intriguing to see that the heyday of Jewish pseudepigraphy coincided with the time when Jewish authors began to sign their work. Ben Sira was one of the first (Sir 50:27). The age of Hellenism witnessed a dramatic increase in literary production, and for the first time in Jewish history people began to write texts that resembled books in the sense we traditionally assign to the term. It is also the first time that authors emerged from the anonymity that was customary until then. Paradoxically, the prevalence of pseudepigraphy in the apocalyptic literature of the time is another manifestation of "author awareness." It uses the notion of the author as a means to facilitate the acceptance of contested texts, by providing the author with a false identity. But the alleged authors are presented as the real authors in the sense that they purportedly wrote the books that go under their name.

If we broaden our scope to include ancient Near Eastern literature outside Palestine, we find that works signed by their author are not entirely a Hellenistic innovation. There are a small number of Mesopotamian texts from the (late) second and first millennia B.C.E. that carry the name of their author. They are not cases of either pseudepigraphy or attributed authorship: it was the real author who signed. This is a known fact. So how does this fit in with the prevailing custom of anonymous authorship? I have argued that the anonymity of literary works is based on the notion of the author as a craftsman: the scribe as a skilled executor of his craft rather than the author of ideas. The existence of some works that were signed by the author supports the idea that scribal authors were primarily celebrated as craftsmen.

Several texts that bear the name of an author are to be excluded from the discussion, such as prayers of petition or thanksgiving, because the statement of identity was there for the gods, who needed to know who was addressing them.[26] Such literary prayers as the Gula hymn of Bullutsa-rabi refer to the author in his or her capacity of suppliant.[27] This is also true for *Ludlul,* a four-tablet text of wisdom modeled on the written prayer of thanksgiving in token of gratitude. Its protagonist, one Šubši-mešrê-Šakkan (*Ludlul,* tablet III, line 43), is purportedly the speaker and the author of the text. However, the author does not mean to identify himself as a writer but as a worshipper.[28]

One text that was signed in a particularly striking way is the *Babylonian Theodicy.*[29] This composition is an acrostic, a technical accomplishment, as the beginnings of its lines in the original language form a sentence in which the author introduces himself as Saggil-kīnam-ubbib. The author is otherwise known only from brief references in the Neo-Assyrian *Catalogue of Texts and Authors* and the Seleucid *List of Sages and Scholars.*[30] They record that he was a royal scholar around 1100 B.C.E. His is the oldest acrostic known in Akkadian literature and this is probably his main claim to fame. The purpose of writing an acrostic was not merely to sign the composition; there were far simpler ways to do that. Saggil-kīnam-ubbib wanted his name to be associated with a scribal *tour de force;* he wanted to be admired by other scribes. This example of claimed authorship is not so much important because of the content of the text, as it is not a particularly significant work, but it does provide evidence of the desire to claim ownership of a display of scribal dexterity.

There is one other acrostic that contains the name of its author.[31] It is a double intercessory prayer by Nabu-ušebši[32] addressed to Marduk and Nabu. The twin prayers both end with a three-line supplication by Nabu-ušebši that pleads for many descendants and a long life. The acrostic is particularly ingenious as it uses signs at both the beginning and the end of the lines to form a sentence describing the author of the text: "By Nabu-ušebši the exorcist, the servant who proclaims your lordship, the servant who deferentially prays to you." The author added a note to his text to alert readers to his clever signature. This explicit self-reference had a double motive. On the one hand, the author wanted the scribal community to acknowledge and admire his mastery of the scribal craft; on the other, he wanted the gods to take note of him that they might bless him.

The composers of acrostics used their texts to display their skills as scribes. This motive is absent from another literary text that mentions its author's name for apparently no other reason than to signify that he wrote it. This is the *Song of Erra,* also known as the *Erra Epic* or *Erra and Ishum.*[33] In the final section of the text, after a three-line summary of its plot, the narrator reveals the origin of the song.

> Its compiler is Kabti-ilāni-Marduk, son of Dabibi.
> In the middle of the night he [i.e., the god] revealed it to him,
> And exactly as he had spoken during his morning slumber,[34]
> He did not skip a single line, nor did he add one to it.
> When Erra heard it, he approved.[35]

This passage is striking in more than one respect. It explicitly mentions the author of the text but hastens to add that the author did not produce the text himself. He took dictation from a god, presumably Erra, the same god who is reported to approve of the text when it is read out to him. The author, in other words, is not the real author. This explains the term "compiler" *(kāṣir kammīšu)* rather than "author" *(ša pî).*[36]

Even if Kabti-ilāni-Marduk was a channel rather than an author, the presence of his signature is puzzling. It is very atypical in Akkadian literature. Various commentators have speculated that the passage in question is a secondary addition to the text.[37] That would make it a case of attributed authorship and thus comparable to the biblical scrolls of the prophets. Kabti-ilāni-Marduk is otherwise unknown, and so is his ancestor Dabibi. Later texts turn him into a hero from before the Flood, but that is a speculation entirely based, it seems, on his status as the author of *Erra*.[38]

The only plausible explanation for the unusual reference to the author in the *Song of Erra* is the nature of the text. Toward the end of the mythological drama, the text assumes traits of a prophecy, as it announces the rise of "a man of Akkad" who will fell the Suteans and bring heavy spoil into Babylon (tablet IV, lines 131–136; tablet V, lines 25–38).[39] The poem was apparently written in support of this new "provider of Esagila and Babylon" (tablet V, line 38), an otherwise unidentified Babylonian king. Being a prophecy—or, rather, a pseudo-prophecy—the text needed the name of the prophet.[40] The name of the alleged "compiler" honors Marduk as the greatest among the gods *(kabti ilāni)* and thereby counterbalances the prominent role of Erra. Because Kabti-ilāni-Marduk has no particular fame, the text stresses that he received the text as a divine revelation. Once again, it is not authenticity but textual authority that is at issue.

Conceptions of Authorship among Assyrian and Jewish Scholars

Various modern scholars have argued that Mesopotamian literature has unfairly suffered from the "stigma of anonymity," as William W. Hallo calls it.[41] Thus Benjamin R. Foster, author of a rightly celebrated anthology of Akkadian literature, states that the Mesopotamian poetic tradition did have "a notion of individual inspiration and authorship."[42] To substantiate his claim, Foster quotes a number of cases, but the only one that holds up to critical scrutiny is that of the *Song of Erra*. The reference or self-reference to Kabti-ilāni-Marduk is highly exceptional, however, and insufficient as evidence to posit the conception of authorship implied by Foster. In ancient Mesopotamia, anonymous authorship was the rule.

An interesting clue to the conception of authorship current in the ancient Near East is offered by the cuneiform *Catalogue of Texts and Authors*.[43] The text is known via copies that came from the library of Assurbanipal. The *Catalogue* sums up all the major texts studied in the scribal schools and gives, for each work, the name of the author or the editor. The *Catalogue* is arranged chronologically. It starts with what were believed to be the oldest texts and ends with the most recent.[44] The expression used to designate authorship is *ša pî,* "from the mouth of," though the same expression is used to introduce the editor. In some cases, information about the author is gleaned directly from the composition in question. Thus, in the case of the *Song of Erra,* the *Catalogue* simply quotes the lines about the nocturnal revelation to Kabti-ilāni-Marduk. In most cases, however, the *Catalogue* derives its information from sources unknown to us.

Though the text has been called a "manifestation of critical scholarship," it is in fact a mixture of mythological lore and scholarly tradition.[45] Some texts are said to be "from the mouth of Ea," the Babylonian god of wisdom, while others are coupled with the name of their editor—as in the case of *Gilgamesh,* said to be "from the mouth of Sin-leqe-unninni." The *Catalogue* has three types of authors: the god Ea, legendary figures, and famous scholars. The oldest works are by Ea, works of the middle period are by legendary figures, and the most recent works by scholars. Nine works are attributed to Ea, and an unknown quantity to antediluvian sages and kings. Their mythological authorship implies anonymity for the real authors in that as no human authors are mentioned, these works must go back to a god or to a legendary hero. Where scholars are mentioned as the authors, it is not always clear whether the *Catalogue* means authors or editors. Judging by the text attached to their names, we can assume that Saggil-kīnam-ubbib and Bulluṭsa-rabi were real authors. However, the other scholars recorded as being authors may well have been editors, as was true in the case of Sin-leqe-unninni.

Irrespective of its historical reliability, the *Catalogue of Texts and Authors* does reflect an interest in issues of authorship among Assyrian scholars. However, there are four observations that must be taken into account. First, the issue of authorship is a matter of interest to later scholars, not particularly to the actual authors of the texts. Second, by adopting a chronological frame, beginning with Ea and various mythological heroes, the *Catalogue* establishes a hierarchy among the classics of Mesopotamian scholarship, with antiquity as the hallmark of authority: the older a work, the greater its value. Works mentioned toward the end of the list are, by implication, less "canonical," which entails that human authorship is associated with works of secondary standing. It is interesting to note, in this connection, that works of entertainment (*Gilgamesh, Etana,* the *Fable of the Fox*) do not enjoy the sacred character ascribed to an astrological compendium or the professional lore of the exorcist. Issues of authorship are intimately connected with scriptural authority. Third, most of the listed texts are, in fact, anonymous. And fourth, the *Catalogue* makes no distinction between authors and editors.

The notion of authorship underlying the *Catalogue* is not that of the author as an individual talent. Had that been the case, authors would have been distinguished from editors. From the fact that the list confuses the two, it may be concluded that its principal purpose was to establish an order of authority. The humans behind the texts are subordinate to the canonical status of the latter. That is why the *Catalogue* records Ea as the author of the standard diagnostic compendium and omits to mention its editor, Esagil-kīn-apli. The authors that are listed (including the editors) are an indication of canonical ranking. In short, the *Catalogue* has no real interest in authorship; it is, rather, about scriptural authority.

A distant Jewish counterpart to the Assyrian *Catalogue of Texts and Authors* is found in the Babylonian Talmud.[46] In reply to the question, "Who wrote the scriptures?" the sages list the various books of the Hebrew Bible and give the names of their writers. The passage merits a full quotation.

Moses wrote his book, the portion of Balaam, and Job.[47] Joshua wrote his book and [the last] eight verses of the Torah. Samuel wrote his book, and Judges, and Ruth. David wrote the Book of Psalms at the instruction of the Ten Elders, namely, Adam, the first human being; Melchizedek; Abraham; Moses; Heman; Yeduthun; Asaph; and the three sons of Korah. Jeremiah wrote his book, the Book of Kings, and Lamentations.

Hezekiah and his associates wrote Isaiah, Proverbs, Song of Songs, and Qohelet. The men of the Great Assembly wrote Ezekiel and the Twelve, Daniel, and the Scroll of Esther. Ezra wrote his book and the genealogies of Chronicles up to his time . . . Who then finished it? Nehemiah the son of Hachaliah.

b. B. Bat. 14b–15a

At first glance, one similarity between this list of books and authors and the Assyrian *Catalogue* is the absence of a clear distinction between author and editor. If the sages say that Jeremiah wrote his book, they presumably mean that he was its author; if they say that Hezekiah and his associates wrote Isaiah, Proverbs, Song of Songs, and Qohelet, they are clearly not implying authorship. They extrapolate Prov 25:1 ("These too are proverbs of Solomon, which the men of King Hezekiah committed to writing") to all of Solomon's writings, while adding Isaiah on account of his relations with Hezekiah (Isa 36–39). The "men of the Great Assembly," too, were presumably editors of the Minor Prophets (the Scroll of the Twelve) rather than authors.

But we probably need to go one step further and say that the sages were not concerned with authorship at all. Otherwise, why would they not have mentioned Solomon as the author of Proverbs, Song of Songs, and Qohelet? Since they followed the doctrine that the Torah is from heaven—as are by extension all the scriptures—human authorship was a matter of little importance to them. Humans were involved in the making of the Hebrew Bible but only in their capacity as transcribers. "The Holy One, blessed be He, dictated, Moses repeated, and Moses wrote" (*b. B. Bat.* 15a). The list in the Talmud does not shed any light on the possible authors of the biblical texts in terms of human authorship. It only tells us what Jewish sages believed was the chronological order in which the texts had been fixed in writing.

Authorship in Antiquity

There does not seem to be a coherent notion of authorship in the texts from antiquity. No single text formulates a theory of authorship, and it is up to us to try to elucidate their ideas on authorship from the disparate data at our disposal. It may be useful to sum up the characteristics of authorship in antiquity by contrasting them with modern notions of authorship.

To us, the author is first of all an individual. A superficial glance at the evidence might give the impression that the ancients shared this view. In the *Catalogue of Texts and Authors,* the author—or editor—is always an individual with a name and, at times, a patronym. The Talmudic list of books of the Bible and their authors, however, twice mentions a collective. Isaiah, Proverbs, Song of Songs, and Qohelet were "written"—meaning "edited"—by "Hezekiah and his associates"; Ezekiel, the Minor Prophets, Daniel, and Esther were the work of "the Men of the Great Assembly." One way to resolve the problem of the individual author and the author as a collectivity is to assume that in the latter case the sages do not refer to the author but to the editors, and perhaps the transcribers, of the books. However, this is not enough. The very fact that both the *Catalogue* and the Talmudic list make no clear distinction between author and editor is significant. But if these two categories were more or less the same in the eyes of the ancients, their distinction cannot be adduced in explanation of collectivities.

Let us assume that to the ancients the author is, in principle, an individual. But what does it mean to be an individual? We think of a human person as a unique individual distinct from all other human beings. This view is the outcome of a long historical process. Earlier cultures put much greater emphasis on the social role of the individual. In ancient civilizations, such as Mesopotamia and Israel, the human person is understood as a character *(personnage)* rather than as a personality *(personne)*. The individual is indistinguishable from his or her social role and social status.[48] That is why the distinction between the individual and the community he or she belongs to is not as rigid as it seems to be in our modern world.

In Mesopotamia and Israel, the author, being a subcategory of the individual, is a particular character or role. The social group the author belongs to and identifies with is that of the scribes. His work expresses the common values, ideological and artistic, of the scribal community.

The author is a craftsman. Individual talent, which would be as real a gift in antiquity as it is today, was not an instrument to express the private and the personal but was a way to attain the pinnacle of a collective art. The signed acrostic, as in the *Babylonian Theodicy,* is a striking illustration of this view: the individuality of the author, symbolized by his signature, is not reflected in original ideas but through the skill to perfect conventional forms.

If the author is a representative of the scribal craft, anonymity is a fitting phenomenon. To us, it would be unusual to publish something in writing without signing it. A book or an article—be it creative writing, journalism, or a scientific study—is the work of one or more persons; acknowledgment of their authorship is almost a moral obligation. Only those who write for a firm or an advertising agency, as a clerk or a copy writer, write anonymously. This modern practice, more than any other, matches the process of producing texts in antiquity. It confirms the fact that the authors of the time did not write as individuals but functioned as constituent parts of a social organism.

Our concept of the author as an individual is what underpins our concern with authenticity, originality, and intellectual property. The ancient Near East had little place for such notions.[49] Authenticity is subordinate to authority and relevant only inasmuch as it underpins textual authority; originality is subordinate to the cultivation of tradition; and intellectual property is subordinate to the common stock of cultural forms and values. Stock phraseology and conventional ideas are no impediment to success as an author.[50] Copying from another author was not a deadly sin.[51] Though Jeremiah inveighed against the misappropriation of oracles (Jer 23:30), the scribes who composed the oracle collections borrowed freely from existing collections.

To us, it would seem wrong to credit an editor with the work of the author. The author, in our mind, is the intellectual source of the text, whereas an editor merely polishes; the former is the creative genius, the latter merely the technician. The distinction was obviously less important to the ancients. They did not place the same value on originality. To them, an author does not invent his text but merely arranges it; the content of a text exists first, before being laid down in writing. The closest counterpart to our notion of invention is perhaps the concept of revelation. Prophets, as channels of revelation, had to be authenticated, which explains why their work had to be signed. This situation is the only instance, in fact, where textual authenticity is tantamount to textual authority. The signature of Kabti-ilāni-Marduk, the composer of *Erra,* should also be seen in this light.

One last aspect of authorship in antiquity that is important to mention is the socioeconomic context of creative and scholarly writing. Modern writers can be economically independent because they are able to sell their books, have academic tenure, or have family to support them. This kind of independence was hardly available to authors in antiquity. Texts were commissioned or written under the auspices of wealthy individuals or powerful organizations. High-ranking individuals, such as a king or some other wealthy citizen, might commission a text. If the author took the initiative, he made sure that he wrote under the auspices of either the palace or the temple.[52] The gentleman author, writing for his own pleasure, did not appear on the scene until the Hellenistic period. Writing practices before then were not conducive to the expression of a personal point of view. On the contrary, writers were the spokesmen of their patrons and, more generally, the institution to which they belonged.

Were there authors in antiquity? Yes, there were. How about individual talent, literary genius, and outstanding artistic skill? All of that existed. The difference between authors then and authors now has more to do with the conditions of literary production, on the one hand, and the perception of authorship, on the other. Both affected the nature of the texts that have come down to us in writing. When reading them, it is necessary to be aware of those differences so as to put the texts in the proper interpretive perspective.

Conclusion

The gist of the present chapter can be summed up in one phrase: authors, in antiquity, were scribes. "Scribe" *(sôpēr)* is the title given to David as the author of Psalms in the Psalms scroll of Qumran.[53] It captures the professional affiliation of those to whom we owe both the books of the Bible and the literary classics of Mesopotamia. Authors belonged to a certain social category or class. Any attempt to enter into the minds of those authors has to be based on knowledge of the class to which they belonged. As an individual, the author was of little consequence. Authors in antiquity did not perceive themselves primarily as individuals, so we are not entitled to, either. The evidence above shows that we will truly understand the authors of antiquity only by studying the scribal milieu. This is precisely what the following chapters will attempt to do.

chapter three

IN SEARCH OF THE SCRIBES, I

Comparative Evidence

So long as we think of the Bible in terms of authors, our understanding of its origins is bound to be impeded. In antiquity, authorship was invoked to assert authority. Those who actually manufactured texts did not see themselves as authors. They did not pursue originality, and what they wrote was not, in their eyes, an expression of talent but a manifestation of craftsmanship. They were scribes rather than authors.

Moreover, the books that the scribes produced were not books in the modern sense of the term. They were not comparable either in form or function. Scribes wrote scrolls (rather than books) for the benefit of other scribes (rather than for private readers). A book market did not exist, nor were there public libraries; in fact, there was no reading public of any substance. Texts reached the people by being read out loud by someone from the literate elite. Writing and reciting were complementary facets of the scribal craft, and the Bible came into being through the agency of the scribes. Its message was proclaimed from the mouths of scribes and it was preserved for later generations through the skill and diligence of the scribes. In many respects, then, the Bible is the fruit of scribal culture.

By studying the texts of the Bible we can tease out information about the scribal culture that produced them. To help us do so it is essential to supplement the biblical data with extrabiblical evidence. To some degree, this can be gleaned from epigraphic discoveries. More fruitful, however, particularly from a heuristic perspective, is the evidence that can be obtained by means of a comparative study of other cultures that are known to have influenced Palestine. The world of the Bible is closely linked to the cultures of Mesopotamia and Egypt, and the scribal culture of Israel is known to be indebted to these neighboring civilizations. While the next chapter will deal with some of the biblical evidence on scribes, this chapter will offer a comparative study of scribes in the Near East.

Scribal Culture in Context

Before launching into a discussion of the comparative evidence, some preliminary comments are in order. First we must consider the objection that evidence from Mesopotamia or Egypt is simply unfit for comparison because such "great civilizations," owing to their social complexity, do not compare with a "small" civilization or culture like biblical Israel. Since the scribal profession arose in response to the need of the bureaucracy in societies with a developed division of labor, so the argument runs, it is unlikely to have flourished in a simple society with a population consisting largely of self-subsisting peasants. And even if there were scribes in Israel, their training was bound to have been far less elaborate than in Mesopotamia or Egypt. An alphabetic script, like the one used for Hebrew, is so much simpler than cuneiform or hieroglyphics.

The fact remains that whatever the complexity, or lack of it, in Israelite society, the presence of professional scribes cannot be contested. Private seals from the monarchic and the Persian periods designating their owner as "the scribe" *(hspr)* confirm the actual existence of a profession that is repeatedly referred to in the Bible.[1] It is true that the meaning of the term for "scribe" (*sōpēr;* variant: *sôpēr*) differs depending on time and context—as I shall demonstrate in the next chapter—but it has always implied active literacy, to be acquired by thorough training; the mere possession of rudimentary writing skills would not have been enough to qualify a person for the professional title of scribe. Like their counterparts in Mesopotamia and Egypt, the Israelite scribes were the educated men of their time.

In addition to the fact that the Israelite scribes are sociologically comparable to the Mesopotamian and Egyptian scribes, there is yet another argument that calls for the use of comparative evidence. The culture to which scribes belonged was cosmopolitan. The scribe portrayed by Ben Sira "appears before rulers and travels through the lands of foreign nations" (Sir 39:4). Scribes interpreted texts and tongues: the knowledge of foreign languages was part of their profession. The cosmopolitan spirit of scribal culture made it open to influences from the outside world. The influence of Egypt, in pre-exilic times, and of Mesopotamia, from the exilic period onward, on the scribal culture of Israel, and thus on the Bible, is widely recognized.[2]

If it must be acknowledged that there are dangers in overly relying on comparative evidence from Mesopotamia and Egypt, it is also true that the data from Mesopotamia and Egypt provide us with a model that can be used as a reference when trying to reconstruct the world of the scribes of the Bible. This model should not be mistaken for a blueprint of reality. It is useful insofar as it puts us on the right track in our investigations. The ultimate test of our reconstruction is not how it fits the model but how it is supported by the data, of which the largest set is the Bible itself.

We will look first at the Mesopotamian evidence, which is, without doubt, the richest available source on scribal culture in the ancient Near East. Though the data come from a period spanning two millennia, we will focus more particularly on the scribes and scholars of Neo-Assyrian and Neo-Babylonian times (ca. 800–500 B.C.E.). This period has the most information and is closest to Israel during a vital phase of its history. To broaden the horizon, we will then proceed to a summary description of the scribal culture of Egypt. While again the data are culled from a wide range of periods, the emphasis will fall on the scribes from the New Kingdom (ca. 1550–1100 B.C.E.). The model of scribal culture obtained from this comparative evidence will help us reconstruct the world of the scribes behind the Bible.

Mesopotamian Scribes

EDUCATION AS A MARK OF SOCIAL STANDING

In ancient Mesopotamia, formal education was the prerogative of the upper classes. The importance of education is illustrated by the fact that even kings boasted of their prowess at school. King Shulgi (ca. 2050 B.C.E.) is on record as having said:

> As a youth, I studied the scribal art in school
> from the tablets of Sumer and Akkad.
> No noble could write a tablet like I did,
> in the place where people try to master the scribal art.
> Adding, subtracting, counting, and accounting:
> I completed the whole curriculum.
> The fair Nanibgal, that is: Nisaba,
> Endowed me generously with wisdom and intelligence.
> I am a dexterous scribe whom nothing impedes.[3]

As a formal institution, the school (Sumerian *é-dub-ba*, Akkadian *bīt ṭuppi*; literally, the tablet house) disappeared after 1900 B.C.E., but the view that formal training as a scribe endowed one with social superiority remained. Kings continued to present themselves as bright students and accomplished scholars. A classic example is that of Assurbanipal (668–627 B.C.E.). He said:

> I have learned the hidden secret of the complete scribal art. With my own eyes I have seen the tablets of heaven and earth. I have discussed in the assembly of the scholars. I have offered interpretations of "If the liver is a mirror of heaven" [a commentary appended to the extispicy series *bārûtu*] with the skilled diviners. I have explained complicated divisions

that had no obvious solution. I have read bilingual compositions whose Sumerian is obscure and whose Akkadian is difficult to decipher. I have examined stone inscriptions from before the Flood which are extremely obscure.[4]

In many of these inscriptions, reference to the king's mastery of the scribal arts is mere rhetoric; it was simply part of the royal ideology that decreed that the monarch should excel in the various branches of scholarship. The emphasis on the esoteric aspects of writing and scholarship (the scribal art being presented as a "hidden secret") served to accentuate the distinction between those who had had the benefit of scribal training from the common masses who had not.

The custom of referring to a king's schooling intimates that a formal education was a social distinction. Only the social elite—the royal family, its entourage, the administrators, the wealthy landowners—could afford to provide their children with a scribal education. Tuition fees were serious, and anything amounting to a tuition waiver was only within reach of the children of the scribes connected to a school. Most girls were not eligible for a scribal education; as a rule only princesses and the like learned to write, as a mark of personal cultivation.[5] In short, the education system of Mesopotamia favored the perpetuation of a small upper class of educated men who were brought up to consider themselves intellectually superior.

SCRIBAL EDUCATION

It is customary to render the Sumerian expression *é-dub-ba* (and its Akkadian translation *bīt ṭuppi*) as "school." Though not incorrect, the English translation is slightly misleading because it conjures up associations with a formal institution, staffed by several teachers, located in a building of some size. In the Old Babylonian period, however, the "tablet house" was often a private house in which a father would instruct his son (or sons) and one or two boys from the neighborhood.[6] There is evidence that the royal administration was involved in establishing the curriculum, but the school itself was not a royal institution.[7]

The school as it was known in the Old Babylonian period (ca. 1900–1500 B.C.E.) did not survive the so-called dark age of Mesopotamian history (ca. 1500–1100 B.C.E.). From the end of the Kassite period onward, scribal education took place in temple schools. In 1960, Wilfred G. Lambert could affirm only that "general considerations would lead us to suppose that the scribal schools were attached to a temple," since he was unable to adduce any evidence to this effect.[8] A sixth-century text from Uruk, published in the 1990s, contains evidence that the temples did indeed serve as centers of scribal training.[9] The discovery in the 1970s of about 1,500 exercise tablets in the temple of Nabû in Babylon illustrates the significance of its educational role.[10] Scribal instruction took place in the temple workshop, or *bīt mummu,*[11] for which reason an apprentice scribe could refer to himself as "son of the temple workshop."[12] Students would often dedicate their exercise tablets to the god of the temple; on the occasion of religious festivals they offered their work to the deity in token of their devotion.[13] Under the auspices of Nabu, the god of writing, students spent years in the temple workshop in order to become accomplished scribes.[14]

The core of a formal education in Mesopotamia consisted of the acquisition of literacy.[15] At school, one learned *ṭupšarrūtu,* "the scribal art." In the first phase of the curriculum, students were taught to write; they were to acquire good handwriting and ease in transcribing. As a Sumerian proverb has it, "A scribe whose hand can keep up with the mouth, he is indeed a scribe!"[16] They developed writing skills first by copying and memorizing lists—of syllables, words, names, sentences, and proverbs—after which they moved on to excerpts from longer literary texts.[17] Aside from belletristic texts, students had to familiarize themselves with grammar, law, business administration, mathematics, science, music, and historiography. The pedagogy was geared toward the mastery of the technical vocabulary of these various disciplines; the emphasis lay on memorization and scribal skills rather than on the intellectual grasp of the subject matter.

Language skills were part of the "scribal art." Sumerian held an important place in the curriculum, especially in the Old Babylonian period. "A scribe who does not know Sumerian, what kind of scribe is he?"[18] Sumerian had a cultural prestige comparable to that of Latin in medieval Europe. Students learned through the reception and reproduction of the classical texts. In the Old Babylonian period, teachers used two sets of classical texts, referred to by Assyriologists as the "tetrad" and the "decad." A total of fourteen Sumerian compositions were standard on the curriculum.[19] Once these texts had been studied, the curriculum allowed a certain freedom of choice when it came to further reading.

It will be clear from this description that instruction in *ṭupšarrūtu* exceeded the acquisition of mere literacy. One who was studying to become a *ṭupšarru,* a scribe, was acquiring what we would call cultural literacy. Over several years students were immersed in the stream of tradition. Owing to this type of education, scribes were not merely penmen and copyists but intellectuals. In fact, the line between "scribe" *(ṭupšarru)* and "scholar" *(ummânu)* is often difficult to draw, since the scribes were the academics of their time; the scribe is by definition an expert *(mūdû,* literally "one who knows") according to a Babylonian gloss.[20] Assurbanipal's description of his own education is characteristic: his mastery of "the complete scribal art" had turned him into a discussion partner of the *ummânū,* the scholars.

The more academic side of *ṭupšarrūtu* had pride of place in the secondary phase of the scribal training. Once a student had acquired a working knowledge of the various branches of expertise for which a scribe might be called upon, he could choose to continue his studies in order to specialize in a particular field. In the first millennium, students could train as an astrologer *(ṭupšar Enūma Anu Enlil,* literally, "scribe [specializing in the astrological compendium] *Enūma Anu Enlil"),* an exorcist *(āšipu* or *mašmaššu),* a diviner *(bārû),* a medical practitioner *(asû),* or a cult singer *(kalû).* For each of these disciplines, there existed a textual corpus (called *ṭupšarrūtu, āšipūtu, bārûtu, asûtu,* and *kalûtu,* respectively) that served as the basis of the curriculum.

Owing to the discovery of a list of works prescribed for the curriculum of the exorcists, it is possible for us to know what kind of training aspiring scholars received. Copies of this list have been found in the cities of Assur, Nineveh, Babylon, and Sippar, which suggests that it constituted a "national" curriculum.[21] The superscription of this list states that the texts that it enumerates "have been established for study and consultation." The verb here translated as "establish" *(kunnu)* implies a kind of canonization of the set teaching texts.[22] More than seventy-five works on exorcism are listed, many running into forty or more tablets of which much had to be memorized by the student.

The curricular list closes with an injunction to the apprentice exorcist that illustrates that his training was not completed once he had read the great texts of exorcism. When the student had mastered the manuals, he moved on to the texts containing commentaries and interpretations, as well as texts in other dialects, such as the Emesal dialect, and the study of bilingual rituals. At this stage the student did not simply learn by rote but had to "apply himself" and to "discuss" with his teachers and fellow students so that they might reach "consensus" on the meaning of the texts.[23] The program was long and arduous. Those who had the endurance and the capacity to successfully finish it could look ahead to a reward: the gods of exorcism would grant them understanding, and their name would last "till distant days."[24]

Letters from court scholars show that many of them combined several specializations. That practice was in keeping with the view that the various branches of scribal knowledge were not separate domains. All disciplines were subsumed under the label of "wisdom" *(nēmequ)*, which, according to the ideology of the time, emanated from the god Ea. In the Neo-Assyrian *Catalogue of Texts and Authors,* the textbooks of exorcism *(āšipūtu),* liturgy *(kalûtu),* and astrology *(Enūma Anu Enlil)* are all said to be "from the mouth of Ea."[25] This is evidence of a scholarly attitude that sees these written texts as all belonging to a single tradition. The authority of the written word, ascribed to the god of wisdom, transcended the disciplinary divisions.

If only because of the daunting demands of the curriculum, specialist studies did not attract students by the numbers. According to the informed estimate of Benno Landsberger, only 10 percent of all students entered such advanced academic programs.[26] Those who had completed the more advanced scribal programs were submitted to a final examination by the Assembly of the Scholars *(puḫur ummâni)*, as the scribal faculty is called.[27] In token of their graduation they received a diploma that allowed them to practice their specialization profession-ally.[28] They had achieved "all the depth of wisdom," as the curriculum calls it.[29] They were scribes in the fullest sense of the term: scribes, scholars, and sages—and living repositories of the stream of tradition.[30]

SCRIBAL CAREERS

Depending on its duration and area of specialization, a scribal training could prepare students for different careers. Most students who had completed only the first phase of the scribal study program would find a place in the administration; there was a steady demand for clerks and scribes. Others might enter the service of private estates and merchant houses; still others would make a living as a public scribe.[31]

The career of those who went through the second phase of the study program was less predictable. Specialist studies did not automatically ensure one a position as a practitioner of that specialization. Temples were the main employers of religious specialists, and most scholars in Babylonia and Assyria in the first millennium were indeed affiliated with temples.[32] The famous scribal families of Uruk, for instance, were connected with the temples of Uruk.[33] Specializing as exorcists, cult singers, diviners, or astrologers, these scholars belonged to the clergy. To call them priests, however, would be somewhat misleading. In spite of their academic expertise, the scholars were subordinate to the real priests of the temple—such as the *aḫu rabû*, or high priest—who were responsible for the daily care and feeding of the gods. Scribal skills and scholarship did not have the same prestige as a position as steward to the gods.[34]

The positions for scholars in temples were limited in number; nor were astrologers, medical practitioners, exorcists, and diviners exclu-sively associated with temples. They were specialists whose work would often bring them into contact with temples, but as professionals they did not necessarily depend on the temples for their income. In fact, some specialists might exercise their profession only part-time, having other sources of income beside their scholarly expertise.[35] We know about a first-millennium ritual designed to bring about brisk business for the diviner, the medical practitioner, and the exorcist.[36] These men operated on the open market, then, which supports Herodotus's report about the way the Babylonians went to the marketplace for advice on disease (*Hist.* 1.198). As a rule, a career as scribe was a secure source of income; there was sufficient demand for the higher scribal skills to permit scribes a life of moderate riches.[37]

Some of the more renowned specialists might obtain a position at the royal court. Though they were a minority of the scholars, they figure prominently in the secondary literature on Mesopotamian scholars because they left a voluminous correspondence with several Assyrian kings.[38] The scholars in question lived in Nineveh, where they acted as counselors to the court. In addition, some had responsibilities in connection with the state cult and others acted as personal tutors of members of the royal family. Their letters offer a remarkable view into the lives and thoughts of the scribal scholars. What they write is perhaps not representative of all Mesopotamian scholars, but it is material that cannot be neglected.

What is striking in the letters of these scholars is the extent of their knowledge and the range of activities in which they were involved. They advised on the health of the king, military tactics, the best ways to keep the gods happy, and the significance of strange events—there seemed to be no limit to what they could advise on. Every piece of advice they gave was based on what they had learned from written lore, and their influence was crucial in both matters of state and the personal life of the monarch. The king had to be sure that his advisors were qualified and trustworthy; his dependence on the expertise of his scholars made him vulnerable and inclined to suspicion.

The ambivalent relationship between kings and scholars is reflected in royal inscriptions in which the kings assert themselves by boasting of their superior wisdom. Assurbanipal portrays himself as the equal of his scholars, and enjoys being called "wiser than Adapa," Adapa being the primordial sage and the patron of scholars. Other kings made comparable claims.[39] However, in day-to-day life the king's knowledge did not match that of his scholars, and he had no choice but to defer to their judgment. It was crucial that he could count on their loyalty. Because the relationship between the king and his scholars was both professional and personal, a change of rule often entailed a change of scholars; the new king brought new confidants into office. Because their positions were always precarious, there was constant competition and rivalry among the scholars. In their letters many praise their own scholarship and describe their rivals as intellectual misfits.

The case of Urad-Gula illustrates how precarious the career of a court scholar could be.[40] Urad-Gula served under the kings Sennacherib (704–681), Esarhaddon (680–669), and Assurbanipal (668–627). Son of the royal exorcist Adad-šumu-uṣur, Urad-Gula seemed destined for a brilliant career. In the reign of Sennacherib he was nominated deputy chief of medical practitioners, and under Esarhaddon he became court exorcist. However, on the accession of Assurbanipal, Urad-Gula was suddenly demoted for reasons that escape us. Father and son both sent several letters of complaint to the new king, who seemed not at all inclined to change his mind. In one of these letters, Urad-Gula points out that he has always been loyal and possesses a record of service that should earn him a position of prominence in the new administration. As it is, however, he is a nobody. Lesser men than he ride in a palanquin, a cart, or on a mule, whereas he, Urad-Gula, has to go on foot without so much as a pair of sandals. A letter by his father reveals that things eventually took a turn for the better. Assurbanipal accepted Urad-Gula once again and allowed him to continue his career as court scholar.

Urad-Gula's career is characteristic of the first millennium Mesopotamian scholars in more than one respect. Family connections, for example, were very important. It is unlikely that Urad-Gula would have obtained such an eminent position as court scholar if Adad-šumu-uṣur had not been his father. A study of the ties between the top scholars that formed the "inner circle" of royal advisors shows that all of them came from a limited number of influential families.[41]

On the whole, the scribal profession was hereditary. "The son takes the profession of his father," according to a Sumerian school text.[42] In the first millennium, knowledge was also passed on from father to son, especially when the son was at a more advanced phase of his studies.[43] Colophons show that junior scribes would often copy tablets for their fathers' collections—collections that they would eventually inherit. In the different cities of southern Mesopotamia, scribes were organized according to families. Many of them traced their ancestry back to the late second millennium B.C.E. In Neo-Babylonian Uruk, for instance, many scribes considered themselves descendants of Sin-leqe-unninni, the composer of the *Gilgamesh Epic*.[44] Whether this is historically correct or not does not matter; the claim shows the importance of birth and descent for a scribe's self-image.

Another characteristic facet of Urad-Gula's career is the way he was able to switch from medicine *(asûtu)* to exorcism *(āšipūtu)*. He had evidently mastered two distinct fields.[45] Proficiency in more than one specialization was not uncommon among Mesopotamian scholars. In a self-recommendation written to the king, a cult singer *(kalû)* points out that he is versed in all the major disciplines.

> I fully master my father's profession, the discipline of hymnology; I have studied and chanted the Series. I am competent in . . ., "mouth-washing," and purification of the palace . . . I have examined healthy and sick flesh. I have read [the astrological omen series] *Enūma Anu Enlil* . . . and made astronomical observations. I have read [the teratological series] *Šumma izbu,* [the physiognomical works] [*Kataduqqû, Alamdi*]*mmû* and *Nigdimmû,* . . . [and (the terrestrial omen series) *Šum*]*ma ālu*.[46]

In addition to being a professional cult singer, the author of this letter claims knowledge in the fields of astrology, exorcism, and divination. Such multidisciplinary knowledge was not exceptional. Scholars were specialists in a particular field, but their training was geared to provide them with the kind of encyclopedic knowledge that was in keeping with the status of an expert scribe.[47]

Because substantial numbers of letters by scholars working for the king have been preserved, we could be misled into thinking that the court was where Mesopotamian scholars usually had their offices. That is not the case. The scholars were religious specialists, and as such the temple was not only their main employer but also their natural habitat. Within the temple compound they were associated more specifically with the temple workshop. In the life of the scholars, the temple workshop and the temple library were important institutions.[48]

The temple workshop, known as the *bīt mummu*, served more than one purpose. It was the place where craftsmen made and repaired cult statues and other ritual objects, but it was also a school for scribes and a center of text production. Nabû and Nisaba, the gods of writing, were "the lords of the temple workshop."[49] The Assembly of Scholars *(puḫur ummânī)* had its seat in the *bīt mummu*.[50] Precisely because it was the meeting place for scholars, it has been suggested that the expression *bīt mummu* should be translated as "temple academy."[51] However, since it was a place where scholars, craftsmen, and students pursued their own activities, it is more appropriate to retain the term *workshop*.

The temples were the obvious place for the Mesopotamian scholars to work. Temples were centers of scholarship and learning because of their libraries; they provided religious scholars with suitable opportunities to practice their craft. The lore of the Mesopotamian scholars was mostly written lore, and when memory failed them, they could consult the tablets. Some scholars had their own personal library, but most of them depended on the texts in the collective libraries of the temples.

The term *temple library* (Akkadian *gerginakku*, etymologically "series [*scil.*] of tablets") is misleading if it is understood to signify a place where librarians actively acquired tablets to make their collection as

comprehensive as possible.[52] The temple collections were based on do-
nations. Colophons often record the names of scholars who wrote or
commissioned a tablet and gave it to the temple library.[53] Copying a
text for the temple was considered a meritorious deed. A scholar who
did this could expect to be rewarded by the gods with good health, intelligence, and a stable professional situation.[54] Once deposited in the
temple, the tablet became the "sacred property" *(ikkibu)* of the deity of
the temple.[55] Tablets were available for consultation, but only for professional scholars. Scribes were allowed to take a tablet home for copying on condition that they would not alter a single line and would return the tablet promptly.[56] The lending periods varied from one day to
a month.[57]

Many of the Mesopotamian libraries are now lost, including the
collections housed in some of the most famous temples, such as the
Marduk temple in Babylon.[58] Nevertheless, a sufficient number of temple libraries have been recovered to allow us to assess the size and the
contents of an average collection.[59] The largest temple library discovered to date is that of the Šamaš temple in Sippar. It is also "the oldest library in history that was found essentially intact on its original
shelves."[60] Its more than 800 tablets include a wealth of scholarly texts
and some traditional literary works, such as *Atraḫasis, Enūma eliš,*
pseudo-autobiographies, and the prologue to the *Laws of Hammurabi*.[61] Other collections are smaller. The Aššur temple in the city of
Ashur and the Nabû temple in Kalḫu (Nimrud) each had about 300
tablets. Tablet series on the various branches of Mesopotamian scholarship made up the bulk of temple collections; lexical lists and lists of
gods have also been found, whereas myths and epics are relatively rare.

The temple workshop was the seat of the Assembly of Scholars and
as such the institutional environment for scholarly debate. Learned discussion was a significant part of the life of the scribes. After all, eloquence was one of the main goals of a scribal education.[62] The epilogue to *Enūma eliš* describes scholars, referred to as "the wise and the
knowledgeable," "consulting one another" about the meaning of the
fifty names of Marduk.[63] The purpose of their discussions is increased

understanding and, ultimately, intellectual consensus.[64] Students also took part in these debates and wrote their tablets "in the meeting of the scholars," profiting from the explanations senior scholars offered them. The study of written texts was accompanied, then, by the verbal exchange of scholarly lore.[65]

SCRIBAL CULTURE

Mesopotamian scribal culture instilled a sense of superiority in its scholars that set them apart from all those without scribal training. Of scribal education in the Old Babylonian period it has been said that "scribal training served to create an *esprit de corps,* a club of those who knew the literary, religious, and scholarly traditions, who acquired the cultural capital to gain legitimate access to the circles of the elite."[66] In today's world we would call them the "in crowd." Scribes in the first millennium were conscious of their membership in a social elite. They saw themselves as initiates, in that the lore of the texts was theirs alone.

The distinction of the Mesopotamian scribes had a material basis in their ability to decipher texts in an arcane language written in a cryptic script. Assurbanipal spoke of the scribal art as a secret and referred to the obscurity of Sumerian and the difficulty of Akkadian. Though the difficulty of cuneiform writing tends to be overrated, both by ancient and modern students, the nonliterate public regarded reading and writing almost as a feat of magic. The scribes cultivated the abstruseness of the cuneiform script through the occasional use of rare signs and unusual logograms.[67] The two languages of the written tradition were Sumerian and Akkadian; by the second millennium B.C.E., Sumerian had already become a language of scholars and jurists, incomprehensible to the general public. By the mid-first millennium, Akkadian was the language of literature and Aramaic was the language of everyday life; while not totally foreign, Akkadian was a serious obstacle to easy access to the tradition.[68] Scribes who could play with the script and had a command of the classical Mesopotamian languages stood apart from the rest of the population.[69]

Secrecy played an important part in the sense of superiority that the scribes cultivated. Students of the various scribal arts had to take a vow of secrecy when they entered their program. A teacher (often father) swore his pupil (son) to secrecy before he taught him his craft.[70] One had to be worthy to enter this closed society of learned men, and a proper social background was an important prerequisite. Teaching the texts of exorcism, divination, or astrology to someone who had not been officially admitted as a candidate-scholar could lead to royal punishment.[71] Successful completion of the training earned the student admission to the circle of the elect. A rite of investiture symbolized his entry into the group of professional scholars: distinctive clothes and paraphernalia marking rank and professional expertise consolidated his sense of belonging to a social elite.[72]

Colophons appended to scholarly works say that the texts are "secret lore of the scholars. The initiate may show it to (another) initiate, but to a non-initiate he may not show it."[73] Such colophons support the idea that Assyrian and Babylonian scribe-scholars were an insular group that had little interaction with the outside world. This impression is counterbalanced, to some degree, by the notion of scholars as teachers. The texts say little about this aspect of their life. One reference comes from *Ludlul bēl nēmeqi*, "I shall praise the Lord of Wisdom," a didactic song of thanksgiving by a court scholar. The protagonist protests his innocence, referring, among other things, to his role as teacher.

> I instructed my land to keep the god's rites,
> And taught my people to honor the name of the goddess.
> I sang the praises of the king as though he were a god,
> And taught the population respect for the palace.[74]

Urad-Gula, whose career as a scholar has been discussed above, makes a similar claim in a similar context. In a letter to the king he points out that he taught the palace servants, "the non-eunuchs and the eunuchs alike," submission and respect for the king.[75] These references are best taken to mean that the scholars offered some form of instruction. Though they did not teach nonscribes the secrets of their profession, they used their authority as men of learning to impress on their fellow citizens the importance of religion and obedience to superiors.

The Assyrian and Babylonian scholars were heirs to, participants in, and perpetuators of a scribal culture that venerated written tradition to a degree seen only in oral cultures. They regarded the scribal craft, including its scholarly specializations, as something beyond the reach of the common masses. Recruited from the aristocracy, they followed in the footsteps of their fathers. Their institutional locus was the temple workshop, situated in the vicinity of the temple library. Their knowledge was mastered through copying and memorizing and honed through discussion and scholarly debate. Whether their own sense of superiority corresponded with a general esteem for scribes and scholars among the population is uncertain. Two or three texts suggest that ordinary people liked to poke fun at scholars on occasion.[76] However, amusement at the expense of the experts does not preclude a fundamental respect for their scholarship; in fact, the two often go together.

Egyptian Scribes

LITERACY AS A MARK OF SOCIAL STANDING

Literacy in Egypt, as in Mesopotamia, was a mark of the elite.[77] The portion of the Egyptian population that was able to read and write (about 5 percent) coincided largely with the aristocracy. Dignitaries, clergy, officials, and anyone with any rank in the royal administration sent their sons to school, or to a tutor. Literacy ran in families, just as scribal offices in practice were often hereditary. The scribal "dynasties" that have left their mark in surviving texts were drawn from the high-ranking families of the land. The typical teaching relationship was modeled on the bond between father and son, which even if merely rhetorical still reflects the importance of birth and family for access to a formal education.[78]

Owing to a series of social changes in the time preceding the New Kingdom, the privilege of a scribal education became accessible to most layers of the population. Egyptologists have argued that the scribal elite changed from an aristocracy into a meritocracy.[79] However, though a scribal career was in principle open to individuals of all social classes, examples of scribes from a modest extraction are rare. The boasting of many officials about their simple descent is often more rhetoric than fact.[80] The few examples of men from simple origins who did manage to achieve a position of influence and fortune as a scribe are the exception, although they do show that the existence of a traditional aristocracy in Egypt did not completely preclude social mobility.

SCRIBAL TRAINING

During the New Kingdom (ca. 1550–1100 B.C.E.), the Egyptian territory expanded, the bureaucracy increased in size, and schools proliferated. Many of them were located in temples.[81] Elementary instruction lasted about four to five years.[82] After an introduction to the principles of writing, students used a manual known as *Kemyt,* "compendium," which contained exercises in epistolary formulas, a model letter, and various kinds of suitable phrases.[83] Lexicographical lists, or so-called *Onomastica,* served the same purpose in Egyptian education as the cuneiform lists of plants, stones, and gods did for the Mesopotamian scribes.[84] A basic education in geography, arithmetic, and geometry was also part of the curriculum.

Pupils with a grasp of the basics continued their education with the study of some of the classical wisdom texts, such as the Satire on the Trades and the various Instructions. The Instructions, known in Egyptian as *sb3yt* (conventionally vocalized as *sbōyet*), consist of counsels and sayings; they exemplify the importance of proverbs and other wisdom texts in the scribal curriculum.[85] The compositions were chanted and memorized; students made copies on the basis of memory.[86] After four years, as the first phase of the curriculum was finished, students were allowed to call themselves "scribe" (*sš* or *sḫ*), a professional title that would generally ensure them a position in the royal administration.[87] Their knowledge of writing did not extend to hieroglyphics, the classical script used for monumental inscriptions and in ancient texts; it did not go beyond mastery of the more simple hieratic script, which was sufficient for most administrative tasks.

Students who wished to master hieroglyphics had to continue their education for a considerably longer period. The advanced curriculum, which included an apprenticeship in one of the professions that could be entered after such literary and scholarly training, like physician or lector-priest, could take up to twelve years.[88] The specialized knowledge students here acquired was based on extensive exposure to more technical texts, broadly comparable to the curriculum followed by the Babylonian exorcists. Most advanced students would have completed their studies by the age of twenty.

TEMPLE WORKSHOP AND TEMPLE LIBRARY

For those entering the priesthood—a term covering a wide array of professions but all connected in some way to the temple—the place for instruction was the "House of Life" *(pr-ꜥnḫ)*.[89] The term refers to a locality near the temple and, by connotation, the body of scholars and specialists attached to it.[90] The Egyptian House of Life was more than a school or a scriptorium. It was a place where doctors, astronomers, mathematicians, and sculptors worked and collaborated on activities designed to promote the welfare of the land. Because it was a center of learning and intellectual life, the House of Life has been compared with the university in premodern Europe.[91] The parallel is apt in the sense that most works of scholarship and religion originated in the House of Life and were copied there for teaching and research purposes.[92] However, since the House of Life was also a place where specialists spoke their spells and artisans made their products, the term *workshop* is more appropriate than *university* or *academy*.[93] In many ways, the Egyptian House of Life is reminiscent of the Mesopotamian temple workshop *(bīt mummu)*.

Under the supervision of the "teacher of the House of Life," scribal students followed a program of advanced studies.[94] The training transformed the scribes into scholars. Books, or rather scrolls, played a crucial role during their study and, later, in their profession. Normally the

69

House of Life would be situated near a library *(pr-mdȝt)* or would have its own; on occasion, the House of Life was coterminous with the library.[95] The Egyptian term that we translate as "library" literally means "house of scrolls." It can refer to an archive as well as to a library.[96] As in the case of the Mesopotamian temple libraries, caution counsels the use of the more neutral term "text collection." These collections included rituals, cultic songs, myths, astrology, astronomy, and exorcism, as well as medical handbooks and funerary literature. To stress their special status the texts were qualified as "secret." The House of Life was the privileged platform for scholarly discussion and philological commentary elicited by the texts. The "scribes of the House of Life" were indeed synonymous with the "learned men" *(rḫ-ḫt);* their culture, as such, was based on the classical texts of literature and scholarship.[97]

EGYPTIAN SCHOLARSHIP AND THE PRIESTHOOD

The existence of a class of priests known as the lector-priests (Egyptian *ḫry-ḫbt)* points to the relationship between literacy and the priesthood. It furnishes us with the occasion to ask about the role of the priesthood in the formation and transmission of the written culture of ancient Egypt. We know that the House of Life was a temple institution; does this mean that the priests were the trustees of the written tradition?

In circumscribing the role of the priesthood as the scribal elite of Egypt, it is important to observe that the Egyptian priesthood was a hierarchical body of three levels.[98] The lowest class of priests were the *wʿb*-priests, the "pure ones," who performed the menial chores in the sanctuary. Most of these men were nonliterate. The lector-priests constituted the middle class. For them, literacy was a prerequisite. They were the ones who recited the spells and performed the rites in temple ceremonies and in funerary rituals. In the Hebrew Bible they appear as "the magicians of Egypt" (*ḥarṭummê miṣrayim,* Exod 7:9, 22) whose powers proved to be inferior to those of Moses and Aaron (Exod 7–9).[99] On murals the lector-priests are often depicted holding or reading from a papyrus scroll. Above them in the hierarchy stood the "servants of God," usually referred to in the secondary literature, following their Greek designation, as "prophets," a somewhat misleading term because these men bore no resemblance whatsoever to the biblical prophets. Because there were four different classes of "prophets," the upper level of the Egyptian priesthood was hierarchically stratified.[100] These "prophets" were certainly literate, but their tasks were primarily the administration of the temple and the performance of the sacrificial rites.

The one group in the priesthood that might appropriately be called the guardians of the holy writ are the lector-priests. In the native perception the lector-priests were the wise men and the sages among the clergy. The well-known prophet Neferti, from the Middle Kingdom, was a lector-priest.[101] In consonance with that fact, lector-priests are documented announcing the verdicts of the oracles that took place at festivals. The chief lector-priest *(ḫry-ḥbt ḥry-tp)* was entrusted with the task of overseeing the preservation and the proper recitation of the sacred texts. Exegetical research was one of his responsibilities.

Two observations merit particular notice in connection with the scribal role of the lector-priests. First, the lector-priests were second in rank to the "prophets"; their prominence as trustees and transmitters of the written tradition notwithstanding, the lector-priests were nevertheless considered a *clerus minor* compared with the upper stratum of the priesthood. Second, nearly all lector-priests were part-time priests. They served the temple on the basis of a rotation system, which meant they were on duty for only three months of the year. According to their letters and administrative records, most of them made a living for the rest of the year as businessmen. Unlike the Babylonian temple scholars, then, their ordinary interaction with the outside world prevented them from becoming an insular group of self-conscious literati.

Conclusion

In many respects, the similarities between the scribal cultures of ancient Egypt and of Mesopotamia are striking. In both civilizations, a formal education, and the literacy this entailed, was normally the prerogative of the upper class. Alongside scribes who had completed only the first level of the scribal education, ready to follow a career in the administration or to gain a living as private scribes, there were those who had followed advanced studies. They spent an extended period of time studying and memorizing a wide array of written lore pertinent to their area of specialization. For the Mesopotamian scribes the higher phase of their education culminated in a formal graduation, including an oral examination and a certificate. Both in Mesopotamia and Egypt, the students who had completed the second phase of the scribal curriculum were the scholars and the "wise men" of their time.

The intellectual center for the scribal scholars was the temple workshop, known as the *bīt mummu* in Mesopotamia and the House of Life *(pr-'nḫ)* in Egypt. There the literati formed an elitist society. Their knowledge was a knowledge contained in, and symbolized by, written texts—texts that they could read but that were inaccessible to the ordinary citizen. These scholars not only studied and used the sacred texts; they also wrote and edited them. The House of Life of the Egyptian temple, much like the temple workshop in Mesopotamia, was a center not only of text study, preservation, and transmission, but also one of text creation.[102] Scribes with scholarly training were instrumental in composing new texts.

Since the search for the scribes behind the Hebrew Bible entails not so much an investigation of individuals as the characterization of a specific social class, the comparative evidence from Mesopotamia and Egypt, which shows that the scribes constituted a professional group with a distinct corporate culture, may prove a useful heuristic device. That is, it may put us on the track toward the identification of the scribes behind the Bible. Informed by the data on the Mesopotamian and the Egyptian scribes and scholars, we shall investigate the biblical evidence on scribes in the chapter that follows.

One issue that will merit special attention is the relationship of the scribes and scholars to the priests. The Mesopotamian and the Egyptian evidence shows that temples were important employers of scribal scholars. In the temple hierarchy, however, the specialists of writing and scholarship stood below the priests, whose duties brought them into closer contact with the deity. It will be part of the investigation in the next chapter to see whether a similar division existed among the Israelite clergy.

chapter four

IN SEARCH OF THE SCRIBES, II

The Biblical Evidence

The books of the Bible would not have seen the light in the oral culture of Israel if it were not for the professional scribes. They are the main figures behind biblical literature; we owe the Bible entirely to them.[1] Who were the scribes behind the Bible? In this chapter we will search the biblical evidence for answers.

The principal difficulty in the search for the Israelite counterparts of the scribes of Mesopotamia and Egypt is the scarcity of written artifacts from pre-Hellenistic Palestine. We owe our knowledge of the Mesopotamian and Egyptian scribes to the records they left us. Due to the corrosive effects of the Palestinian climate on the fragile writing materials that the Hebrew scribes used, relatively few inscriptions have been preserved.[2] In view of the many surviving clay tags that were originally attached to papyrus scrolls, we know that the professional production of written texts must have been significant even in the pre-exilic period.[3] As it is, the principal legacy of the Hebrew scribes is the Hebrew Bible; however, the earliest manuscripts of the Bible at our disposal are from the mid-second century B.C.E. (Qumran). Moreover, the Bible as we know it is canonical literature; the texts have gone through a process of selection and editing. Our evidence on the Hebrew scribes is therefore both indirect and tailored to other needs than those of the historian.

Despite the difficulties in using the Hebrew Bible as an avenue of investigating the Hebrew scribes, there is hardly any other option available to us. The comparative evidence has its heuristic uses, and the epigraphic discoveries (including the Dead Sea Scrolls) highlight aspects of scribal practice, but the main source of information on the Hebrew scribes is the Hebrew Bible itself. Thus I propose to carefully explore the world of the scribes who produced the texts.[4] To that end, I shall attempt to pry loose the data that the biblical texts are able to yield.

The question of the identity of the Hebrew scribes must be tackled in terms of their place in society and their institutional background. The scribes to whom we owe the Hebrew Bible were affiliated with the temple. To understand their mind-set and professional ethics, we have to consider their education. Though the data on scribal education in Israel are scant, they allow a general reconstruction of the curriculum. More forthcoming are the texts, when it comes to the role of the temple scribes in the society of their time. In a religious system that was increasingly based on the authority of written texts, the privileged few who had access to those texts held a position of power and prestige.

"Scribe" and "Sage"

The assertion that we owe the Hebrew Bible to the Hebrew scribes is based on the assumption that oral cultures depend on professionals of writing for the production and preservation of written records. Explicit references to scribes as writers of Bible texts—that is, texts that eventually became part of the Bible—are very rare. When Bible passages mention their writer, the reference is usually to God or a prophet.[5] The two occasions on which the Bible mentions scribes as writers of Bible texts deserve careful consideration. Both references are from the Book of Jeremiah.

An oracle attributed to Jeremiah pictures the scribes as sages who derive prestige from the religious literature they have produced.

> How can you say, "We are sages,
> and we possess the Torah of Yahweh"?
> Assuredly, the deceitful pen of the scribes
> Has turned it into a deception!
> The sages shall be put to shame,
> they shall be dismayed and caught.
> For they have rejected the word of Yahweh,
> so what kind of wisdom is theirs?
>
> Jer 8:8–9

In this passage, the self-styled sages boast of possession of the Torah of Yahweh. From the reference to the "pen" of the scribes it is clear that this Torah is a written document. The author of the oracle—whether the historical Jeremiah or the editor of his collected prophecies—regards this Torah as a "deception" or "lie" *(šeqer)* and denies its divine inspiration. The oracle may reflect a polemic about different versions of the written Torah or about the legitimacy of a Torah in writing as opposed to the oral Torah. Whatever the case may be, the scribes who were responsible for this Torah were not just copyists but composers of the text.

The second reference to a scribe writing the Bible is the account of Baruch recording the oracles of Jeremiah (Jer 36). The narrative insists on the purely instrumental role of the scribe: Jeremiah recited his oracles, and Baruch used pen and ink to write them down in a scroll (Jer 36:18). The emphasis on a literal transcription serves to legitimize a collection of prophecies attributed to Jeremiah. The theological bias of the account should alert us to the possibility that the scribe did in fact produce more than a mere transcription. Contemporaries of Jeremiah suspected Baruch of putting his own words in the mouth of the prophet (Jer 43:2–3).

The term that the two passages use for scribe is *sōpēr* (sometimes

written *sôpēr*), with the plural *sōpĕrîm*. Our quest for the scribes behind the Hebrew Bible has a natural starting point in a study of this Hebrew word. According to the *Hebrew and Aramaic Lexicon* by Koehler,
Baumgartner, and Stamm, Hebrew *sōpēr* has four meanings: (1) scribe,
secretary; (2) royal official, secretary of state; (3) secretary for Jewish
affairs; (4) scholar of scripture *(Schriftgelehrte)*.[6] Let us submit these
four meanings of *sōpēr* to a closer inspection.

(1) The word *sōpēr* primarily denotes the scribe as a craftsman of
writing known by such implements as a "pen" (*'ēṭ*, Ps 45:2; Jer 8:8), a
"writing case" (*qeset*, Ezek 9:2,3), and a "knife" (*ta'ar*, Jer 36:23).[7] He
normally writes in ink (*dĕyô*, Jer 36:18) on a scroll (*mĕgillâ*, Jer 36 pas-
sim), where he disposes his text in columns (*delet*, plural *dĕlātôt*, Jer
36:23).[8]

(2) The earliest use of the term *sōpēr* in a more narrow sense occurs
in connection with the royal court. Seraiah was the "scribe" of David
(2 Sam 8:17); his sons Elihoreph and Ahijah were "scribes" of Solomon
(1 Kings 4:3); Shebna was "scribe" under Hezekiah (2 Kings 18:18;
19:2); Shaphan was "scribe" of Josiah (2 Kings 22); Elishama was
the "scribe" of Jehoiakim (Jer 36); and Jonathan was the "scribe" of
Zedekiah (Jer 37).[9] These men were not ordinary scribes but high-ranking officials. Shebna, for instance, was originally a royal steward (Hebrew *'ăšer 'al-habbayit*, Isa 22:15).[10] As applied to these men, *sōpēr* is a
title best rendered as "chancellor" or "secretary of state." They ranked
higher than penmen or scholars; their position resembled that of the
Egyptian "royal letter-writer of Pharaoh" who, as head of the royal
secretariat, was responsible for the foreign and domestic correspondence of the king.[11] The activities of royal scribes as reported in the Bible have to do with diplomatic encounters (2 Kings 18:17–37); consultation with political advisors (2 Kings 19:1–7); and the management of
temple funds (2 Kings 12:10–16, 22:3–7). The physical act of writing
seems to have been a minor aspect of their duties.[12]

(3) The third meaning of the term *sōpēr*, "secretary for Jewish affairs," is attested only in connection with Ezra. In a classic study on

Ezra, Hans Heinrich Schaeder makes a compelling case for distinguishing between the Aramaic title *sāprā'*, found at Ezra 7:12, 21, and its Hebrew interpretation in Ezra 7:6, 11.[13] In the nomenclature of the Persian government, a scribe is a high-ranking member of the Persian royal bureaucracy, in Ezra's case with a special responsibility for Jewish affairs. In his capacity as secretary for Jewish affairs, Ezra is authorized to draw money from the royal treasury to pay for construction activities on the Jerusalem temple (Ezra 7:21–22).

The Hebrew version of the title of Ezra interprets it in a way that departs from its meaning in Aramaic. Being "an expert scribe in the Torah of Moses" (*sōpēr māhîr bĕtôrat Mōšeh,* Ezra 7:6), Ezra is a scholar rather than an official. An Aramaic parallel to the expression *sōpēr māhîr* is *spr ḥkym wmhyr.* This expression occurs in the *Story of Ahiqar,* a romance from around the fifth century B.C.E., and it qualifies Ahiqar as "a wise and expert scribe."[14] Ezra was a "wise" scribe, too, according to Ezra 7:25. His wisdom, however, is embodied in the Torah of Moses, as a comparison of the quotes from Ezra 7:25 ("the wisdom of your God that is in your hand") and 7:14 ("the Law of your God that is in your hand") demonstrates. Both Ezra and Ahiqar were scholars rather than mere scribes. The area of Ezra's scholarship is specified as being the written Torah. The Torah is his wisdom. In the *interpretatio hebraica* of Ezra's status as a "scribe," Ezra is a Torah scholar.

(4) The Jewish interpretation of Ezra's title *sōpēr* as scholar turns Ezra into the figurehead of the "scholars of scripture" (*Schriftgelehrten*) of the Second Temple. This is the fourth meaning of the term *sōpēr.* The scribes who were scholars of scripture belonged to the group of the Levites (2 Chron 34:13). According to Nehemiah 8, several Levites assisted Ezra during his Torah reading in the temple:

> The Levites explained the Torah to the people, while the people remained in their places. And they read from the scroll, from the Torah of God, interpreting it and clarifying its meaning; so they understood the reading.
>
> Neh 8:7–8[15]

The fact that the Levitical scribes operated as a group is significant. This does not mean that they took turns in reading and explaining. It is far more plausible that they gave instruction simultaneously but at different points and to different audiences. The Levitical scribes were teachers of Torah.

> They offered instruction throughout Judah, and they had with them the Scroll of the Torah of Yahweh. They made the rounds of all the cities of Judah and taught among the people.
>
> 2 Chron 17:9

Having the written Torah "with them" *('immāhem)* as a handbook (compare the expression *tāpaś 'et-hattôrâ*, "to hold the Torah," in Jer 2:8), the Levites were "teaching" *(lmd,* pi'el, 2 Chron 17:9), "interpreting" *(byn,* hip'il, Neh 8:7), "explaining" *(prš,* pi'el, Neh 8:8), and "clarifying the meaning" *(śym śekel,* Neh 8:8) of the Torah. As scholars of scripture, the Levites acted as the successors of Moses who had been the first to "explicate" *(b'r,* pi'el) the Torah (Deut 1:5; compare Deut 30:1–13).

The use of *sōpēr* in the meaning of "scholar" invites us to examine the connection between the terms *sōpēr* and *ḥākām.* The basic meaning of *ḥākām* is "wise," used both as an adjective and as a noun. However, the wisdom implied by the Hebrew term is semantically broader than the concept of wisdom in modern European languages. To us, wisdom stands for prudence, common sense, and balanced judgment, all rooted in a natural disposition of the individual and brought to fruition by experience. In Hebrew, as in most other ancient Near Eastern languages, "wisdom" can also refer to specialized knowledge and learning acquired through education. Where an Israelite would say, "Acquire wisdom!" (Prov 4:5, 7), we would say, "Get an education!" The *ḥăkāmîm* are not only wise human beings but "experts," "sages," "learned men," and, thus, "scholars."

Since wisdom in the sense of learning and scholarship presupposes high literacy, and literacy is to be acquired by a scribal training, it is no surprise to find that *ḥăkāmîm* and *sōpĕrîm* are used occasionally as synonyms. In his attack on the *ḥăkāmîm*, Jeremiah identifies them as scribes (Jer 8:8–9). Centuries later, Ben Sira still regards wisdom as the proper pursuit of the scribe (Sir 38:24). In the conception of the contemporaneous Qumran community, David was the writer of Psalms and therefore, by implication, a "sage" and a "scribe."[16] The rhetorical question, "Who is wise? Let him consider these words," is an admonition to the scribal student who is reading the Book of Hosea (Hosea 14:10; see also Ps 107:43). And when Proverbs says that the fear of the Lord is the beginning of wisdom (Prov 1:7 and elsewhere), it understands wisdom as learning obtained through a scribal education. The accomplished scribe, in other words, is an expert and a scholar—that is, a *ḥākām*.

In light of the preceding observations, the use of *sōpēr* with the meaning "scholar of scripture," the fourth meaning assigned to the term, must be viewed as a particularization of the concept of the scribe as a scholar. The comparative evidence from Mesopotamia and Egypt has prepared us to expect a connection between the scribal art, scholarship, and wisdom. The scholars of the ancient Near East had by definition received a scribal training; they were scribes in the sense of scholars. The scholars of Israel were no exception to the common pattern: they were scribes who had specialized in the classic texts, which in their case made them scholars of the Torah.

The rest of this chapter will be dealing primarily with the scholar-scribes or sages, since they are the ones most intimately connected with the making of the Hebrew Bible. That focus should not lead to an obfuscation of the fact that the term "scribe" covered other meanings as well, especially in the later periods. The Talmud uses the term "scribes" for penmen, drafters of documents, and teachers of elementary subjects and writing; scholars of scripture were called sages.[17] In a study on Jewish scribes in the Second Temple period, Christine Schams emphasizes with good cause that "scribes" were often village scribes, copyists, or government officials.[18] The scribes to whom we owe the Hebrew Bible, however, were scribes whose training and talent made them the intellectuals of their time; they were scribes in the sense of scholars.[19]

Royal Scribes and Temple Scribes

Which scribes were responsible for the writing of the Hebrew Bible? We can narrow down the possibilities by asking after the institution with which the scribes were affiliated, assuming that there were no economically independent scribes in ancient Israel. In the time of the Mishna, there were public scribes offering their services at the marketplace (*m. Git.* 3.1).[20] In the First Temple period the demand for written documents was presumably too limited to allow scribes to subsist as freelance professionals. Private scribes in Mesopotamia worked for large estates and merchant houses; the scale of the economy in Palestine hardly offered such opportunities. The notion that Baruch was a private scribe, as some authors have suggested, is probably an anachronism.[21] Scribes in Israel were attached to the palace or the temple; on occasion private citizens might hire their services, but this did not turn the scribes into private secretaries.

The biblical evidence intimates that the scribes behind the Hebrew Bible were attached to the temple as an institutional and intellectual center; they belonged to the clergy. With this assertion I depart from the view that the bulk of the Hebrew Bible is from the hands of palace scribes. A representative of the latter view is Edward Lipiński; he attributes proverbs, chronicles, and annals to the court scribes.[22] Moshe Weinfeld adds the Book of Deuteronomy to the list.[23] In a study on how the Bible became a book, William M. Schniedewind goes even further by picturing the palace as the place where most parts of the Bible saw the light; in addition to Proverbs, Samuel, Kings, and Deuteronomy, the royal scribes would also have composed the books of the pre-exilic prophets, Psalms, and various other parts of the Bible.[24] What are the arguments that justify such assertions?

All authors agree that a monarchic government entails a bureaucracy, and that a bureaucracy needs scribes. That fact by itself, however, does not mean that the scribes employed by the royal bureaucracy wrote the Bible. The most explicit reference to the effect that biblical texts were composed at the instigation of the king is the superscription of Prov 25:1, which says that some of the Proverbs of Solomon were collected, transcribed, transmitted, or "brought in" (the exact meaning of the verb is not certain) by "the men of Hezekiah."[25] Lipiński, Weinfeld, and Schniedewind think these men must have been royal scribes. Royal patronage, however, need not imply that the scribes held a position in the royal administration. Other arguments are more in the nature of suppositions. In the view of Schniedewind, the political situation in Hezekiah's days "invited, even necessitated, the collection of oral traditions and the writing of literature."[26] Lipiński thinks the royal scribes must have been engaged in writing Davidic ideology and royal propaganda.[27] On the interpretation of the oracle collections of Isaiah, Micah, Amos, and Hosea as pro-Davidic treatises, Schniedewind attributes them to royal scribes from Jerusalem.[28] By construing historiography as royal propaganda, much of the material in Samuel and Kings can also be put to the account of royal scribes. Psalms celebrating the king would have the same origin.[29]

Illustrative of the tendency to see the palace scribes as central figures in the making of the Hebrew Bible is the debate about the background of Baruch. Being the putative composer of the oracle collection of Jeremiah, Baruch is often taken as representative of the scribes who wrote the Bible; his background might give us a clue as to their place in society. In 1970, James Muilenburg argued that Baruch belonged to the inner circle of royal officials, considering the ease with which he moved among personnel from the temple and the palace.[30] The discovery in the 1970s of a bulla (clay tag) impressed with the seal of "Berekhyahu, son of Neriyahu, the scribe" seemed to support his view. Nahman Avigad published the bulla and took it as evidence not only of the historical existence of the biblical Baruch but also of his position in the royal administration.[31] A second bulla with the same seal inscription surfaced in the antiquities market in the 1990s; it also contained the remains of a fingerprint, taken by some to belong to Baruch himself.[32] Since both bullae are not from official excavations ("unprovenanced" is the term), there have been lingering doubts about their authenticity.[33] In 2004, laboratory tests by the Israel Antiquities Authority proved the "fingerprint bulla" to be a forgery.[34] By implication, the Baruch bulla discovered in the 1970s is a fake as well.[35] The biblical data thus remain the only ones available on Baruch.

Once the forged seal is dismissed from the evidence, there are no compelling reasons to say that Baruch was a royal scribe. His brother was "quartermaster" of a diplomatic mission to Babylon (Jer 51:59), but that does not mean Baruch served in the royal administration as well. He was from an aristocratic milieu, as his double patronym indicates (Jer 32:12). This would make him eligible for a position in the administration, but it might just as well have paved the way for a career among the temple clerics.[36] Jeremiah reportedly called upon Baruch once to sign and store a deed of purchase (Jer 32:6–15), once to commit his oracles to writing and to recite them in public (Jer 36); to read the Jeremiah oracles, Baruch took his place in a temple office (Jer 36:10).[37] The texts imply that Baruch was a professional scribe but are hardly forthcoming about his institutional affiliation. As it is, Baruch might have been attached to either the palace or the temple.

To make progress in our understanding of the different roles of palace scribes and temple scribes, we must be aware of some of the pitfalls for Bible scholars who think about these issues; two assumptions often bias their assessment of the role of royal scribes in the making of the Bible. First, the emphasis on the involvement of royal scribes assumes a strong dichotomy between palace and temple. These two great organizations of antiquity are understood as autonomous entities, along the lines of their description in Mesopotamia by A. Leo Oppenheim.[38] On this assumption, any literary work permeated by royal ideology could have been produced only at court; the temple had different interests. Second, temple scribes are treated as a *quantité négligeable* in comparison with royal scribes. Though most authors concede that temple scribes existed, they do not believe that these temple scribes would have been writing for public consumption.[39] This view is based on the contrast between the frequent mention of royal scribes, as opposed to the complete lack of reference to temple scribes under the monarchy.

The two assumptions reflect a serious misunderstanding of the historical reality. Nowhere in the ancient Near East was there a separation between "church" and state. In ancient Israel, the major temples were state temples.[40] The Jerusalem temple started as an annex of the royal palace.[41] Prosopographical studies indicate that there were close ties between the priestly dynasty at Jerusalem and the royal family.[42] The king could appoint priests and had direct access to and disposal of the temple funds.[43] On religious festivals, the temple was the scene of public acts of allegiance to the king.[44] The temple was very much dependent on the support of its royal patron; its priesthood would be receptive to the interests of its principal stakeholder.[45] In short, the temple was not an independent institution.

Nor should the prominence of royal scribes in the biblical record make us underestimate the role of temple scribes. The "scribes" that are mentioned in connection with the court are secretaries of state rather than professionals of writing. Their work was political rather than manual, artistic, or scholarly. The lack of references to priestly scribes in the time of the monarchy is not to be construed as an indication of nonliteracy on the part of the priests. The priests needed writing skills to do their work. They wrote down curses (Num 5:23) and teachings (Hos 8:12; cf. Jer 8:8), certified written records (Isa 8:2; compare Jer 32:10–12), and read the Torah (Jer 2:8; 2 Kings 22). Priests recited formulary prayers for worshippers to repeat; they also wrote down private prayers of thanksgiving in fulfillment of a vow.[46] Literacy was simply a tool of their trade. Relying on the frequency of the word *sōpēr* alone is a poor criterion to determine whether there were skilled scribes at work in the temples.

By way of an instructive aside, it may be helpful to consider the colophon of the Ugaritic *Baal Cycle* as comparative evidence; it demonstrates both the ties of the scribe with the temple and the connection between the temple and the palace. On the last tablet of the *Baal Cycle*, the copyist of the text gives his name and affiliation in a colophon that is separated from the body of the composition by two horizontal lines.

> Scribe is Ilimalku from the town of Shuban,
> Student of Attenu the diviner,
> Chief of the priests,
> Chief of the shepherds,
> Secretary of Niqmaddu,
> King of Ugarit,
> Lord of YRGB,
> Master of ṬHRN.[47]

The colophon presents three individuals: Ilimalku, the copyist of the composition; Attenu, his teacher and supervisor; and King Niqmaddu, the patron of Attenu. Ilimalku is a "scribe" *(spr)*; Attenu is a diviner and attached to the temple as "chief of the priests" *(rb khnm)*; and Niqmaddu is the king and the patron of Attenu in the latter's capacity as royal secretary *(tʿy)*. The copyist of the Ugaritic text was a scribe working in the orbit of the temple under the auspices of the palace.

In light of the foregoing observations, it is to be expected that the temple of Jerusalem was as much a center of literacy as the royal palace; there was no ideological gap between the two institutions preventing temple scribes from engaging in royal propaganda. I now want to go one step further and demonstrate that the temple was the more likely center of production of the traditional literature that came to constitute the Bible. My case is based on three points. First, there is evidence in the Bible for the temple as a center of written law; second, there is evidence, biblical and extrabiblical, for the temple as a center and archive of written oracles; and third, there is evidence for the temple as a center of education and scholarship.

Temples in Israel were traditionally centers of written law. According to the biblical record, the connection between written law and the temple goes back to the very beginning of the monarchy. The figure of Samuel marks the transition between the time of the "judges" and the time of the kings; he had been reared in, and was affiliated with, the temple at Shiloh (1 Sam 1:24–28, 2:18–21, 3:1–21). At the beginning of the rule of King Saul, Samuel wrote "the charter of kingship" *(mišpaṭ hammĕlūkâ)* and deposited the document *(sēper)* in the sanctuary of Shiloh (1 Sam 10:25). It is quite possible that the story is a retrojection of later practice, Shiloh being a forerunner and cipher of the Jerusalem temple (compare Jer 7:12–15, 26:4–6).

By the mid-eighth century, the prophet Hosea spoke of God as the author of written Torah (Hos 8:12); since God writes only in the imagination of believers, the reference is to the priests as producers of written law.[48] More than a century later the priest Hilkiah "found" a scroll containing the Law of Moses (2 Kings 23:24–25) in the temple (2 Kings 22:8). Since the story is meant to promote a recent codification of the Torah, the book was manufactured in the temple rather than found there. It is presumably the same Torah Jeremiah identified as the work of scribes (Jer 8:8). Found in the temple, the Torah was written by temple scribes. The prominent role of temple scribes in the production of written law in Israel goes some way to explain the absence in the Bible of any law book attributed to a king; there are no "Laws of Solomon" to match the *Laws of Hammurabi*. In Israel, the written law came from God—that is, it belonged to the realm of the temple.

The temple was the center, too, of written prophecy. The fact that Ezekiel, commonly regarded as one of the earliest writing prophets, was a priest (Ezek 1:3; compare 1 Chron 24:16) is not without significance for the association of temple clergy with written prophecy. In the story of Ezekiel's calling, dated in 592 (Ezek 1:2), the prophet has a vision in which he sees a hand, stretched out to him, holding a written scroll *(mĕgillat-sēper)*. It is inscribed on both sides with lamentations, dirges, and woes. The prophet is ordered to take the scroll and eat it, that he may henceforth speak God's words (Ezek 2:8–3:4). It is an unusual calling narrative: the familiar motif of God touching the prophet's mouth (Isa 6:6–7; Jer 1:9) is replaced by the consumption of a scroll written by God. The new motif—or the new visionary experience—could occur only at a time in which people like Ezekiel were familiar with the phenomenon of a written collection of prophetic oracles. Ezekiel knew such oracle collections precisely because he was a priest.

The temple was a traditional platform of prophecy; it offered prophets the opportunity to address a sizable audience in a religious context (Amos 7:13; Jer 7:1–12, 26:1–2). Priests not only witnessed the oracles but also reported them in writing (Amos 7:10–11) and authenticated recorded prophecy (Isa 8:1–2). Baruch used the scribal office of the Jerusalem temple to read Jeremiah's prophecies (Jer 36:10). The Book of Balaam from Deir Alla shows that temples in the near vicinity of Israel—or in Israel itself, if Deir Alla is considered to have been within Israelite territory—could have on display written prophecy, copied from a scroll that was kept in the temple.[49] The Balaam text is obviously written prophecy, not just because it has been committed to writing but also on account of its literary character. Prophecies frozen in the biblical psalms also point to the temple as a center where oracles were composed, pronounced, and recycled.[50]

The previous two aspects of the temple—as a center of written law and a center of written prophecy—are linked to the role of the temple as a center of education and scholarship. Sigmund Mowinckel pointed out this role of the temple in 1955. "There is every reason to believe that the school for scribes in Jerusalem, as elsewhere in the Orient, was closely connected with the temple; this is apparent from the very fact that the 'wisdom literature' of Israel was considered to belong to the canonical writings."[51] Mowinckel's argument involves two assumptions. First, that such books as Proverbs were curriculum material for scribal students; and second, that the Hebrew Bible is a collection of texts transmitted in the context of the temple. Comparative evidence from all over the Near East shows that wisdom was indeed common classroom material, and this supports the first assumption. In view of the early presentation of the Bible as a divine revelation, the second assumption is almost a matter of course. This adds up to an understanding of the temple as a place of scribal education. The comparative evidence is also quite compelling; to the data from Mesopotamia and Egypt one might add the location of the school-cum-library between the two great temples at Ugarit.[52] It is to be expected that the Israelite practice would conform to the custom followed by all the surrounding civilizations.

The temple school in Israel need not have been a separate building. Its essence consisted in a master-disciple relationship (see 1 Chron 25:8; Prov 5:12–14; Ps 119:99) that could very well be practiced in one of the temple annexes or the house of a priest-scribe. The assumption of the biblical tradition about Samuel is that he learned his writing skills, implied by 1 Sam 10:25, as an apprentice of Eli in the temple of Shiloh (1 Sam 1:24–28, 2:18–21). Since the priesthood at Shiloh was Levitical, the tradition points to a connection between scribal education and the Levites.[53] It seems likely that the author of the Samuel narratives projected his knowledge about scribal education in his own time upon earlier centuries. Since Shiloh came to be perceived as the single legitimate precedent to the Jerusalem temple, the story reflects scribal instruction by Levites in the context of the Jerusalem temple.

It is uncertain how far back the educational role of the Jerusalem temple might go. The epigraphic evidence from Palestine attests to the existence of a standardized script by 850 B.C.E. Since the uniform script occurs in texts from the north as well as the south, there must have been one institutional center of education having the authority to impose its standards in both Israel and Judah.[54] Though such a center is more likely to have been located in the north than in the south, the Jerusalem temple eventually came to be its successor as a center of scribal education and literary transmission.[55]

The affiliation of the scribal school—more a pedagogical than an architectural concept—to the temple is especially important in view of the role of the school as a center of text production. In the ancient Near East, the men who taught others to read texts were also the men who wrote texts themselves. All over the Near East, schools were not merely centers of text transmission but also of text composition. While the temple scribes in Israel were responsible for teaching the scribal craft, they were also the ones who created the bulk of the biblical literature.

The Levitical Scribes

If the scribes behind the Bible were indeed temple scribes, they were the forerunners of, and partly identical with, the Levitical scribes from the days of Ezra and later. These Levites were scribes in the fourth meaning of the term: scholars of scripture. They are referred to in this capacity in post-exilic sources; it is likely that they had pre-exilic antecedents in the milieu of the Levites, but it is usually difficult to separate historical information on that time from projections onto the past of situations that obtained in the time of the authors. Prudence counsels us to begin by looking at evidence of Levitical scribes in the post-exilic era.

An important source of information on the Levites is Chronicles, a rewritten history of Judah composed in scribal circles toward the end of the fourth century B.C.E.[56] There are quite a lot of data in Chronicles to corroborate the hypothesis that the Levites were involved in activities that required high literacy. There are four roles that the Levites are said to perform. First, the Levites offer Torah instruction: they explain, interpret, and teach. People come to seek Torah from their mouth. As guardians of the Torah, the Levites are the only ones allowed to carry the ark, the shrine of the Scroll of the Torah.[57] Second, the Levites are liturgists: they lead in prayer, confession, praise, and blessings; conduct musical performances in a cultic context; and address the homily to the congregation.[58] Third, the Levites act as civil servants, both in Jerusalem and throughout Judah: they distribute justice; collect tithes and taxes; and keep the records of the civil state.[59] Fourth, the Levites maintain order in the temple: they protect the gates and supervise construction activities.[60]

Though Chronicles rarely designates Levites as scribes (1 Chron 24:6; 2 Chron 34:13), there is no doubt that responsibilities for Torah instruction and jurisdiction could be held only by people who had had the proper scribal training.[61] For those Levites who worked as liturgists, magistrates, tax collectors, or clerks, literacy was also a basic requirement. It can be concluded, in view of their various responsibilities, that the Levites were part of the literate elite of the Second Temple period.

Extrabiblical texts from the Hellenistic period confirm the impression that the Levites were the scribal experts of Jewish society. In the Aramaic *Levi Document,* an important source of the Greek *Testament of Levi,* Levi enjoins his children to perpetuate their scribal knowledge.[62]

And now, my sons, teach [*'lp,* a verb derived from the practice of alphabet instruction] scribal craft, instruction [and] wisdom [*spr wmwsr ḥkmh*] to your children . . . and read the books [?] . . . and they will be heads, and magistrates, and judges.[63]

This injunction to the children of Levi attests to a high rate of literacy among the Levites. The majority of scholars date the *Levi Document* to the middle of the third century B.C.E.[64] It seems warranted, then, to conclude that the role of the Levites as experts of the scribal craft continued in the Hellenistic period.

Further evidence on the Levites as scholars of scripture is found in the Book of Jubilees (ca. 150 B.C.E.).

And he [i.e., Jacob] gave all of his books and his fathers' books to Levi, his son, so that he might preserve them and renew them for his sons until this day.

Jubilees 45:15

This passage bears a close resemblance to the transmission of sacred writings by Levi and his lineage mentioned in the *Testament of Qahat* and reflected in the *Visions of Amram,* both known from the Qumran scrolls.

And they gave to Levi, my father, and my father Levi [gave] to me
All my writings [*ktby*] in testimony, so that you might be forewarned by
   them.

4Q542, fragment 1, ii, 11–12 (compare 4Q543, fragment 1, 1–2)

The significance of these references does not reside in the implications about the writing proficiencies of the Levites but rather in the emphasis on the Levites as the transmitters of the sacred literature of the Jews.

But what does it mean if we say that the scribes of the Second Temple were Levites? Who are the Levites? The question is legitimate and to the point; if it does not receive an answer, the statement that the Levites were the temple scribes of the Persian period adds little to our knowledge. The Levites of the Second Temple period are best described as a branch of the Jewish priesthood specializing in the transmission and interpretation of scripture, and, by extension, in jurisdiction, liturgy, and administration. How did the Levites become the professionals of writing among the priests?

The position of the Levites is a classic problem in biblical scholarship and the subject of numerous studies.[65] By way of a succinct statement of the problem, it suffices to compare the terminology of Deuteronomy with Chronicles. Deuteronomy speaks about "the Levitical priests" *(hakkōhǎnîm halwiyyîm)*, whereas Chronicles distinguishes between "the priests *and* the Levites" *(hakkōhǎnîm wěhalwiyyîm)*.[66] In the pre-exilic view of Deuteronomy all legitimate priests are by definition Levites and all Levites are priests; in the post-exilic view of Chronicles, Levites are by definition nonpriests. How are we to explain the difference?

The most satisfying solution to the problem invokes a historical development in the role of the Levites. An early text transmitted in the Book of Deuteronomy shows that the Levitical clergy originally had two functions.

> They shall teach your laws to Jacob, and to Israel your Torah;
> They shall offer you incense to savor, and whole-offerings upon your
> altar.
>
> Deut 33:10

The names "Jacob" and "Israel" are designations of the Northern Kingdom; therefore the text presumably dates from before the fall of Samaria in 722. In pre-exilic Israel, the Levitical priests were both teachers and cultic servants: they gave Torah instruction, and they offered incense and sacrifice. They were, so to speak, full priests with all the attendant rights and duties.

In the wake of the fall of Samaria, groups of Levitical priests from the north migrated to the Southern Kingdom; they tried to find employment at the temple of Jerusalem and other sanctuaries in Judah.[67] Ancient rivalries between priests from the south and priests from the north flared up again; the conflict increased in intensity when Josiah decided to centralize the cult in Jerusalem. The consistent manner in which Deuteronomy speaks about "the Levitical priests" is an effort to defend the sacerdotal rights of the Levites; the rule that every Levite who joins the Jerusalem priesthood shall have an income equal to that of the other priests is quite explicit on this score (Deut 18:6–8).

Not all priests were on the side of Deuteronomy. As a spokesman of the priestly elite from Jerusalem who was deported to Babylonia in 597, Ezekiel took a very different position toward the Levites. In his visionary design of the new temple (Ezek 40–48), Ezekiel distinguishes between "the Levitical priests descended from Zadok" (Ezek 44:15) and the other Levites. In the view of Ezekiel, the Zadokite priests were the ones who maintained the service of the temple at the time Israel went astray from Yahweh (Ezek 44:15). They had thereby earned the right to act as sole priests.

> They shall declare to My People what is sacred and what is profane, and inform them what is clean and what is unclean. In lawsuits, too, it is they who shall act as judges; they shall decide them in accordance with my rules. They shall preserve My teachings and My laws regarding all My fixed occasions; and they shall maintain the sanctity of My Sabbaths.
>
> Ezek 44:23–24 (NJPS)

Ezekiel blamed the Levites for cultic aberrations in the pre-exilic period (Ezek 44:10). As their punishment, the Levites were to be demoted from the priesthood and made responsible for all the menial chores in the temple. They could remain temple servants, but they forfeited their priestly prerogatives.

The dispute about the position of the Levites continued in the early Persian period. In the oracle collection attributed to Malachi, the Levites are still designated as priests (Mal 2:1–9), though the prophecy emphasizes the role of the Levites in giving reliable instruction in the

Torah (Mal 2:6–7). By the time of the Chronicler (ca. 350 B.C.E.), the conflict had reached a solution by means of a division of labor between the Levites, on the one hand, and the traditional Jerusalem priesthood descending from Zadok, on the other. In the new scenario, the Levites were responsible for the teaching of Torah and the distribution of justice; in addition they served as temple singers and as guardians of the sanctuary. This division of tasks turned the Levites from priests into preachers and public teachers of Torah.

The "priests" in the more narrow sense of the term (i.e., those with Jerusalemite ancestry) remained responsible for the sacrificial cult. In the hierarchy of the temple, the priests had higher rank because they had a greater intimacy with the sacred; only they had the right to enter the sanctuary to approach the table of Yahweh (Ezek 44:16). In the long run, however, the influence of the Levites would be more significant than that of the Zadokites. As the religion of the Jews became more and more a religion of the Book, the power shifted from the servants of the altar to those who guarded the written tradition and held the keys to its interpretation.

The *Levi Document, Jubilees,* and the *Testament of Qahat* show that the division of labor as described in Chronicles continued to obtain through the Hellenistic period. The fact that such Qumran writings as the Rule of the Community consistently distinguish between priests and Levites shows that the Levites remained a separate group among the clergy. By the Roman period, however, the Levites disappear from our sources. According to the synoptic Gospels, the temple clergy consists of "the priests" *(archiereis)* and "the scribes" *(grammateis)* instead of "the priests and the Levites" as in Chronicles.[68] The terminological development underscores that the division between "priests" and "Levites" came to be perceived as one of labor rather than ancestry.

Two further arguments support the view that the "scribes" of the Gospels are the descendants and successors of the Levites from the days of Ezra, Nehemiah, and Chronicles. One is the association of the scribes with the study and teaching of Torah. According to the Gospel of Luke, the "scribes" are coterminous with "the teachers of the law" (*nomodisdaskaloi*, Luke 5:17) or "lawyers" (*nomikoi*, Luke 7:30). The other argument is based on a comparison of lists of temple staff as found in Nehemiah (ca. 350 B.C.E.); the Seleucid Charter of Antiochus III (222–187); and the synoptic Gospels (ca. 70 C.E.).[69] Nehemiah enumerates Levites, singers, gatekeepers, and priests (Neh 13:5).[70] The Seleucid Charter grants tax exemption to "the council of elders, and the priests, and the scribes of the temple, and the temple musicians."[71] In the Gospels, the list consists of elders, priests, and scribes.[72] Apparently the "scribes [of the temple]" in the later lists (Antiochus III charter, Gospels) have taken the place of the Levites in the earlier one (Nehemiah).

In light of the historical differentiation within the priesthood after the Exile, the forerunners of the Levitical scribes of the Second Temple are to be sought among the priesthood of the First Temple. The "scribes" to whom Jer 8:8 attributes the forerunner of Deuteronomy belonged to the same group as the priests who are said to "hold" or "handle" (Hebrew *tāpaś*) the (written) Torah (Jer 2:8). Jeremiah identifies these scribes with the "sages" (*ḥăkāmîm*, Jer 8:8–9). To understand the significance of that term, it is necessary to know that, in Jeremiah, the sages are a professional group alongside the priests and the prophets. The *locus classicus* that mentions the three groups (Jer 18:18) makes it clear that together they constituted the religious establishment. The sages, then, were scribes who, on account of their access to the written tradition, claimed superior knowledge (compare Jer 9:22–23; note the use of verbs denoting insight [*śkl*] and knowledge [*yd'*] in verse 23). They were the scholars of the temple.

Another piece of evidence on the temple scribes is the Book of Deuteronomy. As witnessed in their preoccupation with "the Levitical priests," the scribes who wrote Deuteronomy had affinities with, and may have belonged to, the Levitical priesthood.[73] A telltale occurrence of the "Levitical priests" is found in connection with a ruling concerning the king.

> And when [the king] accedes to the royal throne, he shall have a copy of
> this Torah written for him on a scroll from before the Levitical priests.
> And it shall be with him and he shall read from it all his life.
>
> Deut 17:18–19

Several modern Bible translations (e.g., NJPS) render the expression
"from before" *(millipnê)* as "by," implying that the Levitical priests
were to provide the king with a copy of the Torah. Literally, however,
the preposition implies that the copying takes place "in the presence
of" the Levitical priests, because they are the guardians of the original
Torah. The latter interpretation is entirely in keeping with the role of
the Levites as guardians of the ark (Deut 31:24–26).

The Levitical scribes and scholars of the Persian era, then, had predecessors among the priesthood of late pre-exilic times. The predecessors
of these predecessors are shrouded in darkness. We must be content
with observing that the Levitical scholars of scripture from the days of
Ezra, Nehemiah, and Chronicles, on the one hand, and the priests who
promoted the Book of Deuteronomy, on the other, spring from the milieu of the temple scribes that were involved in collecting and composing earlier parts of the Bible. These professional scribes were more than
mere professionals of writing; they were scholars committed to the transmission, interpretation, and divulgation of the traditional scriptures
they had received from their fathers and ancestors. They were the Hebrew counterparts to the scribal scholars from Mesopotamia and Egypt.

Scribal Education in Israel

To understand the mind-set, the traditions, and the values of the scribes
who wrote the Hebrew Bible, we have to look at the ways in which
they were trained. A scribal education not only imparted skills and
knowledge; it also inculcated ways of thinking and a professional ethics. Most people are, for better or worse, the product of their education. So were the biblical scribes. What was their training like?

The debate on scribal training in Israel has often focused on the exis-

tence of schools. Controversy surrounds this issue. While some specialists confidently claim the existence of schools throughout the biblical
period and in various parts of the country, others are very skeptical.[74]
As argued above, the essence of scribal training does not reside in
buildings that can be identified as schools, but in a teacher-student
relationship in which the transmission of scribal skills is based on a
curriculum. Such a program of study is to be distinguished from the
acquisition of basic literacy for simple chores like accounting and run-
of-the-mill administrative tasks. The epigraphic evidence suggests that
training in rudimentary scribal skills was available throughout Palestine, but the formation of scribes who were "expert and wise" required
a program of study provided only in the temple school.[75]

The official scribal training may at times have been a one-on-one experience, especially since the scribal profession tended to run in families
and a father would be a natural teacher of the son. At times, though,
students refer to their teachers in the plural (Ps 119:99; Prov 5:12–14,
mělammědîm, môrîm). Students presumably sat at the feet of their
teachers, as the disciples of Elisha sat before him (2 Kings 4:38, 6:1), the
elders of the exiles sat before Ezekiel (Ezek 8:1), and as Paul received
instruction at the feet of Gamaliel (Acts 22:3). Though none of the
three instances cited is a case of scribal instruction in the narrow sense
of the term, the examples illustrate the setting of a learning situation.

An anonymous prophet from the mid-sixth century B.C.E. draws on
the typical classroom situation to explain the source of his oracles.

> The Lord Yahweh gave me a tongue of students
> to know how to comfort the weary with words.
> Morning by morning he rouses,
> He rouses my ear,
> to listen as students do.
>
> Isa 50:4

The prophet likens the verbal inspiration by God to the daily instruction by a teacher. The teacher speaks the text first, and his "students"

(limmûdîm) repeat it after him in order to write it down.[76] Such metaphors and such language were apparently clear to the audience, which suggests familiarity on their part with the practices of scribal education. Though the "school" may have been a phenomenon unknown before the Hellenistic era (Sir 51:23 is the first mention of a "school," *bêt midrāš*), scribes had been receiving formal training for centuries.

Our knowledge about the scribal curriculum in Israel is almost nil. Nothing comparable to the Babylonian list of textbooks and reference works for apprentice exorcists has been found for Hebrew scribes. The rare textual discoveries that have been interpreted as school exercises are usually susceptible of other interpretations as well. Most of the so-called abecedaries, for example, are more plausibly interpreted as sample texts for potters and engravers than as scribal scriblings.[77] We are thus reduced to guesswork when trying to reconstruct what might have been the curriculum. The comparative data from Mesopotamia and Egypt are helpful to some degree; so are the indications of Ben Sira and the collection of the Qumran library as reconstructed on the basis of the discoveries in the Judaean desert; but any reconstruction involves a certain amount of speculation.

The scribal curriculum in the Second Temple period is likely to have consisted of two phases, just like the scribal curriculum in Mesopotamia and Egypt. In the first phase, students acquired the basic skills of writing, composition, and eloquence. The second stage of the curriculum was devoted to the memorization and study of the classic texts of their trade and their culture. Further specialization is likely to have occurred, presumably in the form of an individual traineeship.

The basic scribal skills of writing were acquired in the initial phase of the program. Though the twenty-two characters of the Hebrew alphabet are easily mastered, apprentice scribes could not satisfy themselves with the mere reproduction of the letters. They had to learn to write them with speed and in a clearly legible hand. Calligraphy and speed being the result of exercise and practice, scribal students were made to copy texts containing all the letters of the alphabet. In the Persian and Hellenistic periods students probably copied alphabetic acrostics such as Psalms 25 and 119. These biblical acrostics are comparable to the *Babylonian Theodicy*, a cuneiform acrostic used for the instruction of Mesopotamian scribes.[78] The use of psalms as teaching material for beginners supports the view that the scribal school was connected with the temple.

Psalm 25 is a simple acrostic; it has twenty-two verses, each beginning with a different letter of the alphabet.[79] Psalm 119 is more complex; it consists of twenty-two stanzas; the eight lines of each stanza all begin with the same letter; the stanzas follow the order of the alphabet. By copying these texts, the pupil automatically worked his way through the entire alphabet. The use of these psalms as exercises for apprentice scribes explains why their protagonist is typically a young man. Thus the "I" of Psalm 25 worries about his "youthful sins" (v. 7), and the speaker of Psalm 119 is a "young man" (v. 9) who claims to have gained more insight than his teachers (v. 99). Some of the other biblical acrostics are plausibly explained as study material as well.[80]

The comparative evidence from Mesopotamia and Egypt shows that a scribal education was aimed at mastering the technique of writing as much as acquiring a large vocabulary. For the latter purpose, the teachers used lists like the Babylonian lexical texts and the Egyptian onomastica. Such Hebrew lists now survive only in fragments used in other compositions.[81] The list of clean and unclean animals in Deut 14 (compare Lev 11) is a good illustration: it orders the animals according to their habitat (heaven, earth, water) and physical characteristics. Other lists or catalogues that merit mentioning are the topographical list in Num 33:1–49, the list of female jewelry in Isa 3:18–23, and the lists of revealed things in apocalyptic literature from the Hellenistic and Roman periods.[82] Passages such as Job 38 may have drawn their inspiration from educational lists.[83]

Closely associated with the mastery of a rich vocabulary is the ability to understand and use the terminology that was particular to specialized fields of activity. Scribes had to be able to draw up deeds and contracts (compare Jer 32:9–15); all sorts of transactions, such as a sale or a divorce, required a written document using the proper legal idiom

(Deut 24:1, 3; Isa 50:1; Jer 3:8). In their training, then, scribes had to learn the language of notaries. In litigation, writing was essential too; the bill of accusation, the confession of innocence, and the judicial verdict were laid down in documents (Ps 149:9; Job 31:35). Scribes also needed to know how to keep financial records and how to draw up a balance sheet; they were the accountants of antiquity. The composition of a list of curses, as mentioned in Num 5:23, presupposes on the part of the scribe a working knowledge of the typology of the genre; the affinity between the curses in Deut 28 and Assyrian treaty curses probably reflects access to a common stock acquired through education.[84] In short, the basics of scribal training taught students to be conversant with the technical language of all activities for which writing might be needed.

Instruction in the idiom of particular professions and written genres could be seen as part of the larger program of language instruction. The linguistic skills of the scribes would normally have included the mastery of one or more foreign languages. Around 700, the officials of King Hezekiah were able to conduct a conversation in Aramaic, which to the common people was incomprehensible (2 Kings 18:26). In addition to Aramaic, the scribal program may have taught other languages as well, such as Egyptian and, later, Greek. In the words of Ben Sira, the accomplished scribe "will travel through the lands of foreign nations" to increase his knowledge (Sir 39:4). Such exploits presume that training in foreign languages was part of the scribal education.

Ease in writing and language skills were only part of the scribal craft. Scribes also had to acquire eloquence. The comparative evidence from Mesopotamia and Egypt shows that scribes were as much speakers as they were writers and readers; the Israelite scribe, too, was a master of the pen as well as the tongue (compare Ps 45). Scribes had to be able to compose their own texts, and composition being largely an oral art, scribes thus had to acquire rhetorical skills.

To develop rhetorical skills in their students, teachers had recourse to proverbs. That proverbs were a regular item on the curriculum is to be expected by virtue of the analogy with Mesopotamia and Egypt.[85] The

didacticism of the proverbs, their pithiness, and their rhythmic quali-
ties made them eminently suitable as teaching material. Proverbs such
as the one cited in Qoh 7:1 have an unmistakable oral quality.

ṭôb šēm miššemen ṭôb
wĕyôm hammāwet miyyôm hiwwālĕdô
A good name is better than fragrant oil,
And the day of death than the day of birth.

Many other texts might be quoted in example of the rhetorical characteristics of proverbs. Their place in the teachings of the sages is explicitly mentioned in Qoh 12:9. The references in Proverbs to "writing on
the tablet of the heart" (Prov 3:3, 7:3) use the image of students writing
down proverbs from dictation as a metaphor and thereby attest to
the educational practice of memorizing and copying proverbs. Because
Qohelet and Ben Sira had been immersed in proverb collections as students and teachers, they adopted the format of maxims for large parts
of their own writing.

The secondary phase of the scribal program was devoted to the study
of the classics. In a book on schools and the making of the Hebrew Bible, André Lemaire advances the hypothesis that the books of the Bible
were preserved and canonized by virtue of the fact that they were on
the curriculum of the scribal schools.[86] It has been objected that there is
no evidence to support the contention "that advanced scholars in Israel
used literature as instructional aids."[87] The prologue of Ben Sira is
quite explicit, however, about the use of "the books of the fathers" for
purposes of instruction (see also Sir 39:1–3). The internal evidence
from a book like Isaiah is likewise in favor of a transmission through
the schools; the sedimentary character of the text is best explained by a
growth over the centuries through a process in which oral commentary
by teachers became part of the written text.

To find out which classics had the greatest place in the scribal curriculum, we may look at the library of Qumran. About 25 percent of
the Dead Sea Scrolls are scriptural. Except for the Scroll of Esther, all

books of the Hebrew Bible are represented by at least one copy. The three books represented by the most manuscripts are Psalms (thirty-nine in total, including twenty-two manuscripts from Cave 4), Deuteronomy (thirty-one, including twenty-one from Cave 4), and Isaiah (twenty-two, including eighteen from Cave 4). As Eugene Ulrich comments on these statistics, "It is interesting, but not surprising, that these three books are also the most frequently quoted in the New Testament."[88] I propose to understand the "popularity" of Deuteronomy, Isaiah, and Psalms as an indication of their position in the scribal curriculum.

Confirmation of the central place of Deuteronomy, Isaiah, and Psalms in the scribal curriculum may be found in the Levitical signature of the final redaction of these books. The place of the Levites in the closing chapters of Deuteronomy is particularly prominent; the Levites keep the written Torah as guardians and interpreters (Deut 31:9–13, 24–26). The section in question belongs to the final edition of Deuteronomy, as I will demonstrate in Chapter 6. The Psalter in its canonical shape is a Levitical compilation as well.[89] The mention of "the House of Levi" in a psalm outside the five collections (Ps 135:20) is significant, as is the emphasis on the study of Torah in the introduction to the Psalter (Ps 1:2). A Levitical hand in the redaction of Isaiah seems less obvious. The final chapter of that book, however, makes a striking reference to the Levites in the promise that God will take from among the nations that will gather in Jerusalem some "for priests and for Levites" (Isa 66:21). This prediction gives the eschatological redaction of Isaiah a Levitical ring.

Since scribal education in the Persian period was in the hands of the Levites, the Levitical role in the shaping of Deuteronomy, Isaiah, and Psalms is corroborating evidence for the use of these books in the training of scribes. Their selection as textbooks was based in part on their presumed antiquity and authority, in part on their usefulness as tools for scribes and teachers. The scribes taught the Torah to the people; the Book of Deuteronomy provided them with a textbook. The scribes assisted worshippers in their devotional duties, including the recitation of prayers and, if need be, the composition in writing of songs of thanksgiving; the Book of Psalms was the handbook for these liturgists. The Book of Isaiah, finally, taught the scribes ways in which to construe the past, the present, and the future; it provided them with a means of dealing with history and its vicissitudes.

The scribes in training studied the classics through immersion in the text. The quotations of, allusions to, and stylistic affinities with the classics in the "secondary literature," such as the nonbiblical writings from Qumran, the pseudepigrapha, and the New Testament, betray a thorough knowledge of the written tradition. Students chanted the texts, copied them from dictation, and committed them to memory; it was a process of "enculturation" through memorization.[90] Psalm 119, exercise material for elementary students, conveys the image of a scribe murmuring the text of the Torah; in what is like an opening statement to the entire Psalter, Psalm 1 does the same (Ps 1:2).

Instruction in the classics in the context of scribal education was not a matter of merely memorizing. Teachers explained the texts to their students. If scribes were to elucidate the sense of the scriptures (*śôm śekel*, Neh 8:8; *hēbîn*, Dan 11:33), they had to receive exegetical training themselves. An example is found at Neh 8:13–18, which contains a halakhic ruling on the various types of branches to be used for the construction of booths for Sukkoth. A prophecy by Haggai contains an echo of the question-and-answer commentary on rules of purity and contagion (Hag 2:11–13). And Qohelet's counsel against rash vows (Qoh 5:1–6) reads like a commentary on Deut 23:22–24.

The scribal education passed on what in Mesopotamia was called "the oral lore of the masters" *(ša/šūt pī ummâni)*. What the oral lore on the prophets may have looked like may be inferred from the *pesharim* ("commentaries") from Qumran. Like the *pišru* in Mesopotamia, the Jewish *pesher* offered an explanation of the written tradition.[91] The first and the second *pesher* on Isaiah are based on the notion, common to other Qumran *pesharim*, that everything God had spoken through the prophets pertained to the end of time. And since the end of time was imminent, or had already begun, everything in the prophets was interpreted in the light of current events. The same hermeneutical principle commands Daniel's interpretation of the seventy-year desolation of Jerusalem prophesied by Jeremiah (Dan 9). This type of commentary is no innovation by the author of Daniel or the teachers at Qumran. The fact that similar readings of the prophetic material have become part of the Book of Isaiah proves the antiquity of this line of interpretation.

In sum, the scribal education in Israel provided students with much more than the mere skills of reading and writing. Scribes received training in speaking as well. They knew how to address an audience and they knew how to interpret the scriptures. In an "Age of Prose" (the phrase is from a book by Tamara Eskenazi on Ezra-Nehemiah), the scribes were the new prophets; by virtue of their professional training, they were the repositories of the Word of God.[92]

Status of the Scribes in the Second Temple Period

Scribes in the civilizations surrounding Israel were conscious of their powerful position. The most striking instance is offered by the Mesopotamian scholars. During the Neo-Assyrian and the Neo-Babylonian periods, the Mesopotamian scribes cultivated a corporate spirit based on their membership in the community of the initiates as opposed to the mass of the noninitiates. The secrecy with which they surrounded their written traditions, though in truth more rhetorical than real, was essential to their sense of belonging to an exclusive elite; and exclusiveness was essential to their self-esteem. Though they were at times derided by the public, the very same public accepted the premise of the social superiority of the scribes.

We need to understand the status of the Hebrew scribes because it has repercussions for the way in which we see the making of the Hebrew Bible and the coming about of a biblical canon. These are issues to which we will return later in this book, but they are intimately related to the public position and the self-perception of the Hebrew scribes. It matters whether these men saw themselves as guardians of a secret or as teachers of the ignorant; whether the writings they studied were accessible to all or the preserve of the fortunate few; and whether their authority was based on their knowledge or on their affiliation with those in positions of political power.

The first point to be noted when it comes to the status of the scribes is the fact that they constituted a "publicly founded scholarly guild."[93] By instituting a tax on agricultural produce, Nehemiah secured the income of the Levites.[94] Unlike the Egyptian lector-priests, then, their devotion to the scribal profession was full-time. As Ben Sira notes, "The wisdom of the scribe depends on the opportunity of leisure" (Sir 38:24). In view of their social-economic situation, the Levitical scribes can be likened to civil servants with no financial worries. They could apparently afford to pay for the education of their children; for them, a tuition fee consisting of "a large sum of silver" (Sir 51:28) was not prohibitive (compare Prov 4:5, 17:16 on the "acquisition" of wisdom). While it is conceivable that mere copyists and lower clerks were drawn from the lower strata of society, scribes belonged to what we would call the upper middle class.

A scribal education, moreover, held the promise of upward social mobility. According to Ben Sira, the accomplished scribe "attains eminence in the public assembly," "sits in the judge's seat," "serves among great men," and "appears before rulers" (Sir 38:31–39:5). Such career perspectives are predicated on the assumption that the wisdom of the scribe will command general respect. The same assumption underlies the post-exilic "wisdom frame" of the Book of Deuteronomy, extant in chapters 4 and 30. There the written Torah is presented as the wisdom of Israel that will be recognized and valued by the other nations (Deut 4:6–8). On this view, wisdom, and more especially the wisdom acquired through the study of "the Law of the Most High" (Sir 39:1), is universally accepted currency. If Ben Sira is speaking for the average Hebrew scribe, the latter aspired to be recognized by the public for his talents.

Social success and membership in an exclusive elite can boost each other. The Israelite scribes were distinct from their compatriots and coreligionists on at least three counts. First, they were the literate minority in a culture that was still basically oral. Second, they were privy to the deeper meaning of the sacred writings—a meaning hidden from the common crowd. Third, they were the inheritors of Moses and the prophets; no other group could claim the office and authority of the spiritual ancestors of the nation. All three points merit closer inspection.

Literacy is a mark of social distinction inasmuch as the illiterate majority holds the written word in high esteem. What would be the social advantage of reading skills if books were irrelevant to the masses? In the Persian era, Judaism developed into a religion of the book—that book being the Book of the Torah of Moses and ultimately, by extension, the Hebrew Bible as a whole. The impetus for this development was the Hellenistic era, when books and libraries became the symbol of a nation's cultural capital. But veneration for the "ancestral books" (Prologue to Ben Sira) did not mean that everybody had access to them. Simple reading skills were insufficient, as the language of the "holy books" differed significantly from the colloquial language of the day; for an uneducated audience, the Hebrew writings needed to be paraphrased in Aramaic.[95] The skills of the scribes—of reading, understanding, and interpreting—commanded general respect. The scribes held the key to the symbolic capital of the nation.

The social esteem that the scribes enjoyed bordered on awe in the face of their textual interpretations. Ben Sira emphasizes that the scribe has privileged access to the "subtleties" *(strophais)*, "hidden meanings" *(apokrypha)*, "obscurities" *(ainigmasi)*, and "secrets" *(apokryphois)* of the scriptures (Sir 39:1–8). The protagonist of Psalm 119, held out as an example to apprentice scribes, immerses himself in the Torah in order to penetrate its "mysteries" *(niplā'ôt,* Ps 119:18, 27). Like Daniel, the scribe sits down to consult the books and discover their meaning (Dan 9:2). Thus he finds that seventy years stands for seventy weeks, and that these weeks are no ordinary weeks but eschatological weeks. The true scribe, in other words, has learned to see what others could not see even if they were given the ability to read. For the scribe, reading is a source of revelation, and his audience knows this. The more ingenious the interpretation, the greater the fame of the scribe (compare Sir 39:6–11).

The social position of the scribes is anchored, ultimately, in their role as successors of Moses and the prophets. Applied to the Levites, this type of legitimation is already prominent in the Book of Deuteronomy. According to the last verses of Deuteronomy, there never has arisen in Israel a prophet like Moses (Deut 34:10–12). The revelation that he received and put down in writing was passed on to the Levites; as the inheritors of Moses's office (Deut 31:9), they were the guardians of the master copy of the Law (Deut 17:18–19). Being the precursors of the scribes and sages of the Hellenistic period, the Levites passed on their prophetic authority to their successors.[96] According to a rabbinical doctrine that goes back to the late Hellenistic period, the spirit of prophecy had ceased; the authority of the prophets now lay with the scribes.[97] From this ideological perspective, the prophets of old can retrospectively be qualified as "scribes" and "teachers" themselves.[98] The scribes were, in a way, the new prophets.[99]

A circumstance that is particular to the position of the Levitical scribes from the Second Temple is the rivalry between scribes and priests. In the temple hierarchy, the Levites were subordinate to the priests. To us this may seem strange, because we tend to value intellect higher than holiness. But in a religious system in which holiness is the core value, those with access to the altar have a higher rank than those with access to books. Due to the gradual transformation of Judaism into a religion of the Book, the scribes eventually transcended their secondary status in the hierarchy. For a long time, however, the scribes of the Second Temple had an uneasy relationship with the servants of the altar.[100]

The transformation of Judaism into a religion of the Book promoted the scribes to a prominent position. Through the doctrines of the Mosaic succession and the departure of the spirit of prophecy, the scribes claimed, in fact, a monopoly on religious instruction. Indeed it should not be overlooked that public instruction was crucial to the position and power of the Jewish scribes. They were, to quote an expression from the Book of Daniel, the "knowledgeable among the people" and had a duty to give insight to many (Dan 11:33). Jerusalem was their power base. From there they went out to the towns to offer instruction from the "Book of the Torah of Yahweh" (2 Chron 17:7–9). Their power resided not so much in their possession of a secret as in their position as mediators and brokers of a body of knowledge that was, for all practical purposes, inaccessible to those not initiated into the arts of writing and interpretation.

chapter five

MAKING BOOKS

Scribal Modes of Text Production

According to the postscript to the Book of Qohelet, "There is no end to the making of many books" (Qoh 12:12). This warning is meant for an audience of scribes, addressed in the person of an apprentice ("my son"). Allowing for the fact that the word for "books" refers to all sorts of written documents and that "making" can mean copying, the scribes of antiquity were indeed the labor force of text production; they were the ones responsible for the "making of books" *('ăśôt sĕpārîm).*[1] This chapter examines the way in which scribes were involved in that process; we shall look at the various modes of text production in use by the ancient scribes and exhibited in the Hebrew Bible.

To properly appreciate the role of the ancient scribes, it is necessary to take leave of the common conception of the scribe as a mere copyist. The traditional distinction between authors, editors, and scribes is misleading because it obfuscates the fact that authorship and editorship were aspects of the scribal profession.[2] In the words of James Muilenburg, scribes "were not only copyists, but also and more particularly composers who gave to their works their form and structure, and determined to a considerable degree their wording and terminology."[3] The Qumran scrolls qualify King David as a "scholar" and a "scribe" because he supposedly wrote the Book of Psalms; text production is the province of the scribal profession.[4] Scribes were also responsible for the transmission of the written tradition, as succeeding generations of students learned the scribal art by copying the classic texts. However, the involvement of scribes in the process of literary production exceeded that of mere copyists. They had an active part in the formation and the transformation of the tradition.

In this chapter we will concern ourselves with the role of the scribes in the production of texts rather than in their reproduction. We can distinguish six ways in which scribes produced written texts. They might engage in (1) transcription of oral lore; (2) invention of a new text; (3) compilation of existing lore, either oral or written; (4) expansion of an inherited text; (5) adaptation of an existing text for a new audience; and (6) integration of individual documents into a more comprehensive composition. The transition between the various modes and techniques of text production is fluid; many texts of the Bible or from Babylonia or Egypt exhibit traces of several techniques. For the sake of clarity, however, it is useful to treat each mode of text production separately, and to illustrate them with actual instances from the Bible and other works of Near Eastern literature.

Transcription

The scribe who transcribes writes out a text that is not of his own making but that originates with an oral source. In the technique's crudest form, the transcriber is purely instrumental, writing down what someone else dictates; he copies from hearing rather than seeing. The biblical model of the scribe as secretary is Baruch. According to the account in Jer 36, we owe the Book of Jeremiah to the fact that the scribe Baruch wrote down the oracles "from the mouth" of the prophet (Jer 36:4). In this image, the scribe is a faithful recorder who neither omits nor adds a single word; he simply transforms an oral artifact into a written text.[5]

The apologetic angle of the story about Baruch producing the scroll of Jeremiah is obvious; the tale is designed to legitimize a scroll containing prophecies attributed to Jeremiah. Nevertheless, the phenomenon of dictation to a scribe was common enough in the ancient world; on occasion, a prophet might use a secretary. A Mesopotamian letter from the royal archives of the city of Mari tells about a prophet asking a royal official for a "discreet scribe" to "make him write down the message which the god Šamaš sent me for the king."[6] The etymological equivalent of *mār bīt ṭuppi naṣram* ("a discreet son of the tablet house") is our term *secretary,* since the Babylonian word for "discreet" primarily conveys the notion of secrecy. Here, then, is a historical instance in which a prophet wants to dictate his oracle to a scribe. The Baruch story may or may not be fictitious, but the phenomenon of a prophet dictating to a scribe was not pure fantasy.

According to the biblical portrayal of Baruch as model secretary, the scribe remains invisible in the text he writes from dictation. In reality, however, the transformation of speech into scripture was not a mechanical recording in writing of the oral performance. As the scribe committed the spoken word to writing, he adapted it to meet the conventions of the written genre. In the ancient Near East the most common genre for which scribes acted as transcribers was the letter. Given the modest rate of literacy in the population, many correspondents made use of a scribe. To judge by cuneiform letters that have been preserved, scribes did leave their imprint on the text dictated to them. Trained as they were in the niceties of the epistolary genre, the terminology and phraseology the scribes used were proper to the art of their profession as well as their personal talent; their style was hardly a reflection of the rhetorical gifts of their patrons. In the Amarna letters from Palestine, the citations of and allusions to proverbs betray the scribal education of the writers.[7]

Although transcriptions are rarely if ever literal, the changes secretaries make in dictated text remain limited. As a rule of thumb, we may say that the part the scribe plays in the wording of the text increases in proportion to the distance between the oral performance and the product in writing. In the case of dictation, the distance is minimal; when the scribe acts as a reporter of an event he has witnessed, his part in the written record is larger; he gives *his* version of the event. This may seem like stating the obvious, but it tends to be overlooked when it comes to the written record of the specifically oral genre of the prophetic oracle. Prophets, as a rule, do not write, nor do most of them have secretaries; they speak, and if we have a record of their oracles it is because scribes wrote down a report of their speech.[8]

Since it is materially impossible to compare the written record of ancient prophecy with its spoken performance, we are unable to establish the changes operated by the scribe; we have only his recollection of the oracle. In a few cases, however, the same oracle is reported in three witness accounts. The original has vanished into the air, so to speak, but the three versions in which it survives allow us to make a tentative assessment of the part played by the scribe in the recorded oracle.

Again my example comes from the Mari archives. The circumstances are slightly more complex than I just intimated. The three accounts are reports not by scribes but by two royal officials and a priestess of royal descent, each of whom used a scribe; and the oracle they quote has been given on three separate occasions. But in all three reports it is the same oracle by the same prophetess that is being cited.[9]

The next day a prophetess [*qammatum*][10] of Dagan of Terqa came to me [i.e., Sammetar, the governor of Terqa] and spoke to me in the following terms: "There is water running beneath the straw. They keep sending messages proposing peace, and they even send their gods [i.e., images of the gods, to serve as witnesses to a formal treaty], but it is deceit they are harboring in their hearts. The king must not commit himself without first consulting the god." . . . She also delivered her oracle in the chapel of Bēlet-ekallim to the priestess Inibšina.[11]

A prophetess [*qammatum*] of Dagan of Terqa came to me [i.e., Inibšina, sister of King Zimrilim and "wife" of the god Addu of Terqa] and spoke to me in the following terms: "The friendship of the man of Ešnunna is deceptive. There is water running beneath the straw. In the very net that he is spreading I will catch him, and his time-honored possession I will put to utter waste." This is what she said to me. Now take care of your-self. Do not enter the treaty without [first obtaining] an oracle.[12]

And from a letter by Kanisan, a royal official based at Terqa:

[I heard] the words that are being said [in the temple of Dagan]. This is what they are saying: "There is water running beneath the straw. The god of My Lord went and delivered his enemies into his hand." . . . For his own good, My Lord must not be negligent about making oracular in-quiries.[13]

The one literal quote on which the three reports agree is the saying about water running beneath the straw. It is a phrase with the quality of a proverb and thus likely to be remembered. On the rest, the re-ports differ. They all contain the advice to the king to consult the god through extispicy, but in the one case the warning is part of the oracle and in the two others, a counsel from the writer. All three reports refer to peace negotiations with the ruler of Ešnunna, but the terms they use differ considerably.[14] Except for the one saying about water beneath straw, the texts give only the gist of the oracle of the prophetess, each using its own words while pretending to quote hers.

This example from the Mari archives illustrates the impossibility of retrieving the actual text of the oracle as it was spoken, even where three written reports are available. A biblical example that demon-strates the same point comes from the Book of Jeremiah. The book contains two parallel records of a single prophecy that the historical Jeremiah reportedly delivered in 609.[15] The oracle is known as the tem-ple sermon because it was spoken in—and, in a sense, against—the Je-rusalem temple. Chapter 7 gives a lengthy report of the speech of the prophet; chapter 26 focuses on the opposition triggered by Jeremiah's performance but quotes his oracle as well. The central point on which the two versions of the prophecy agree is the comparison between the temple in Jerusalem and the sanctuary at Shiloh; abandoned and destroyed, the fate of the latter is a warning to the former (Jer 7:12–15, 26:6, 26:9).

Because the two reports exhibit one literal correspondence, some commentators conclude that these were the authentic words of Jeremiah.[16] Since both the idea and the terms in which it is phrased are characteristically Deuteronomistic—that is, proper to the scribal circles that produced the Book of Deuteronomy and much of the historical texts of the Bible—it is questionable whether the historical Jeremiah ever drew a parallel between Shiloh and Jerusalem or phrased it in this way.[17] Prudence counsels us to say that the comparison between the two chapters demonstrates that it is almost impossible to distinguish the part of the prophet from the intervention of the scribe. While it is unnecessary to posit that the temple sermon is a pure invention, there is no way for us to penetrate beneath the scribal interpretation of the event.

If the room for scribal license increases in tandem with the distance between the transcriber and his oral source, whether in time or in social location, it is particularly great when it comes to folktales.[18] Some of the stories from the Book of Genesis fall into this category. They circulated in the oral tradition before the scribes put them down in writing. In the process of transmission, one story might be told in different versions; it remained open to modification until a scribe fixed its form. The threefold occurrence of tales with the wife-sister motif in Genesis illustrates both the flexibility of the oral tradition and the impact of the scribes on their written form.

Tales with the wife-sister motif tell about a man traveling abroad who passes off his wife as his sister because he fears that other men might kill him out of envy. Inevitably, one of the locals takes a fancy to the wife and, believing her to be the sister of the first man, adds her to his harem. The plot is common in folklore. In the Book of Genesis, it occurs in three versions.[19] In Gen 12:10–20 the protagonists are Abraham, Sarah, and Pharaoh; in Gen 20:1–18, Abraham, Sarah, and Abimelech; and in Gen 26:6–11, Isaac, Rebekah, and Abimelech. What were the names and the words that the first storyteller used? Impossible to say. We only know the versions as different scribes saw fit to phrase them. Whether one refers to those scribes as the Elohist (E) and the Yahwist (J) on the criterion of the divine names they use (Elohim as opposed to Yahweh) does not matter for my purpose, as it suffices to observe that the language of each version is characteristic of a particular scribe or scribal tradition.[20]

Summing up, we may say that scribes, even in their most instrumental of roles, impose their style, language, and ideas on the text. Acting as secretaries and transcribers, they are not phonographs in writing; they mold the material that reaches them orally. As prophecy turns into scripture, when tale becomes text, the scribe transforms his data to suit the conventions of the written genre and his interpretation of the oral tradition. Much in the Hebrew Bible goes back to the oral tradition: from the tales of the patriarchs to the oracles of the prophets, and from priestly laws to genealogies and proverbs. Our only access to that tradition passes by its transcription; by the same token, there is no way of getting around the scribe.

Invention

What transcription and invention have in common is the fact that the text the scribe writes is not an extension of an anterior text. Unlike in many other modes of text production, the scribe who transcribes and the scribe who invents both produce an original text. The transcriber transforms oral data into writing; the scribe who invents composes a text of his own contrivance. Different though they are, the two modes of text production are at one in that they create the written data on which other modes of text production are dependent. In this sense, transcription and invention are the two primary modes of text production.

Because no text from the Hebrew Bible is explicitly the invention of a scribe, we must turn to other Near Eastern literature to identify characteristics of compositions that are typically scribal. A famous composition by a scribe is the *Babylonian Theodicy*.[21] The ingenious acrostic of the poem tells the reader that Saggil-kīnam-ubbib was its author; tradition has it that this man was a court scholar in the service of Nebuchadnezzar I (1125–1104) and Adad-apla-iddina (1068–1047).[22] Trained as a scribe with a specialization in exorcism, the author of the *Theodicy* composed a dialogue between two scholars.[23] Considering the traditional link between wisdom and the scribal art, it is natural to assume that the two protagonists are representatives of Mesopotamian scribal culture. In this context, the reference to their scribal training makes sense.[24] The characteristics that mark this composition as scribal, then, are the technique of the acrostic, the form of the dialogue, the focus on wisdom, and the references to the scribal context.

Partly on the strength of this Babylonian text, we may venture to suggest that the biblical acrostics are scribal inventions as well. The mere fact that acrostics can be fully savored only by people who know how to read—and to read well, at that—qualifies them as typically scribal products meant for the instruction and enjoyment of scribes and apprentice scribes. In the preceding chapter I showed that the alphabetic Psalms 25 and 119 were in use as teaching material in the schoolroom; hence the references to youngsters and teachers. It is likely that teacher-scribes composed these texts. Another scribal composition in the form of an acrostic is the praise of the virtuous woman in Prov 31:10–31, since it combines the technique of the acrostic with wisdom teaching. The admonition to "sons" (that is, pupils) in the acrostic Psalm 34 ("Come, my sons, listen to me: I will teach you what it is to fear Yahweh," v. 12) is another indication that acrostics were used in an educational context.[25]

On account of the close association of wisdom and the scribal art, both in Mesopotamia and in Israel, there can be little doubt that the Book of Job goes back to a scribe as well. In addition to its focus on the theodicy issue and its use of dialogue, the book betrays its scribal origins through its display of rare vocabulary and knowledge of natural phenomena. The text exhibits the influence of compendium lists as they were used in scribal schools.[26] Other wisdom compositions, such as Qohelet (Ecclesiastes) and Ben Sira, are evidently scribal inventions as well; Qohelet because of its citation of proverbs and the scribal identification in the postscript (Qoh 12:9–10); Ben Sira because its author refers to himself as the teacher of a school (Sir 50:27, 51:23).[27]

One of the characteristics that mark Qohelet as a scribal composition is the citation of proverbs. It was not the use of proverbs, specifically, that was current practice among scribes, but the use of material extant in other written sources. A text by a Babylonian scholar illustrates the practice. In the hymn to the goddess Gula, the author Bulluṭsa-rabi makes extensive use of names and epithets from existing lists and texts.[28] It is unlikely that he was copying these elements from tablets he had before him; intimately acquainted with the written tradition, Bulluṭsa-rabi was presumably quoting from memory.[29] The procedure of using texts to produce new texts is a phenomenon of scribal culture attested in a variety of cuneiform compositions. It also occurred in Israel.

A biblical instance of a composition that draws heavily on earlier compositions is the Book of Chronicles. Its anonymous author (or authors, as the case may be) emphasizes time and again that the book is a work of scholarship. Throughout the work there are references to written sources such as "the book [*sēper*] of the Kings of Israel" (1 Chron 9:1); "the Words of Samuel" (1 Chron 29:29); "the Words of Nathan" (2 Chron 9:29); "the Midrash of the Prophet Iddo" (2 Chron 13:22; cf. 12:15); "the Words of Jehu" (2 Chron 20:34); "the Prophecy of Isaiah" (2 Chron 32:32); "the Lamentations" (2 Chron 35:25); and several others. Some of these works are known to us while others are not, at least not under that title.[30] To a large extent these references are a "mere show" of wide learning.[31] There can be no doubt, however, that the Chronicler did in fact use written sources for his work.[32] Both by the actual mode of production and by the self-conscious parading of scholarship, Chronicles is evidently a product from the scribal workshop.

Less obviously the work of scribes, many of the Psalms also fall into the category of scribal inventions. The fact that the composer of Psalm 45 compares his tongue to the pen of an expert scribe is evidence of the close association between cult singers and scribes.[33] In the vision of Chronicles, the temple singers are Levites and, as such, the "brothers" of the temple scribes. In a way, the cult singers *are* scribes, just as the Mesopotamian *kalû* ("liturgist, lamentation singer") was a scribe who had specialized in liturgical lore. The prayers and hymns brought together in the Psalter are, for the major part, the work of liturgists with a scribal background. This is true not only of the alphabetic prayers and the wisdom psalms, but of the majority of the individual laments and the congregational hymns as well. These texts are not spontaneous expressions of grief or joy but fixed liturgical chants designed to be recited or sung. They are the work of cult specialists trained to translate situations and sentiments into the proper words of prayer and thanksgiving.[34]

When invention is the mode of text production, the scribe who writes acts as an author. If anonymity prevails, it is because the scribe does not think of himself as an author in the modern sense of the term; he practices the craft of literary composition using the tools and techniques he acquired during his scribal education. The predilection for traditional terminology, formal language, citation, allusion, and a display of learning is characteristic of the spirit of the scribal workshop. Alongside transcription, invention is a primary source of biblical texts; it is especially prominent as a mode of text production with respect to wisdom literature, historiography, and the Psalms.

Compilation

Another mode of "making books" was the scribal art of compilation. Proverbs 25:1 introduces a subseries of proverbs with the words, "These too are proverbs of Solomon, which the men of King Hezekiah of Judah have transcribed." The transcription here referred to implies by the same token the formation of a written collection or compilation.[35] Compilation may concern items of either the oral or the written tradition; in the first case it involves transcription, in the second it is aimed only at creating a series. The essence of compilation, in either case, is juxtaposition; its logic "is additive and aggregative rather than subordinative and analytic."[36]

Among the cuneiform texts from Abu Salabikh (mid-third millennium B.C.E.) there was already a proverb collection, known as the Instructions of Šuruppak.[37] It attests to the antiquity of a genre of compilation that remained popular with scribes all over the Near East. How many of the gnomic sayings are in fact scribal creations, we do not know. Although the biblical Book of Proverbs presents itself as the "Proverbs of Solomon" (Prov 1:1, 10:1, 25:1), the "Words of the Wise" (Prov 22:17, 24:23), the "Words of Agur son of Yakeh" (Prov 30:1), and the "Words of Lemuel, king of Massa" (Prov 31:1), it contains in fact much popular lore. If the collection as a whole can be considered the work of scribes, it is because compiling was a classic scribal technique of composition. Scribes made the Book of Proverbs by collecting striking sayings and by presenting them in a series of written compilations.

Compilation is a scribal mode of production that has spawned a great variety of texts in the ancient Near East. Its primal form is that of the list; the scholarship contained in such lists is referred to as *Listenwissenschaft*.[38] Apart from the lists of syllable signs, the cuneiform equivalent of abecedaries for alphabetic scripts, the Mesopotamian lists are not only aids for instruction but also scribal ways of ordering the universe. So-called lexical lists arrange words and names thematically rather than in alphabetic or syllabic order. A Mesopotamian example is the following passage from a bilingual list of professions and occupations. Each entry consists of a Sumerian term followed by its Babylonian equivalent, to which I append an English translation.

[maš]-maš	*mašmaššu*	exorcist
nar-balag	*āšipu*	exorcist
ka-pirig	*āšipu*	exorcist
muš-la-la-aḫ	*mušlalaḫḫu*	snake-charmer
lú-^{giš}gam₃-šu-du₇	*muššipu*	exorcist
la-bar	*kalû*	lamentation singer

gala-maḫ	*galamaḫḫu*	chief lamentation singer
i-lu-di	*munambû*	wailer
i-lu-a-li	*lallaru*	mourner
lú-gub-ba	*maḫḫû*	ecstatic
lú-ni-zu-ub	*zabbu*	madman
kur-gar-ra	*kurgarrû*	transvestite
ur-SAL	*assinnu*	catamite[39]

To list all the names of professions, trees, rivers, towns, or musical instruments is a way of organizing knowledge in an encyclopedic fashion.[40] The same procedure informs the Egyptian *onomastica* and the Hebrew lists of related terms and concepts.[41] Of the Hebrew lists only fragments survive; they are sufficient, however, to serve as evidence of the practice of *Listenwissenschaft* among the Hebrew scribes.[42]

There is a connection between *Listenwissenschaft,* on the one hand, and certain hymns of praise, on the other. One way of extolling the deity is to list her names, virtues, and deeds. An example of *Listenwissenschaft* in the service of hymnology is the list of the fifty names of Marduk appended to *Enūma eliš,* or the *Epic of Creation:* the names are a poetic version of the traditional genre of the god list. By identifying various minor deities with Marduk, each name is an occasion for the scribe to expound one of the virtues of the chief god of Babylon.[43] Some of the Hebrew lists of natural phenomena are alluded to in hymnic contexts, as in Job 38, Psalm 148, Sir 43, and the Septuagint version of Dan 3:52–90.[44] The authors of these passages neither copied nor invented; they used the format of the list—and perhaps the substance of an existing list—as a springboard for their praise of the deity.

Lexical lists can be considered the first level of the scribal art of compiling. At a more sophisticated level we find the list of observations; instead of words and names, the scribes list such phenomena as the various configurations of animal entrails. The extispicy handbooks of Babylonia are indeed constructed as compilations of omens and their interpretation. The tablet series read like a dictionary or an encyclopedia, listing the complete array of particulars and anomalies by anatomical order. A sample passage illustrates the scribal method of compiling variants of a theme.

> If the apex of the heart is bright to the right:
>> elation, my army will reach its destination.
> If the apex of the heart is bright to the left:
>> elation, the enemy's army will reach its destination.
> If the apex of the heart is bright to the right and dark to the left:
>> My army will establish victory over the enemy's army.
> If the apex of the heart is bright to the left and dark to the right:
>> The enemy's army will establish victory over my army.
> If the apex of the heart is both bright and dark to the right:
>> Terror will befall my army.
> If the apex of the heart is both bright and dark to the left:
>> Terror will befall the enemy's army.[45]

The origin of such compilations goes back to historical observations of the connection between portent and event on the basis of the reasoning *post hoc ergo propter hoc*.[46] On the assumption that the gods write their intentions in the entrails of animals, the omen lists are comparable to cuneiform sign lists, with the scribe acting as a collector of signs written by the gods.[47] Since the true collector suffers from the compulsory desire for a complete collection, the scribe will complete the list of signs observed with signs of his own invention.[48] In fact, the great majority of the omens in the lists are invented omens; in this sense, compilation triggered invention.

There are many types of omen lists, ranging from astrology to the particulars of human behavior. At first glance, the cuneiform omens have no counterpart in the Bible. This does not mean, however, that the Hebrew scribes did not resort to compiling cases as a mode of text production. The earliest law collections, such as the one preserved in the Covenant Code (Exod 21:1–22:16), bear a formal resemblance to the omen lists.[49] Every entry in an omen list consists of two parts: the protasis describing the ominous situation (the configuration of the entrails, the movement of the stars, or any particular event), and the apodosis spelling out its meaning—which is, in a sense, a divine verdict.

> If white fungi fill a man's house:
>   The owner of that house will become poor.
> If fungus is seen on a south wall:
>   The mistress of the house will die.[50]

The casuistic laws of the Bible have a similar structure; after the definition of the legal case in the protasis, the apodosis gives the pertinent verdict.

> If a man strikes the eye of his slave, male or female, and destroys it:
>   he shall let him go free on account of his eye.
> If he knocks out the tooth of his slave, male or female:
>   he shall let him go free on account of his tooth.
> If an ox gores a man or a woman to death:
>   the ox shall be stoned and its flesh shall not be eaten.
>
> Exod 21:26–28

Both the omens and the laws are a mixture of historical and hypothetical cases. As is the case for the cuneiform omens, many of the biblical cases and verdicts are scribal inventions; compilation led to invention.

The priestly laws of the Bible, too, can be viewed as a compilation of separate instructions. The Hebrew word for such a priestly instruction is *tôrâ*; under normal circumstances, "instruction does not fail from the priest" (Jer 18:18; compare Ezek 7:26). The instruction the priest provided was casuistic. The one who came to the priest for instruction asked a specific question and obtained a specific answer (Hag 2:11–13; Mal 2:6–7). The Book of Leviticus is a compilation of such priestly instructions. The various "laws" are marked off from one another by postscripts:

> This is the instruction concerning the burnt offering.
>
> Lev 6:2

This is the instruction concerning the meal offering.

Lev 6:7

This is the instruction concerning animals, birds, all living creatures that move in water, and all creatures that swarm on earth.

Lev 11:46

This is the instruction concerning the leper at the time he is to be cleansed.

Lev 14:2

To signal the end of the compilation the scribe has added a postscript saying, "These are the . . . instructions that Yahweh gave . . . on Mount Sinai through the agency of Moses" (Lev 26:46). The book, then, is a scribal compilation of *tôrôt,* endowed with a divine origin and attributed to Moses.[51]

Much in the prophetic collections goes back to the scribes in their capacity as compilers as well. A comparison with the Neo-Assyrian oracle collections may be illuminating.[52] The cuneiform evidence suggests that, at the time of its delivery, the prophetic oracle was first transcribed on a small tablet (including the name of the prophet), and afterward copied onto a larger multicolumn archival tablet. The collection tablets were scribal compilations on the basis of written oracle reports. We may imagine that the genesis of the prophetic collections in the Bible followed similar lines, although recollection and collective memory may have been as important a source as the archives. It is clear, at any rate, that the prophetic collections of the Bible are basically compilations of separate oracles.

An analysis of Jeremiah 2 illustrates the fact that some sections of the prophetic books are compilations of separate oracles. Though secondarily reworked into a larger unit, the thirty-seven verses of Jeremiah 2 are divided over some ten oracles. The chapter is interspersed with stereotyped formulas, such as "Thus says Yahweh" (*kōh 'āmar yhwh,* vv. 2, 5); "oracle of Yahweh" (*ně'ūm-yhwh,* vv. 3, 12, 29; see also vv. 19, 22); "Hear the word of Yahweh" (v. 31, emendation), indicating the presence of a multitude of oracles. Commentators are divided about the correct division of the chapter into its constituent oracles, but their analyses are on the whole remarkably similar.[53] Other prophetic books are like Jeremiah with respect to its character as a collection. That fact is underscored by the occasional occurrence of the same oracle in two different collections, such as the prediction of a universal pilgrimage to Jerusalem (Isa 2:2–5, compare Mic 4:1–5). These instances demonstrate that the context of the collection is secondary to the separate oracle record.

Much of what is true for the prophetic collections of the Bible is true for the Book of Psalms. Aside from the part the scribes played in the formation of the separate psalms, the scribes created the book by compiling psalms in five different collections. Hymns, prayers, laments, and meditations that once circulated independently were brought together in five different scrolls, four of which close with a more or less standard doxology.

Blessed is Yahweh, God of Israel,
from eternity to eternity. Amen and Amen.

Ps 41:14

Blessed is Yahweh Elohim, God of Israel
Who alone does wondrous things;
Blessed is his glorious name forever,
His glory fills the whole earth. Amen and Amen.
End of the prayers of David son of Jesse.

Ps 72:18–20

Blessed is Yahweh forever. Amen and Amen.

Ps 89:53

Blessed is Yahweh, God of Israel, from eternity to eternity.
Let all the people say: "Amen." Hallelujah.

Ps 106:48

Since 1 Chron 16:36 quotes the doxology of Collection Four (Psalms 90–106) as part of Psalm 106, the division into books goes back at least to the time of the Chronicler. Though now brought together in one "book," the five collections had a prior existence as books in their own right. Some psalms made their way into two different collections. A good illustration is Psalm 14 from Collection One (Psalms 1–41), which returns in a slightly modified version as Psalm 53 in Collection Two (Psalms 42–72). The principal difference is the use of the name "Yahweh" in Psalm 14 and the use of "Elohim" in Psalm 53. Other psalms that occur in two different contexts are Psalm 18 (= 2 Sam 22) and Psalm 60:8–14 (= Ps 108:8–14).

Expansion

Expansion occurs where scribes enlarge an existing document with additions of their own. Except for annotations scribbled in the margins, usually referred to as "glosses," expansions normally required the scribe to prepare a new copy of the text. The format of a cuneiform tablet or a Hebrew scroll did not allow a textual amplification of any consequence on the tablet or scroll that carried the text; unless the scribes were prepared to write the whole text anew, they could not incorporate new material.

The preparation of a new copy of the text, enlarged with supplementary data of various kinds, could conceivably take place either in the course of a new text edition or in the far more common process of reproduction from a master copy. It is important to be aware of this distinction. In the terminology of biblical scholars, the phenomenon of textual expansion goes by such names as *Fortschreibung* or *relecture;* the one term conveys the notion of a steady process of text amplification as successive scribes add data to a text they are copying; the other has the scribe giving a creative reading of his text that somehow becomes part of the text itself. Both terms have the connotation of a slow and gradual process, as implied by the English expression "textual growth." It bears emphasizing that such growth is not a natural and organic process but the outcome of deliberate interventions in the texts. Scribes were averse to such interventions while copying from a mother text. Expansion is therefore most likely to be explained as an activity in the context of a new edition.

Text expansion is indeed a striking phenomenon because it seems to contrast with the veneration of scribes for the written tradition. It suffices to look at cuneiform compositions represented by copies from different periods to be struck by the scrupulous adherence on the part of successive generations of scribes to the "master copy" *(gabarû)* or the "original" *(labīru)* of their text.[54] They copy the text as they find it, including its lacunae. "Recent break" *(ḫipi eššu)* is the conventional expression for such damages. The frequent occurrence of the notation underscores the scribal ethics of fidelity to the received text. The scribes normally refrained from restoring a defective copy, even if the reader was encouraged to supply an appropriate phrase.[55] To ensure that he had not skipped a line or copied one twice, the scribe made a line count and noted it on the tablet. Faithful reproduction of the text as received was the scribal norm. The dutiful scribe neither added to nor removed from his text.

If expansion seems an infraction of the scribal code of conduct, it is because we tend to confuse the scribe as copyist with the scribe as editor. Expansion is a well-attested phenomenon in the context of a new edition; the scribe as editor is at liberty to do what would be considered a sin for a copying scribe. Owing to the Mesopotamian use of clay tablets as writing material, it is possible at times to compare different editions of the same cuneiform composition. A classic example is that of the *Gilgamesh Epic*. Because we possess copies of the Old Babylonian text of the epic—or at least substantial parts of it—and also copies of the Standard Babylonian version, more than 500 years younger, we are able to see how the scribe of the later version expanded the material at his disposal.

The Old Babylonian edition of the *Gilgamesh Epic* was called, after its opening line, "Surpassing all other kings."[56] It is a third-person account of the great deeds of Gilgamesh. The epic conveys the message that the way to a good life requires acceptance of one's mortality and a readiness to enjoy the good things in life. This is the wisdom Gilgamesh eventually learns from the mouth of Shiduri the tavern-keeper. The scribe of the Standard Babylonian edition added a prologue of twenty-eight lines. Line number one in the Old Babylonian version became line twenty-nine in the new one. The new prologue emphasizes that the epic is about wisdom *(nēmequ)*.[57] It pictures Gilgamesh as a man who obtained secret wisdom inaccessible to others.

> He who saw the Deep, the country's foundations,
> Who knew everything, was wise in all matters! . . .
> He learnt the sum of wisdom of everything.
> He saw what was secret, discovered what was hidden,
> He brought back a message from before the Flood.
>   *Gilgamesh* I i 1–2.6–8[58]

The theme of the prologue returns at the end of the text, in tablet XI. There the author reveals what kind of wisdom Gilgamesh did learn. It is not the wisdom of the tavern-keeper, whose *carpe diem* counsel has disappeared from the text. In the Standard Babylonian version, Gilgamesh receives his wisdom from Uta-napishti, also known as Atraḫasis, the hero who survived the Flood. The example shows that a revision may not only expand but also suppress earlier material.[59]

The episode of the encounter with Uta-napishti was already part of the epic in Old Babylonian times, as the last part of the Old Babylonian Sippar tablet suggests. Yet it is evident from the literal correspondence between the closing lines of tablet XI and lines 18–23 of the prologue (XI 322–328 = I i 18–23) that the editor who added the prologue was also responsible for a thorough expansion of tablet XI (that is, the corresponding passage in the Old Babylonian edition).[60] He added the Flood account, the homily by Uta-napishti, and an epilogue.[61] The most striking modifications of the text are to be found at the very beginning and the end of the epic.

Informed about the editorial techniques of Sin-leqe-unninni—the scribe who wrote the standard version of *Gilgamesh*—we must ask whether similar techniques can be detected in the Hebrew Bible. A basic rule of editorial expansions of the kind we find in *Gilgamesh* is that they occur at the borders of the text. Knowing that we must look for scribal interventions at the beginning and the end of literary units, we cannot fail to discover a number of editorial expansions in the books of the Bible. In view of the colophon-like notice in Lev 26:46 ("These are the laws, rules, and instructions . . ."), chapter 27 is evidently an editorial expansion. The analysis of Deuteronomy indicates that the book has several beginnings: one in Deut 1:1 ("These are the words") and an earlier one in Deut 4:44 ("This is the Torah"); as a matter of consequence, chapters 1 through 4 must be viewed as expansions added in a revision of the earlier work.

Textual expansions at the borders of a text are often a way of reframing a composition in the course of a new edition. Most expansions, however, occur within the body of the text. To understand the occurrence of such intratextual expansions, we must pay attention to the oral tradition surrounding the transmission of written texts. Often the origins of textual expansion are to be found in the oral explanations that teachers gave as they transmitted written texts to their students. In Mesopotamian scribal circles, this oral tradition was known as *ša/šūt pî ummâni*, "oral lore of the masters."[62] The oral lore of the Mesopotamian scholars is comparable to the Jewish oral Torah (the Torah "through the channel of the mouth," *šebbĕ'al peh*) that, as rabbinic tradition has it, was handed down alongside the written Torah.

The phenomenon of intratextual expansion is best understood as a process in which the oral lore of the masters entered the written text. As in the case of paratextual expansions, that is, those at the beginning or the end of the text, intratextual expansions have their most plausible setting in the context of a new edition, as opposed to a reproduction, of a traditional text. Such editing should not be confused with publishing; textual revisions and expansions performed in the course of a new edition usually remained within the confines of the scribal elite. Nor need a new edition acquire the status of *textus receptus*. The cuneiform tradition has several instances of works circulating in different versions, none of which could lay claim to a position as the canonical version.

Once again, actual cases of intratextual expansion are easier to demonstrate for cuneiform literature than for the books of the Bible because in the case of Mesopotamia we can see the textual development by comparing copies from different periods. The astrological compendium *Enūma Anu Enlil* offers a good illustration.[63] Celestial omens were written down from Old Babylonian times onward. Once put down in writing, the tradition remained in constant need of interpretation and supplementation. So long as the tradition remained alive, the series *Enūma Anu Enlil* never became fully fixed. As David Brown puts it, "The later second millennium redactors felt free not only to gather existing omens and elaborate on them using the rules of textual play, but to *include* omens that could only have been invented at that time."[64] In the process of transmission, textuality interferes with orality as the oral lore of the masters is incorporated in the written text of the series. The same phenomenon is documented for cuneiform texts outside the astrological tradition, such as the exorcistic series *Utukkū lemnūtu*, "Evil Spirits," as indicated by the comparison with its "forerunners," and the ritual series *Maqlû*, "Combustion."[65]

To illustrate the fact that intratextual expansion took place in scribal circles all over the Near East, it may be useful to point to an example from Egypt. The ancient Egyptian mortuary texts have a written tradition of millennia extant in the Pyramid Texts (Old Kingdom), the Coffin Texts (Middle Kingdom), and the *Book of the Dead* (New Kingdom). The scribal transmission of these texts was both reproductive and productive.[66] The scribes were involved in "an ongoing process of composing and editing, rather than simply recopying, spells."[67] A comparison of the *Book of the Dead* with the preceding bodies of funerary texts shows that the early spells were an inspiration and a source for later ones; alongside the inherited spells, the Egyptian scribes of the New Kingdom also added new literary creations.[68] The notion of the traditional literature as a heritage that scribes transmitted unchanged over the centuries does not agree with the actual transformations and growth in the written tradition. Such changes are best understood as the reflection of a lively oral tradition that continued alongside the transmission in writing.

The examples of intratextual expansion in the Hebrew Bible are legion, but for most of them there is no proof other than the internal evidence in the text itself, to be detected only by a critical analysis of its redaction. One such piece of evidence is the repetitive resumption, also known by the technical term *Wiederaufnahme*.[69] Where an expansion causes an interruption in the flow of the text, the movement resumes with a repetition of the words found just before the expansion; the inserted text is thereby bracketed by two phrases that are very similar if not identical. It is not always easy to decide whether the scribe responsible for the expansion wished to signal his intervention in the text by deliberately creating a bracket, or whether the bracket was extant even before the insertion as a way of linking two textual blocks. In the second case, the repetitive resumption served as a kind of catch-line. Two examples may help us to understand the phenomenon.

The Book of Judges follows the Book of Joshua and continues its historical narrative. The sequence is evident from a comparison between Josh 24:28–31 and Judg 2:6–9. The passage in Judges repeats almost literally the verses from Joshua: Joshua dismissed the Israelites to their "inheritance"; the people served Yahweh during the time of Joshua and the elders; Joshua died at the age of 110 and was buried. These interlocking passages now bracket Judg 1:1–2:5. The assessment of the territories not in the possession of the Israelites (Judg 1:1–36) as well as the etiological tale of Bochim (Judg 2:1–5) have ostensibly been added to an earlier edition of Judges. In that previous edition, the text probably began with Judg 2:6–9; the passage originally served to make the link with the Book of Joshua, and became a *Wiederaufnahme* due to the insertion of Judg 1:1–2:5.

A rather similar case is extant in the repetitive resumption of Exodus 40:33 in Numbers 7:1.[70] The verse from Numbers,

On the day that Moses finished setting up the Tabernacle, he anointed and consecrated it and all its furnishings, as well as the altar and its utensils, echoes Exodus 40:33,

> And he [i.e., Moses] set up the enclosure around the Tabernacle and the altar, and put up the screen for the gate of the enclosure. When Moses had finished the work, the cloud covered the Tent of Meeting, and the presence of Yahweh filled the Tabernacle.

Exodus 40:33 and Numbers 7:1 now serve as brackets for the corpus of sacerdotal law contained in the Book of Leviticus and Numbers 1–6. The compilation of "instructions" *(tôrôt)* once had an independent existence but has now become an expansion of the Exodus narrative. Secondarily introduced by a passage concerning the presence of Yahweh in the Tabernacle (Exod 40:34–38), the priestly law was presented as divine revelation (compare Lev 1:1–2).

Internal textual evidence for expansion is hardly ever beyond dispute. By good fortune there is one case of textual expansion where the evidence is uncontested—even though scholars differ about its interpretation. I am referring to the two versions of the Book of Jeremiah. The Greek translation of Jeremiah as extant in the Septuagint is shorter by one-seventh than the text of the book in the Hebrew Bible. Its arrangement of the material, moreover, differs considerably from that in the Hebrew text. Discoveries in the Judean Desert have yielded a fragment of a Hebrew version of Jeremiah (4QJer^b) that agrees with the Septuagint against the Hebrew text known from the Masoretic tradition. Based on this fragment, tiny though it is, scholars have concluded that the Greek translation goes back to a Hebrew text that preceded the version of Jeremiah as we have it in the Hebrew Bible.[71]

By comparison with the Septuagint and 4QJer^b, the Masoretic version of Jeremiah represents an expansion of the earlier text of the book in a number of ways. Many expansions read like explanations by the teacher to his students as they were reading the text. The "first year of King Jehoiakim son of Josiah of Judah" was indeed synchronous with "the first year of Nebuchadnezzar king of Babylon" (Jer 25:1). The scribe adds patronymics (29:21, 36:8); specifies Baruch's profession

(36:26, 36:32); explains the topographical setting of events (37:17, 41:1); emphasizes the chronology (28:1); fills in names (21:2, 28:4, 40:9, 52:16); and clarifies the significance of the descriptions by adding details to the point of redundancy (36:6, 41:2, 41:7). All these are expansions best understood by analogy to an oral recitation by a teacher who paraphrases his text as he reads it.

Expansion of a different order is at issue in Jer 33:14–26.[72] The thirteen verses added by the scribe are not a clarification of the preceding passage but an extended paraphrase of the "promise" (literally, "the good word") mentioned in Jer 29:10 ("I will fulfill my good word for you"); the prophecy of a scion for the royal dynasty of David in Jer 23:5–6 (quoted in 33:14–16); and the parallel that Jer 31:35–37 draws between the immutable laws of nature and the steadfast commitment of God to his people (paraphrased in 33:19–26). The scribe who added 33:14–26 elaborated on the earlier restoration oracles and gave them a particular twist by emphasizing the central role of the Davidic dynasty and the Levitical priests (33:17–18, 33:22, 33:26). The perspective is clearly post-exilic, since the expansion contemplates a restoration of both the kingship and the priesthood along the same lines as the oracles of the prophet Zechariah (Zech 3–4, 6:9–13).[73]

The expansion in the Masoretic text of Jeremiah 33 is an instance of a teacher explaining the meaning of received oracles for his own time. Introducing his commentary with the standard phrase, "See, days are coming," he gives a free quotation of earlier oracles, paraphrases them, and interprets them in such a way that he produces in fact new oracles. Yet this type of expansion remains a commentary by the scribal teachers on the written text as they had received it. It was oral lore of the masters before it was incorporated in the written text. The phenomenon could occur only at a time in which the prophetical books were still "under construction." After the closure of the books of the prophets such commentary did not disappear, but the written form was kept apart from the prophecy itself. The *pesharim* from Qumran illustrate the new scribal practice.

Adaptation

Neither the scribe who transcribes nor the scribe who invents has a written text at his disposal for text he produces. The compiler, on the other hand, will often work with written material, and expansion presupposes the presence of a written text. Adaptation, too, is a mode of text production that requires an anterior text. The scribe will use that text as a model for his own; instead of writing a text, he will be rewriting one. His adaptation can take various forms. It may be a mere translation from the one language into the other; the translation may transform the text substantially by appropriating it for an audience with different religious loyalties; the adaptation can result in a variant version of the text with no hint of competition; and adaptation may be a way of rethinking a classic case and updating the written tradition. There is no shortage of examples to illustrate these various procedures.

Translation from one language to another was not uncommon as a mode of text production in the Near East. The twelfth tablet of the standard edition of *Gilgamesh* is a more or less literal translation in Akkadian of (the second part of) the Sumerian composition known as "Gilgamesh, Enkidu, and the Netherworld."[74] The Mesopotamian *Gilgamesh Epic* also existed in a Hittite and a Hurrian version.[75] An example of a translated text in the Bible is Proverbs 22:17–24:22. In 1924 Adolf Erman discovered that it depended on the *Teachings of Amenemope*.[76] This Egyptian wisdom text has thirty chapters; hence the reference in Prov 22:20 that reads, "Indeed, I wrote down for you the thirty chapters."[77] Gary A. Rendsburg has proposed a slight emendation of Prov 22:19 to obtain a reference to the very name of Amenemope.[78] Even if his proposal is judged to be too fanciful, there is no doubt about the Egyptian background of the chapters from Proverbs. Nor need there be cause for surprise; both as a scholarly pursuit and as a literary genre, wisdom belonged to the common heritage of the Near East.

Another instance of adaptation through translation is extant in Psalm 20 of the Hebrew Bible. In the 1980s two Dutch and two American scholars discovered that a Demotic papyrus in the Amherst collection of the Pierpont Morgan Library in New York contained an Aramaic blessing that corresponded almost word for word with the first part of Psalm 20.[79] The Aramaic text goes back to a Phoenician original, as indicated by the divine names Bethel and Baal Shamayn and the mention of Zaphon as the holy mountain.[80] The striking similarity between the Aramaic text and Psalm 20 is best explained by assuming that both are revisions of the same Phoenician original. This postulated Phoenician text is now lost, but the parallelisms between the Aramaic and the Hebrew texts suffice to reconstruct the Phoenician original. When a scribe working in Egypt translated the text into Aramaic, he substituted the name Horus for Baal.[81] The motive for the substitution is not entirely clear. While it has been claimed that the inhabitants of the Nile delta identified Baal Zaphon with Horus, there is very little evidence to this effect.[82] A religious appropriation for the greater glory of Horus cannot be excluded.[83]

On the assumption that the Aramaic psalm is a largely accurate translation of the Phoenician original, the adaptations performed by the Jewish scribe who wrote Psalm 20 are clear. Name substitution is the most striking feature. Instead of the name "Baal," replaced by "Horus" in the Aramaic, the Jewish scribe put in the name "Yahweh." The name "Zaphon" for the divine abode, retained in the Aramaic, became "Zion" in the Hebrew version. In addition to such obvious changes, the Hebrew scribe also intervened in his text in more subtle ways. He changed "our trouble" into "the day of trouble," and "tomorrow" into "the day that we call." The scribe revised a pagan poem into a Yahwistic psalm, and made the references to the actual circumstances so vague that it lent itself to use in a wide array of contexts.

It is not superfluous to point out that text appropriation through name substitution, as exemplified by Psalm 20, can equally occur where no translation is involved. A classic example of the procedure is found in the Neo-Assyrian version of the so-called *Epic of Creation*, also known by its opening words *Enūma eliš*. This Babylonian composition was created toward the end of the second millennium as an official charter of the position of Marduk as supreme god of the universe. It is a document of Babylonian nationalism, as Marduk is the chief deity of Babylon. In the Assyrian version of the poem, the name of Marduk is replaced by Anshar, a primeval deity identified in later times with Assur, the national god of Assyria. The revision of the text is intentional. Focused on a single name (though necessitating a change of identity for some other gods as well), the substitution transforms the text from a Babylonian piece of propaganda into an Assyrian one.[84]

Adaptations need not be designed to supersede their models. A literary genre from Mesopotamia in which it is common for texts to exist in multiple versions is that of the royal annals. The examples at our disposal come from Assyria. At various intervals, the scribes working for such kings as Assurbanipal had to produce display inscriptions extolling the glorious deeds of the monarch. The various stones they inscribed relate the same events in basically the same terms, yet often the one text differs from the other by the insertion of one or two names or another version of a common episode. The analysis of the successive "editions" shows that the scribes did not simply copy a mother text but used various written sources to adapt an existing annal.[85] The case of the royal annals demonstrates that a new version of the text was not necessarily a substitute of a previous one; the various Assurbanipal inscriptions existed alongside each other, embodying slightly different perspectives on the same events.

A more competitive relationship between model text and adaptation exists among the various cuneiform law collections. From the late third millennium onward, it was customary for Mesopotamian rulers to publish a series of exemplary verdicts in demonstration of their wisdom and devotion to the ideals of justice. These law collections ("codes" is their traditional misnomer) were written on commission. The scribes who produced them found their model in the collections put together by their predecessors. The laws in question are casuistic. Some of them go back to historical cases, but many more use the model of a case as a means of establishing general legal principles for which there is no precedent. A typical instance is the case of abortion and miscarriage due to assault.

The earliest example comes from the *Laws of Lipit-Ishtar* (ca. 1930 B.C.E.). Three possibilities are dealt with: assault on a free woman resulting in abortion of the fetus; the same circumstance when the assault is also fatal to the woman herself; and assault on a slave woman causing her to miscarry. The verdicts, respectively: a fine of thirty shekels of silver; the death penalty; a fine of only five shekels of silver.[86] A Sumerian law exercise tablet from ca. 1800 treats two cases: the fine for abortion due to assault depends on whether the man "jostled" the woman or "struck" her: the latter offense is punished twice as severely.[87] About fifty years later, the case of *abortus provocatus* is dealt with in the *Laws of Hammurabi.* Six cases pass in review, the main concern of the scribes being the distinction of three social classes to which the woman might belong, her assault carrying a penalty in keeping with her social status.[88] The topic makes yet another appearance in the Middle Assyrian Laws (ca. 1050 B.C.E.). They add the case of a pregnant prostitute and of abortion provoked by the woman herself.[89]

The fact that the issue of miscarriage due to assault occurs in four different Mesopotamian law collections is hardly to be explained by the frequency of the event; incidents of the sort are statistically rare. Yet once the case made its way into the *Laws of Lipit-Ishtar,* it became a standard topos in nearly all subsequent law collections from Mesopotamia. Moreover, as a result of the spread of the legal tradition of Mesopotamia to other civilizations of the Near East, the topic of an assaulted woman having a miscarriage also made its way into the *Hittite Laws* (paragraphs 17–18) and into the earliest laws preserved in the Bible (Exod 21:22). Jacob J. Finkelstein interprets this borrowing as a literary phenomenon as opposed to a legal one.[90] It illustrates how scribes went about their work. They used the written tradition, either native or adopted, as a model for their own writing.[91]

There is another example of adaptation of written law in the Bible. The oldest law collection of the Bible says that someone who acquires a

Hebrew slave—note the term "Hebrew" *('ibrî)* as distinguished from "Israelite" or "Judaean"—must release him as a freedman in the seventh year (Exod 21:2–11). The legal section of Deuteronomy returns to the issue, quoting from Exodus by using the term "Hebrew," and determines that the act of manumission should be combined with a generous supply of livestock, food, and drink (Deut 15:12–18). A third law, found in the Holiness Code, adapts the earlier rules by prohibiting the turning of an indebted compatriot into a slave; the status of the indebted individual should be that of a hired or bound laborer (Lev 25:39–46). A careful comparison between the three law collections reveals various other points of dependence and distinction. For the present purpose, however, it suffices to show that successive generations of scribes used the case as a classic on which they made their own variations. The different laws have all been preserved and collected in the biblical tradition, in spite of their conflicting views.[92]

Integration

The English word "text" comes from Latin *textus,* which literally means "woven." The term evokes the image of the written composition as a piece of cloth woven from multiple threads. In Mesopotamia, scribes and scholars used this very image for a text that had been produced on the basis of several documents.

The diagnostic series *Sakikkû,* a textbook for Babylonian practitioners, is an example of a scholarly work that reached its standard form through the integration of separate and diverging source texts.[93] Its editor was a scribe by the name of Esagil-kīn-apli.[94] Born from a scribal family that traced its origins back to the time of Hammurabi, Esagil-kīn-apli was the leading scholar of Babylonia under King Adad-apla-iddina (1068–1047). Authorized by a royal mandate, this man created what came to be the canonical version of the diagnostic compendium. In a subscript to the catalogue of the forty tablets of *Sakikkû,* Esagil-kīn-apli is credited with the production of a "new text" (written with the Sumerian signs *sur gibil*).[95]

> The lore that from old time had not been given a new [authorized] text,
> but that was like twisted threads for which no master copy was available
> . . . Esagil-kīn-apli . . . using the splendid intelligence which Ea and
> Asalluḫi had granted him, deliberated with himself, and produced a new
> text of *Sakikkû,* from head to foot, and established it for instruction.[96]

The Sumerian verb *sur* has the meaning "to spin, to twist, to weave."[97]
According to a Sumerian hymn, words may be "woven like into a net
[*sa*]."[98] Since the next line of this hymn says that "it was written on
its tablet and was being laid to hand," the metaphor of weaving or
spinning refers here to the establishing of a standard edition written
down for ready reference.[99] In the description of the editorial activity
of Esagil-kīn-apli, the reference to manuscripts as "twisted threads"
(written with the Sumerograms *gu.meš gil.meš*) likens the work of the
scribal editor to that of a weaver.

The scribal activity of Esagil-kīn-apli on the diagnostic corpus
Sakikkû was both critical and compositional. Not only did he attempt
to define the correct text, he also brought disparate materials together
into a single series. His revision of the extant written sources served the
purpose of creating a definitive work. The materials he assembled had
not, until then, been part of a single tradition; some were diagnostic observations, others were physiognomic lore, yet others were behavioral
omens.[100] By putting them together in a series of exactly forty tablets,
Esagil-kīn-apli put them under the authority of Ea, the god of wisdom,
since forty is precisely his numerological figure.[101] In the case of Esagil-
kīn-apli's work on *Sakikkû,* then, revision and compilation go in tandem. His scribal activity can serve as a model for conceptualizing the
work of Hebrew scholar-scribes on biblical books with multiple
sources.[102]

Editorial activity on the basis of source texts is visible in the Hebrew Bible as well. Given two documents, the Hebrew scribe could
follow different strategies to weave them into a single text. If he chose
to preserve both documents intact, he would use the technique of
conflation.[103] Without sacrificing anything of either source text, the

scribe would put them together through juxtaposition or, more elegantly, by dissolving the two texts into their constituent elements, which he would then piece together into a new configuration. Another way of preparing an integrated text was to take one document as the master text and to eclectically use the second document to supplement it. Deuteronomy 12 offers an example of the first technique; the Flood narrative from the Book of Genesis illustrates the second procedure.

Deuteronomy 12 prohibits worship of Yahweh in places other than "the one place that Yahweh shall choose." Analysis of the chapter shows that its redundancy, noted by many commentators, is the result of the conflation of two parallel sets of stipulations. The editor used the cut-and-paste variant of the conflation technique; he cut the texts he worked with into sections and pasted them together. As a result, Deut 12:4–27 consists of two sections, each having two parallel sets of stipulations (12:4–7//12:8–12 and 12:13–19//12:20–27).

> You shall not continue current practices . . . [4//8];
> Yahweh shall choose one place . . . [5//9–11a]
> where you will bring all your sacrifices and gifts [6//11b].
> There you will rejoice before Yahweh . . . [7//12].
> If you desire to eat meat, you may slaughter and eat in your settlements [13–15a//20–21].
> Since the slaughter is profane, it does not require ritual purity [15b//22].
> Do not partake of the blood [16//23–25].
> The various sacred gifts may not be consumed locally but must be brought to the one place Yahweh shall choose [17–19//26–27].

In combining his two sources, the scribal editor was apparently aiming at completeness. He wrote a text that was in no way deficient.

The editor of the Flood narrative took a slightly different approach. Ever since the rise of the historical-critical study of the Bible, the story of Noah's ark has been used as a textbook case of source-critical analysis.[104] Generations of students have been taught to read Genesis 6–9 as a composite account integrating narratives from a Yahwistic document (J) and a priestly source (P). Despite occasional attempts to defend the original unity of the chapters, the prevailing opinion views the Flood narrative as the work of an editor who conflated two accounts into one.[105] The repetitions (e.g., Gen 6:5–8//6:9–13), contradictions (e.g., Gen 6:19–20 versus 7:2), and redundancies (e.g., Gen 7:7//7:13; 7:17// 7:18) are indeed unmistakable. In contrast to Deuteronomy 12, the editor of the Flood narrative took one document as his master text (P) and made eclectic use of his second source (J). At the beginning and the end of the narrative, the two documents are clearly identifiable; in the middle section, however, the editor worked phrases and expressions from J into the P account in such a way as to leave few distinct traces of J.[106]

The technique of weaving separate documents into one text requires access to, and is based on, a variety of written sources. Such a scholastic procedure strikes some Bible scholars as anachronistic.

> Specific issues in the logistics of literacy . . . argue against the documentary hypothesis . . . At the heart of the documentary hypothesis . . . is the cut-and-paste image of an individual . . . having his various written sources laid out before him as he chooses this verse or that, includes this tale not that, edits, elaborates, all in a library setting . . . Did the redactor need three colleagues to hold J, E, and P for him? Did each read the text out loud, and did he ask them to pause until he jotted down his selections, working like a secretary with three tapes dictated by the boss?[107]

The ironic questions Susan Niditch asks are rhetorical; in her mind there is no doubt that the image of a scribe working with two or more texts is a mirage of nineteenth-century European scholars. The Mesopotamian evidence demonstrates, however, that by the end of the second millennium B.C.E. scribes already engaged in such editorial activities. The scribal workshop of the temple in Jerusalem may have been an enclave of literacy in an oral world, but it was not for that reason any less sophisticated than the scriptoria of the medieval monasteries.

One last question, finally, concerns the motives of the scribes in weaving together distinct and at times disparate traditions. Why did they want to compose a "new text" out of "twisted threads"? They would seem to have been inspired by the wish to create a "canonical" document. Working under the patronage of the royal court, Esagil-kīn-apli produced an "authorized" edition of the diagnostic lore. The scribes who edited the biblical Flood narrative, or even the Pentateuch as a whole, aimed to produce a document that would have the support of different textual communities. By writing a work that integrated documents with different ideas and perspectives, the scribes were creating a national written heritage that transcended earlier divisions.

From Survey to Sample

The survey of scribal modes of text production offered in this chapter is, to some degree, artificial in the sense that it separates methods and techniques scribes normally used in conjunction. Adaptation and expansion, for instance, will often go hand in hand, just as one text might well be the fruit of both transcription and compilation. Very few texts represent a single mode of production in its pure state. If the present discussion has treated the various production modes separately, it was primarily for the purpose of analysis, not because this is the way actual texts present themselves.

Having established the role of writing and authorship, the place of the professionals of writing, and the methods and techniques these professionals used, we can now proceed to study two books of the Bible as samples of scribal culture. Chapter 6 will deal with the Book of Deuteronomy as an instance of the legal and narrative traditions of the Bible; Chapter 7 looks at the place of written prophecy, mainly on the basis of the Book of Jeremiah. The two chapters will illustrate the various scribal modes of text production by looking at concrete examples; in so doing, the analysis will show that the authorship that the tradition attributes to Moses and Jeremiah has to give way to the scribes as the actual producers of the biblical texts.

chapter six

THE TEACHING OF MOSES

Scribal Culture in the Mirror of Deuteronomy

The Hebrew Bible is both a product of and a monument to the scribal culture of ancient Israel. If we want to get acquainted more closely with the Hebrew scribes—their way of thinking, their values, and their working methods—the best way to do so is by studying the texts they produced. That is why, in this chapter, I shall submit one of those texts to a close reading. It is a sample of scribal culture not only as a literary artifact but also for the views and values it contains.

The text that will serve as a means of entry into Hebrew scribal culture is the Book of Deuteronomy. The choice takes its cue from the disparaging reference in the Book of Jeremiah to "the Teaching of Yahweh" *(tôrat yhwh)* as the product of "the deceitful pen of the scribes" (Jer 8:8). Karl Marti argued in 1889 that the "Teaching of Yahweh" that Jeremiah was denouncing as a fraud has to be identified with the Book of Deuteronomy.[1] In view of the obvious connection between Deuteronomy and "the Book of the Teaching" *(sēper hattôrâ)* underlying the religious reform carried out by King Josiah in 622, it makes sense to think that it was indeed an early edition of Deuteronomy that provoked Jeremiah's criticism.[2] On the assumption that Deuteronomy is a product of "the pen of the scribes," then, it can be read as a mirror in which scribal culture is reflected.

The Composition of Deuteronomy in Light of Scribal Practice

On the surface, the structure of Deuteronomy is simple. The book contains the farewell speech delivered by Moses shortly before his death. In the context of his address, Moses renews the covenant between God and the Israelites; Deuteronomy is the text of the second covenant, concluded in the land of Moab forty years after the first covenant at Mt. Horeb. The solemn address of Moses consists of a rehearsal of past events (Deut 1–3); a series of exhortations (Deut 4–11); an exposition of the "rules and verdicts," also known as the Deuteronomic law code (Deut 12–26); speeches on the occasion of the covenantal ceremony, including conditional curses and blessings (Deut 27–30); and speeches and poems in light of the death of Moses (Deut 31–34). The genres of valedictory oration, treaty text, and law code seem to blend into a harmonious whole.

Closer inspection of the text, however, reveals the harmony to be deceptive. The perspectives of a final teaching or Torah, on the one hand, and a treaty, on the other, are scarcely compatible; even if many commentators find no tension between the two, either by highlighting the one at the expense of the other or by glossing over the difference, most of them acknowledge the existence of redundancies and inconsistencies in the text.[3] Such observations have led to a near consensus that the Book of Deuteronomy as we know it is the end product of more than 200 years of scribal activity.[4] However, the unanimity about the complex history of the book translates into a bewildering diversity of opinion as to the details of its making.[5]

Leaving aside the prehistory of the text, there are basically two models on which to conceptualize the development from Josiah's reform document (the so-called *Urdeuteronomium*, presumably the first edition of the book) into the Book of Deuteronomy as we know it. The one model says the scribes added substantial sections in the course of three or four editions; in this model Deuteronomy is an assemblage of literary blocks: the scribes expanded the original text with a few major supplements.[6] The other model views the process as one of steady revi-

sion and expansion in piecemeal fashion; in this model Deuteronomy is
a deposit of many sediments rather than blocks.[7] If Deuteronomy were
an altarpiece, the one model would say it consists of panels, while the
other would say it is one picture to which many artists have added a
stroke of the brush.

The usual way to make a choice between the two models is to ask
which model provides the most satisfying explanation of the final version of Deuteronomy. Much of the secondary literature takes this van-
tage point. A preliminary question, however, concerns the attitude of
the scribes toward a written text from the stream of tradition. How are
we to conceive of their interventions in a text they had received? Since
the phenomenon of textual growth is not growth in the biological sense
of the term but the result of scribal activity, we must be clear about the
usual mechanics of that activity.

To put the problem of textual growth into focus, it is helpful to recall
that the first edition of Deuteronomy (the *Urdeuteronomium*) was not
an ordinary text. Promoted as a lost document from long ago, the reverence and respect it commanded were sufficient to legitimize a major
cult reform. By the witness of Jer 8:8–9, the sages who boasted possession of this scroll regarded it as a divinely inspired document; to them it
was Holy Writ. A text of such prestige does not readily lend itself to revision, correction, expansion, or supplementation; alterations of any
kind would have to be made with caution, since sacred texts may not
be tampered with. While it is true that Deuteronomy has gone through
several editions, the document on which the editions were performed
had a status that rendered revision a kind of sacrilege.

The text of Deuteronomy itself contains evidence to demonstrate
that the preservation of the correct text was a matter of concern to the
scribal circles that produced it. The injunction not to alter the text by
additions or deletions (Deut 4:2; 13:1) proves the importance attached
to textual integrity.[8] This so-called canon formula was meant to fix the
text into a book. According to Deut 31:9, Moses wrote down his teaching and entrusted the priests with safeguarding it. Earlier in Deuteronomy the priestly responsibility for the written Torah comes to the fore

in the rule according to which the King should procure a copy of the Torah from the priests (Deut 17:18). The priests are the authority, then, charged with preserving the purity of the Torah; a copy needed their certificate.

While the priests were officially to prevent textual alterations, the evidence shows that the text did not remain untouched. Due to scribal interventions of various kinds, Deuteronomy developed from a reform document into the book as we know it. Textual interventions would not have occurred unless three conditions were met: without (1) an occasion, (2) a motive, and (3) a warrant, textual developments would not have taken place. An occasion alone would not suffice to explain a textual revision; nor would, by itself, a motive; and without a warrant, any change would be an infraction on the integrity of the text. Only the conjunction of occasion, motive, and warrant made scribes actually revise and alter the venerated text. The occasion, I suggest, was furnished by the necessity, every so often, to replace a scroll grown threadbare with a new one; the motive resided in the wish to make the text reflect the ideas and insights that had developed over time; and the warrant came from a priestly authority supervising the scribes.

Let me first comment on motive and warrant. As for the motive to revise, expand, and adapt the received text, the mere fact that the redactions of Deuteronomy are spread over 200 years indicates that we should reckon with the wish of scribes to attune the text to changing historical circumstances and interpretive perspectives. Designed in the late pre-exilic era as a charter of a religious reform, Deuteronomy had to serve a different function in the time of the Exile, when the temple lay in ruins; its meaning for the post-exilic community had to be defined along different lines yet. Precisely because Deuteronomy was surrounded by a halo of antiquity and authority, it was able to provide new ideas, triggered by new situations, with a Mosaic ancestry and authority.

If the responsibility for preserving the book intact lay with the priests, the warrant that allowed scribal interventions to take place would have to come from them. It is difficult to believe, however, that a collective would be able to formally authorize a new edition. One would expect the priests to be represented by a supervisor empowered to pronounce a *nihil obstat*. The doctrine of the Mosaic succession, adumbrated in Deut 18:15–18, might indeed be taken to imply the existence of a position of leadership among the priests in charge of the Torah. Hilkiah, who found the Book of the Torah, held the position of high priest; Ezra, who promulgated the Book of the Law, was a priestly authority as well; at the beginning of the Common Era, the office of high priest was believed to endow its holder with prophetical insight (John 11:51); such data suggest that the scribe or scribes who prepared a new edition of Deuteronomy worked under the auspices of the priestly leadership.[9]

This brings me, finally, to the occasion. If the occasion for a textual revision coincides with the time when an old scroll has to be replaced by a new one, the text in question must have existed in a single master copy. Such is indeed the impression conveyed both by the Book of Deuteronomy and by the account of Josiah's reform (2 Kings 22–23). According to Deut 31:9, Moses wrote down his teaching and gave it to the priests. Only the king was entitled to a second copy (the "double" of the Torah, *mišnēh hattôrâ*), which he had to obtain, precisely, from the priests in charge of the text (Deut 17:18). The story of the discovery of the Book of the Torah by the high priest Hilkiah presumes a single copy as well; being a relic of the Mosaic age, it was stored in a safe place and handled with the utmost care. The public at large owed its knowledge of the text to instructions from the king, both written and oral, and to public readings by the clergy.[10]

The biblical evidence that the Book of the Torah existed in a single master copy finds support in a consideration of the logistics of textual revision. Even the hypothesis of literary blocks or supplements assumes several editions of Deuteronomy. If the book existed in a substantial number of copies, it would have been virtually impossible to prevent a proliferation of variant texts; each new edition would require the authorities to suppress all extant copies of the previous edition. If no copies existed but the master copy, the priests were in full control of the text, its transmission, and its editions—including the scribes, who worked under the priestly patronage.[11]

If a text exists in a single master copy written on a papyrus scroll, the opportunities for a steady accumulation of slight changes, deletions, minor expansions, and the like are almost nil. The physical format of the text allows for little else than annotations in the margins; writing between the lines is hardly possible in view of the neat script, and erasures were probably too brutal an intervention in the text. To integrate new data into the text, the entire scroll has to be rewritten. Considering these restraints on text revision, it is highly unlikely that we should conceive of the process of textual growth as a steady accretion of new textual data. The odds are overwhelmingly in favor of a limited number of text editions, each new edition allowing the scribes to enrich the text with new material as it had accumulated over time.

The life span of a papyrus scroll was limited; at the end of its life cycle, the scribes prepared a new copy and put the old scroll away (in the Roman period and later, in a storage facility known as the *genizah*, from Persian *ginzakh*, "treasury").[12] The significance of the event may be illuminated by the analogy with the cult image. In the religious life of the Mesopotamians, the cult statue was as important as the written Torah came to be for the Jews.[13] Unlike the gods, the cult image was subject to decay. At some point, therefore, a new image had to be made. According to the official doctrine, the new image was a reincarnation of the old one; even though it could not materially be an exact copy of the previous one, the theology of the cult image says that it is a representation of the god in the canonical shape, that is, as it was revealed in the beginning. Actual changes, either by accident or on purpose, were treated as though they had always been present in the image. The divine image was an *effigies ne varietur*, much like Deuteronomy was a *textus ne varietur*—in spite of the obvious changes in the successive editions.[14] Since very few people would get a close look at the image, most changes would pass unobserved; moreover, the burial of the previous statue made a comparison impossible.

If a new edition replaced a scroll whose condition had deteriorated, the number of editions must be related to the average life cycle of a papyrus scroll. Depending on the quality of the papyrus, the climate, and the storage conditions, a scroll that was used as a reference text would last two or three generations. Judging by its expansions, the scroll of Deuteronomy was intensively studied and commentated; heavy use might have reduced the time of its viability. There would have been cause, then, every forty years or so, to prepare a new master copy. That was the occasion, I submit, that allowed the scribes to revise and expand the received text.[15]

When it comes to the historical plausibility of the two models of textual growth, the hypothesis of a limited number of editions incorporating each various assemblage of new material wins on all scores. The notion of an ongoing *Fortschreibung* is simply not consistent with ancient Near Eastern scribal practice. A comparison with the works of cuneiform literature, such as the *Epic of Gilgamesh,* confirms the point. We know for a fact that the standard version of *Gilgamesh* was a new edition incorporating new sections and deleting some earlier scenes, that it was prepared under the supervision of a leading scholar, and that it was promoted by the authorities as the definitive edition. Though the material that entered the new edition may have accumulated over time, the redaction of a new text was a rare occurrence, both preceded and followed by periods in which the received text was left unchanged.

My analysis of the textual history of Deuteronomy shall therefore proceed on the assumption that the charter document of Josiah's reform went through a limited number of editions before it reached its present form. Taking forty years as a plausible interval between editions, the scribes would have prepared revisions around 580, 540, and 500, assuming the original version of Deuteronomy goes back to ca. 620 B.C.E. Though one or more of these editions were presumably undertaken in the larger context of the writing of the Deuteronomistic History or the composition of the Pentateuch, I shall focus on the Book of Deuteronomy as a literary unit in its own right.[16] The attempt to delineate the successive editions of Deuteronomy is not an exercise for its own sake but is designed to open up a perspective on the social and intellectual milieu of successive generations of Hebrew scribes.

The Four Editions of Deuteronomy

Having established that the Book of Deuteronomy in its present form is most likely the outcome of a limited number of successive editions, I now turn to the text itself in an attempt to identify those editions. The only evidence we can work from is the final edition of the text; in this respect, there is quite a difference between Deuteronomy and a Mesopotamian classic like *Gilgamesh*. The two major editions of *Gilgamesh* are each extant in several copies, a circumstance that allows us to see how the composer of the second edition transformed the text of the first.[17] In the case of Deuteronomy, we have to reconstruct previous editions on the basis of traces and clues left in the final one; the procedure inevitably involves a certain amount of speculation.

What traces and clues are we to look for? Many scholars proceed on the assumption that each edition of Deuteronomy exhibited a different style and idiom. While one had a preference for addressing the audience in the singular, for instance, another would consistently use the plural.[18] However, an analysis based on stylistic criteria alone fails to yield convincing results, as each new edition necessitated the production of a new scroll on which the entire text had to be rewritten; the editors were at liberty to put the stamp of their style on the text as a whole, including those parts they had inherited. While we should not ignore such matters as literary style and idiom, we must primarily look for a difference in perspective. Usually the motive for producing a new edition was the wish to give a new interpretive frame to existing material; more so perhaps than to add new material, the scribes made a new edition so as to lay down a new understanding of an ancient text.

The comparative evidence from the Mesopotamian classics illustrates how the scribes proceeded as editors. If we stay for a moment with the *Epic of Gilgamesh*, we can see that the standard version (ca. 1100 B.C.E.) reframed the Old Babylonian edition (ca. 1700 B.C.E.) by adding a prologue and recasting the final episode. To convey a new perspective on the text, the editor expanded the beginning and the end, thus providing a new interpretive horizon. It is true that he also deleted a scene, added some new material, and gave the epic an appendix that was principally connected with the *Gilgamesh* story by the name of its protagonist, but the angle of the new edition becomes visible in the framework of the text.[19]

Taking the editorial technique of the Babylonian scribe as a model, we should expect to find evidence of the successive editions of Deuteronomy at the borders of the book. It seems simple enough to say where a text begins and where it ends, but in the case of Deuteronomy the matter is not so clear; the book has several beginnings, just as it has several endings. There are three rubrics that open the book (1:1, 4:44, 4:45) and three colophons, or rather postscripts, that close it (28:69, 29:28, 34:10–12). That fact by itself is significant; the three sets of rubrics and colophons correspond with three different editions of Deuteronomy. In what follows I shall demonstrate that the book has in fact received four editions, the fourth one having neither a rubric nor a colophon of its own. In their chronological order we can distinguish (1) the Covenant Edition, (2) the Torah Edition, (3) the History Edition, and (4) the Wisdom Edition; the names are modern inventions meant to characterize the editions.[20]

Both in distinguishing and naming the editions, I have anticipated the demonstration. Let me substantiate my views first with an analysis of the closures of Deuteronomy. All commentators agree that the body of Deuteronomy consists of chapters 12–26. The original core of this collection of rules and verdicts, ending in Deut 26:16–19, is closed by a section of blessings and curses (Deuteronomy 28 minus an expansion) and a colophon (Deut 28:69). The second edition has expanded the section of curses in chapter 28 and added chapter 29, which ends with a colophon in 29:28. A third closure occurs in Deut 34:10–12, which concludes a section that contains the last words of Moses (Deut 31–34); the third edition also inserted chapter 27.[21] The fourth edition, finally, inserted chapter 30. The three closures belong to three successive editions; the fourth edition has no proper colophon and thus stays within the perspective of the third edition.

I shall say more about the nature of these editions in a moment. For now, let me point out that each of the three closures has a counterpart at the beginning of the book. The Covenant Edition, which ended with 28:69, opened with the rubric of Deut 4:45, originally followed by Deut 6:4–9; the Torah Edition opened with the rubric in 4:44 and had Deuteronomy 5 as its first section; the History Edition added Deuteronomy 1–3 as a prologue to the text, with a rubric preserved in 1:1; and the Wisdom Edition inserted Deuteronomy 4 as an opening after the prologue, but added neither a rubric nor a colophon. A close reading of the beginning and the end of Deuteronomy, then, leads me to conclude that there were four editions before the book reached its final form. The next step is to assess the perspective of each of these editions.

THE COVENANT EDITION

The first edition of Deuteronomy, also known in the secondary literature as the *Urdeuteronomium,* is the Covenant Edition. The Hebrew term that is crucial here is *bĕrît,* "treaty, covenant"; the Covenant Edition of Deuteronomy is the *sēper habbĕrît,* "the book of the covenant," as it is referred to in the account of Josiah's reform (2 Kings 23:2, 23:21).

The treaty perspective of the Covenant Edition comes to the fore in its rubric and its colophon. The rubric refers to the text as "the treaty stipulations" *('dwt).*[22]

These are the treaty stipulations—the decrees and the verdicts—that Moses spoke to the people of Israel when they had left Egypt.

Deut 4:45

The colophon uses the more common word "covenant" *(bĕrît).*[23]

These are the terms of the covenant which Yahweh commanded Moses to conclude with the Israelites in the land of Moab, in addition to the covenant which he had made with them at Horeb.

Deut 28:69

The treaty perspective is not confined to a label; the very structure of Deuteronomy follows the pattern of a treaty, as is clear from the comparison with Hittite and Neo-Assyrian treaty texts.[24] The treaty structure of Deuteronomy consists of three parts: first a prologue (beginning with Deut 6:4–9), then the treaty stipulations (Deut 12:1–16:17, 26), and, finally, conditional blessings and curses (Deut 28). In addition to the treaty structure, scholars have noted the presence of "treaty language" in Deuteronomy.[25]

Why did the first editor of Deuteronomy feel the need to label and structure his text as a treaty? The reason for his choice has to do with the religious reform implemented under King Josiah. This reform was based on a covenant with the leadership of Israel, on which occasion the king read the scroll that was found in the temple (2 Kings 23:1–3). The first edition of Deuteronomy presents itself as the text of that "scroll of the covenant." To legitimize the measures taken by the king, the scribe of the Covenant Edition of Deuteronomy invented the notion of a previous covenant concluded in the land of Moab when Israel was about to enter the Promised Land (Deut 28:69), to serve as a historical precedent for the covenant of Josiah with the people.

The reform of Josiah consisted of a variety of measures, but its main objective was to centralize the Yahweh cult in the temple at Jerusalem.[26] It should be expected, therefore, that the doctrine of a single legitimate place of worship would constitute the core of the Covenant Edition. Such is indeed the thrust of the first edition: One God, one temple, to summarize its message. As Albrecht Alt observed in 1953, the famous passage known as the *Shema* ("Hear, O Israel! Yahweh is our God, Yahweh is One!" Deut 6:4) constitutes the beginning of the Deuteronomic reform document.[27] The call for the exclusive worship of Yahweh as a single deity lays the foundation for the central chapter of the Covenant Edition (Deut 12), now opening the series of "rules and verdicts" (Deut 12–26). Just as Yahweh is one, so his temple must be one; Israel may worship Him only at the one site that He will choose. Though the name of Jerusalem is not mentioned, there is little room for doubt that this is the place the editors had in mind.

It would be a misconception to believe that the scribe of the Covenant Edition was simply producing a forgery to provide his royal patron with a license for his reform plans. Close inspection of his work reveals that he did not write his text before the reform, but that he was reflecting on it after the fact.[28] The analysis of the chapter on the single place of worship (Deut 12) shows that its redundancy, noted by many commentators, is the result of the conflation of two parallel sets of stipulations.[29] The editor did not write this program himself; he used existing texts, most likely reflecting royal decrees sent out to local officials ordering them to discontinue worship at provincial shrines and temples.[30] Whatever the particular background of the texts the editor used, he composed the chapter not before but after the reform—even if the reform was still recent.[31]

If the Covenant Edition is in fact posterior to Josiah's reform, it cannot be interpreted as a pamphlet. Another look at the substance of the edition offers support for this conclusion. In addition to the chapter on cult centralization (Deut 12), the Covenant Edition includes a variety of laws, some of which are only remotely related to the issues at stake in Josiah's reform. The rules on clean and unclean animals (Deut 14:3–21) are related to the cult, but not specifically to the centralized cult. There is no consensus among scholars about which chapters of Deut 12–26 go back to the Covenant Edition; most would agree, however, that Deut 12:1–16:17 were part of it. These chapters have not been invented from scratch; they constitute a revision of the earlier Covenant Code (Exod 21–23).[32] What the Covenant Edition contains, then, is a theological reflection on the reform, and an *aggiornamento* of existing law in light of the reform.

Judging by his work, the scribe behind the Covenant Edition was a legal scholar and theologian rather than a politician or a pamphleteer. He may have worked under royal patronage, but the scope of his work is wider than the king's agenda. Cloaked with the authority of Moses, the lawgiver of old, he reinterpreted, adapted, and rewrote the legal traditions he was familiar with. His work was work in writing; it is possible he was also familiar with an extensive oral tradition, but the edition he produced used written material as its sources.

The literary and scholarly nature of the Covenant Edition finds support in the thesis that the editor was using the Neo-Assyrian treaty texts as his model. Many scholars have argued that Deuteronomy followed the layout of the Assyrian texts as a means of subverting them by focusing the allegiance of Judah exclusively on God instead of the Assyrian king.[33] Detailed comparison between the curses in Deuteronomy and in the vassal treaties of Esarhaddon may indicate borrowing on the part of the Judaean scribe.[34] Even if the case for a literary borrowing is not entirely compelling, the structure and idiom of the Covenant Edition leave no doubt about the fact that the editor was well versed in the particularities of the treaty genre. He was a professional with a thorough knowledge of the legal tradition and the conventions of international treaties.

THE TORAH EDITION

Let us now turn to the second edition of Deuteronomy, which I have dubbed the Torah Edition. The defining term of the Torah Edition is, indeed, the word *tôrâ*, "teaching, ruling, law." If the Covenant Edition is the *sēper habbĕrît* (2 Kings 23:2, 21; cf. 23:3), the Torah Edition is the *sēper hattôrâ* (Deut 28:61, 29:20, 30:10). Moses is its reputed author; later tradition identifies the *sēper hattôrâ* as the *tôrat mōšeh* (Josh 8:31, 23, 23:6; 1 Kings 2:3; 2 Kings 14:6, 23:25) or the *sēper mōšeh* (Neh 13:1; 2 Chron 25:4, 35:12).

In the Torah Edition, the Book of Deuteronomy opens with the rubric of Deut 4:44:

This is the Torah which Moses set before the children of Israel.

It ends in Deut 29:28 with a conclusion that reads like a colophon:

The hidden things belong to Yahweh our God; but the things that have been revealed belong to us and to our children, that we may do all the words of this Torah.

In the presentation of the Torah Edition, then, the text of Deuteronomy is a Torah, that is, an instruction, by Moses, the legendary founder of the nation; that instruction, moreover, is not based on human insight but has been revealed (a passive form of the verb *gālâ*) by God.

The Torah Edition highlights the special role of Moses in a prologue. That prologue is found in Deuteronomy 5, inserted between the rubric of the Covenant Edition (Deut 4:45) and its opening section (Deut 6:4–9). The new prologue reminds its readers how Yahweh made a covenant with the Israelites at Mt. Horeb, where He addressed them face to face; all the people heard the Ten Words He spoke (5:2–18).[35] When Yahweh had "stopped speaking," He inscribed his words on two tablets of stone and gave them to Moses (Deut 5:19).[36] Because the people feared they would die if they would hear God's voice again (5:22), they asked Moses to act as their go-between.

> You go closer and hear all that Yahweh our God says, and then you tell us everything that Yahweh our God tells you, and we will willingly do it.
>
> Deut 5:24

God approved of their attitude, and Moses accepted his role as mediator. Thereupon Moses climbed Mt. Horeb to receive "the whole Commandment—the decrees and the verdicts" (5:28).

The implication of this passage is that the words written on the two tablets do not constitute "the whole Commandment" *(kol-hammiṣwâ)*. God had stopped speaking—not because He had nothing more to say, but because the people could not bear to hear His voice any longer. Nevertheless God continued to speak, this time to Moses in private. Alongside the written commandment—written by God, that is—there is a spoken commandment, of which Moses is the sole human repository.[37] The oral revelation that Moses received followed on the presentation of the stone tablets, which signifies that the written Law is not complete without its oral complement. This complement—defined by the pair *ḥuqqîm ûmišpāṭîm,* "decrees and verdicts"—is the subject of the Torah Moses sets out to expound shortly before his death.[38] What he imparts to his people is what in Babylonia would be called "oral lore of the master" *(ša/šūt pî ummâni)*—the oral being by no means inferior to the written but rather its authoritative interpretation.[39]

By means of the construct of an oral revelation, the scribe of the Torah Edition created room to insert new material into the law book that he had inherited. Prior to an assessment of the innovations he introduced, however, it may be helpful to determine the context of his views by establishing the date of the Torah Edition. A first clue to its time of origin comes from the expansions in the curse section (Deut 28:58–68). The intervention of the editor of the Torah edition is evident from such expressions as "the terms of this Teaching that are written in this book" (28:58) and "diseases and plagues not mentioned in the book of this Teaching" (28:61), "teaching" being a translation of *tôrâ*. The editor has supplemented the curses with a reference to the Judaean Diaspora; in case of disobedience, the Israelites would be dispersed among the nations, where they would worship gods of wood and stone (Deut 28:64–65). I take this curse to be *ex eventu;* that is to say, it was coined on the basis of the Diaspora after the fall of Jerusalem in 568. Even more explicit is the reference in Deut 29:27: "Yahweh . . . cast them into another land, as is still the case" (*kayyôm hazzeh;* literally, "as today"). The editor lived in the exilic era.[40]

In the absence of further information, it is difficult to narrow down the time frame to a specific part of the exilic period. In the entire Torah Edition of Deuteronomy there is not a single allusion to a return from exile, unlike the Wisdom Edition, in which such an allusion does occur. By the witness of Second Isaiah (Isa 40–55), speculation about the possibility of a return to Judah started to flourish when Cyrus was conquering Babylonia; by this token, the Torah Edition is from the beginning rather than the end of the Babylonian captivity. Another indication comes from the "Deuteronomic Constitution," which the editor incorporated in his text (Deut 16:19–18:22). In anticipation of the discussion below, this constitution may be qualified as a Utopian document at home in a time in which dreams had to make up for lost realities. The temple vision of Ezekiel (Ezek 40–48) partakes of the same genre and belongs in the same period. The years between 590 and 570 are a plausible setting.[41]

The main contribution the Torah Edition makes to the law code is the section on the various public offices (Deut 16:18–18:21), also known as the Deuteronomic Constitution.[42] The section opens with rules concerning the local distribution of justice (16:18–20); treats the paradigmatic case of private apostasy (17:2–7); affirms the supreme authority of the central judiciary (17:8–13); defines the position of the king (17:14–20), the priests (18:1–9), and, in conclusion, the prophets (18:9–22).[43] The effect of the addition is significant: what in the Covenant Edition had been a law code in the vein of earlier law codes became the constitution of a theocratic state; a reform document turned into a program for the establishment of a theocracy—or perhaps "hierocracy" is a more accurate term, since it is in fact the priests who are to run the show.

The primacy of the priests is evident throughout the Torah Edition. In the vision of the editor, the priests constitute the highest court of law (17:8–13; cf. 19:17, 21:5); where formerly the king had been supreme judge, the priests now take his place.[44] The remaining role of the king is largely ceremonial; save for reading his copy of the Torah, to be obtained from the priests, he has very little to do (17:14–20). The primary concern of the editor is to make sure that the monarch should be subservient to the priests. Hence the stipulation that the king be chosen by God; this is another way of saying that the candidate for kingship had to have the approval of the priests.

The Torah Edition also redefines the role of prophets (Deut 18:9–22). Prophecy, in the view of the Torah editor, is the Israelite answer to the divinatory practices of the heathen nations. Yet not every prophet is a godsend; the true prophet is one like Moses. According to the promise put in the mouth of Moses,

> Yahweh your God will raise up for you a prophet from among your own people, like myself; him you shall heed.
>
> Deut 18:15

The context makes it clear that this "prophet like Moses" is not a single figure but one in a succession of prophets; otherwise prophecy would offer no viable alternative to the proscribed means of divination. By making Moses the model prophet, the editor redefines prophets as teachers of Torah. By so recasting the prophets, however, he turns them into extensions of the priests who possess the Torah; in the vision of the Deuteronomic Constitution, priests are the leading actors, while king and prophet play supporting parts.

The substance of the inserted Constitution is consistent with the historical context earlier suggested for the Torah Edition. In view of the symbolic role assigned to the king, the editor did not live in the time of the monarchy; Josiah would not have consented to sponsor such views, any more than other men in his position.[45] The ideal fits a time in which the head of state had little political power; the first decades of the Exile saw Jehoiachin in this position. Another indication of the time frame is the criterion for distinguishing between reliable and unreliable prophets; the simple advice of the Torah Edition is to check whether the oracles of a prophet have come true or not (Deut 18:21–22). This criterion, obviously of little use at the time the prophet delivers his prediction, presupposes a situation in which events have proved some prophets right and others wrong; the events in question are most likely related to the fall of Jerusalem.

The scribe who wrote the Torah Edition of Deuteronomy was active in the first decades of the exilic period. Faced with national disaster and a temple in ruins, he was trying to come to terms with a venerated text that seemed strangely at odds with the realities of his time. Putting himself in the seat of Moses, he supplemented the revelation by Moses with a vision of the future state of Israel. In that state to be, political power, legal authority, and religious expertise were concentrated in the hands of the priests.

What does the Torah Edition tell us about the scribe who wrote it and his milieu? By putting the priests in charge of the written Torah (see especially Deut 17:18), the editor is obliquely implying something about his own social background. It certainly looks as though he identified with these priests. By asserting a monopoly on the Torah, the author promoted a group that claimed to detain privileged information. It is this information, available to them in the form of a written text, that was to legitimize the leadership they aspired to. The scribe who wrote the Torah Edition did not describe a situation of fact but an ideal; since he felt compelled to assert the prerogatives of the priests, they must have been facing opposition. By promoting a priesthood focused on written texts, the editor portrayed the ideal clergy after his own image.

By claiming a priestly milieu for the author of the Torah Edition, my analysis faces the objection that the language of the Torah Edition is hardly recognizable as priestly. But what exactly is priestly language, one may ask. The usual parameters that define priestly idiom are based on the P sections in the Pentateuch, the Holiness Code (Lev 17–26), and the Book of Ezekiel. In my view, the Book of Deuteronomy reflects a division in the priesthood between servants of the altar, on the one side, and administrators, judges, and scholars, on the other. This second group came to be identified with the "Levitical priests," the forerunners of the Levites as we find them in texts of the post-exilic era such as Chronicles. It is the interests of this second group that the scribe of the Torah Edition was promoting.

THE HISTORY EDITION

The History Edition of Deuteronomy is posterior to both the Covenant and the Torah Editions and fuses their distinct perspectives into one. In the perspective of the History Edition, Covenant and Torah are interchangeable notions; though the *sēper habbĕrît* and the *sēper hattôrâ* were originally distinct editions of Deuteronomy, the History Edition treats them as one.[46]

The promiscuous use of *sēper habbĕrît* and *sēper hattôrâ* occurs elsewhere in the Bible in the books that constitute the Deuteronomistic History. Thus the description of Josiah's reform, found at 2 Kings 22–23, refers to the charter document now as the "Book of the Torah" (2 Kings 22:8, 22:11; compare 23:24), now as the "Book of the Covenant" (2 Kings 23:2, 23:21; compare 23:3). This parallel between the History Edition of Deuteronomy and the Deuteronomistic History is not a coincidence: the author of the third edition of Deuteronomy rewrote the text so that it might serve as the beginning and the basis of a much larger historical work. From a reform document and, later, a theocratic vision, Deuteronomy became part of a historiographic project.

The scribe of the History Edition added chapters 1–3 at the beginning and chapters 27 and 31–34 at the end. In its new version, Deuteronomy opened with the rubric

> These are the words that Moses addressed to all Israel on the other side of the Jordan.
>
> Deut 1:1

It ended with a concluding observation about Moses as a prophet without an equal:

> Never again did there arise in Israel a prophet like Moses, whom Yahweh knew face to face, with respect to all the signs and portents which Yahweh sent him to perform in the land of Egypt, against Pharaoh and all his courtiers and his whole country, and with respect to the great might and awesome power that Moses displayed before all Israel.
>
> Deut 34:10–12

More so even than the Torah Edition, then, the History Edition focuses on Moses. Whereas the Torah Edition presented Moses as the model and prototype of a succession of prophets (Deut 18:15–18), the History Edition corrects that notion by saying that never again has there arisen a "prophet like Moses."[47] The observation implies a view of the post-Mosaic era as a time that fatally lacks the greatness and purity of the past.[48]

The scribe of the History Edition did indeed take a dim view of the national history. Cast as a historical summary, Deuteronomy 1–3 commemorates the events during the forty-year journey from Horeb to Moab. Martin Noth has demonstrated that this summary was designed to open and set the tone of the Deuteronomistic History.[49] The chapters portray the people in a rather unfavorable light (Deut 1:12, 1:26–28, 1:32, 1:34–36, 1:41–45; 3:26). The note of criticism is sharper in the final chapters of the book. The scribe of the History Edition added disparate materials from the Moses tradition (notably the Mt. Ebal episode, the Song of Moses, and the Deathbed Blessing of Moses), and framed them with references to the sins and apostasies that the Israelites would commit after the death of Moses (Deut 31:16–21, 31:27–29).[50] In this conception, even the Book of the Torah is a witness against the Israelites (Deut 31:26).

Some of the pieces in the homiletic sections of Deuteronomy (Deut 5–11) emphasize the rebellious nature of the Israelites as well; they, too, are presumably from the hand of the History Edition editor. To him, Mt. Horeb is a symbol of rebellion rather than a place of revelation (Deut 9:7–10:11).[51] If Moses had to stay on the mountain for forty days and forty nights, with neither food nor drink to sustain him, it was because he had to move God to pity after the unhappy incident with the golden calf. In the end he did obtain a new copy of the stone tablets in token of the enduring covenant; the editor displays no interest in an additional oral revelation, however.

If the Hebrew scribes bear any likeness to the History Edition editor—who is, after all, a scribe too—they are also historians, even if their kind of history has the scent of religion. They read the national history as a theodicy of the Exile. Embedded in their theological reading of the past, however, is a scholarly interest in the footnotes of history, evidenced in observations about "archaeological, topographical, chronological . . ., and statistical details—matters of scholarship that have nothing to do with religion."[52] In the History Edition of Deuteronomy, the scribes come across as educated clerics who find it as difficult to curb their curiosity as to avoid moralizing. The history they practice is a written genre; though they strike a homiletic chord, the scribes are writers rather than preachers.

THE WISDOM EDITION

Though the Wisdom Edition of Deuteronomy does not coincide with the final stage of the book, it does represent its last major redaction. The scribe who wrote the edition was less concerned with the notion of a covenant than with the intellectual significance of the Jewish way of life based on the Torah. He refers to the Law of Moses as *tôrâ* and *miṣwâ*, "teaching" and "commandment," terms that are prominent in the editorial frame of the Wisdom Edition.

The proper contribution of the Wisdom Edition is extant in chapters 4 and 30, which serve as a new frame of Deuteronomy.[53] The chapters in question provide a clue as to the time of the editor. Deut 30:1–5 contemplates the possibility of a conversion of Israel followed by a return of the exiles, then scattered all over the world; a similar allusion to a national conversion occurs in Deut 4:29–31. This note of optimism is lacking in previous editions of Deuteronomy from the Exile; it most likely means that the editor lived in the time after the Exile.

A study of the wisdom framing of Deuteronomy yields evidence of influence of scribal traditions from Mesopotamia.[54] Like his predecessors who wrote down the Torah and History Editions, the scribe of the Wisdom Edition presumably had a background in Babylonia. In view of his crusade against cult images and his message of monotheism, he may in fact have been living in Babylonia when he prepared his edition. In this reconstruction, then, the Wisdom Edition was written by a Babylonian Jew in the early Persian period.

The Wisdom Edition gives a new dimension to Deuteronomy. This dimension consists in the self-confident affirmation of the superiority of the Jewish way of life. The frame of reference of the editor is cosmopolitan: his vision embraces the beginning of history, "when God created man on earth" (4:32), and it includes humankind "everywhere under heaven" (4:19). The criterion by which he measures the distinction of the Jewish way of life is wisdom. Wisdom, in his experience, is an international currency; it can be recognized for what it is, irrespective of the mother tongue or nationality of the observer. Concomitant with his high regard for wisdom, the editor displays a trust in the value of argumentation.

Thus the editor condemns the worship of images under reference to an argument from experience—invented experience, to be sure, but experience nevertheless. Leaning heavily on the revelation at Mt. Horeb as described in the Torah Edition, the Jewish scribe reminds his core-ligionists that they saw no shape *(tĕmûnâ)* when Yahweh spoke to them (4:15); Jews should therefore refrain from making images of any shape whatsoever (4:16–18). Experience is adduced, too, as grounds for monotheism. Since there is no parallel to the experience of Israel in recorded history (4:32–34), there is no further need for demonstration that "Yahweh alone is God; there is none beside Him" (4:35). To modern readers the validity of the argument may seem doubtful, but whether convincing or not, the author of the Wisdom Edition does appeal to arguments rather than to religious authority.

In a similar line, the editor preaches faithfulness to the Torah on the grounds that it is a superior form of wisdom. Once again, the argument is not from authority ("You have to do this because God says so") but from the recognizable virtue of the teaching:

> Observe them [viz. the decrees and verdicts] faithfully, for that will be proof of your wisdom and discernment to other peoples, who on hearing of all of these laws will say, "Surely, that great nation is a wise and discerning people."
>
> Deut 4:6

In consonance with his presentation of the laws as wisdom, the editor emphasizes that the laws are commensurate with the human intellect.

> Surely, this Commandment [*miṣwâ*] . . . is not beyond your comprehension [*lō' niplê't hî' mimmĕkā*] nor is it too remote. It is not in heaven, that you should say, "Who among us can go up to heaven and get it for us and impart it to us, that we may observe it?" Neither is it beyond the ocean, that you should say, "Who among us can cross to the other side of the ocean and get it for us and impart it to us, that we may observe it?" No, the Word is very close to you, in your mouth and in your heart, to observe it.
>
> Deut 30:11–14

By using the imagery of scaling heaven and crossing the sea, the scribe of the Wisdom Edition borrows a theme from Babylonian wisdom texts. The *Dialogue of Pessimism* puts it as a rhetorical question:

> Who is so tall as to ascend to the heavens?
> Who is so broad as to encompass the underworld?[55]

In various forms, the question occurs time and again in texts concerned with matters beyond human reach, such as life eternal and, more specifically, knowledge of what the gods design and desire.[56] The theme also made its way into Hebrew wisdom texts.[57] In the Wisdom Edition of Deuteronomy, the scribe has applied it to the Torah as a rhetorical means to imply that, precisely, the mind of God is not a secret. On the contrary, the Law is intelligent and intelligible; Jews have no reason to withdraw into skepticism.

The scribe of the Wisdom Edition of Deuteronomy read the Torah of Moses with a view to comprehending its wisdom; he wanted to understand and explain why the "rules and verdicts" make sense. Where he intervened in the body of Deuteronomy, his contribution is likely to be found in the legal sections. It is not clear whether Deut 19–25 should be attributed in its entirety to the Wisdom Edition; however, the author of that edition did leave unmistakable traces of his intervention.[58] Time and again in this section, the text explains the rationale of the laws: "otherwise . . .; that is why . . .; so that . . ." (Deut 19:6, 19:7, 19:10; see also Deut 21:14, 22:26–27, 22:29, 23:15, 24:6). The author stresses that application of the laws will serve as a deterrent (Deut 19:20, 21:21); in warfare, trees must be spared because they are defenseless (Deut 20:19); rules for building serve to prevent accidents (Deut 21:8); a counsel of prudence occurs in the midst of rules of conduct (Deut 23:23).[59] In short, the Torah Edition culls wisdom from the Law.

Later Jewish scribes have used the Deuteronomic association between law and wisdom as a springboard for speculations about the preexistence of the Torah; in this line of reasoning, the revelation of the Law at Mt. Horeb can be viewed as a descent from heaven of wisdom personified (Sir 24; Bar 3). Such ideas were not in the mind of the Wisdom editor of Deuteronomy. He did not transform the concept of wisdom but tried to apply the logic of wisdom to the realm of law. By interpreting the Torah as an expression of wisdom, he created room for scholarship in which devotion to the Torah need not inhibit the exploration of the riches of experience and reason. If we were to apply a theological dictum to his view of the Torah, it would be a variation on St. Thomas Aquinas's *gratia non tollit sed perficit naturam* (*Summa Theologica*, Quaestio 62): the Torah does not annul human wisdom but leads it to perfection.

The Wisdom Edition reveals yet another aspect of Hebrew scribal culture. The prominence of terms for "teaching" (*lammēd*, Deut 4:1, 5, 10, 14), in conjunction with the focus on wisdom, throws the scribes into relief as teachers. They are the forerunners of Ben Sira, who in his classroom combined praise of the Law with the exploration of human nature in all its manifestations. The tone of the Wisdom Edition is also reminiscent of a teacher: there is the reasoned explanation; the shifting from the plural *you* to the singular *you*; the use of the list (e.g., Deut 4:16–18)—all pedagogical devices fit for communicating knowledge. The scribe behind the Wisdom Edition is likely to have been a teacher himself.

Moses as Model of the Scribes

The successive editions of Deuteronomy provide us with an insight into the methods, mind-set, and ideas of successive generations of scribes. We have seen their interests shifting from the legal consequences of cult centralization to the exploration of the wisdom of Torah, with a Utopian design of a theocracy and a theological reading of the national history in between. In their work, these scribes manifest themselves as intellectuals and scholars with an evident interest in cultic matters.

A special way in which the scribes of Deuteronomy are saying something about themselves is through their portrayal of Moses. At several places in Deuteronomy it is clear that the scribes consider themselves the heirs and successors of Moses. The chapter devoted to the succession of Moses designates the priests as the trustees and custodians of the Torah he has written (Deut 31:9, 25–26); as Moses imparted his teaching to the Israelites in his day, so the priests are to read his Torah to their contemporaries (Deut 31:10–13). Only they have access to the Torah; for a copy, even the king has to turn to them (Deut 17:18–19). The priests these texts refer to are consistently qualified as "Levitical." We will have occasion to dwell on the significance of this specification; for now it suffices to observe that these Levitical priests are apparently professionals of writing, since they keep (Deut 31:25–26), copy (Deut 17:18), and read from the Torah (Deut 31:11). There is every reason to believe, then, that these are self-references of the scribes; they claim the legacy of Moses.[60]

The fact that the scribes of Deuteronomy view Moses as their ancestor and their patron is significant of their background. The figure of Moses, like the motif of the Exodus, is at home in the religious traditions of the Northern Kingdom; if both eventually became part of the Judean heritage, it was through the agency of disenfranchised clergy who had found refuge in Judah after the fall of Samaria. The scribes to whom we owe the Book of Deuteronomy, then, are presumably from priestly families from Israel. For several generations these families had been living in Judah, yet they still maintained a distinct identity through their focus on Moses and the Exodus tradition. The mere fact that the authors of Deuteronomy are scribes indicates that they belonged to the social establishment; since they were deported to Babylonia, they must have been part of the leading elite of Judah.[61]

The northern roots of the scribes of Deuteronomy explain the combination of priestly concerns (such as sacrifice, purity rules, and the festival calendar) and the use of a language that does not strike one as specifically priestly. The language of Deuteronomy is Deuteronomic, if the tautology be permitted; it differs from the idiom of the Holiness Code (H), the Book of Ezekiel, and the priestly document (P). Yet the fact that the scribes of Deuteronomy do not use the idiom of Ezekiel, H, or P does not mean they were not priests. We must differentiate between parties in the priesthood; the scribes of Deuteronomy were Levitical priests as opposed to Aaronite or Zadokite priests.

Strictly speaking, the expression "Levitical priests" is redundant in the perception of the Deuteronomic scribes, since to them, all legitimate priests are descendants of Levi (see, e.g., Deut 33:8–11). Yet in the context of the polemic concerning the legitimate priesthood, as reflected in Ezekiel 44, the qualification of priests as Levitical becomes a defense of clergy whose sacerdotal rights were not being honored. At several places in the book, Deuteronomy is quite explicit about those rights (see, e.g., Deut 10:8–9, 14:27–29, 18:1–8); in a more subtle fashion, however, the scribes promote the Levitical priesthood by casting the priests in the role of scribes and legal scholars in the tradition of Moses. In the perspective of Deuteronomy, the Levitical priests have the monopoly on Torah and legal expertise; the focus on instruction and jurisdiction throws other sacerdotal prerogatives into the shadows. Deuteronomy promotes a new conception of the priests as experts in the written Torah; the scribes behind Deuteronomy thus attempted to redefine and revalorize their own area of expertise.

It is a debated point among critics whether Moses was actually mentioned in the first edition of Deuteronomy; many authors believe he entered the scene only in the second or third edition.[62] It is true that the reference to the "Torah of Moses" in 2 Kings 23:25 is later than the first edition of Deuteronomy, but it is difficult to reconstruct a first version of Deuteronomy without mention of Moses. At the same time, it must be conceded that if Moses was part of the Covenant Edition, he was not a prominent character. His role in the subsequent editions is far more significant; the Torah Edition offers a good starting point for a study of the image of Moses in Deuteronomy.

If Moses has a title in the Torah Edition, it is that of prophet. Thinking of Moses, the term "prophet" is perhaps not the first qualification that comes to mind; Elijah was a prophet, and Amos and Isaiah, but Moses is more commonly perceived as a priest and a lawgiver. It is significant, however, that the Torah Edition chooses to ignore the sacerdotal aspects of Moses's ministry. By presenting Moses as a prophet, the scribe of the Torah Edition was transforming the concept; to him, a prophet is not an ecstatic or a diviner but someone who gives Torah and communicates God's Law. The Deuteronomic prophet, in other words, acts as a Torah scribe.

It is no coincidence that the passage that refers to Moses as a prophet links this title to Moses's role as intermediary at Mt. Horeb. The prophetic revelation of Moses consists in the oral Torah, which he put down in writing not long before he died and entrusted to the priests. Along with the written Torah, the priests inherited the office of Moses. The law on the referral of baffling cases stipulates that the local authorities are to go to the priests to receive from them an oral ruling (17:8–13). The word used in this connection is *tôrâ:* the priests dispense an oral teaching, much like the teaching of Moses (see also Deut 24:8).[63] Cases that are not provided for in the Book of the Torah, then, are to be decided by the oral Torah of the priests, who have inherited the office of Moses. What is adumbrated here is the doctrine of the Torah *šebbe'al-peh.*[64]

It might seem strange that the priestly scribes would think of themselves as prophets, but other parts of Deuteronomy confirm the fact that they do claim this role for themselves. It is well known that the promise concerning a prophet like Moses (Deut 18:18) was not written to be read as the prediction of the coming of one particular prophet, but as a legitimization of those who were sitting on "the seat of Moses" (Matt 23:2).[65] The author of the Torah Edition thought of scholars like himself as the successors of Moses in his prophetic office. They claimed the authority to interpret and to update traditional law in light of the insights revealed to them. Like Moses, they mediated between God and the people.

While Moses was a prophet of revelations in the Torah Edition, the editor of the History Edition turned him into a preaching prophet. The History Edition has little interest in Moses as a mediator of revelations; it is primarily concerned with the lessons of history that Moses had taught. What is traditionally known as the homiletic quality of the first part of Deuteronomy is most likely due to the scribe of the History Edition. His sermons are sermons in writing; to take them as the transcript of actual performances does not take into account their literary character.[66] Yet we are dealing with a literary phenomenon that cannot have been without its oral counterpart; if the editor used the form of the homily, he drew on his oratory experience. After all, a scribal education taught skills of both writing and speaking.[67]

In the Wisdom Edition of Deuteronomy, finally, Moses is not so much a prophet or a preacher as, first of all, a teacher. The introductory statement in Deut 1:5 is instructive in this respect:

> On the other side of the Jordan, in the land of Moab, Moses began to expound this Torah.

Where the Torah Edition would say that Moses revealed the Torah as a prophet would, the Wisdom Edition makes Moses "expound" or "explain" (in Hebrew, an intensive form of the root *b'r*) the Torah. Both editions contain the episode at Mt. Horeb: in the Torah Edition Moses mediates a revelation of "decrees and verdicts" (Deut 5:19–28), whereas the Wisdom Edition makes him a teacher of "decrees and verdicts" (Deut 4:10–14).[68] The Torah is treated as a given, which Moses and his successors have to interpret. The rubric says that Moses "began" this activity, thus suggesting that he had successors who would continue his work.[69] In their capacity as teachers and exegetes of the Torah, the scribes regarded themselves precisely as the heirs of Moses.

Conclusion

This chapter has presented the Book of Deuteronomy as a sample of scribal culture, both when taken as a literary artifact and when read as a reflection of scribal concerns; in addition, the text has served as a window on the social and historical background of the scribes.

The Book of Deuteronomy as we know it from the Hebrew Bible is the work of several generations of scribes. The book was conceived and composed in their milieu; there it was taught and transmitted; and in the course of its transmission it received three new editions, each separated from its predecessor by some forty years. For almost two centuries, the text existed in a single copy. It had the value of a relic from the Mosaic age, to be renewed only when the material condition of the scroll had deteriorated to the point at which it was deemed incompatible with the dignity of the text. Each edition of Deuteronomy entailed a revision of the entire manuscript; the scribes added each time a new interpretive framework, inserted some new material, and rephrased the text as they had received it.

The four editions of Deuteronomy grant us an insight into changes and continuity among a particular scribal milieu. The scribes behind Deuteronomy descended from priestly families that had moved, after 722, from the Northern Kingdom to Judah. They traced their origins back to Levi. Being Levites, they considered themselves entitled to serve at the temple, yet instead of a focus on the sacrificial cult they developed a profile as legal scholars. Throughout the four editions of Deuteronomy they promoted their own area of expertise as the central concern of the priesthood and as the main source of its authority. They were lawyers, albeit lawyers of a particular kind; their scholarship embraced both the written and the oral Torah, and the Torah to them was more than just a work of law. The Torah stood for a way of life and a certain vision of history.

The distinct accent of each of the four editions of Deuteronomy reflects a development in the scribal view of the Torah. In the Covenant Edition, the Law serves to establish a religious orthodoxy; it prescribes a format for human devotion in which there is a place for one God only and only one place to worship Him. The Torah Edition presents the Law as a design for the future as revealed in the past; it describes a theocratic utopia, which was a source of inspiration rather than a law to be applied. In the History Edition, the Law has become an enduring witness against past generations; their unwillingness to uphold its norms explains the disasters that have struck Judah and Jerusalem.

Finally, in the Wisdom Edition, the Law is taken to embody a superior form of wisdom to be appreciated as such by every human being under heaven.

The successive editions of Deuteronomy attest to the broadening horizon of the scribes. At first they do not look beyond the borders of Judah; in the end, their vision has become cosmopolitan. In conjunction with the broad scope of their vision, the scribes developed a new perception of their own position. They are no longer parochial clerks but see themselves as men of the world, propagating a way of life that must command the respect of others. The religion they teach is in no way backward; on the contrary, the Jewish way of life is an enlightened way of life glowing with the wisdom of the Torah.

Owing to its long history, the Book of Deuteronomy bridges the time of the late monarchy to the Persian period. Starting out with a revision of the written law inherited from the mid-monarchic era (i.e., the Covenant Code), Deuteronomy takes its readers to the time of Ezra, who held out the Torah as the ultimate form of wisdom (Ezra 7:14, 25). In response to two centuries of national history, the scribes reconceptualized the Torah and, by the same token, their own role as legal scholars. Deuteronomy takes us from Hilkiah to Ezra; both are priests and both are associated with the Book of the Torah. Ezra, however, is also a scribe. As he is described in the books of Ezra and Nehemiah, Ezra incarnates the priestly scribe, whose ideal prototype and ancestor the editors of Deuteronomy had portrayed in the figure of Moses.

chapter seven

MANUFACTURING THE PROPHETS

T𝒽e Book of Jeremiah as Scribal Artifact

The previous chapter looked at the Book of Deuteronomy as a sample of scribal culture; by highlighting the role of the scribes in the making of the "Book of the Torah," it offered a model for understanding the involvement of the scribes in the production of the legal and narrative texts of the Bible. In this chapter we turn to the prophetic collections. Within the section known as the Neviim (Prophets), the Bible has fifteen books attributed to named prophets, from Isaiah to Malachi. This literature is of a rather different kind than Deuteronomy; the history of its making is bound to be different as well. What were the production mechanisms, who were the writers, and what was the social setting of the prophetic literature?

The Earliest Books of the Prophets

The books of the prophets as we know them date from the Persian and the early Hellenistic periods. There is solid evidence, however, that written collections of prophetic oracles were already in existence in the period of the monarchy, in the seventh and sixth centuries B.C.E. The First Book of Kings mentions a prophet by the name of Micaiah son of Imlah; in the days of King Ahab, this man had a vision of God on his heavenly throne (1 Kings 22:6–28). Concluding the account of Micaiah's prophecy, the editor of Kings observes that Micaiah also said, "Hear, you peoples, all of you!" (1 Kings 22:28). This phrase is the opening line of the Book of Micah the Morashtite (Mic 1:2). The editor of Kings has confused the two prophets, attributing the Book of Micah to Micaiah ben Imlah. He made a mistake, but in so doing left a testimony to the existence of a scroll of Micah oracles.

There is no consensus about the precise date of the edition of Kings, but only a handful of scholars would put it later than the early exilic period (ca. 560 B.C.E.). In the first half of the sixth century, then, scribal circles were familiar with the Book of Micah. A second witness to the circulation of the Micah scroll is the quotation of a Micah oracle in the Book of Jeremiah. After Jeremiah's temple sermon in 609 (Jer 26:1), the elders of Judah came to the defense of Jeremiah by pointing out to the population that in the days of King Hezekiah, about a century before, Micah the Morashtite had also announced the destruction of the Jerusalem temple (Jer 26:17–19). The literal citation of Mic 3:12 reflects the existence of an oracle collection attributed to Micah. Whether it was actually known and studied by the "elders" of Judah is questionable, but there can be little doubt that the editors of the Book of Jeremiah knew the Micah collection. Since they were active in the early exilic period, the Book of Micah was by then an object of study.

It is more than likely that the Book of Jeremiah, too, was in circulation in the community of the exiles. According to Jeremiah 36, Jeremiah dictated his collected oracles to the scribe Baruch in 605. The scroll to which the latter committed the text ended up being burned, which made it necessary to produce a second scroll. The historical accuracy of this account is suspect; it has presumably been composed to serve as an authentication narrative of an early Jeremiah scroll. This scroll is described in considerable detail: it was written in ink (Jer 36:18), disposed in columns (Jer 36:23), and it contained, in addition to Jeremiah oracles from the first part of his prophetic career, "many [other] words like these" (Jer 36:32). The story would be pointless if, in fact, there were no such scroll; we must therefore assume that, by the time of the story's composition, a written Jeremiah collection was in existence.

We have another witness, from roughly the same period, for the existence of written oracle collections. In the story of Ezekiel's calling, dated in 592 (Ezek 1:2), the prophet has a vision in which he sees a hand, stretched out to him, holding a scroll *(mĕgillat-sēper)* inscribed on both sides with lamentations, dirges, and woes. The prophet is ordered to take the scroll and eat it, that he may henceforth speak God's words to his people (Ezek 2:8–3:4). It is an unusual calling narrative: the familiar motif of God touching the prophet's mouth (Isa 6:6–7; Jer 1:9) is replaced by the consumption of a scroll written by God. The new motif—or the new visionary experience—can occur only at a time in which people like Ezekiel are familiar with the phenomenon of a written collection of prophetic oracles.[1]

Such evidence proves the existence of pre-exilic prophecies written down on scrolls; the pre-exilic prophets thus had a counterpart in oracle collections from before the exile. It is hardly surprising that the references to this tradition of written prophecy are almost all from the period of the early exile; after the disastrous events of 597 and 586—the first deportation to Babylon and the second deportation after the capture of Jerusalem—the study of the prophets was a way of coming to terms with the national catastrophe. The Torah Edition of Deuteronomy mentions fulfillment of predictions as the main criterion by which true prophets are to be distinguished from impostors (Deut 18:21–22); the editor formulated this criterion after, and in light of, the fall of Jerusalem and the destruction of the temple. True prophets were those who had foreseen those events, as Micah had when saying Jerusalem would become heaps of ruins (Jer 26:18; Mic 3:12). The Deuteronomic criterion of true prophecy presupposes the existence of written prophecy, for otherwise it would hardly be possible to check whether a prophet had been right or wrong.

The biblical evidence for written prophecy in the time of the monarchy finds extrabiblical support from the Book of Balaam discovered in 1967 at Deir Alla.[2] Deir Alla is a site in East Jordan close to, if not identical with, the place known as Succoth in the Bible.³ The Aramaic text of the Book of Balaam was written on plaster that was originally applied to the entrance of a large building thought to have served as a temple. Because the plaster came from the wall, we know that the text was originally for public display, not unlike the display inscriptions on temples and palaces known from Egypt and Mesopotamia. Certain characteristics of the inscription indicate that it was copied from a scroll.⁴ The layout of the text follows the model of a scroll: it is written in ink, arranged in columns, and has rubrics (titles and transition passages) marked in red, in conformity with a scribal practice known from Egyptian papyri.⁵

Written in red, a rubric opens the text:

Book [*spr*] of [Ba]laam, [son of Beo]r, seer of the gods.

The text continues with a description of the gods visiting the seer at night and communicating to him an oracle of El. As he wakes up, Balaam is in distress. In reply to their solicitous questions, he announces to his people what the gods are about to do. His oracle is one of doom, implying that the natural order will turn into a kind of counterorder.

Several details of the Balaam prophecy have parallels in biblical prophecy. The crucial point in the present connection, however, is the light the Balaam text sheds on the formation of the prophetic collections of the Bible. The text is generally dated between 800 and 750 B.C.E. At that time, then, there was scroll—the master text of which the wall inscription is a copy—containing the collected words and deeds of someone regarded as a prophet—or, rather, a "seer of the gods" (*ḥzh 'lhn*). This collection is contemporaneous with such early biblical prophets as Hosea and Amos (both ca. 760 B.C.E.). Coming from an area that was adjacent to, and in some periods perhaps part of, the state of Israel (compare Pss 60:8, 108:8), the Book of Balaam shows us what the pre-exilic books of the prophets may have looked like.

If it is an established fact that there were prophetic collections in the monarchic period, the volume and nature of these collections are yet to be determined. We have seen that there was a collection of Micah oracles, since two texts from the early exilic period quote from it. However, the two citations are from the beginning of chapter 1 (1 Kings 22:28 quoting Mic 1:2) and the end of chapter 3 (Jer 26:17–19 quoting Mic 3:12). It is theoretically possible, therefore, that the pre-exilic Micah collection consisted of only the first three chapters of the present book—precisely the part that many critics regard as the original core.[6] Much the same is probably true of other prophetic collections; the pre-exilic scrolls were forerunners of the later books, and presumably considerably smaller.

One characteristic the prophetic books of the Bible share with their pre-exilic forerunners is their composite nature, manifesting itself in the juxtaposition, often without any apparent transition, of oracles about different subjects and from different periods. Interspersed between and among the oracles, moreover, are laments, prayers, eulogies, and more of the like, as a result of which most books give an impression of incoherence and disorder. In the eyes of a modern reader, the prophetic books of the Bible "are not the kind of literary works which follow from the master plan of a single creative mind."[7] This judgment is likely to hold good for the first prophetic collections as well; they were anthologies and compilations of quite heterogeneous materials.

Comparative evidence from contemporaneous Mesopotamian sources shows how Assyrian scribes went about the composition of oracle collections. From the time of Esarhaddon and Assurbanipal (first half of the seventh century B.C.E.), there are some thirty oracles that have been preserved in writing.[8] The oracle records come in two formats: in collections written on vertical, multicolumn tablets, and as single oracles written on small horizontal tablets. The small tablets were suited for reports and letters, the multicolumn tablets for archival storage and reference purposes. This evidence suggests that the oracle was first transcribed on a small tablet (including the name of the prophet), and afterward copied onto one of the larger archival tablets. Since the originals were routinely destroyed, we have no way of confirming this procedure on the basis of a specific oracle. But the oracle collections do presuppose an earlier record of the individual oracles; the proposed reconstruction, based on what is known for other types of records, makes good sense.

The Neo-Assyrian evidence is relevant to the discussion of the formation of the prophetic collections in the Bible on two scores. First, it shows that scribes of the temple administration kept a written record of the individual oracles pronounced in the temple, and second, it attests to the custom of collecting prophecies on larger tablets kept for future consultation. The organizing principles of the Assyrian oracle collections were subject matter and date; the storage tablets contain oracles attributed to various prophets and prophetesses. In this respect, then, they differ from the biblical collections, which find their unity in the—presumed—author of the oracles. The point of comparison, however, is clear: the recording of separate oracles preceded the composition of the collections.

In the perception of the later biblical and much of the postbiblical tradition, the prophetic books of the Bible have prophets as their authors; the rubrics to the books do not distinguish between prophet and author. However, if the books in question have not been designed by "a single creative mind," the presumed authorship of the prophets applies at best to the separate units of the compositions, their compilation being the work of later editors. Since the quest for the origins of the prophetic books has to begin by identifying the composers of the constituent parts of the whole, we can start off with the question of whether the prophets actually wrote down their oracles—or any other parts of "their" books.

Prophets and Writing

The early prophets of Israel did not write; they were men—and women—of the spoken word, who delivered their oracles to an audience largely incapable of reading. This is the impression conveyed by the biblical picture of the pre-exilic prophets, and this has been the dominant view among scholars and historians since the early twentieth century.[9] On occasion, however, the Bible does speak about prophets writing. Instead of dismissing this evidence as editorial fantasy, we had better establish the extent, purpose, and historical plausibility of the phenomenon.

The references to pre-exilic prophets in the act of writing can be counted on the fingers of one hand. Leaving aside the cases of dubious historical authenticity, there are four records of a prophet writing that strike many critics as reliable.[10] We have (1) Habakkuk recording a prophecy on tablets (Hab 2:2), (2) Isaiah writing down an enigmatic phrase on a large sheet (Isa 8:1), and (3) Jeremiah sending a letter to the exiles in Babylon (Jer 29:1); to these biblical instances we must add (4) the reference to a written message from "the prophet" mentioned in an early sixth century ostracon from Lachish (Lachish Letter 3, lines 20–21). I will discuss the texts in the above order.

Although the four references are not of one kind, they all illustrate the use of writing for the purpose of communicating a message to a contemporaneous audience. Habakkuk is instructed to write down his prophecy so a herald may run to proclaim it.

> Write down the prophecy,
> And inscribe it clearly on the tablets,
> So that a [town] crier may run with it.
>   Hab 2:2[11]

The prophet is to write down a single prophecy as a means of publication by the intermediary of a herald. The procedure resembles the one employed by King Sennacherib, who, according to 2 Chron 32:17, wrote "letters" *(sĕpārîm)* to be read by messengers in order to persuade the Judaean population to surrender. Thus the speech the royal officers delivered in Jerusalem (2 Chron 32:9–16) echoed throughout the Judaean countryside. Habakkuk, for his part, used writing as a means of broadcasting an oracle.[12]

Whereas Habakkuk was to write an oracle for public broadcasting, Isaiah was instructed to paint his text on a poster.

> And Yahweh said to me: "Get yourself a large sheet and write on it with a brush: 'Pillage hastens, looting speeds.'"
>
> Isa 8:1

Four words are all Isaiah writes by way of an enigmatic oracle ("Maher-shalal-hash-baz") designed to arouse the curiosity of the viewer. No one who came by could escape seeing it; Isaiah used a "large sheet" and a "brush" to paint his words in bold characters.[13] The prophet made Uriah, the high priest, countersign the poster as a witness (Isa 8:2; compare 2 Kings 16:10–16); since the second witness bears a name that was popular in priestly circles (Zechariah son of Jeberechiah), he may also have been a priest. In view of the witnesses, Isaiah is likely to have hung his poster in the temple.

Isaiah's enigmatic oracle written large in the temple resembles the strange writing on the wall mentioned in the Book of Daniel (Dan 5:1–29). Written by "the fingers of a human hand" (Dan 5:5), the four words that appeared on the plaster of the wall—*mene mene tekel upharsin*—were just as mysterious as Isaiah's poster. It required the intervention of Daniel to illuminate their meaning. Isaiah used the medium of writing as a visual means of communication, but the message he wrote down was deliberately obscure. Its purpose was to raise questions. The first question voiced by most people who saw the poster would be a request for someone to read it; second, they would ask for an explanation.

An Assyrian dream report from the days of Isaiah shows that the notion of a prophecy published as a display inscription was not totally foreign in the ancient Near East. In the annals of King Assurbanipal there is an unusual dream report involving a young man in Babylon.

> In these days, a certain man went to bed in the middle of the night and saw a dream. Upon the pedestal of the god Sin was written: "Upon those who plot evil against Assurbanipal, King of Assyria, and resort to hostilities, I shall bestow miserable death. I shall put an end to their lives through the quick dagger, conflagration, hunger, and pestilence." When I heard this, I put my trust in the words of Sin.[14]

Even if dreams are a distorted reflection of events from the waking life, the report attests to the phenomenon of written prophecy displayed in a public place. A variant version of the text has the god Nabu read the text to the dreamer, which shows that most onlookers would need the assistance of a scribe to understand the writing.[15]

In the third instance of a pre-exilic prophet's using writing as a means of communicating his message, the writer is Jeremiah. According to the account of Jer 29:1–3, Jeremiah sent a letter *(sēper)* to the exiles in 594 B.C.E. In that year King Zedekiah sent a diplomatic mission to his Babylonian overlord Nebuchadnezzar to protest his innocence and persuade him of his loyalty.[16] Members of the mission carried Jeremiah's letter calling on his deported compatriots to accept their situation and integrate themselves in the Babylonian society. Whether the whole text of Jer 29:4–23 was in Jeremiah's letter is doubtful, but the report that the prophet sent a letter along the lines of the oracle in Jer 29:4–9 is quite plausible. The message of the prophet was entirely in consonance with the purpose of Zedekiah's mission: he recommended what must have been perceived as a pro-Babylonian attitude bound to please Nebuchadnezzar and his entourage.

The practice of transmitting a prophetic oracle by letter is confirmed by an extrabiblical reference on an ostracon from Lachish. The Lachish ostraca are usually referred to as the Lachish letters because they contain copies (less likely, drafts) of letters written on papyrus, sent from Lachish.[17] They all date to the years 587/586 B.C.E. and are thus contemporary with Jeremiah. Lachish Letter 3 speaks about a letter *(sēper)* "from the prophet" *(mē'ēt hannābî')* that opened with the word "Beware!" *(hiššāmer)*.[18] The letter in question has been lost, but its mention shows that a prophet in sixth-century Judah did use the medium of a letter to communicate his message. A few letters sent by prophets to the King of Mari, more than a millennium earlier, show that the Judaean custom has early antecedents in the Near East.[19]

There is no compelling reason not to take seriously these reports about prophets writing; on the contrary, both the comparative evidence from Mesopotamia and the inscriptional evidence from Lachish corroborate the biblical data. On occasion, then, the pre-exilic prophets did write. Their purpose in writing, however, was confined to communicating a message to their contemporaries. They resorted to the written word when they judged an oral delivery less apt to reach their intended audience. Not a single time, though, did they write in view of preserving their words for future generations. Yet this was precisely the purpose of the prophetic collections as we know them from the Hebrew Bible. The books of the prophets were composed for an audience that would consult them after the prophets had gone.

Scribes and Prophets

Though prophets may have written on occasion, they did not record the oracles they delivered. Considering the existence of pre-exilic oracle collections, however, somebody must have taken the initiative to commit the oracles to writing. So who did? The nature of the prophetic books makes it clear that the literary fixation of separate oracles preceded the composition of the collections. In our quest for the writers, we can narrow down the field, in a first analysis, to those who recorded the texts that were later included in the collections. There are basically two possibilities: either the separate oracles go back to archival records kept by officials, or they are the recorded recollections of followers of the prophets. In the first case the chronological interval between the delivery of the oracle and its fixation in writing was relatively brief; in the second, the time gap between delivery and writing may have been significant, in which case the oral tradition may have served as a bridge.

The comparative evidence from Assyria is in favor of the first solution. We know that the Neo-Assyrian oracle collections go back to individual oracle reports drawn up by officials for the benefit of the crown. There is some evidence in the Hebrew Bible that might be marshaled in support of a similar practice in Israel and Judah. The Book of Amos describes an encounter between the prophet Amos and Amaziah, the priest of Bethel (Amos 7:10–17). Alarmed by the subversive oracles Amos delivered at the temple of Bethel, Amaziah sent a message to the king in which he reported what Amos had been saying (Amos 7:11;

compare 7:9, 7:17). In the days of Jeremiah, the Jerusalem counterpart of Amaziah was Zephaniah son of Maaseiah. Having been appointed as priest, it was his duty to act as superintendent of the sanctuary; if a prophet disturbed the order, the priest was to put him "into the stocks and into the pillory" (Jer 29:24–28; compare 20:1–6). Such measures were presumably an occasion for a report to the political authorities.

The references in the books of Amos and Jeremiah suggest that prophets had a predilection for the temple as a platform for their performances. After all, prophets belonged to the religious establishment on a par with priests and sages (see, e.g., Jer 18:18); the temple was, in a way, home territory for them. Practically speaking, moreover, on religious high days the temple was the place where they were sure to find an audience.[20] The high priest being the official under whose authority the prophets delivered their oracles, there is reason to surmise that the temple scribes recorded the prophecies; the high priest would thus have been able to check what a prophet had been saying even if he had not been present on the occasion. In light of the comparative evidence of the Neo-Assyrian oracles, it is possible that the archives of the Jerusalem temple kept records of the oracles delivered in the precincts of the sanctuary.

Yet comparative evidence does not amount to compelling evidence; the existence of a file of oracle records in the archives of the temple, either at Jerusalem or in Bethel, remains a matter of informed speculation. Also, the hypothesis faces two serious objections. Reading through the books of the prophets, the oracles one encounters seem often too general to have been of interest to the temple officials; many of them are artful and literary, and not very specific in content. Nothing in the Book of Amos, for example, is as particular and specific as the prophecy Amaziah reports to the king. It is possible that the historical Amos, just like other prophets, was in fact quite specific in his predictions. If so, the distance between the oracles in his book and his actual performances is considerable. In sum, the contents of the books of the prophets do not correspond with what one would expect in the records of the temple archive.

The second objection concerns the nature of the prophetic collections in the Bible. Unlike the Assyrian oracle collections, the biblical books derive their unity from the person of the prophet. In Assyria, the scribes made a selection of those oracles in favor of the king and arranged them by theme and date of delivery; one tablet will contain oracles from different prophets. The biblical books of the prophets, in contrast, gather various oracles attributed to a single prophet; as if to underscore the importance of the person of the prophet, the collections often contain narratives about the prophet as well. In this respect, then, the prophetic books of the Bible resemble the Book of Balaam more than they do the Assyrian oracle collections.

The mixture of oracles from, and narratives about, one prophet suggests that the early Hebrew collections were the work of followers and sympathizers. Even if the composers owed their knowledge of the prophet's oracles to the temple files, it is very unlikely that they obtained the information on his life and times from the official archives. Recollection, either personal or mediated, seems a more plausible source. But if the authors of the biographical pieces on the prophets worked from memory, whether individual or collective, why would not the writers of the oracles have worked from memory as well? It would have been easier, in a sense, than going through the temple archives looking for relevant records. In brief, while there may have been oracle records on file in the temple archive, it is unlikely that they played a decisive role in the composition of the prophetic books of the Bible.

There is one biblical document that describes the coming about of a prophetic book. It is the story of the scroll in which the scribe Baruch wrote the collected oracles of Jeremiah (Jer 36). In previous remarks about the pertinent chapter from the Book of Jeremiah, I have stressed its ideological slant; the narrative has been designed as proof of the authenticity of an early scroll of Jeremiah oracles. Notwithstanding the bias of the account, however, it contains several facts about the production of the prophetic collections that merit careful attention. First, the composer of the collection is a professional scribe from the entourage of the prophet; second, the oracles in the collection are the written recollections of oral performances of the prophet; and third, the collection that survives is not the original scroll but a rewritten one to which many things have been added. I will use these three points as propositions about the formation of the prophetic books in general.

According to the account in Jeremiah 36, the writer of the earliest collection of Jeremiah oracles was a professional scribe (*hassōpēr,* Jer 36:26, 36:32). At the request of the prophet, the scribe Baruch put down in writing oracles from a period of some twenty years. Some time later he read the scroll to assembled worshippers in the temple; his connection to the prophet was not confined, apparently, to his role as transcriber. Other passages from Jeremiah suggest that Baruch was a close companion and, in a sense, collaborator of Jeremiah's. People suspected that he was Jeremiah's inspiration (Jer 43:2–3); the personal oracle addressed to him implies he shared in the afflictions of the prophet (Jer 45:1–5). Baruch was not merely a scribe, then, but a scribe with a personal affinity with Jeremiah and his message.

It would be incorrect to assume that Baruch was alone in his support of Jeremiah; he represents a larger community of followers and sympathizers. A study of the Book of Jeremiah yields an astonishing number of names of people who were either opponents or supporters of the prophet; both camps were influential in the royal bureaucracy and among the temple officials.[21] Defenders of Jeremiah's cause included, notably, various members of the Shaphan family.[22] While it might be mistaken to designate these people as "disciples" of the prophet, they did constitute a support group that was receptive to Jeremiah's message. Baruch belonged to a wide circle of sympathizers of the prophet, then, many of whom were scribes by profession or belonged to the literate elite.[23]

Being a scribe, Baruch combined his personal sympathy for Jeremiah and his message with the ability to compose a literary text. The conjunction of these two conditions in one person predisposed Baruch to act as the chronicler of the prophet. The importance of his role can hardly be overrated. It matters little whether or not it was actually one Baruch who wrote the first collection of Jeremiah oracles; the significance of the reference to Baruch concerns the involvement of a professional scribe in the creation of the collection. This means that the earliest prophetic collections were already the work of professionals of writing, and that we should therefore expect to find evidence of the usual practices and techniques of the scribal craft.

The second element that may be inferred from the story about Baruch and the scroll of Jeremiah concerns the relation between the written oracles and their oral delivery. The text of Jer 36:2 intimates that Baruch the scribe wrote down the text of the oracles that Jeremiah had delivered over a period of some twenty years; he composed, indeed, an oracle collection. A crucial question here is the method that Baruch employed in establishing the text of these oracles. According to the biblical account, he wrote at the dictation of the prophet. This part of the tale, however, is historically suspect because it is obviously designed to prove that the collection had the authority of the prophet: *ipse dixit,* or as the Semitic idiom has it, the oracles were "from the mouth" of the prophet. It is highly unlikely that Jeremiah took the initiative to put his oracles on record, and it was certainly not at the command of God. Prophets, as we have seen, were not in the habit of writing their messages; nor were they accustomed to dictating them to others.

If Baruch did not write from dictation, his knowledge of the oracles came from another source. While it cannot be excluded that he had access to oracle reports from the temple archives, the more likely possibility is that he worked on the basis of recollection. His scribal education had trained his powers of memorization, and it is quite possible that for much of what he wrote he could consult his own memory. It is unlikely, however, that he had been a witness of all the oracles he recorded; the oral tradition as it circulated among Jeremiah's supporters must have supplied him with other material. In this reconstruction, it is not necessary to posit the existence of an oral tradition spanning several generations, as had been the trend for a while in the 1930s and 1940s. The oral tradition that Jer 36:2 might imply does not exceed twenty years. It was part of a group culture in which the acts and oracles of Jeremiah were an important topic of conversation and discussion.

The account of Baruch and the Jeremiah scroll is relevant to yet a third aspect of the production of early oracle collections. The story of the scroll is not only about its making but also about its destruction and its reproduction in an expanded form. According to the biblical narrative, the first scroll ended up in the flames of the brazier of King Jehoiakim; in stark contrast with the awe King Josiah had shown for the Book of the Torah (2 Kings 22–23), Jehoiakim displayed only contempt for the oracle collection and burned it, column by column. To make up for the loss of the first scroll, Jeremiah received word of God telling him to write a second one. In a stunning feat of memory, he dictated the text of the first scroll all over again to Baruch, who was thus able to write a second scroll. In addition to the earlier text, this second scroll contained "many [other] words like these" (Jer 36:32).

Though the biblical narrative focuses on Jehoiakim's refusal to listen to the word God spoke through Jeremiah, it is significant for the history of biblical literature on account of the theme of the reinvented text. The same motif occurs in the tale of the two tablets containing the Ten Commandments; because Moses destroyed the first tablets, God had to make a new copy. Both stories reflect an awareness among the scribes that the texts at their disposal were not originals but copies going back to a lost original. In the case of the Jeremiah scroll, moreover, the scribe who wrote the Baruch story realized that the Jeremiah scroll as he knew it contained parts that had not been in the earlier scroll. The legitimizing narrative of Jer 36:27–32 is a witness to the textual growth of the Jeremiah tradition.

It is useful, at this point, to confront the witness of Jer 36:27–32 with the textual history of Deuteronomy. As discussed in Chapter 6, a close analysis of Deuteronomy demonstrates that the book went through four major editions in order to reach its present form. Each edition was physically coterminous with a scroll; a new edition, with revisions and expansions, required the production of a new scroll, which took the place of an earlier one thereafter discarded and reduced to oblivion. The growth of the literary tradition, whether legal, narrative, or prophetic, materialized in a succession of scrolls, the interval between them being normally dictated by the life span of a scroll. Particular incidents, symbolized in Jeremiah 36 by Jehoiakim's act of book burning, might accelerate the development.

On the strength of the biblical account of the making of the scroll of Jeremiah, it is possible to formulate a model for the way in which the prophetic books came into being. In this model, scribes are instrumental in the making of the collections. Their work naturally exhibits all the characteristics of scribal procedure, including transcription, invention, and expansion. The scribes' principal means of access to the words and acts of the prophets was memory; personal memory, in some cases, but mostly collective memory as extant in the minds of the supporters and followers of the prophets. In addition, the scribes could incorporate in the collections oracle records from the temple files. In the course of the transmission of the prophetic collections, the scrolls received additions. These additions were in a way "like" the earlier material but were not necessarily from the same prophet; the further removed from the first collection they were, the more significant the contribution of the scribes who made the additions.

Jeremiah as a Scribal Artifact

If the account about the Jeremiah scroll in Jer 36 allows us to develop a model for conceptualizing the coming about of the prophetic collections, the Book of Jeremiah supplies us with the material to test the validity of that model. Three propositions make up the model; translated to the Book of Jeremiah they hold that (1) the Book of Jeremiah is a scribal artifact; (2) the core of the book is based on personal and collective memory; and (3) the scribes expanded the original Jeremiah collection with material associated with Jeremiah but not necessarily from him. The following sections will offer evidence demonstrating the accuracy and significance of these propositions.

In demonstrating that the Book of Jeremiah is a scribal artifact, I wish to make two points. First, the book is a scribal composition as opposed to a prophetic memoir; those parts of the book that present themselves as a genuine autobiographical document by Jeremiah, namely the so-called Confessions, are in fact the work of scribes. And second, the scribal nature of the book is revealed by its use of existing oracle collections to create new oracular material; the oracles against the nations, collected in chapters 46–51 of the Masoretic text, offer some striking illustrations.

Scattered over the first twenty chapters of Jeremiah we find the Confessions of Jeremiah; they consist of complaints of the prophet and answers by God (Jer 1:4–19, 6:9–11, 6:27–30, 9:1–6, 11:18–12:6, 15:10–21, 17:14–18, 18:18–23, 20:7–18). It is the view of many scholars that the Confessions of Jeremiah constitute a unique document that qualifies the prophet as an individual of great sensitivity and exceptional literary merit.[24] The usual designation of these individual laments as "confessions" is significant of the value attached to them. Borrowed from Augustine's *Confessiones,* it identifies Jeremiah's laments as one of the oldest introspective texts in human history. The trouble, however, resides in the fact that these texts, if indeed authentically autobiographical, are truly unique. There is nothing like them in the ancient Near East. No one kept this kind of personal diary.[25]

The fact that the ancient Near East has no documented parallel to a private record of an inner struggle with one's destiny does not mean that the Confessions of Jeremiah are without literary parallels. Some of the laments from the Psalter, such as Psalm 69, would not be out of place in the mouth of Jeremiah.[26] The parallels with the Book of Job are even stronger in some respects, since they extend to the divine replies.[27] However, the individual laments in the Psalms are not personal documents but formulaic prayers intended for multiple use and for purposes of edification. And the Book of Job is not really about Job but about the problem of the theodicy. The laments and the divine responses are didactic literature.

The laments of Jeremiah and the accompanying divine replies have a striking parallel outside the Bible in the Babylonian wisdom composition known as *Man and His God.*[28] The cuneiform poem consists of three parts. After a short introduction of the protagonist, the subject of the text launches into a lament that is quite like the laments of the Bible. At the end of the text the deity responds with an oracle of salvation and encouragement. The text compares with *Ludlul bēl nēmeqi*, which is also an account of individual misfortune ending with the delivery of the sufferer by a merciful god.[29] Unlike *Man and His God* and the Book of Job, *Ludlul* lacks a divine discourse. A common characteristic of the three texts, however, is their didactic nature. Though they present themselves as (auto)biographical narratives, they are in fact scholarly wisdom texts.

In view of both the biblical and the extrabiblical parallels, the Confessions of Jeremiah are best interpreted as a literary creation for purposes of instruction and edification. They are not a genuine ego-document but a scribal composition designed to create a certain image of the prophet Jeremiah. Its author wanted to construct a prophetic identity for Jeremiah. To reach his aim, he focused on Jeremiah's inner struggle to come to terms with his prophetic calling as a way to show what it means to be a real prophet. In so doing, he contributed in no small measure to the romantic perception of the biblical prophets as tormented individuals of great literary talent.

The fact that the composer of the Confessions was indeed constructing a *prophetic* identity is clear from the correspondences between the Confessions and the account of Jeremiah's calling in the first chapter of the book. Some of the parallels are astonishingly close.

And I will make you . . . a fortified wall of bronze;
They will attack you, but they shall not prevail over you,
For I am with you to save you and deliver you.

Jer 15:20

And behold, I will make you today a fortified city,
And a wall of bronze . . .
They will attack you, but they shall not prevail over you,
For I am with you . . . to deliver you.

Jer 1:18–19[30]

Other correspondences are less striking but nonetheless substantial. According to Jer 1:4, Jeremiah was destined to become a prophet because God had set him apart even before he was born. In the Confessions the prophet acknowledges his special position by saying that he is called by God's name (Jer 15:16). God put His word in the mouth of the prophet (Jer 1:9), and the prophet claims that "when Your words were offered, I ate them" (Jer 15:16). "Do not be a cause of dismay for me," prays the prophet (Jer 17:17), echoing God's injunction "not to be dismayed by them, lest I dismay you before them" (Jer 1:17).

The connection between Jeremiah's calling (Jer 1:4–10, 1:11–19), on the one hand, and the Confessions, on the other, is seldom taken into account, because commentators feel that the two belong to different genres. Yet the narratives of Jeremiah's calling are a mixture of divine speech ("I make you a prophet," "I make you a fortified city," "Fear not, for I am with you") and individual complaints ("I do not know how to speak, for I am only a youth") very much like the Confessions. With their mixture of laments and divine speeches, the Confessions are a sequel to the calling of the prophet. The author intended to show that inner conflict does not attend only the beginning of a prophetic career but accompanies it all along. A real prophet is always pursuing an inner dialogue with God.

One reason why many students of the Book of Jeremiah find it hard to believe that the Confessions are a scribal invention is that they contain implicit—and at times explicit—references to the life of the prophet. Was the scribe of the Confessions so bold as to simply make up a spiritual biography of the prophet? It does not seem so. In addition to a rich store of Psalms phraseology from which he did borrow, he had some well-known prophets as models for Jeremiah. Their careers and experiences served as a source for the spiritual autobiography outlined in the Confessions. Two models are mentioned in Jer 15:1–3: Even if Moses and Samuel were to stand before God, God would not be won over to the people. Jeremiah is supposed to be like Moses and Samuel. Other prophets, such as Elijah, though not mentioned in the Book of Jeremiah, provided supplementary data to flesh out the inner life of Jeremiah. Another model prophet was Micah; he also announced doom to Jerusalem and was proved to be right (Jer 26:17–19).

The model prophets supplied, first of all, certain elements for the portrait of Jeremiah as a prophet. In response to the divine calling, Jeremiah objects that he is only a youth *(na'ar)* and that he does not know how to speak (Jer 1:6). The youthfulness is borrowed from Samuel's calling (1 Sam 3:1–10) and the lack of rhetorical ability echoes Moses's alleged speech impairment (Exod 4:10, 6:11, 6:29). The role of the prophet as an intercessor, mentioned in the Confessions (Jer 15:11, 18:20) and referred to in the sermons (Jer 7:16, 11:14, 14:11), goes back to Moses (Num 11:1–13, 21:4–9; Deut 9–10) and Samuel (1 Sam 7:5, 8:6, 12:19, 12:23). That people do not listen is a problem confronting all prophets—as Moses (Exod 6:8, 6:11) and Samuel (1 Sam 8:6–8) knew before Jeremiah (Jer 6:10, 20:8). Jeremiah faced enmity (Jer 11:18–21, 12:6, 15:10, 18:18–23, 20:10) and found life unbearable (Jer 20:14–18), just like Elijah (1 Kings 19:1–14) and Moses (Num 11:15). Even the desire to withdraw to the desert (Jer 9:1) is copied from Elijah (1 Kings 19:4).

The correspondence between Jeremiah and Micah is even closer.[31] The writer of Jer 26:17–19 refers to Micah as a precedent of Jeremiah. He quotes from Micah's oracles and thereby attests to the existence of the written collection. The author of the Confessions borrowed from the Book of Micah to enrich Jeremiah's experience with certain particulars.[32] In fact, the Micah collection may have given him the idea for the Confessions, since it contains a personal lament much in the vein of those by Jeremiah (Mic 7:1–6). Enmity from Micah's own household (Mic 7:5–6) and attempts to keep him from prophesying (Mic 2:6) find many echoes in Jeremiah's Confessions. As Micah (Mic 3:8), Jeremiah is filled to the brim with God's anger, to the point where he cannot keep it in (Jer 6:11, 15:17, 20:9). Specific images, such as that of the "incurable wound" and the "deceitful spring" (Jer 15:18) come from Micah (Mic 1:9, 1:14), as does the image of the prophet gleaning leftovers from the harvest (Jer 6:9, based on Mic 7:1).

It would be tedious to draw out the complete list of all the correspondences between Jeremiah's Confessions and other parts of the Hebrew Bible, including the Book of Psalms. The parallels that have been mentioned should suffice to show that the Confessions are not a *creatio ex nihilo;* their author had access to a mine of materials from which to borrow all sorts of elements and expressions for the construction of Jeremiah's prophetic identity. These materials were literary, and the scribe who used them worked on the basis of texts that he had memorized. Jeremiah's own life was just a minor source of inspiration. The only reference in the Confessions to a specific detail from the life of Jeremiah is the mention of "the men from Anathoth" (Jer 11:21), and that could simply depend on the fact that Anathoth was known to be the birth town of the prophet. Everything else in the Confessions is the result of creative use of topics, texts, and phrases from the written stream of tradition.

The importance of the written tradition as a source for material attributed to Jeremiah is more conspicuous yet in the case of the section known as the Oracles against the Nations (Jer 46–51). Several of these oracles are artificial in the sense that scribes manufactured them by borrowing bits and pieces of other oracles and merely changing some of the names. One oracle is entirely a montage of citations from other oracles. The phenomenon of literary borrowing is further evidence of the use the scribes made of existing written sources. In composing the Book of Jeremiah, the scribes operated as scribes used to do; they drew from written sources to produce new literature.

In the oracles against Babylon (Jer 50–51), the scribes recycled material from earlier parts of the Book of Jeremiah. Verses 41–43 of chapter 50 speak about a people coming from the north, "a great nation and many kings . . . from the ends of the earth"; this nation will wage war "against you, Daughter of Babylon." The oracle is almost literally a citation from Jer 6:22–24. In the earlier context, however, the nation from the north marched "against you, Daughter of Zion" (Jer 6:23); "the King of Babylon" who hears the report (Jer 50:43) was originally the anonymous population of Judah: "we" (Jer 6:24). In chapter 51 something similar occurs. The hymn to God the Creator, who is vastly superior to the lifeless idols (Jer 51:15–19) has been taken, verse by verse, from Jer 10:12–16. The two instances show that the Jeremiah tradition grew by a process of *relecture:* the scribes studied the received text and reapplied it to new situations.

The most striking instance of a prophecy that is a scribal construct is the prophecy against Edom (Jer 49:7–22, LXX 30:1–16). The prophecy in question is a patchwork of fragments from existing oracles. Almost every verse has a correspondence, often literal, elsewhere in the prophets or in the Book of Jeremiah itself. Verse 7 compares to Obadiah 8; verse 8 is an adapted quote from an oracle against Hazor in Jer 49:30a and 49:32c; verses 9 and 10 have an analogue in Obadiah 5–6; verses 12 and 13 are a variation on Jer 25:15–29 and 25:8–11, respectively; verses 14–16 have a variant formulation in Obadiah 1–4; verse 17 is also found in Jeremiah's prophecy against Babylon in Jer 50:13b; verse 18 is paralleled by Jer 50:40 with minor variations; verses 19–21 have an almost exact parallel in Jer 50:44–46 (LXX 27:44–46), with the substitutions of "Edom" for "Babylon" and "the inhabitants of Teman" for "the land of Chaldea" (LXX, "the Chaldean inhabitants"). Verse 22, finally, occurs also in Jer 48:40–41 (not in the LXX) with the same formulation but applied to Moab. For "Bozrah" and "Edom" in Jer 49:22 the parallel in Jer 48:40–41 has "Moab" twice.

The text is an anthology of oracles, much as the psalm of Jonah (Jon 2:3–10) is an anthology of lines from the Psalms. The anthology is the work of a man who was well versed in the written tradition of the prophets; outside the circle of professional scribes, such men did not exist. The Edom prophecy is most likely a composition based on quotations from memory. Variants in vocabulary and orthography, free citations, and the like, suggest that the scribe who wrote the text was not surrounded by manuscripts from which he simply copied. He freely drew from the oracles stored in his memory to create a new oracle, which he added to the oracles of Jeremiah.[33] It was, typically, a scribal technique to make the prophet speak again, posthumously.

Prophets from Memory: The Acts and Oracles of Jeremiah

The second proposition in our model for the making of the prophetic books concerns the role of memory, both individual and collective. While not excluding the possibility that scribes consulted the temple archives when writing the Book of Jeremiah, the model attributes a crucial role to recollections about the prophet that were shared among his followers and admirers. This implies that many stories about the prophet, and oracles attributed to him, circulated for some time in the oral tradition before scribes committed them to writing.

The text that I will use to illustrate the "memory hypothesis" is a work that may be dubbed the Acts and Oracles of Jeremiah. It is a document now disassembled into pieces scattered through the Book of Jeremiah. To bring the fragments together again, it is helpful to be aware of the structure of the Book of Jeremiah in its present form. The differences between the Greek and the Hebrew version of Jeremiah demonstrate that the book consists of three parts. In the Greek translation of the Septuagint, based on a Hebrew edition of Jeremiah still partially extant in the Qumran documents, the Oracles against the Nations (Jer 46–51 in modern Bible translations) follow right after Jer 25:13 (Jer 25:14–31:44 LXX); as a matter of consequence, Jer 26 in the Masoretic text is Jer 33 in the Septuagint. The different position of the Oracles against the Nations allows a division of the book into three parts. Part One runs from chapter 1 through 25; Part Two runs from chapter 26 through 45; and Part Three is the Oracles against the Nations (46–51). Chapter 52 is, by all accounts, an appendix to the book as a whole.

Part One of the book differs from Part Two in its focus on the words of the prophet. Whereas Part Two contains the *acta* of Jeremiah, Part One contains his *dicta*. The difference comes to the fore with particular clarity when we compare the parallel accounts of Jeremiah's sermon in the temple in chapters 7 and 26. Whereas chapter 7 contains an extensive report of the words of Jeremiah, chapter 26 is very concise about his sermon. It focuses instead on the hostile reactions to the prophet and the protection he received from Ahikam son of Shaphan. The difference is characteristic of the respective angles of Jeremiah Part One and Part Two.

Within Part One there are a number of sermons whose ideas and phraseology are reminiscent of Deuteronomy and the Deuteronomistic History. These prose sermons begin in 7:1–8:3 and continue in 11:1–14, 13:1–14, 16:1–18, 18:1–12, 19:1–20:6, 21:1–10, 22:1–5, 24:1–10, 25:1–13. Several sermons presuppose a particular context without telling the reader what that context is. For example, in the sermon against the people who refuse to comply with the terms of "this covenant" (Jer 11:1–14), we must guess what covenant the prophet is talking about. Something similar is true for the sermon in chapter 7, the Tophet prophecy in 19:1–13, and the reference to "this book" in 25:1–13. This out-of-context phenomenon is presumably the result of an editorial strategy by which the orations were lifted from their narrative framework because the composer was interested only in collecting the oracles. This explanation presupposes the prior existence of a source in which sermons and context were joined, which postulated text we may call the Acts and Oracles of Jeremiah.

To reconstruct that source, we must look at chapters 26–45. The composer of Part Two wanted to portray Jeremiah as a true prophet and a true patriot. He therefore highlighted Jeremiah's conflicts with rival prophets (such as Hananiah, and the false prophets in Babylon) and his attitude toward the Babylonians. Most of the material that Part Two uses is of the same cloth as the prose sermons in Part One. In fact, some of the stories in Part Two supply the original context of the sermons in Part One. The tale about the temple sermon in Jer 26 provides the context of that sermon in Jer 7; the rubric in Jer 7:1–2 (missing in the LXX edition) is entirely based on Jer 26. The proper understanding of Jer 25:1–13 requires knowledge of Jer 36. Part Two supplies the background of the sermon about "this covenant" as well; the text refers to the act of manumission to which Hezekiah committed the population by covenant (Jer 34:8–22).

Because of the connections between the prose sermons of Part One and the narratives of Part Two, Sigmund Mowinckel suggested that the sermons are Deuteronomistic elaborations of the biographical narratives of Part Two.[34] This implies a unilateral dependence of the sermons in Part One on the narratives of Part Two. However, there are also instances where Jeremiah Part Two refers back to the prose sermons of Part One. The reference to "the loathsome figs so bad that they cannot be eaten" in Jer 29:17 presupposes knowledge of Jer 24:1–10. The mutual dependence of sermons and narratives shows that they were originally part of a single source, the one I have dubbed the Acts and Oracles of Jeremiah. Except for some later additions (e.g., Jer 30–31, 33), it is basically coterminous with Part Two plus the sermons from Part One.

The Acts and Oracles of Jeremiah has its roots in the oral tradition among scribes of the early exilic period. Proof of the point is the occurrence of several doublets. The story of the delegation sent by King Zedekiah to the prophet Jeremiah, found at Jer 37:3–10, is a doublet of Jer 21:1–7. According to the one version, Zedekiah sent Zephaniah son of the priest Maaseiah and Jehucal son of Shelemiah (37:3); according to the other he sent Zephaniah and Pashhur son of Malchiah (21:1). The one version has the delegates asking Jeremiah to intercede with God on their behalf (37:3), the other has them asking the prophet to inquire of God on their behalf (21:2). The tenor of the answer that they receive is the same in both cases. Instead of taking these narratives as referring to two consultations of the prophet, I understand them as reflecting slightly diverging traditions about the same event.[35]

Much the same can be said about the doublet concerning the incarceration of Jeremiah on the charge of treason, his liberation from jail, the secret consultation by the king, and Jeremiah's subsequent confinement in the prison compound (Jer 37:11–21//38:1–28). The similarity between the stories, with respect to both general structure and specific details—such as the identification of "the house of the pit" (*bêt habbôr*, 37:16) or simply "the pit" (38:6 and elsewhere) with the house of the scribe Jonathan (37:15, 20, 38:26)—is such that they must go back to the same events. The occurrence of these doublets shows that we are not dealing with "an eyewitness account of events by a contemporary observer such as Baruch son of Neriah."[36] The composition stems from a milieu in which variant oral traditions have been circulating for some time. The scribes who put these traditions in writing knew them from hearsay.

I have argued that the prose sermons in Jeremiah Part One were amputated from the Acts and Oracles of Jeremiah, now found in Jeremiah Part Two. The fact that chapters 26–45 do contain a few full-blown sermons in the vein of the sermons of Part One demonstrates that the oral tradition about Jeremiah was not only retentive but also creative. The tradition kept producing new oracles, whether based on invention or recollection or a mixture of both. Jeremiah's sermon about the Rechabites (Jer 35) is an example; the written version came into existence after the editor of Jeremiah Part One had composed his oracle collection. Both the doublets and the new sermons attest to the vitality of the oral traditions about Jeremiah.

In the 1930s and 1940s, Scandinavian scholars emphasized the importance of the oral tradition behind the books of the prophets. In the view of Henrik Samuel Nyberg, Harris Birkeland, and Sigmund Mowinckel—and many others in their wake—the prophetic books as we know them are the outcome of a long process of oral tradition.[37] Nyberg and Birkeland even suggested that the aggregation of separate oracles into collections was an oral phenomenon. These views are no longer in favor among biblical scholars. Studies done in the 1950s and the 1960s observed that the formation of the prophetic collections was essentially a literary process.[38] About the same time, social anthropologists demonstrated the flexibility of oral traditions and their unreliability as a source of historical information.[39] In the model developed in this chapter, the formation of the prophetic books was neither a purely literary nor a purely oral phenomenon. The scribes who composed the collections used written texts (such as the Acts and Oracles of Jeremiah) that had a limited period of oral tradition behind them. At the same time, though, the oral tradition remained productive of new texts.

As the oral tradition was committed to writing, the oracles of the prophets borrowed their style from the scribes who wrote them down. The style of the Jeremiah sermons is generally qualified as Deuteronomistic because their outlook and phraseology are akin to what we find in the Book of Deuteronomy and the Deuteronomistic History. This could mean that the scribes behind the Book of Jeremiah (or much of the material in the book) had the same background as, or were even identical with, the scribes behind Deuteronomy and the Deuteronomistic History. As Andrew Dearman observes, though, "Deuteronomistic prose is similar to . . . scribal prose."[40] The prose sermons of Jeremiah are essentially a scribal version of prophecy.

Expanding the Prophets

The third element of the production model we are testing concerns the growth of the prophetic collections through the addition of "many [other] words like these" (Jer 36:32). Our examination of the Oracles against the Nations (Jer 46–51) has revealed how the scribes recycled existing Jeremiah oracles as well as oracles attributed to other prophets, as a means of expanding the Jeremiah tradition with "new" materials. Such expansions occurred in the course of successive editions of the book. Usually we can reconstruct these various editions only on the basis of intratextual traces; rubrics and colophons proved to be such traces in the case of Deuteronomy. With the Book of Jeremiah, however, we are in the fortunate circumstance of having two different editions at our disposal; the one is extant in the Masoretic text of the Hebrew Bible, the other in the Greek translation of the Septuagint. Our study of expansion in the books of the prophets will be based on a comparison of these two editions.

Biblical scholars have long been aware of the fact that the Greek translation of Jeremiah as extant in the Septuagint is shorter by one-seventh than the text in the Hebrew Bible. Its arrangement of the material, moreover, differs at some points from that in the Hebrew text. The most striking instance is the position of the Oracles against the Nations. Whereas the Septuagint places them right after 25:13 ("And I will bring upon that land all that I have decreed against it, all that is recorded in this book—that which Jeremiah prophesied against all the nations"), the Hebrew Bible has them at the end of the book (chapters 46–51). The discoveries in the Judean Desert have yielded a fragment of a Hebrew version of Jeremiah (4QJer^b) that agrees with the Septuagint (henceforth Jer^LXX) against the Hebrew text known from the Masoretic tradition (henceforth Jer^MT). Based on this fragment, scholars have concluded that the Greek translation goes back to a Hebrew text of Jeremiah that differs in important respects from the Masoretic text as we know it from the Hebrew Bible.

The differences between Jer^MT and Jer^LXX are such that they cannot be attributed to scribal errors in the process of transmission. Nor can the Hebrew vorlage of the Septuagint be interpreted as an abbreviated version of the book. In view of their different placement of the Oracles against the Nations, Jer^MT and Jer^LXX represent two different editions of the same book. Chronologically, the edition reflected in Jer^LXX precedes the one extant in Jer^MT. Although a new edition may delete parts of a previous one (the Standard Babylonian edition of *Gilgamesh* skipped the encounter between Gilgamesh and Shiduri known from the Old Babylonian edition), each successive edition entails, as a rule, an expansion of the text. There are no indications to the effect that this rule does not apply for the two editions of Jeremiah.[41]

A study of the expansions made in Jer^MT demonstrates that the scribal modes of textual production as evidenced in the Oracles against the Nations continued to be practiced after the completion of the Hebrew vorlage of Jer^LXX. On the basis of a compositional analysis, chapters 30–31 and 33 are generally considered secondary insertions in Part Two of Jeremiah (Jer 26–45).[42] After the Hebrew vorlage of the Septuagint had been written, this inserted part of the book remained under construction. In the edition represented by the Masoretic text, a scribe added another thirteen verses to what is now chapter 33 (Jer 33:14–26).[43] They contain an extended paraphrase of (a) the "promise" (literally, "the good word") mentioned in Jer 29:10 ("I will fulfill my good word for you"); (b) the prophecy of a scion for the royal dynasty of David in Jer 23:5–6 (quoted in 33:14–16); and (c) the parallel that Jer 31:35–37 draws between the immutable laws of nature and the immutable commitment of God to His people (paraphrased in 33:19–26). The scribe who added 33:14–26 elaborated on the earlier restoration oracles and gave them a particular twist by emphasizing the central role of the Davidic dynasty and the Levitical priests (33:17–18, 33:22, 33:26). The perspective is clearly post-exilic, since the verses contemplate a restoration of both the kingship and the priesthood along the same lines as the oracles of the prophet Zechariah (Zech 3–4, 6:9–13).[44]

Expansion by the addition of thirteen verses is a conspicuous way of altering a received text. The scribes of Jer^MT expanded their text in a more subtle fashion by adding various references to King Nebuchadnezzar and the reign of the Babylonians. A comparison of Jer 25:1–13 in Jer^LXX and Jer^MT provides a good illustration. Jer^LXX dates the oracle in "the fourth year of King Jehoiakim son of Josiah of Judah," thereby establishing a link with Jer 36:1–2. Jer^MT adds that the fourth year of Jehoiakim coincided with "the first year of Nebuchadnezzar king of Babylon" (Jer 25:1). The addition is not fortuitous but part of a new perspective that the editor of Jer^MT imposed on the text. In verse 9 he refers to Nebuchadnezzar as the servant of Yahweh ('abdî, "My servant"); verse 11 predicts that all the nations shall serve the king of Babylon for seventy years; verse 12 announces that Yahweh will punish the king of Babylon and the Chaldeans for their sins; and verse 14 repeats that they (i.e., the Babylonians) will bear the consequences of their sin.

All of the references to Nebuchadnezzar, Babylon, and the Chaldeans just mentioned are lacking in Jer^LXX. In contrast with the Jer^LXX edition (Hebrew vorlage), the editor of Jer^MT hints at the doctrine of a *translatio imperii* in which the reign of Nebuchadnezzar inaugurates seventy years of Babylonian supremacy.[45] The scribal editor based his conception of the historical succession of empires on an understanding of the verdict on King Jehoiakim in Jer 36:30. In response to the destruction of the Jeremiah scroll by the king, the prophet announces the end of the Davidic dynasty (Jer 36:29–30); the oracle of doom combines the earlier oracles of Jer 22:18–19 and 22:30 in a "new" prediction. By emphasizing that the year in which Jehoiakim sealed the fate of his dynasty coincided with the accession of Nebuchadnezzar, the editor of Jer^MT was implying that Nebuchadnezzar would execute God's plan; Nebuchadnezzar was, as Jer^MT 25:9 has it, the "servant" of Yahweh.

The different versions of Jer 25:1–13 show that the scribes of the Jeremiah tradition were not only adding "many [other] words like these"; they were also reframing the message of the prophet in such a way as to make it relevant for their own time. The doctrine of the succession of world empires occurs in full-blown form in the Book of Daniel and other apocalyptic writings; its purport is to show that God rules world history. Human kingdoms have their day until, at the end of time, God will establish His reign. The Jeremiah edition extant in the Masoretic text marks an intermediate stage between prophecy as a commentary on national history and prophecy as a global vision of world history.

The comparison between Jer^MT and Jer^LXX proves the importance of expansion as a scribal mode of text production. In the vast majority of cases, however, such formal proof is not available. And with Jeremiah, when the texts of Jer^MT and Jer^LXX agree, we cannot prove that some parts of the book were additions to the original collection because we do not possess a manuscript of that collection. It is very possible, for instance, that Jer 2:1–4:2 contains oracles from before the time of Jeremiah.[46] The Northern Kingdom had ceased to exist as a political reality in 722; why address it some one hundred years later and upbraid it for seeking help from Assyria and Egypt (Jer 2:18.36)?[47] The reproof would fit the time of Hosea (ca. 730 B.C.E.) much better. In fact Hosea makes a very similar reproach (Hos 7:11), and there are quite a number of other parallels between Jer 2:2–4:2 and the Book of Hosea as well. The resemblances might well follow from the circumstance that the Jeremiah oracles against Israel are not actually from Jeremiah but from a contemporary of Hosea. The scribes may have expanded the Jeremiah collection with pre-Jeremiah material, as they expanded the Isaiah collection with post-Isaiah material (the so-called Deutero-Isaiah and Trito-Isaiah).

The "Scribalization" of Prophecy

The Book of Jeremiah is paradigmatic of the books that the Bible attributes to pre-exilic prophets: the prophets who gave their names to the books wrote neither those books nor the oracles they contain; the Neviim are the work of scribes. The scribes who composed the books used written records based on the recollections of partisans and supporters of the prophets; separate oracles existed in written form before the collections took shape. Narratives about the prophets also had their source in memories cultivated and transmitted by the prophets' sympathizers. Working with written sources of various kinds, the composers of the prophetic books expanded the prophetic materials by a process of *relecture*, creative citation, and appropriation of written oracles from anonymous prophets.

By the early exilic period, written oracle collections had become an established phenomenon with the literate elite of the Jews; as a result, the authority of the prophets became a scriptural authority. This development would have several consequences, one of which was the "scribalization" of prophecy. Once prophecy had become a written genre, new prophets employed writing as the principal means of disseminating their ideas. The anonymous individual known as Deutero-Isaiah is likely to have been a prophet of the new stamp: he wrote his message, instead of preaching it in the streets. In the late Persian and the early Hellenistic periods, the posthumous transformation of prophets into writers was complete; those wishing to emulate the prophets, such as the author of the visions of Daniel (Dan 7–12), presented their work as a scribal activity.

Another consequence triggered by the scribalization of prophecy was a new paradigm of revelation. As I shall demonstrate in the next chapter, the transition of authority from the spoken word to the written text led to a reinterpretation of the notion of revelation. Just as prophecy had become written prophecy, so the concept of revelation would become coterminous with the book. Without their knowing it, the scribes who wrote down the oracles and composed the prophetic collections were sowing the seeds of a radical transformation of Israelite religion.

chapter eight

INVENTING REVELATION

The Scribal Construct of Holy Writ

In the course of their transmission, the books of the Bible came to be viewed as divine revelation. As Josephus writes in the first century C.E., the Jews held their scriptures to be "oracles of God" (*theou dogmata, C. Ap.* 1.42).[1] The early church adopted the same view and passed it on to most Christians of the Middle Ages and the early modern period. In fact, much of the Bible's impact on the history of Western civilization has been due to the belief that it is, in one way or the other, the "Word of God." To deal with the origins of the Bible without explaining its status as Holy Writ would yield a truncated account of its making. This chapter will therefore offer an analysis of the factors behind the claim that the Bible is a revelation.

The Hebrew Bible is the product of the scribal culture of its time; its status as divine revelation is a construct of the Hebrew scribes as well. Though the scribes did not invent the notion of revelation as such, the framing of the books as Holy Writ was their doing. To understand their concept of revelation, it is helpful to observe that the Bible is not the only set of ancient Near Eastern texts to claim supernatural origins. The scribes and scholars of Mesopotamia, too, believed that the key texts of their literary canon were from the mouth of the gods. In fact, the cuneiform canon presents both a precedent for and a parallel to the transformation of the Hebrew scriptures into the Word of God.[2]

This chapter focuses on the development of the revelation paradigm as applied to the Hebrew Bible. After making some preliminary observations about the notion of revelation, we will study how Babylonian and Assyrian scribes used the revelation paradigm. We will then turn to the biblical evidence, to see how the Hebrew scribes sought to legitimize the texts they produced and transmitted by qualifying them as revelation.

Revelation: From Oral to Written

The notion of revelation is probably as old as religion itself; if religion is defined as human interaction with culturally postulated superhuman beings, revelation may be defined as human knowledge from a culturally postulated superhuman source.[3] Knowledge, in this context, covers more than a stock of information; it embraces a grasp of things, intelligence, know-how, and insight into matters hidden to others. Diviners, prophets, and priests are the ones who claim access to such extraordinary knowledge. They derive their power and authority from the privileged intelligence they possess.

In the civilizations of the ancient Near East, knowledge from revelation is in origin oral lore; predictions, oracles, and instructions are found in the mouth of religious specialists: diviners answer their clients' queries, prophets deliver their oracles as the divine inspiration moves them, and priests tell worshippers what behavior pleases the gods. The experts transmit their know-how by oral instruction among themselves, as well. So long as this special knowledge is not available without the mediation of religious experts, it is not thought of as something with a separate existence. In its oral manifestation, revelation is lodged and anchored in its human transmitters.

Matters change to the extent that we may speak of a paradigm shift when written texts supplant the oral tradition as the main channel of information. When the notion of revelation is transferred from the spoken word to the written text, the concept gains a new significance. Applied to a collection of texts, revelation denotes a product rather than an interaction. Since the written text has an objective existence outside its producers and consumers, it is a source of authority by itself. Where, before, religious specialists derived their legitimacy from the revelation they possessed in person, they now have to refer to the sum of knowledge laid down in a body of texts. The related changes in the concept of revelation affected the nature and the role of religious experts: revelation became the province of scribes and scholars; the art of interpretation supplanted the gift of intuition.

To discover the internal logic of these developments we shall first look to Mesopotamia. The cuneiform evidence indicates that the concept of revelation as a characteristically scribal construct emerged at the end of the second millennium B.C.E. under the influence of the increasing role of literacy in the transmission of religious lore. In tandem with the new view of revelation, the role and position of religious experts went through significant changes. The insights derived from a study of the Mesopotamian evidence will illuminate comparable developments in Israel.

Revelation as a Scribal Construct in Mesopotamia

A key text for understanding the Mesopotamian concept of revelation is the *Catalogue of Texts and Authors*.[4] The *Catalogue* is a sophisticated work of scholarship; it lists all the classic texts studied in scribal circles of the seventh century B.C.E. and gives for each text the name of its author. In the discussion of the *Catalogue* in connection with the Mesopotamian concept of authorship (Chapter 2) it became clear that the *Catalogue* does not distinguish between author and editor. Nor is the list concerned with authorship for the reasons modern readers would find it relevant; the primary interest of the Mesopotamian scholars lies with the authority of the traditional texts.

The *Catalogue* lists the works of the cuneiform tradition in their order of presumed antiquity.[5] Though the text has been preserved only in fragments, it is still possible to see that it distinguishes three successive eras in the literary production. The earliest group of texts are "from the mouth of Ea," the second group of texts are by sages from before the Flood, most notably Adapa, and the third and largest group of texts are by various postdiluvian scribes and scholars of great repute. Antiquity is the yardstick of authority: the older the work, the higher its rank among the classics.[6] The divine authorship attributed to the oldest texts underscores the fact that they enjoy the greatest authority. For the purpose of the present discussion, it is this group that merits our particular attention.

The core of the cuneiform canon consists of the large reference works of the various scholarly disciplines of first-millennium Mesopotamia. Everything that falls within the categories of incantation literature *(āšipūtu)*, liturgical lore *(kalûtu)*, astrology *(Enūma Anu Enlil)*, medical prognostics *(sakikkû)*, and various types of omen literature (physiognomy, malformed births, and chance utterances) is traced to Ea, the Mesopotamian god of wisdom. In addition to these compendia, the *Catalogue* mentions two Sumerian myths as being "from the mouth of Ea" *(ša pî ᵈE[a])*; the scribes used these literary texts as scholarly literature.[7] By giving pride of place to the professional literature of the literate scholars (the *āšipu*, the *kalû*, the *ṭupšar Enūma Anu Enlil*, and the *asû*), the *Catalogue* proves to be a scribal composition. Also, the concept of revelation it employs is a scribal construct. An explanatory passage toward the end of the text implies that Ea spoke these texts and that "Adapa wrote them down at his dictation" *([Ada]pa ina pîšu isṭuru)*.[8] These texts "from before the Flood" *(ša lām abūbu)* were transmitted down the generations through the intermediary of Adapa and other celebrated sages from the past.[9]

Without actually using the word "revelation," the *Catalogue* applies that concept to a major part of the written tradition. It thus reflects a new paradigm of revelation; no longer an interaction between gods and religious specialists, revelation is now encoded in a set of written texts. The *Catalogue* was written around 700 B.C.E.[10] Other texts from that time also attest to the new paradigm of revelation. In an almost casual manner, Sargon II (709–705) refers to hemerological lore "which Niššiku [a name of Ea] the lord of wisdom wrote down on an ancient tablet."[11] A literary prayer to Marduk refers to an incantation for appeasing an angry god as "the writing of Ea" *(šiṭru ša ᵈEa)*.[12] A minor myth from the first millennium mentions Ea as the author of directions for preparing various medicinal poultices.[13] All of these texts say that the professional literature of the scholars springs from the subterranean deep *(apsû)*, the "house of wisdom" that is the home of Ea.[14] By 700 B.C.E., then, the new paradigm of revelation seems to have been well established.

According to the new paradigm of revelation, the textual lore of the Mesopotamian scholars comes, in more than one respect, from another world. It is from the gods; from the time before the Flood; and from an extraterrestrial place that ordinary humans can never reach. Where Ea is identified as its divine author, that place is the abyss, the watery abode underneath the earth. Other texts from the first millennium indicate that the extraterrestrial source of revelation could also be situated in heaven.[15] Two texts demonstrate the latter point; the one is the *Myth of Enmeduranki,* which goes back to about 1100 B.C.E.;[16] the other is the *Myth of Adapa,* in its Neo-Assyrian version.

According to the *Myth of Enmeduranki,* the gods Shamash and Adad, patron deities of divination, brought Enmeduranki, an ancient king of Sippar, into their assembly.[17] Though the text does not specify the location of this divine assembly *(puḫru),* the reference to "a golden throne" implies that it was in heaven.[18] Having seated Enmeduranki before them, Shamash and Adad revealed to him the art of divination by showing him the proper techniques. They gave him the "tablet of the gods," that is, the liver, that he might read its signs as an encrypted message. After he returned to earth, Enmeduranki assembled "the men of Nippur, Sippar, and Babylon" before him and transmitted to them what he had learned from the gods. The myth serves as an introduction to instructions for a teacher ("father") who intends to teach a novice ("son") the lore of divination. The genealogy of the discipline makes it a heavenly revelation. It is, as the text says, "a mystery of Anu, Enlil, and Ea" (*niṣirti* ᵈ*Anu* ᵈ*Enlil u* ᵈ*Ea,* lines 7, 13, 17) and "a secret of heaven and underworld" (*piriŝti ŝamê u erṣetim,* lines 8, 14, 16); the same applies to its written lore, including the commentary texts, the astrological series *Enūma Anu Enlil,* and the calculation tables.[19] Through his heavenly journey, Enmeduranki learned "the wisdom of Shamash and Adad."[20]

Another human who traveled to heaven is Adapa, patron and founding father of the art of exorcism *(āŝipūtu).*[21] The Old Babylonian version of his myth tells about his breaking the wing of the South Wind; his trial in heaven by Anu; and his return to earth without the gift of immortality.[22] The Neo-Assyrian version, dating to ca. 750 B.C.E., has added a summary that serves to introduce an exorcistic procedure. It repeats that Adapa went up to heaven and saw all its secrets; though still a human being, he thus gained divine knowledge. Adapa's heavenly knowledge is invoked, in the Neo-Assyrian expansion, as a means to cure disease.[23] In first-millennium texts, the wisdom of Adapa is indeed proverbial.[24] His wisdom is no ordinary wisdom; it has its source in heaven.[25]

Summing up the relevant evidence from first-millennium Mesopotamia, we find that the concept of revelation is applied to a restricted group of texts within the cuneiform canon, most notably the professional compendia of the main scholarly disciplines. According to the new doctrine, these texts go back to the gods, and more especially to Ea; even the extispicy corpus, known as *bārûtu,* though hailed as "the wisdom of Shamash and Adad," has been "proclaimed" *(nabû)* by Ea, as one text has it.[26] Since the gods have their abode in extraterrestrial locations, their revelations are either from the cosmic deep or from heaven. As an oft-repeated saying has it, no human being can climb to heaven or go down to the underworld; those are inaccessible places.[27] If the gods had not revealed them, no one would ever know "the secrets of heaven and underworld."[28]

In the conception of the Mesopotamian scribes, revelation takes the form of written texts. Gods did not, as a rule, write revelations themselves, however; in Mesopotamia there was no tradition of a divine *autographon* comparable to the two tables of the Ten Commandments.

Ea dictated his revelation to Adapa, who transmitted it in turn to the sages after him. The legacy of these *apkallu*s was still being transmitted among the first-millennium scholars. They studied texts "from the mouth of the ancient *apkallu*s from before the Flood."[29] To stress the reliability of the tradition, one colophon claims that the copyist of hemerological lore inherited "from the seven *apkallu*s" had access to master copies from "Sippar, Nippur, Babylon, Larsa, Ur, Uruk, and Eridu."[30] The seven cities correspond with the seven *apkallu*s, and the reference to these "master copies" *(gabarû)* is intended to convey the message that the text is the faithful transcript of the words of the sages from before the Flood.[31] Through the written tradition, then, the scholars claim to have access to "the wisdom of Ea" *(nēmeq ᵈEa).*[32] The chain of tradition links the scribes and scholars of the present to their distant forebears from the past. Not even the great Flood has been able to break the chain; as by a miracle, the revelations from before the Flood have been preserved intact.[33]

Dating the New View of Revelation

When did the Mesopotamian scribes begin to think of their texts as revelations? A study of some of the younger cuneiform classics demonstrates that this new concept of revelation is older than the first millennium B.C.E. In looking at the references to revelation in the more recent additions to the scribal canon, it is possible to trace the emergence of the concept back to the end of the second millennium B.C.E.

One of the latest texts in the scribal stream of tradition is the *Song of Erra.* Written around 800 B.C.E., it is one of the rare cuneiform texts to present itself as a revelation.[34] According to its postscript, the god Erra revealed the text at night; as the author woke up, he committed it to writing without skipping a single line; he then read it again to Erra for checking, and Erra spoke his approval.

> Its compiler is Kabti-ilāni-Marduk, son of Dabibi.
> In the middle of the night He [i.e., the god] revealed it to him,
> And exactly as He had spoken during his morning slumber,[35]

> He [the author] did not skip a single line, nor did he add one to it.
> When Erra heard it, he approved.[36]

This story of origins is striking on two counts: first, because it gives the name of the author of the text, one Kabti-ilāni-Marduk; second, because it defines the composition as a literal transcript of a divine revelation. The identification of the author is probably due to the prophetic prediction the text contains; the description of a nocturnal revelation is designed to endow the new composition with the same status as the classics. If the classics go back to the gods, a new text aspiring to become a classic has to invoke the same paradigm. Indirectly, then, the *Song of Erra* attests to the view that the classics are from the mouth of the gods.

Another latecomer of cuneiform literature is the Babylonian *Epic of Creation,* known among the Mesopotamian scribes as *Enūma eliš.* *Enūma eliš* is a propagandistic myth in praise of Marduk, the city god of Babylon. It was written at the end of the second millennium, when Babylon rose to a political prominence it had not possessed for centuries. By raising Marduk to the top of the pantheon, the poet meant to consolidate the position of Babylon on the political map. To promote his composition, the author added a postscript in which he claims a divine origin for his work.

> This is the revelation which an Ancient, to whom it was told,
> wrote down and established for posterity to hear.[37]

The text uses the fiction of a divine revelation granted to an anonymous author from the past, here simply referred to as "an Ancient" *(maḫrû).* The word for "revelation" is *taklimtu,* literally a "demonstration"; the term preserves a reminiscence of the time in which revelation was primarily thought of as a visual experience.[38] In this case, however, "they," that is, the gods who had earlier recited the fifty names of Marduk, told the text to an Ancient, meaning that they had been dictating it. Said Ancient put it down in writing and "established" it *(šakānu)* for future generations to hear, which probably means that he placed the work on the scribal curriculum.[39]

It makes sense for the author of *Enūma eliš* to resort to a special strategy to get his text accepted, because his work is not just a new text but also a theological innovation. By making Marduk number one among the gods, *Enūma eliš* disturbs the traditional hierarchy of the pantheon. To legitimize this theological move, the author invokes the paradigm of revelation as applied to written texts. That paradigm, in other words, must already have been in place. Since *Enūma eliš* was written in the reign of Nebuchadnezzar I (1125–1104), the concept of written texts being divine revelations must go back to the late second millennium.[40]

Another piece of evidence in support of the view that the notion of revealed writings arose in the late second millennium is the Standard Babylonian version of the *Epic of Gilgamesh*. The Old Babylonian edition of *Gilgamesh* is a third-person account of the great deeds of Gilgamesh. The epic conveys the message that the way to a good life requires acceptance of one's mortality and the mental disposition to moderately enjoy the good things in life. The standard version, written around 1100 B.C.E., changes the mood of the epic. The editor has added a prologue of twenty-eight lines in which he pictures Gilgamesh as a man who obtained hidden wisdom, inaccessible to others.

> He learned the sum of wisdom of everything:
> He saw what was secret, discovered what was hidden,
> He brought back a message from before the Flood.
> *Gilgamesh* I i 6–8

The theme of the prologue returns at the end of the text, in tablet XI. That tablet describes the encounter between Gilgamesh and Utanapishti, the hero who survived the Flood. This Utanapishti "reveals" *(petû)* various secrets, referred to as "a hidden matter" *(amat niṣirti)* and "a secret of the gods" *(pirišti ša ilī, Gilgamesh* XI 9–10, repeated in 281–282).

Even if the language of secrecy is largely rhetorical, the standard version of *Gilgamesh* reflects a significant shift in the concept of wisdom. Whereas in the Old Babylonian edition wisdom is human knowledge painstakingly acquired through a lifetime of experience, half a millennium later wisdom has become divine. A deified hero from before the Flood has supplanted Shiduri, the female innkeeper who gave Gilgamesh good counsel in the Old Babylonian text. The wisdom Utanapishti discloses is out of reach for ordinary mortals. It is from before the Flood—that is, chronologically remote—and beyond the ocean and the waters of death, from the realm of the gods. Unless revealed, this wisdom remains hidden.

I do not mean to imply that the standard version of *Gilgamesh* presents the text of the epic itself as a revelation. That is not the case; on the contrary, the editor defines his text as a *narû*, a literary testament, by Gilgamesh himself.[41] What it does attest to, however, is a preoccupation with esoteric knowledge (hence the language of secrecy) and an interest in the notion of revelation. The edition by Sin-leqe-unninni reflects a spiritual climate in which scholars were looking at ways to redefine the written heritage that was theirs. In their attempts at redefinition, revelation proved to be a helpful paradigm in establishing the authority of the written lore of their craft.

Explaining the Emergence of the Revelation Paradigm

The cuneiform evidence attests to the emergence of the revelation paradigm as a means to assert the authority of the written tradition. Scrutiny of the relevant data allows us to date the new view of revelation around 1150 B.C.E. What the texts do not tell us, however, are the reasons that prompted the scribes to shift to the revelation paradigm. Why did the scholars of the period feel compelled to invoke the notion of revelation, and why just then?

Let us first look at one answer to this question that does not withstand critical examination. It merits a reassessment because it is the principal explanation to have been advanced thus far.[42] The theory holds that the scribal doctrine of revelation was designed to combat a mood of skepticism about traditional values. The concept of revelation would have been used to buttress the plausibility structures, to use the terms of the sociologist Peter Berger.[43] This thesis assumes, first, that skepticism was a striking characteristic of the period around 1150 B.C.E., which corresponds, in Mesopotamian history, with the early post-Kassite era, and second, that the revelation paradigm was designed to lend credibility to a tradition otherwise assailed by doubt and disbelief.[44] The first assumption can in principle be checked by means of a historical inquiry; the second is more in the nature of a conviction that is beyond falsification, but that a few sobering observations can put in perspective.

To show that the early post-Kassite era was marked by skepticism, one could refer to the *Babylonian Theodicy*, reportedly written sometime between 1125 and 1050.[45] This clever acrostic reflects a mood of pessimism and a temperate form of agnosticism, as shown by a handful of quotations.

> The design of the god is as remote as the netherworld.[46]

> The strategy of the god [is inscrutable] like the innermost of heaven,
> The decree of the goddess cannot be understood:
> Teeming humanity is well acquainted with hardship.
> The plans concerning them are [a deep mystery] to humans,
> To understand the way of the goddess [is beyond them.]
> Their destiny[47] is close, [but its meaning is far away.][48]

> The divine mind is remote like the innermost of heaven,
> It is very hard to understand, and people do not know it . . .
> Try as one may, humans do not know the design of god.[49]

The emphasis in these reflections is on human ignorance of the plans and purposes of the gods. In the view propagated by the *Theodicy*, this ignorance is an implication of divine transcendence. Heaven and underworld, the classic habitat of the gods, are out of human reach; they are also beyond the intellectual grasp of humans. Gods, in this view, are not just physically remote and distant but intellectually, as well.

Another text from roughly the same period is the poem in praise of Marduk known as *Ludlul*.[50] *Ludlul* tells the story of Shubshi-meshre-Shakkan, brought to disgrace by envious colleagues but returned to high office through the intervention of Marduk.[51] The plot offers a setting for sombre speculations in a vein familiar from the *Theodicy*.

> What is proper to oneself is an offense to one's god,
> What in one's own heart seems despicable is proper to one's god.
> Who can learn the reasoning of the gods in heaven?
> Who could understand the intentions of the god of the depths?[52]
> Where might human beings have learned the way of a god?
>
> *Ludlul* II 33–38

This passage combines the familiar notion of the remoteness of the gods (they are either in heaven or in the subterranean depths) with doubts about the validity of our moral values. How can we be sure that the gods use the same yardstick that we do when it comes to measuring human integrity? It is not implied that the gods hide their desires and designs on purpose, but that humans are incapable of knowing what the gods mean and what they want.[53] This is the voice of skepticism.

In an attempt to link the skepticism of the *Theodicy* and *Ludlul* to the socioeconomic circumstances of the time, Rainer Albertz has argued that both were written in response to the social transformations that were taking place just then.[54] Sources from the aftermath of the Kassite period speak about repeated occurrences of famine, raids by Aramaeans and Sutaeans, and a central authority seriously impaired by local manifestations of insubordination.[55] The emergence of a new upper class and the demise of the traditional aristocracy fostered a climate in which doubts about divine justice were rampant. The theological expression of these doubts emphasizes the transcendence of the gods and the insufficiency of the human intellect to know them. This religious skepticism, then, would be a phenomenon typical of the decades surrounding the end of the Kassite era.

Two considerations impair this theory. A first objection is the fact that no one historical period has a monopoly on social turmoil. It is true that the early post-Kassite era was a time of unrest, economic distress, and social uncertainty, but it is not difficult to point to other times that witnessed disturbance on a comparable scale; if one has an eye for it, almost every period contains evidence to the effect that society was going through incisive changes. The ubiquity of social crisis imperils the explanatory power of the theory that regards the *Theodicy* and *Ludlul* as typical products of the turbulent years of the twelfth century B.C.E.

The second objection concerns the date of the two compositions; as it is, the evidence for a twelfth-century date is not entirely satisfactory. Though the possibility has never been seriously considered, the *Theodicy* could be from the first millennium B.C.E.[56] And while *Ludlul* is likely from the late Kassite period, it has a precursor from Ugarit (ca. 1400 B.C.E.) that itself is likely to go back to an Old Babylonian forerunner.[57] The subject matter, in other words, is hardly the exclusive property of any one particular period.

The second tenet of the skepticism theory is that the revelation paradigm is primarily a means of conferring plausibility on contested traditions. This assumption is far from compelling. As a rule, periods of social crisis are apt to elicit manifestations of faith as much as they foster skepticism. Skepticism, moreover, does not necessarily lead to disaffection from tradition and its institutions. It is difficult to believe that the argument from authority, or divine revelation, would persuade Mesopotamian skeptics to put their faith in the experts who handled the tradition.

Instead of looking for a cause in the social history of Mesopotamia, it may be preferable to explain the emergence of the revelation paradigm as a consequence of the shift in the tradition from the oral to the written.[58] The hypothesis that takes the revelation paradigm as a consequence of literacy is based on the following considerations. So long as religious lore is the oral treasure of a society of specialists, it is in a way impervious to criticism. Oral traditions are characteristically in a state of flux; research in oral cultures shows that the alleged antiquity of the tradition does not inhibit its spokesmen from adapting and reshaping it as they see fit. The tradition is the preserve of the specialists who keep and maintain it; the audience is unable to check the version of the performing expert against the original, for there simply is no "original."

Once the knowledge of the experts has been put down in writing, the tradition obtains an existence outside the mind of the initiate. The transition from an oral to a written tradition is neither abrupt nor complete; for centuries the written tradition runs alongside the oral one, the one fructifying and supporting the other and vice versa.[59] Yet at some point the written tradition takes the lead; from that moment on, new experts are formed on the basis of textual instruction. Quotation becomes a means of persuasion; the phrase "it is written" gives additional force to an argument.[60] The oral lore does not die, but its authority is subordinate to that of the written texts. As the tradition develops a separate identity in the process of codification, its users are faced with a problem of legitimacy.

My explanation assumes that the decisive turning point in the balance between the oral and the written occurred around 1300 B.C.E.; from that time on, orality gave way to writing as the first source of authority. An important indicator of the change is the cuneiform lexicographical tradition. A study of the lexicographical texts from before 1300 B.C.E. shows that oral instruction played a central role in the training of scribes. Students wrote from dictation, while teachers used their memory rather than a textbook. From 1200 B.C.E. on, the lexicographical texts occur in a stabilized form that remains essentially the same for centuries. From that moment on, students began to acquire their knowledge by copying texts rather than listening to a teacher; the master copy took the place of the master.[61]

The evidence of the lexicographical lists is contemporaneous with the evidence for attempts at creating a kind of literary canon. Under the Second Dynasty of Isin (ca. 1150–1030), Esagil-kīn-apli published the authorized text of the diagnostic compendium *Sakikkû* in a standard series of forty tablets.[62] In the same period, Sin-leqe-unnini made a new edition of *Gilgamesh* meant to take the place of all earlier and diverging versions.[63] We know that the astrological series *Enūma Anu Enlil* also reached its canonical shape in the late second millennium.[64] In conjunction with the publication of the authorized series, Esagil-kīn-apli redesigned the curriculum for the exorcists on the basis of reference works and textbooks. Although writing and written texts had been characteristic features of Mesopotamian civilization since the early third millennium, the culture went through a development in which written texts ousted the oral tradition from its privileged place.

Once the written tradition supplanted oral knowledge, it needed an authority that did not derive from those who transmitted it. The problem facing the scribes was legitimacy rather than credibility. Once the written texts came to serve as the standard of tradition, the tradition could not derive its authority from the experts who used the texts. The scribes found their new source of authority in the concept of divine revelation. Through the construct of an antediluvian revelation from Ea to the *apkallu*s, transmitted in an unbroken chain of sages, scribes, and scholars, the written tradition could claim a legitimacy issuing from the gods.

In support of the theory that the revelation paradigm was an answer to a legitimacy problem, one can point to the emergence of the rhetoric of secrecy.[65] At about the same time that the Mesopotamian scribes and scholars began to speak of the tradition as having been revealed, they started to emphasize its secret nature. An early literary expression of the turn to esoteric knowledge is the standard version of *Gilgamesh*. By means of several expansions, the editor turned Gilgamesh into someone who had been initiated into secrets from before the Flood. Both the cuneiform tradition and modern scholarship assign these changes in the epic to ca. 1100 B.C.E.

Another indication of the scholarly preoccupation with secret lore is furnished by the so-called secrecy colophons. These colophons qualify the texts as "privileged information," using the terms *nişirtu* (from *naṣāru,* "to guard, to preserve") and *pirištu* (from *parāsu,* "to cut off, to separate"); the one term emphasizes that the text is secret, the other that it is exclusive. The secrecy colophons add that the texts are for initiates only, the classic term for "initiate" being *mūdû,* literally "the one who knows, the expert" (from *idû,* "to know"). This is what a standard secrecy colophon looks like:

> Secret of the scholars. The initiate may show it only to another initiate; the noninitiate may not see it. Forbidden thing of the gods.[66]

This type of colophon is characteristic of first-millennium texts and flourished particularly in Neo-Assyrian times. It made its first appearance, however, toward the end of the second millennium. The earliest examples are from the library of Tiglath-pileser I (ca. 1114–1076) and from late-second-millennium B.C.E. Nippur.[67]

To qualify a text as a revelation is not exactly the same thing as to say that it is secret. On the contrary, one might argue that once something is revealed, it is no longer a secret. And yet the notions of revelation and secrecy are intimately connected in the cuneiform tradition, both in time and in their reference to written lore. I would suggest that they both are related to the shift from the oral to the written. To legitimize the written tradition, the Mesopotamian scholars qualified it as divine revelation; to preserve their privileged position as brokers of revealed knowledge, they declared it to be secret knowledge. The insistence on secrecy became necessary when the tradition began to circulate in writing, for as Plato said, "It is not possible that what is written down should not get divulged."[68]

That the prohibition against disclosure meant that the general public was wholly ignorant of the written lore of the specialists is doubtful. In the history of religions, "secrets" often turn out to have been public secrets.[69] The motto of secrecy was mainly a matter of rhetoric; the rate of literacy in Mesopotamia was too low for written lore to be in danger of excessive dissemination. Nevertheless, the injunction not to show the text to outsiders served its purpose so long as it gave insiders the idea that they belonged to the happy few. The principal function of the secrecy colophon was to preserve a sense of privilege among the experts.[70]

If the real target group of the secrecy colophons was the society of scholars themselves, it stands to reason that the revelation paradigm was addressed to them in the first place as well. Both the revelation paradigm and the ethics of secrecy were scribal constructs to convince the scholars of the time of the validity of their written lore and of the privilege of their profession. There was no need to persuade the public; the ancient Mesopotamians consulted their specialists as doggedly as we turn to our doctors, therapists, and lawyers, whether they solve our problems or not. Once the professional lore of the Mesopotamian scholars had become written lore, both the status of the knowledge and the position of the experts had to be reinvented, so to speak. Revelation was a construct of scribes for an audience of scribes, just as scribes enjoined secrecy on other scribes for the benefit of all who belonged to the scribal profession.

The Written Torah as Revelation

The insights gained from a study of the Mesopotamian evidence provide an interesting angle from which to approach the concept of revelation in the Hebrew Bible. In attempting to determine when the revelation paradigm was applied to written texts in Israel, we will work from my hypothesis, developed on the basis of the cuneiform material, that this moment coincides with the development of the written tradition into the primary source of authority.

The biblical record of the history of Israel and Judah tells about many priests and prophets who provided oral instruction to the people and their leaders; they disclosed God's designs through advice, oracles, and sermons. The first time the historians refer to a book as a source of instruction, however, is on the occasion of the cult reform of King Josiah in 622. The biblical narrative about this event attests to a turning point in the relationship between the oral and written traditions.

According to the account in 2 Kings 22–23, the priest Hilkiah was searching in the temple for silver when he discovered "the Book of the Torah" (*sēper ḥattôrâ*, 1 Kings 22:8; 2 Chron 34:14). He reported the find to the royal secretary Shaphan, who in turn informed King Josiah (1 Kings 22:8–10). Josiah had the book brought and read to him. On hearing the text of the Torah, the King realized that he and his forebears had long been acting against God's commandments. He therefore decided to carry out a reform: cult symbols of deities other than Yahweh were destroyed, local sanctuaries were burned, and the Passover festival was celebrated in accordance with the rites as God had prescribed them (2 Kings 23). When he centralized the cult in Jerusalem, King Josiah took his cue from a written text; the Book of the Torah had proved traditional custom to be corrupt; the oral lore of the specialists stood corrected by a book.

This outline of Josiah's reform is based on the second book of Kings, which closes the larger work of the Deuteronomistic History. Since the Deuteronomistic History achieved its final form during the Babylonian Exile, it is theoretically possible that the notion of a book as the basis for a reform is a secondary construct; it is even conceivable that the reform in question is a later fiction. The archaeological record, however, indicates that Josiah did indeed carry out a reform, even if it was less comprehensive in its effects than the author of Kings intimates.[71] We have, moreover, the testimony of Jeremiah, who was active as a prophet from the reign of Josiah onward (Jer 1:1). In an early oracle he joins issue with opponents who refer to the Torah of Yahweh as something they possess in writing (Jer 8:8–9).[72] Jeremiah also attacked those who took the temple of Jerusalem to be *the* house of Yahweh and therefore an inviolable safe haven (Jer 7, 26). By this witness, the doctrine of the Jerusalem temple as the single legitimate place of worship and the existence of a written Torah both go back to the days of Josiah.

The combined evidence of 2 Kings 22–23 and the Book of Jeremiah implies the existence, toward the end of the seventh century B.C.E., of a book known as "the Book of the Torah" or "the Torah of Yahweh." In 1805, Wilhelm de Wette made a convincing case for identifying this

Book of the Torah with Deuteronomy.[73] Cult centralization, icono-
clasm, and the Passover sacrifice are indeed central to both the Book of
Deuteronomy (Deut 12, 16:1–8) and Josiah's reform. After the discovery by De Wette, it took almost another century before Bible scholars
decided that the book that Jeremiah had denounced as a fraud must
also be identified with Deuteronomy.[74] Once the connection had been
made, the identification seemed obvious; the reason it took so long was
the reluctance on the part of many scholars to admit that one book of
the Bible would qualify another book of the Bible as a fraud.

The qualification of Deuteronomy as a fraud is not my point,
though; what I want to demonstrate is the connection between the reference to a book as an ultimate source of authority and the invocation
of the revelation paradigm. We know that the Book of the Torah that
Josiah referred to is to be identified with Deuteronomy; if my theory is
correct, then, we should expect to find in Deuteronomy a reference to
its own status as revelation. Such references are indeed not lacking;
they are most explicit in the second edition of the text, which I have
dubbed the Torah Edition, a product of the early exilic period.

In the Torah Edition, the Book of Deuteronomy opens with the rubric of Deut 4:44:

This is the Torah which Moses set before the children of Israel.

It ends in Deut 29:28 with a conclusion that reads like a colophon:

The hidden things belong to Yahweh our God; but the things that have
been revealed belong to us and to our children, that we may do all the
words of this Torah.

In the presentation of the Torah Edition, then, the text of Deuteronomy
is a Torah—that is, an instruction—by Moses, the legendary founder of
the nation; that instruction, moreover, is not based on human insight
but has been revealed (a passive form of the verb *gālâ*) by God.

The perspective of the Torah Edition comes to the fore in more elaborate fashion in its opening chapter, now Deut 5:1–6:3. Here the editor makes a distinction between the revelation God gave publicly and the revelation that He granted Moses in private. God spoke the Ten Words in the presence of all the Israelites (Deut 5:22); afterward, however, He spoke to Moses alone and revealed to him all the "rules and verdicts" he was to teach his people (Deut 5:28–31). In this view, Deuteronomy is the Torah that Moses wrote not long before he died, on the basis of the revelation God had given to him on Mt. Horeb.

The Torah Edition of Deuteronomy combines the doctrine of a revelation in writing with a characteristic "book awareness." Although the reference to Moses writing down his Torah does not occur before Deut 31:9, the closing sections of the Torah Edition, to be found in the last part of Deuteronomy 28 and all of Deuteronomy 29, emphasize that the Torah has become a book: "all the words of this Torah which are written in this book" (Deut 28:58); "the book of this Torah" (Deut 28:61); "all the curses of the covenant written in this book of the Torah" (Deut 29:20; cf. 29:19, 29:26). These expressions are at odds with the fiction that Deuteronomy is a valedictory oration; this is Moses the author speaking. The scribes of the Torah Edition thought of Deuteronomy as a book containing a revelation, and they put their conception in the mouth of Moses.

Though allegedly written by Moses, the Book of Deuteronomy did not see the light before the reform of Josiah in 622 B.C.E.; the story of its spectacular discovery in the temple is an invention designed to convey a false aura of antiquity. The parallel with *Enūma eliš* is striking: *Enūma eliš* presents itself as the work of an anonymous Ancient who wrote down what the gods revealed to him; Deuteronomy refers to Moses as the author who wrote down what Yahweh had revealed to him. In both cases we are dealing with a theological innovation—the promotion of Marduk to the summit of the pantheon, in the first case; the restriction of cultic worship to Jerusalem, in the second—presented as an ancient revelation. The notions of antiquity and revelation reinforce each other. In reality, Deuteronomy is a recent text and the notion of revelation it promotes is a scribal construct formulated in the early sixth century B.C.E.

The Jeremiah oracle about the Torah of Yahweh (Jer 8:8–9) demonstrates that the notion of a book as divine revelation was already familiar in the late seventh century.

> How can you say, "We are sages,
> and we possess the Torah of Yahweh"?
> Assuredly, the deceitful pen of the scribes
> Has turned it into a deception!
> The sages shall be put to shame,
> they shall be dismayed and caught.
> For they have rejected the word of Yahweh,
> so what kind of wisdom is theirs?
>
> Jer 8:8–9

The prophet speaks about a written document, produced by scribes, qualified as Torah, and attributed to Yahweh. The scribes proclaimed the book to be a revelation, because they referred to it as "the Torah of Yahweh." As a source of authority, it has obviously supplanted the oral tradition, since those who proclaim themselves "sages" derive their wisdom from the possession of the written law; instead of boasting of their mastery of the oral lore of their profession, they exult in their access to a written text.

Deuteronomy, Jeremiah, and the Deuteronomistic History speak about Deuteronomy as Torah revealed in writing. Deuteronomy was not the first manifestation of a written tradition of laws and customs, however. Since much of Deuteronomy is in fact a revision of the Covenant Code, now incorporated in the Book of Exodus (chapters 21–23), the book stands in a tradition of written law.[75] The innovation of Deuteronomy lies not in the fact of its being written Torah, then, but in its claim to be a source of authority overruling the oral tradition. Until Deuteronomy, the written word had been an aid in the oral transmission of the tradition; Deuteronomy stands for a reversal of roles: it turns oral exposition into a handmaid of the written text.

Once the written Law supplanted the oral Torah as the primary source of authority, the concept of revelation became a subject of theoretical reflection. Jewish scholars from the Hellenistic period developed a theology of the Torah and, by the same token, of revelation. Drawing on the imagery of Proverbs 8, Job 28, and Deuteronomy 30:12–14, Ben Sira equated the Torah with Wisdom personified (Sir 24).[76] Issued from the mouth of God, Wisdom came down from heaven and received a resting place in Jerusalem, where she invites all those who desire her to eat their fill of her produce. "All this," Ben Sira writes, "is the book of the covenant of the Most High God" (Sir 24:23). The Book of Baruch, a pseudonymous work of the late second century B.C.E., also takes "the book of the commandments of God" (Bar 4:1) as the ultimate embodiment of wisdom. The author alludes in unmistakable fashion to Deuteronomy 30:12–14 ("Who has gone up to heaven and taken her? . . . Who has gone over the sea and found her?" Bar 3:29) as corroborating evidence for his argument.

The rabbinical theology of the Torah developed two other notions. The sages focused on the preexistence of the Torah, and they speculated about the way in which the divine Torah came within human reach. The doctrine of the preexistence of the Torah is foreshadowed in Ben Sira's reference to its having been created "from eternity, in the beginning" (Sir 24:9). Rabbi Aqiba picked up the idea and argued that the Torah was "the instrument by which the world has been created."[77] The *Midrash Rabbah* on Genesis understands this to mean that God consulted the Torah before He created the world, much like a craftsman consults his parchments and tablets before he starts building (*Midr. Rab. Gen* 1/1). This image implies that the Torah contains information from which even God can learn; such is indeed the idea underlying the view that God spends the first hours of each day studying the Torah (*b. Ab. Zar.* 3b).

Faced with the problem of explaining the transfer of the Torah from heaven to the human realm, the sages offered different solutions. These imply different modes of revelation. The more traditional view holds that God revealed the Torah to Moses using the mode of dictation. "The Holy One, Blessed be He, dictated; Moses repeated; and Moses wrote" (*b. B. Bat.* 15a). Because Moses was a meticulous scribe, he made a transcript of God's words that was faithful to the smallest detail; even the tiniest dot is from God (*b. Sanh.* 99a). Another view takes it that Moses received the Torah through the mediation of angels (Acts 7:53; Heb 2:2). This theory implies that Moses himself did not write it, but that he received a heavenly copy of the Torah. The two views concur, however, in assigning to Moses a role of receptor rather than mediator: revelation has become an act of God in which the human party is a passive instrument.

The Prophets as Revealed Literature

So far this history of the concept of revelation in Israel has focused on the Torah, the Book of the Torah being, first, a designation of Deuteronomy and, second, a name of the first section of the Hebrew Bible (Genesis through Deuteronomy). What I want to look at now are the books of the prophets.

The thesis that underlies my historical analysis assumes that the revelation paradigm is invoked when written texts supplant the oral tradition as the principal source of authority and the main channel of information. In the area of prophecy, this moment occurs later than it does with the Torah. To understand the emergence of the revelation paradigm in connection with the prophetic literature, we must establish both when this literature came into being and when it came to supplant the spoken delivery of oracles as the principal conduit of prophecy.

The earliest prophetic collection of the Bible that presents itself explicitly as a book is the Book of Jeremiah. According to the narrative in Jeremiah 36, the scribe Baruch made a complete transcript of the prophecies of Jeremiah, which he wrote down in a scroll. Whether fact or fiction, the story proves the existence of a written oracle collection attributed to Jeremiah. Elsewhere in Jeremiah, too, there is evidence that the composers of the text were deliberately creating a book. The text repeatedly refers to itself as a scroll (*sēper*; see in addition to Jer 36, Jer 25:13, 30:2, 45:1, 51:60). In the narrative of Ezekiel's calling, dated in 592 B.C.E., God makes the prophet eat a scroll containing all the words he was to prophesy (Ezek 2:8–3:4). In this conception of prophecy, the oracles existed in writing even before the prophet pronounced them; he became the mouthpiece of a book.⁷⁸ The evidence shows that prophetic books had become a normal phenomenon in the early sixth century B.C.E.

As is clear from both the cuneiform texts and the Hebrew Torah, the emergence of written texts need not entail the simultaneous eclipse of an oral tradition. Applied to the phenomenon of prophecy, this means that the literary fixation of oracles need not replace prophets performing orally. Some of the exilic and post-exilic oracle collections from the Bible may have originated in writing (Deutero-Isaiah is a case in point), but it is unlikely that Joel, Haggai, Zechariah, and Malachi were books from the start. Most commentators understand these collections as literary reflections of oral performances. At any rate, the references to prophets in Nehemiah 6:7 and 6:14 demonstrate that oral prophecy was still alive in the Persian era. The emergence of written prophecy, then, did not immediately reduce oral prophecy to a subordinate position; until the mid-fifth century, prophets were still performing.

In the second century B.C.E., however, the books of the prophets had taken the place of the prophets themselves. According to a text from about 160 B.C.E., Daniel understood "from the books" *(bassĕpārîm)* the number of years Jeremiah had given as the time of Jerusalem's desolation (Dan 9:2). Instead of turning to a living prophet, Daniel consulted a book. In the Prologue to Ben Sira, the grandson of the author refers to "the Law, and the Prophets, and the other books" (Prologue Ben Sira, lines 24–25)—implying that to him the prophets were first and foremost books. Ben Sira himself mentions Isaiah, Jeremiah, Ezekiel, and the Twelve in his Praise of the Fathers (Sir 48:22–25, 49:7–10). He knew these men from the scrolls that carried their names, as is apparent from the citation of the Malachi postscript (Mal 3:22–24) in Sir 48:10. By the second century B.C.E., then, the authority of the prophets had passed on to their books.

The publication of the Scroll of the Twelve in the third century B.C.E. marked the increasing impact of written prophecy. As I shall argue at some length in Chapter 9, the publication of the Minor Prophets in one book—physically a scroll—amounted to a declaration by the scribes that the era of prophecy had come to an end. That is why they created a twelfth prophet, by attributing several anonymous oracles to a fictitious prophet by the name of Malachi. Twelve is the number of plenitude and completeness; as the last prophet of the Twelve, Malachi concluded the prophetic era. To judge by the internal evidence, the Scroll of the Twelve did not see the light before the Hellenistic age, which means that it came into being in the third century.

As the term "Prophets" came to designate a collection of scrolls, the Hebrew scribes began to develop a new understanding of the prophetic experience. This new conception of prophecy comes to the fore in the apocalyptic literature of the late third and the early second centuries B.C.E. In the modern appreciation of biblical genres, there is quite a difference between prophecy and apocalypticism.[79] Although there is no point in denying the distance between the two, it is important to understand that the apocalyptic literature reflects a particular perception of prophecy. Those who wrote under the names of Enoch and Daniel were trying to imitate the prophetic genre. The fact that they produced something quite distinct from traditional prophecy shows that their perception of prophecy bears all the marks of their own time.[80]

Let us take, as key witnesses, the Book of the Watchers (1 Enoch 1–36, third century B.C.E.) and the Book of Daniel (ca. 160 B.C.E.). These texts present Enoch and Daniel as scribes and sages rather than prophets in the vein of Elijah. The author of the Book of the Watchers calls Enoch "the scribe of righteousness" (1 Enoch 12:4, 15:1; compare 92:1) and describes him more than once in the act of writing or reading (1 Enoch 13:4, 6; 14:4; 33:3, 4). Daniel had received a scribal formation (Dan 1:4) and had knowledge of all sorts of writings (Dan 1:17). Enoch and Daniel owe their special wisdom to visions; transported into the heavens, they are able to see hidden matters and to converse with angels. Their god is a "heavenly God who reveals mysteries" (Dan 2:28; compare 2:47). In the perception of the scribes of the Hellenistic period, then, prophets were sages who had seen heavenly secrets; their books are filled with superior wisdom, to be grasped by illuminated readers (1 Enoch 5:8; compare Hos 14:10).[81]

Both in Daniel and in the Book of the Watchers, the rhetoric of revelation occurs in conjunction with an emphasis on writing as the primary vehicle of prophecy. Daniel and Enoch recorded their visions in a book (1 Enoch 14:1, 14:7; Dan 7:1, 12:4). Books were important, too, in their visionary experiences. The future that Daniel saw in his visions was written in heavenly books (Dan 10:21, 12:1); the apocalyptic experience permitted the prophet to read those books. At the same time, we find him consulting the books of the prophets of the past (Dan 9:2). Enoch, for his part, could look up the names, the laws, and the companies of the stars in the text the angel Uriel had written for him (1 Enoch 33:4). In more than one way, then, books are prominent in these Hellenistic texts.[82] The Book of the Watchers and Daniel exhibit a focus on the written word that reflects a transfer of prestige from the spoken oracle to the prophetic book.

The new conception of prophecy affected the way in which the scribes viewed the prophets of the past, which is reflected in the superscriptions to the prophetic collections.[83] When prophecy became primarily a literary genre, the prophets were posthumously transformed into authors. Though early oracle collections include some scattered references to prophets writing (Isa 8:1, 30:8; Hab 2:3), the Chronicler is the first to systematically present the prophets as authors. He describes the prophet Isaiah as the writer of a chronicle about Uzziah (2 Chron 26:22; compare 32:32) and the prophet Jeremiah as the author of Lamentations (2 Chron 35:25; compare Josephus, *Ant.*, 10.5.1). In addition to Isaiah and Jeremiah, the Chronicler refers to works written by "Samuel the Seer" (1 Chron 29:29); "Nathan the Prophet" (1 Chron 29:29, 2 Chron 9:29); "Gad the Seer" (1 Chron 29:29); "Ahijah the Shilonite" (2 Chron 9:29); "Iddo the Seer" (2 Chron 9:29, 12:15; cf. 13:22); and "Shemaiah the Prophet" (2 Chron 12:15). The attribution of historiography and liturgical laments to the prophets demonstrates that the prophets had come to be perceived as men of letters.

When the Hebrew scribes adopted the revelation paradigm in connection with the prophetic literature, they took the vision *(ḥāzôn)* to be the classic mode of prophetic revelation. That is why the rubrics of the prophetic books often use the terminology of the visionary experience as the technical vocabulary for prophecy, even for prophets whose oracles do not refer to any vision (Isa 1:1, 2:1; Amos 1:1; Hab 1:1; Ob 1; Nah 1:1; compare 2 Chron 32:32). This particular construction of the prophetic experience is related to the legitimizing accounts contained in the prophetical scrolls. The calling narratives of the prophets, inserted in their books as proof of their credentials, are often related to visionary experiences in which the prophet communicates with God (Isa 6). The scribes have turned this element of the prophetic experience into a kind of dogma of prophetic revelation.

There should be no mistake about the antiquity of the notion of revelation in connection with prophecy; prophets have always claimed to act as the mouthpiece of God. The novelty of the scribal construct of prophecy as a revelation lies in the reference to written texts. The scribes developed the notion of the prophet as a scribe, and of his message as a secret revealed by heavenly figures, to legitimize the fact that the prophets had become books. Prophets were men of the past; the scribes had taken their place. The only way in which God would now speak to human beings was through the written text.

Conclusion

In the title of this chapter I call revelation a "scribal construct." It will be clear by now that this expression was not intended to mean that scribes invented the notion of revelation as such; their invention was rather in the nature of a radical transformation. They used the concept of revelation as an epistemological category to qualify a body of literature. By identifying revelation with a circumscribed group of texts, the scribes shifted the focus of the concept. Until then revelation had been understood as an interaction between superhuman beings and human individuals in which the former imparted knowledge to the latter; in the conception developed by the scribes, revelation became an object rather than an interaction: it was coterminous with a set of texts.

The shift of focus had implications for those who had acted as mediators of revelation in the past. The charismatics of old, whether prophets, priests, or sages, were posthumously transformed into scribes. Some might think of Isaiah or Jeremiah as the authors of their books, but in the scribal construct of revelation, the real author is God. The emphasis on the status of the text as revelation meant that its presumed author had actually been writing down dictation; Adapa wrote what Ea said, just as Moses transcribed the words of God. The mediator became a mere channel; not an author and composer, but a scribe and transcriber.

The trigger for the new scribal concept was the increasing importance of the written text as a medium of information, to the detriment of the oral tradition. The book became the norm, as illustrated by the account of Josiah's reform. Textbooks supplanted oral lore as the main source of instruction and reference. The growing reliance on the written tradition required a legitimization. The scribes found such legitimacy in the construct of revelation.

The consequences of the new concept of revelation have been tremendous. Once the text became a revelation instead of an aid to the expert or an archival record, it turned into a store of hidden treasures and secret meanings. The scribal doctrine of revelation spawned an exegetical tradition in which the quest for the meaning of a text came to resemble an oracular inquiry. The book became an icon, and reading and copying, acts of devotion. By redefining the concept of revelation, the Hebrew scribes laid the foundations for a cult of the book, the repercussions of which are still perceptible in the modern reception of the Bible.

chapter nine

CONSTRUCTING THE CANON

The Closure of the Hebrew Bible

Throughout this book we have looked at the making of the Hebrew Bible from the perspective of the Hebrew scribes; we now conclude with an account of the canon, because the canon is the final act in the making of the Bible. The previous chapters have demonstrated that the books of the Hebrew Bible are products from the scribal workshop. However, the production history behind the books of the Bible does not explain how the separate scrolls became one book, and why this one book—and this book only—had canonical status. Why precisely this collection of texts, to the exclusion of others? And whence did they derive their claim to canonicity?

To speak about the canon of the Hebrew Bible is a little awkward, since the very term is a Christian coinage.[1] The dictionaries show that Greek *kanōn* developed the meaning of "table." Astronomical tables, for instance, could be referred to as *kanones*. In ecclesiastical usage, the *kanōn* is a table or list of books received by the church as divine revelation. The first examples of such a list are from the second century C.E.[2] Employed in the sense of "list" or "table," the term *kanōn* can alternate with the word *katalogos*, "catalogue."[3] A "canon" or a "catalogue" gives the number, the names, and the order of the books.[4]

Without calling it a canon, Jewish scholars of the Common Era were familiar with the phenomenon of an authoritative list of books. A discussion in the Babylonian Talmud about the order and the authors of the works of the Hebrew Bible lists twenty-four books; the Twelve Minor Prophets are counted as one, and Ezra-Nehemiah as well (*b. B. Bat.* 14b–15a). Though the Talmud is a document from later times, it here preserves an early tradition.

Two testimonies from the first century C.E. prove the antiquity of the Talmudic list of canonical books. In his elegant defense of Judaism, Flavius Josephus contrasts the "myriads of inconsistent books" of the nations with the twenty-two books of the Jewish people ("our books") that are "justifiably relied upon" *(dikaiōs pepisteumena)* (*C. Ap.* 1.38–40). The second text is found in an apocalyptic work attributed to Ezra. It records how Ezra, under divine inspiration, dictated the text of ninety-four lost works of Moses to five scribes. Twenty-four books he made public so that they might be read by "the worthy and the unworthy" alike; the remaining seventy he kept under seal for "the wise" (2 Esdras 14:44–46). The twenty-four books of Ezra correspond with the twenty-four books of the Bible as counted by the Talmud; the twenty-two books mentioned by Josephus probably refer to the same books in a different count and a different division.[5] By specifying the number of the books, both Josephus and the author of 2 Esdras 14:44–46 implicitly rely on a list.

It is important to acknowledge that the canon is originally a list and not a volume. We think of the Bible as a book, but the physical shape of a book goes back to the codex, and the earliest codex of the Hebrew Bible that we have is the Aleppo codex from the ninth century C.E. Earlier evidence of the Bible in the form of a codex concerns the Greek version only.[6] The Hebrew Bible was a list before it was a book. In view of the *numerus fixus* given in several first-century C.E. texts, moreover, the list was apparently considered to be closed. The question, then, is how did this list come about?

The classic view of the history behind the biblical canon is the so-called three-stage theory developed in 1871 by the German scholar Heinrich Graetz and elaborated and disseminated in the works of Frants

Buhl, Gerrit Wildeboer, and Herbert E. Ryle.[7] It assumes that the Bible was canonized in three phases: first the Law (Hebrew *tôrâ*, also known as the five books of Moses, from Genesis through Deuteronomy), then the Prophets (Hebrew *nĕbî'îm*, consisting of the former and the latter prophets; that is, the historical books and the prophetical collections), and finally the Writings (Hebrew *kĕtûbîm*). The entire process took some 500 years and was brought to a close in 100 C.E. by a rabbinical meeting at Jamnia known in the literature as the Council of Jamnia; there the Jewish authorities reached an agreement on the boundaries of the canon.

Today this theory of canonization is no longer in favor with the scholarly community. Its fatal flaw is the alleged Council of Jamnia. A critical reading of the rabbinical sources has led most scholars to conclude that there never was a Council of Jamnia; it is a historical chimera of dubious Christian inspiration.[8] Because the Council of Jamnia is not a historical detail but the cornerstone of the theory, its dismissal disqualifies the theory as a whole. The history of the canonization of the Hebrew Bible has to be written anew. Most biblical scholars are well aware of this challenge, but they are hardly of one mind about the way to handle it.

In reaction against the classic theory of canonization, there is a widespread tendency today to explain canonization as an organic process. The following sentences from *The Oxford Dictionary of the Jewish Religion* are fairly typical.

> No record exists . . . of a particular time and place at which the biblical canon was established, and no single authoritative institution ever existed in Jewish history that would have had the power to establish the canon. Rather, the canonization of the Bible was a natural, gradual process, by which those writings popularly believed to be of great antiquity and divinely inspired were accorded sacred status.[9]

Other treatments of the canon, too, describe it as the outcome of "a natural, gradual process."[10] On this view, the canon is the spontaneous creation of the community of the faithful, persuaded as they were by a power intrinsic to the scriptures.

The theory of organic growth presents no great advance over the classic three-stage theory. Though the proponents of the theory avoid theological categories, they promote in fact a close parallel to the Protestant notion of the *logos autopistos,* the "self-authenticating Word."[11] According to this view, the books of the Bible are canonical because of their content; that content has the virtue of persuasion, which is why the books were eventually recognized to be sacred. This theory draws its inspiration from a sense of unease about the notion of authority. The modern ideal of individual freedom and dignity does not sit well with the idea of a canon that requires submission. If the solution is a kind of crypto-fundamentalism, however, the cure is worse than the disease.

Contemporary scholars advance two other models that could serve as an alternative to the three-stage theory. One model is that of the library catalogue; the other is that of the scribal curriculum. The one assumes that the canon derives from the list of books available in the library, more specifically the library attached to the temple in Jerusalem. The other derives the canon from the list of works established for the classroom. Both models are not just models for the process of canonization; they serve as precedents as well. The library catalogue and the school curriculum are presented as the precanonical phase of the books of the Hebrew Bible. Both models relate the canon to institutions intimately associated with the scribal culture of the day, and in this respect they fit the perspective adopted in this book. Let us have a closer look.

The Library Catalogue as Precursor of the Canon

Since the canon is originally a catalogue of sorts, the library catalogue seems to offer a close analogy. Being a collection of books, the Bible compares to a library—a portable library perhaps, but a library nevertheless; St. Jerome called the Bible a "sacred" or "divine" library.[12] In light of such considerations, the library model appears to offer a promising avenue for conceptualizing the canon. Perhaps the books of the Hebrew Bible were once the holdings of the temple library at Jerusalem. Several authors have embraced this theory and used it to explain the nature of the canon and the order of the biblical books.[13]

The library hypothesis—"library hypothesis" being short for the theory that the canon of the Hebrew Bible goes back to the catalogue of the temple library in Jerusalem—is based on three assumptions. According to assumption one, there was a library in the temple at Jerusalem; assumption two says that the holdings of that library were regarded as special, that is, protocanonical, which implies a discriminating acquisition policy on the part of the Jerusalem librarians; and assumption three holds that there was a library catalogue as a precedent of the canon. Let us assess these three assumptions.

The first assumption, namely that there was a library connected to the temple in Jerusalem, seems fairly unproblematic.[14] According to a pseudonymous letter from about 60 B.C.E., cited in the introductory section of the second book of Maccabees (2 Macc 1:10–2:18), there was a temple library (*bibliothēkē* is the Greek word) in Jerusalem.[15] This is what the Jews from Jerusalem wrote to their coreligionists in Alexandria:

> The same things are also reported in the records and in the memoirs of Nehemiah, and also that he founded a library in which he collected the books [*biblia*] about the kings, and of the prophets, and the writings of David, and royal letters about votive offerings. In the same way Judas too collected all the books that had been lost on account of the war that had come upon us; they are in our possession. So if you should lack some of them [in your collection], send people to get them for you.
>
> 2 Macc 2:13–15

The letter mentions Nehemiah as the founder of the library and Judas Maccabee as the one who replenished its holdings by collecting all the books that had been lost during the war. Proud of their well-stocked library, the authors of the letter extend an invitation to the Jews in Alexandria to have copies made of those books lacking in the Alexandrian collection. Though the founding of the library by Nehemiah may belong to the realm of legend, the library's existence in Jerusalem seems assured.

The evidence for a temple library in Jerusalem is not confined to the reference in 2 Macc 2:13–15. The report of the discovery of the Book of the Law by the priest Hilkiah (2 Kings 22) presupposes the practice of keeping books in the temple in the pre-exilic period. Another witness to a temple archive or library is the story of Samuel depositing a scroll (*sēper*) recording the rules of the monarchy in the sanctuary ("before Yahweh," 1 Sam 10:25); the narrative probably projects later customs back onto the time of the incipient monarchy. Parallels to the temple library of Jerusalem abound, both in the Near East and in the classical world. In the words of Moshe Greenberg, "The existence of a temple library . . . is a commonplace in the ancient Near East; indeed, it would have been odd had the Jews not had such an archive at Jerusalem."[16]

If the existence of a library connected to the Second Temple can be accepted as a historical fact, it remains to be established what kind of institution it was. In our minds, the term *library* designates, more or less by definition, a public library. Before the Hellenistic era, however, public libraries were unknown.[17] Temple libraries were not public, even though we would define temples as public institutions. Not all temple areas were open to the public. Access to the library was limited to authorized personnel only. For Mesopotamia, this fact comes to the fore in the colophons appended to copies housed in the library. They often specify that the tablet in question is sacred property of the temple. It was secret lore and accessible only to the initiate.[18]

The fact that the libraries of antiquity were not public blurs the distinction between library and archive. Most of these libraries were not libraries in our sense of the word; they were storage rooms for precious objects, some of which were written texts. According to Josephus, the priest Hilkiah (Eliakias, as he has it) found the sacred books of Moses as he was bringing out the gold and silver from the temple treasuries.[19] Josephus thus establishes a link between the library of the temple and its treasuries. Other evidence points to the same connection. According to Ezra 6:1, the royal library of Darius, literally "the house of the books" *(bêt siprayyā'),* was also the place where the treasures *(ginzayyā')* were stored. The Talmud says that the king should order two copies of the Law, one for his personal use and one for his treasury *(bêt gĕnîzāw, b. Sanh.* 22a). Copies of official decrees were routinely stored in the temple treasury as well (1 Macc 14:49; compare the reference to "royal letters about votive offerings" in 2 Macc 2:13).[20]

While the existence of a temple library in Jerusalem is not in doubt, its nonpublic character marks a difference between library and canon. Unlike the esoteric books preserved for the privileged few, the twenty-four books of the canon are public property, available to "the worthy and the unworthy" alike (compare 2 Esdras 14:44–46). If the parallel between library and canon is maintained, then, one must assume a transformation of the rules of entry. Strictly speaking, however, assumption number one is borne out by the evidence: the temple at Jerusalem did indeed possess a library.

How about assumption number two? Did the librarians of Jerusalem accept into their collection only books that they judged to be holy and, in a manner of speaking, protocanonical? Proponents of the library theory are quite certain that this was indeed the case. Thus Roger Beckwith, in a monograph on the canonization of the Bible, writes that "the primary reason for laying up books in the Temple was not their liturgical usefulness but their sanctity . . . [U]ncanonical books would not normally be brought into the Temple, which was the place for laying up holy books."[21] Beckwith makes much of the fact that Josephus uses the verb *anakeimai* when he speaks about the "scriptures" being stored in the sanctuary.[22] The verb would imply that the texts in question were regarded as votive offerings, and thus sacred.[23] This argument is not very impressive, since the sanctity conferred on written scrolls housed in the temple does not imply that their contents were canonical. In the oral culture of the ancient Near East, written artifacts, whether scrolls or tablets, were items of value irrespective of their actual content.

We have no evidence about the acquisition policy of the Jerusalem library; in fact, we do not even know what the temple collection contained. The only clues for our speculation on the subject are (1) the summary description of the Jerusalem library holdings in 2 Macc 2:13–15; (2) assumptions about the texts likely to be needed and stored in the temple; and (3) the comparative evidence from the ancient Near East, ranging from the libraries of Mesopotamia and Egypt to the scroll collection of Qumran. Since the comparative evidence yields data about both the actual possessions of libraries and, in some cases, the methods by which the owners built up their collections, it offers the most solid starting point for our investigation.

Ouside of Palestine, there were libraries all over the ancient Near East.[24] They were of two types: while most libraries were what we would call reference libraries, a few were designed as comprehensive libraries, with collections that aimed to be complete.[25] The Mesopotamian temple libraries were nearly all text collections for the use of priests, scribes, and scholars affiliated with the temple; hence the predominance of learned textbooks over works of a more literary nature. The largest temple library discovered so far had some 800 tablets; the private family libraries of exorcists and other scholars were smaller but essentially similar.[26] Temple libraries in Egypt were comparable to the Mesopotamian ones in that they, too, were usually of a modest size.[27] A catalogue from Edfu demonstrates that the temple there had a collection confined to scrolls needed for practical purposes. The list runs to some thirty-five titles; a small room sufficed for the storage of the scrolls.[28]

Compared with the reference libraries of the temples, the palace library (or libraries) of King Assurbanipal belonged to a different world.[29] Being about twenty times as large as a temple library, it could pretend to be comprehensive. King Assurbanipal pursued an aggressive acquisition policy for his collection of texts; in addition to the tablets and writing boards that he confiscated, he had scribes and scholars copy numerous texts.[30] Correspondence between the palace at Nineveh and the scholars of Borsippa and Babylon shows that the king was willing to pay a good price for the texts he commissioned.[31] Administrators kept track of the tablets that came in; in the end, the library had collections totaling some 10,000 tablets.[32] This, then, was a library that aimed to have the complete range of cuneiform science, law, and literature.

It does not seem that Assurbanipal used selection criteria for the texts that entered his libraries other than comprehensiveness. In one letter the king orders his servants to collect every text that is "suitable for my palace (library)."[33] The phrase has been understood to mean "beneficial to my governance," but that is stretching the meaning of the term for "palace" *(ekallu)*.[34] Another letter shows that the king was interested in obtaining "all the scribal learning" *(kullat ṭupšarrūtu)* from the temple libraries of Borsippa and Babylon.[35] Assurbanipal shows a preference for scholarly texts over fiction, but he strikes us primarily as a collector with an "obsessive desire to possess everything."[36] There is no evidence that he was trying to make a canonical or official collection.[37]

The library of Assurbanipal is one of the few Near Eastern libraries of the past that sought to obtain copies of every written work worthy of preservation. The Ptolemaic library of Alexandria falls into the same category; its scope was even more ecumenical. Did the temple library of Jerusalem belong to the same type, or was it a reference library of the kind found in many other temples of the Near East? The answer probably lies in between.

The most important archaeological event for biblical scholarship in the twentieth century was the discovery of the Dead Sea Scrolls at Qumran. This extraordinary collection of texts gives us an idea of what a major Jewish library of the Hellenistic era may have looked like. The Qumran library was, broadly speaking, comprehensive; it contained copies of works with opposite views, such as the Aramaic Levi document, Jubilees, and 1 Enoch, on the one hand, and Ben Sira, on the other.[38] Except for the Scroll of Esther, we know of no Jewish literary text clearly dating from before 150 B.C.E. that was not represented. In fact, Qumran has yielded many Hebrew texts that never made it into the Hebrew Bible. It is theoretically possible that the temple library of Jerusalem was smaller than the library of Qumran. This, however, seems highly unlikely. The authors of the letter quoted in 2 Macc 2:13–15 assume that the Jerusalem library has various works not available to the Jews in Alexandria. Ben Sira was available at Qumran and Alexandria; it must have been present in the Jerusalem library as well. The fact that it was not included in the Hebrew Bible shows that there is no one-to-one correspondence between the Masoretic canon and the holdings of the temple library in Jerusalem.

According to 2 Macc 2:13–15, Nehemiah founded a library in which he collected "the books [*biblia*] about the kings, and of the prophets, and the writings of David, and royal letters about votive offerings." This summary is striking on two accounts. For one, it fails to mention the Torah—that is, the Pentateuch; second, it refers to "royal letters about votive offerings," which we are unable to identify with any texts from the Hebrew Bible. The summary description of the collection is apparently eclectic, since the library surely had a copy of the five books of Moses. In fact, the reference to the royal letters suggests that it contained various texts not found in the Hebrew Bible as we know it. Whether the Jerusalem library had a copy of the corpus of writings attributed to Enoch, as was the case at Qumran, is doubtful. It is unlikely the temple authorities of Jerusalem accepted the authorship of Enoch; that may have been sufficient reason not to admit the texts to their collections. Be that as it may, the temple library of Jerusalem surely contained more texts than those found in the Hebrew Bible.

Assumption number three still remains to be investigated. Can we establish a link between the list of the books of the Hebrew Bible and the catalogue of the Jerusalem library? Despite the presence of libraries all over the Near East, the evidence for actual library catalogues is scant. There are lists and inventories that have been interpreted as library catalogues, but closer inspection shows that they in fact represent four distinct functions, none of which is that of a library catalogue in the modern understanding of that term.[39]

First, some of the Mesopotamian catalogues are in fact curricular lists, that is, enumerations of works to be studied by scribes and scholars to be; I will return to these texts in the discussion of the curriculum hypothesis.[40] Second, other catalogues are lists of texts belonging to one specific genre or to a particular series. A third group of catalogues, dating from the reign of Assurbanipal, are lists of recent library acquisitions. And fourth, some "catalogues" are inventories. Such inventories are comparable to library catalogues in some respects, but they are primarily an account rather than a tool for visitors to the library. There is no proof that the order of the inventory corresponds to the order of the tablets on the shelves.[41] Nahum M. Sarna has proposed to interpret the Talmudic list of the books as a library catalogue (*b. B. Bat.* 14b–15a), but the order is by presumed antiquity rather than disposition on the shelves.[42]

Since there is no conclusive evidence of library catalogues in the ancient Near East, it is difficult to take the biblical canon as the transcript of a library catalogue. The only type of catalogue that really compares to the Hebrew canon is from the West rather than the East. The Hellenistic era saw the emergence of the prescriptive library catalogue, a subcategory of the Greek *pinakes,* "indexes," that were in use as normal library catalogues.[43] Because the selective *pinakes* listed only the foremost among the poets, orators, historians, and philosophers, they functioned in fact as a kind of canon. Those who wished to constitute their own library could use them as a guideline.[44] It has been suggested that the Jewish sages composed the list of Hebrew books in imitation of the Hellenistic lists of exemplary works; such lists being the basis for the canon, the canon would be selective without being exclusionary.[45]

It is doubtful whether the selective catalogues of the Hellenistic era had a formative influence on the canon of the Hebrew Bible. The parallel is primarily relevant for the way in which the canon may have functioned. Most Jews of the early Common Era owed their knowledge of the Hebrew scriptures to their local synagogues. Every Jewish place of worship owned a collection of scrolls used for public readings; every synagogue, in other words, had a reference library. The canon resembles the *pinakes* in that it can be viewed as a list of works ideally present in every synagogue library. If the library hypothesis fails to account for the formation of the Hebrew canon, then, the selective catalogues for a model library may illuminate the way in which the canon functioned in the centuries before the printing press.

If we have to abandon the interpretation of the canon on the basis of the library analogy, does this mean that the library model is entirely without value? I do not think so. The existence of libraries prepared the ground, so to speak, for the emergence of canons. Though the presence of a text in a library need not imply canonicity, it does mean that the text in question had entered the stream of tradition. Libraries embodied the literary and scholarly heritage. And a work had to be perceived as "traditional"—or "ancestral" *(patrōios)*, as the Prologue of Ben Sira has it—as a precondition for becoming canonical. In this sense, inclusion in the library was a condition for inclusion in the canon; however, inclusion in the library was not a ticket to canonization.[46]

The Scribal Curriculum as a Precedent of the Canon

The second model put forth as a way to conceptualize the process of canonization is that of the scribal curriculum. Let me emphasize once again that the curriculum, like the library, serves as a model and a precedent for canonization. It is intended both to illuminate the mechanics of the canonization process and to explain the role of the books of the Bible before they became the books of the Bible. Whereas the library hypothesis says that they were library books, the curriculum hypothesis takes them as textbooks.[47]

Between a school curriculum and a library catalogue there is an obvious similarity. Both are lists of texts with a claim to the status of "classics." Within this general correspondence, there is room for a distinction, however, given that the curriculum is selective whereas the library is not. Since every study program is by definition constrained by limitations of time and means, we know that the scribal curriculum could accommodate only a limited number of works. If only for practical reasons, it was subject to closure.

Precisely because a curriculum is subject to closure, texts are in competition for a place. Unlike a place in a library, inclusion in a curriculum asserts the superiority of a written text over other texts. In this respect, the scribal curriculum could be viewed as a laboratory from which the canon was issued. The case of newly created texts offers a good illustration of the process. New texts have to vie with other compositions, both from the past and from their own time, for a place in the stream of tradition. Take a newcomer among the classics of Mesopotamia: *Enūma eliš,* written at the end of the second millennium. It is an ancient text by our standards, but young by comparison with *Gilgamesh* and the story of the Flood.

The postscript of *Enūma eliš* makes it clear that the composer hoped his text would achieve lasting fame through its use in scribal education. Just after celebrating Marduk by means of an ingenious exegesis of his fifty names, the poet adds:

> The wise and the learned should ponder them together,
> The teacher should repeat them and make the pupil learn by heart.
> The ears of the shepherd and the herdsman should be open
> In order not to neglect Marduk, the champion of the gods,
> That his land may prosper and he himself be safe . . .
> This is the revelation which an Ancient, to whom it was told,
> wrote down and established for posterity to hear . . .
>
> *Enūma eliš,* VII:145–150, 157–158

Preservation in writing does not guarantee admission to the ranks of the classics. That is achieved by "establishing" the text for future generations to hear. The verb here translated as "established" *(šakānu)* is used for putting a text on the scribal curriculum, which is likely what is being referred to here.[48] We know that the scribal curriculum was established under the auspices of the king.[49] That is why the text explicitly solicits endorsement by the king, poetically called "the shepherd and the herdsman"; he had to agree with a major addition to the textbooks.[50] That the school was the context for the transmission of the text is implied, too, by the reference to the "wise" *(enqu)* and the "learned" *(mūdû),* the teacher ("father," *abu)* and the pupil ("son," *mari).*[51]

On the crucial point of closure, the curriculum compares to the canon. Its boundaries may have some elasticity, but every teacher knows that there are limits to what the curriculum can accommodate. Decisions about the content of the curriculum, moreover, are an exercise of authority, just as the canon represents an act of authority. In the Mesopotamian context, jurisdiction over the curriculum ultimately lies with the king. The curriculum is imposed, just as the canon is. Though the curriculum of the Jewish scribes in the Second Temple period did not have a royal sanction, it could hardly have been established without the approval of the temple authorities. The curriculum, then, does provide a model for the concept of a selection of texts from the stream of tradition.

The parallel between curriculum and canon becomes even more compelling if we distinguish between a core and an elective curriculum. By assuming the presence of electives on the curriculum, we broaden the concept to include a longer list of works that are deemed suitable for teaching purposes. This opens up the possibility that—for instance—all the prophetic books of the Hebrew Bible were potentially curriculum material, but that only some were actually studied. The situation would thus compare to the literary curriculum in modern schools, where students only read a few titles from a list of approved and suitable books. The curriculum—that is, the list of works fit for scribal students—is more comprehensive than the actual study program.

In his study published in 2003, the Belgian Assyriologist Herman Vanstiphout argues that some of the literary catalogues from ancient Babylonia attest, in fact, to a core curriculum.[52] Although these lists are not identical, they overlap considerably when it comes to the classics to be studied by scribal students. When properly understood, these catalogues are a witness to what Vanstiphout calls "the first canonization in history."[53] A sobering comment is nevertheless in order. What these texts attest to is at best a virtual canon, since no two catalogues are the same. Moreover, this virtual canon is unlike the biblical canon in that it is open to fluctuations; different times and different places cultivated different canons. While the term "canon" is perhaps not inappropriate, such cultural canons are not to be confused with the canon of the Hebrew Bible.

A major objection against the curriculum hypothesis concerns the technical nature of the curriculum. Since there was no formal education for all in the ancient Near East, the curriculum was designed for the training of professional scribes and specialized scholars. Assuming that the parallel with the Mesopotamian curriculum is valid, it is highly unlikely that the curriculum for Hebrew scribes would be coterminous with the biblical canon. In the initial phase of their training, the Mesopotamian scribes had to study lexicographical lists of various kinds; in the program for advanced studies, the textbooks of the Mesopotamian students dealt with exorcism, divination, and various other sciences or pseudo-sciences. There was only very limited room in the curriculum for epics and other types of literature. In the biblical canon, the more "technical" textbooks are underrepresented whereas works of literature are overrepresented in comparison with the curriculum. In my reconstruction of the curriculum of the Hebrew scribes, there is only a partial overlap between the curriculum and the—later—canon.

Neither the library catalogue nor the scribal curriculum provides a perfectly adequate model for understanding the origins of the biblical canon. The parallels between the three distinct phenomena is nevertheless striking inasmuch as the selective library catalogue, the curriculum, and the canonical list are all discriminatory as well as authoritative. Moreover, they deal with written compositions of particular prestige and are thus typically expressions of a culture of literacy. In a world without libraries or schools, there could hardly have been a canon. Yet the biblical canon cannot be reduced to either a library catalogue or a curriculum; it is a reality of its own kind. To grasp that reality in its proper perspective, we must look at the historical stages leading up to the canon.

Ezra and the Canonization of the Law

Although neither the library catalogue nor the scribal curriculum provides an adequate model for understanding the origins of the biblical canon, they do have the merit of alerting us to the fact that the canon was at home in the scribal culture of antiquity. Both the library and the curriculum are manifestations of scribal culture; the canon, too, is a phenomenon that would not have seen the light if it were not for the Hebrew scribes.

Scribes in fact played a crucial role in the emergence of the biblical canon. Around 450 B.C.E. Ezra the scribe took the first step toward its creation. Mandated by the Persian authorities to provide the province of Judah with a national constitution, Ezra promulgated the Torah of Moses as the law of the land. The Torah that Ezra imposed constituted the beginning of the canon; it was its earliest form and remained its lasting core. The second step occurred two centuries later, when the Jerusalem temple scribes published an edition of the Prophets, the Psalms, and Proverbs. The scribes regarded their edition as definitive because they considered the era of revelation to be closed. There was no canon as yet but all the ingredients were present; the canonical era being closed, the closure of the canon was only a matter of time.

My reconstruction of the process leading up to the biblical canon departs from the classic three-stage theory in two respects: instead of three stages, I distinguish only two, and instead of a closure of the canon, I prefer to speak of a closure of the canonical era. Aside from the speculation about a Council at Jamnia, the three-stage theory errs fundamentally on two counts. First, by interpreting the Masoretic division of the Bible into three sections as the historical order of canonization, the theory ends up in hair-splitting discussions about the status and the number of books in the section known as the Writings. In the Hellenistic and Roman periods the division between the Prophets and the Writings was everything but watertight. Josephus counted much of what is now in the Writings as belonging to the Prophets; the fundamental division was that between the Law and the Prophets. Second, the classic theory approaches the history of canonization in terms of its outcome; this is another error. The outcome of the process being a canon—that is, a closed list of books—the theory views the preceding stages as canons as well. This leads to the self-contradictory notion of a closed list that was twice expanded. In fact, however, the Hebrew scribes of the Hellenistic period did not make a list but developed the notion of the era of revelation; the later list merely names the works believed to be genuinely from the canonical era.

The first stage in the making of the Hebrew canon was the canonization of the five books of Moses, known as the Torah. The Law of Moses received canonical status under the impetus of the Persian authorities. In their dealings with conquered nations, the Persians sought to provide their rule with a solid base by sanctioning the codified law of the land as the law of the Persian king.[54] Those nations that did not possess a national law were urged to create one. Egypt is an example. According to the *Demotic Chronicle*, the Persian king Darius ordered the governor of Egypt in 518 to install a commission of priests, scholars, and military leaders to put the laws of Egypt into a written code.[55] The work took them more than ten years. Around the same time, Darius sent an Egyptian priest by the name of Udjahorresnet from Elam to Egypt. His mission was to restore the workshops of the Egyptian temples, thereby creating the necessary infrastructure for the implementation of the law.[56]

The parallel between the mission of the Egyptian priest Udjahorresnet and that of the Jewish priest Ezra is striking. Ezra was sent from Babylonia to Jerusalem to reorganize the province of Judah in accordance with the rules of the Law. The Persian authorities referred to Ezra's law code as "the Law of your God that is in your hand" (Ezra 7:14). Since Ezra was an expert in the Law of Moses (literally, a "proficient scribe of the Law of Moses," Ezra 7:6), it is legitimate to equate the "Law of your God" with the Torah of Moses. The Persian king explicitly endorsed the mission of Ezra by adopting Jewish national law as the law of the Persian king (Ezra 7:26).

For the implementation of the Torah as the national law, Ezra had to create an infrastructure that would render it possible to administer the Torah at a local level. To achieve this goal, Ezra established a network of regional centers for public instruction and jurisdiction; these were the ancestors of the later synagogues.[57] Ezra put Levites in charge of the local centers. The Levites were a scribal elite that gave regular readings of the Torah, adjudicated local disputes, and fulfilled various administrative duties (compare 2 Chron 17:7–9). The local administration was subordinate to the central temple authority in Jerusalem, in conformity with the Deuteronomic Constitution. The synchronization of the religious calendar, for instance, was determined by the authorities in Jerusalem.

The identification of Ezra's law book is a topic of ongoing scholarly debate.[58] It has been strongly put forth that the law that was "in the hand" of Ezra was in fact Deuteronomy, or the Priestly Code, or a document now lost to us. None of these solutions satisfies. It was Ezra's mission to implement a national law; to that end he had to fuse partisan documents (such as Deuteronomy and the Priestly Code) into a higher unity, which ultimately resulted in the Pentateuch, or the five books of Moses.[59] The veneration of the Pentateuch by the Samaritans forces us to posit its acceptance well before the schism with Judaism occurred.[60] The work must have been composed and published before 400 B.C.E.; 450 is a plausible date.[61] Ezra was a scholar who received his scribal training in Babylonia. His work on the Pentateuch compares to the editing of the *Gilgamesh Epic* by Sin-leqe-unninni and the editing of the prognostic compendium *Sakikkû* by Esagil-kīn-apli. The latter used disparate sources ("twisted threads," in the scribal idiom) to produce a "new text" (Sumerian *sur gibil*).[62] Ezra did the same for the Law of Moses. Whether he did so in person or as supervisor of an editorial committee hardly matters. His name is attached to the edition; the Pentateuch is as much the Book of Ezra as it is the Book of Moses.

In Jewish historiography, Ezra is a symbol of the Jewish restoration in the Persian era; in the history of religions, Ezra counts as the founding father of Judaism: what some see as a restoration is for others the beginning of something distinctly new. Ezra was indeed an innovator in the sense that he fused separate and at times conflicting legal and narrative traditions—the various strands of the Pentateuch—into one literary work and defined it as the Law of Moses. It is a feat of scribal acumen because it incorporates early legal texts, such as the Covenant Code, alongside law that was meant to supersede them, such as Deuteronomy; it has different visions on the temple and the priesthood cohabiting under the single authority of Moses; it succeeds in weaving parallel historical traditions into one narrative. Ezra's work has been characterized as a compromise.[63] It is indeed artificial and replete with redundancy, but it stands as a symbol of Jewish identity. That identity, embodied in the Law, was a scribal creation.

Without the Persians, there would not have been a Pentateuch. The Persians are responsible, too, for the transformation of the Torah into the Law, because the codification of the legal traditions did not leave their nature unaffected. It is often said that Greek *nomos* is a mistranslation of Hebrew *tôrâ; tôrâ* means "instruction, advice," whereas *nomos* is "law." The Greek translation, introduced by the Septuagint, turns an act of personal interaction into an impersonal and abstract notion. But the Greek language is not to blame. Well before the Septuagint, the Persian authorities defined the Torah of God as "law" *(dāt)*. They thus brought to a conclusion a development that had been going on for some time. The Book of Deuteronomy, written in the seventh century B.C.E., had already transformed the plural *tôrôt,* oral instructions delivered by the priests (see, e.g., Jer 18:18; Ezek 7:26; Hag 2:11–13), into a single *tôrâ,* the written instruction of Moses. By virtue of being written, the Torah became binding as a general rule; particular situations became cases, and for each case, the law did provide.

Codification is a form of canonization.[64] And in this case, canonization is not the outcome of some organic and natural process but the result of the editorial activity of Ezra—either as actual editor or as editorial supervisor—and a decree by the Persian government. Scribes like Ezra can make a book from separate documents, but it is not within their power to impose that book as binding. The power to impose belongs to the authorities—the Persian authorities, in this case.[65]

The Closing of the Canonical Era

Two distinct but closely connected events marked the second phase in the canonization of the Hebrew scriptures. Between 300 and 200 B.C.E., the scribes of the temple workshop at Jerusalem prepared an edition of the Prophets, the Psalms, and the Book of Proverbs to meet the demands of a growing class of literate laymen; their edition was meant to be definitive and to be put at the disposal of the public, to be read in local places of worship, in schools, and by private individuals. At the same time, the temple scholars formulated the doctrine of the closure of the prophetic era. According to this new doctrine, the Spirit of prophecy had departed from Israel after the days of Ezra. Direct revelations were believed not to occur any longer; thenceforth, divine illumination could be obtained only by a study of the Law and the Prophets.

The third century B.C.E. was a period of important editorial activity of the Hebrew scribes. To appreciate the scope and significance of their work, we can start by looking at their edition of the Minor Prophets. Originally most of the Minor Prophets—so called because the books in question do not match the volume of the Books of Isaiah, Jeremiah, and Ezekiel—were works on separate scrolls, some of which were in existence in pre-exilic times. Both the First Book of Kings and the Book of Jeremiah contain a reference to the Micah scroll (1 Kings 22:28, compare Mic 1:2; Jer 26:18, compare Mic 3:12); the oracle collections of Hosea and Amos also presumably existed in the First Temple period as separate scrolls.[66] Around 250 B.C.E., however, the Jerusalem scribes decided to publish all the Minor Prophets on a single scroll. Moreover, they artificially turned their number into twelve by inventing a prophet by the name of Malachi.

Originally Malachi was not a name but a title, meaning "My Messenger." It is taken from Mal 3:1, where God is quoted as saying, "Behold, I am sending My Messenger to clear the way before Me." The scribes took this reference as an allusion to the name of the otherwise anonymous author of the oracles. In fact both the name Malachi and his book are artificial, since the three chapters of Malachi were originally part of a collection of three anonymous "pronouncements" (*maśśā'*, Zech 9:1, 12:1; Mal 1:1); two were added to the Zechariah collection, and the third was turned into a separate book.[67] The scribes' motive for creating a twelfth prophetic book had to do with the number twelve: twelve stood for plenitude and, by implication, for closure. The publication of the Twelve Minor Prophets as a single scroll conveyed the message that the time of the prophets had come to an end; no new prophet would thenceforth arise.

If Malachi is a scribal construct created to obtain the canonical number of twelve, it follows that the Book of Malachi would originally have been placed at the end of the Minor Prophets. In this respect, the Masoretic manuscripts of the Minor Prophets preserve the original order.[68] Further corroboration of the position of Malachi at the end of the Minor Prophets is provided by the occurrence of an editorial postscript or epilogue, less aptly called a colophon, that pertains to the Minor Prophets as a whole.[69]

> Be mindful of the Law of My servant Moses, whom I charged at Horeb with decrees and verdicts. Lo, I will send the prophet Elijah to you before the coming of the awesome, fearful day of Yahweh. He shall turn the hearts of fathers to their children and the hearts of children to their fathers, lest I come and strike the whole land with utter destruction.
>
> Mal 3:22–24

This postscript closes the Book of Malachi and, by the same token, the Book of the Twelve as a whole. It is highly significant of the doctrinal outlook of the scribal editors.

The epilogue to the Twelve Prophets consists of two parts. The first part urges the reader to be loyal to the Law of Moses, while the second one predicts the return of the prophet Elijah. The double edge of the epilogue reflects the two major concerns of the editors. The Torah of Moses is the ultimate source of authority they acknowledge; attributed to Moses in his capacity as "servant" of the Lord, it contains the "decrees and verdicts" *(ḥuqqîm ûmišpāṭîm)* for every Israelite. Both the tenor and the phraseology are strongly reminiscent of the Book of Deuteronomy. The scribal editors imply that the publication of the Prophets is not meant to take the place of the Torah but to serve as a reminder of its importance.

The second part of the epilogue has a Deuteronomic flavor as well. Since the era of the prophets has come to a close, the editors do not predict the coming of a new prophet but the return of a famous prophet of old. Their source of inspiration is Deut 18:15–18, where God announces that He will raise up a prophet like Moses. The Samaritans read this text as an announcement of the Taheb, the "Restorer," who would put an end to the age of disfavor before the Day of the Lord.[70] The Jerusalem editors of the Minor Prophets identified this Restorer with Elijah; he would "restore" *(šwb,* hip'il*)* the heart of the fathers to the sons and vice versa.[71] Elijah was indeed "like Moses," as both Elijah and Moses had been transferred to heaven.[72] Elijah's return would be a return from on high. The editors believed that the end of time—the Day of Yahweh—was near; Elijah's mission would be to prepare the people for the event. This suggests that the publication of the Prophets is to be situated in a time of Messianic expectations.

The epilogue or colophon of the Minor Prophets is important not only for the insight it provides into the doctrinal stance of the editors, but also as an indication of the scope of their editorial work. The reference to the Torah of Moses creates a literary bracket that links the scroll of the Minor Prophets to the first scroll of the entire section known as the Prophets (Joshua, Judges, Samuel, Kings, Isaiah, Jeremiah, Ezekiel, the Twelve). Mal 3:22 echoes Josh 1:7.

> But you must be very strong and resolute to observe faithfully the entire Law that my servant Moses enjoined upon you.

The scribal technique of the *inclusio*—the technical term for such a bracket—is a subtle way of marking the beginning and the end of a literary unit—a unit that, here, consists of the entire collection of the

Prophets, from the former to the latter.[73] The edition of the Minor Prophets, then, was designed as the final piece of a larger literary edifice.

The Malachi epilogue contains a very general indication of the historical background of the edition of the Prophets. There are several data that allow us to be more specific about its chronological place. Ben Sira, who is writing between 200 and 180 B.C.E., quotes from the epilogue to Malachi (Sir 48:10) and refers to "the bones of the twelve prophets" (Sir 49:10). He can have done so only because he was familiar with the published scroll of the Twelve Prophets. Copies of the Twelve Prophets were also found among the texts at Qumran; they go back to the first half of the second century B.C.E. In the Book of Daniel, finally, dating from ca. 160 B.C.E., the protagonist is presented as studying a prophecy of Jeremiah that he found "in the books [of the prophets]" (*bassĕpārîm*, Dan 9:2). By 200 B.C.E. at the latest, then, the publication of the Prophets, including the scroll of the Twelve, was a fact.

From various references to Greece in the prophetic corpus it is clear that the publication of the Prophets cannot have preceded the Hellenistic era.[74] A rough estimate puts the edition somewhere between 300 and 200 B.C.E. At that time, Judah was under the rule of the Ptolemies. The Ptolemaic period in Palestine is characterized by increasing tensions between a social upper class of landed gentry and the leading priestly families, on the one hand, and the general population of peasants, craftsmen, retailers, and Levites, on the other.[75] The discontent of disinherited classes bred speculation about an imminent divine intervention. The edition of the Prophets is an expression of the eschatological expectations of the time. It is a call to return to the values of the old-time religion (the Torah of Moses) in the face of the Day of the Judgment, which was to come very soon.

The creation of a twelfth Minor Prophet (Malachi) and the edition of the Minor Prophets as one work demonstrate that the scribes believed that the prophetic era had come to a close. It was only because no new prophet would arise that the prophets of old could be published in a definitive edition. The doctrine of the end of the era of revelation is not formulated in the Hebrew Bible itself; we conclude that it existed by inference from the edition of the Minor Prophets and from its editorial epilogue. Later Jewish sources are more explicit. According to the Tosephta on the Mishna tractate Sotah, "When the latter prophets, Haggai, Zechariah, and Malachi, died, the Holy Spirit departed from Israel."[76] In the first century c.e., Josephus wrote that the time of revelation had come to a close under Artaxerxes (*C. Ap.* 1.40–41), the Persian king from the time of Ezra.[77]

Even though its explicit formulation is later than the canonization of the Hebrew scriptures, the doctrine of the era of prophecy is of crucial importance for the correct understanding of the logic underlying the biblical canon. The era of prophecy is the era of revelation, and thus, by the same token, the canonical era; Moses stands at its beginning and Ezra at its end. Everything written that is holy and inspired can have come only from their time. The scribes of the early Hellenistic period did not draft a list nor did they close the canon; they simply enunciated the principle that the time of revelation belonged to the past. Supernatural authority attached only to writings by inspired men from the era of prophecy. Such men could indiscriminately be referred to as "prophets," a term that came to signify all authors inspired by the Holy Spirit.[78]

If there was a criterion of canonicity, then, to use an anachronism, it was a formal one. For a written text to have divine authority, it had to pass the test of antiquity. The books of true value were the "ancestral books," as the grandson of Ben Sira calls them (Prologue to Ben Sira, line 10).[79] Hence the proliferation of pseudonymous authorship in the Hellenistic and Roman periods; a writer who wanted his text to gain the same status as the holy books had to convince his audience that his work was of high antiquity.[80] Some authors succeeded in this stratagem and others failed; the author of Daniel found credence, but the authors of the Enoch literature did not—or found it only in limited circles. There was a critical readership that was well aware of the possibility of forgery; many authors tried to pass off their work as ancient, but most of them failed to persuade their audience.[81]

Acting on the conviction that the productive era of inspired texts had come to an end, the temple scribes of Jerusalem prepared final editions of other works from the past as well. Both the Book of Psalms and the Book of Proverbs, the one attributed to David and the other to Solomon, received a new edition in the third century B.C.E., around the same time the scroll of the Minor Prophets saw the light. Although the Psalms, the Proverbs, and the Minor Prophets are quite different types of literature, the scribes who edited them in the form in which we know them took these texts to belong to one and the same written heritage; these were the works of inspired authors and were full of divine wisdom.

The spirit in which the editors prepared these texts for publication is evident from their comments at the beginning and the end of their editions. The prefaces and postscripts ("colophons" is the term often used) are notices to the reader; the scribes have thus left instructions concerning the purpose of the sacred literature and the way in which the reader should approach the text. A comparison of the postscript to Hosea (the book that opens the scroll of the Minor Prophets), the introduction to the Book of Psalms, and the preface to the Book of Proverbs are illuminating. The three texts are given below.

He who is wise [*ḥākām*] will consider these words,
He who is prudent [*nābôn*] will take note of them.
For the ways of Yahweh are straight;
The righteous [*ṣaddîqîm*] will go in them,
But the sinners [*pōšě'îm*] will stumble on them.

Hos 14:10

Fortunate the man who does not go in the counsel of the wicked
   [*rěšā'îm*],
Or take the way of the sinners [*ḥaṭṭā'îm*],
Or join the company of the insolent [*lēṣîm*];
Rather, the Torah of Yahweh is his delight,
And he studies [lit.: mutters] His Torah day and night . . .

Therefore the wicked [*rĕšāʿîm*] will not survive the judgment,
Nor will sinners [*ḥaṭṭāʾîm*] in the assembly of the righteous [*ṣaddîqîm*].
For Yahweh knows the way of the righteous [*ṣaddîqîm*],
But the way of the wicked [*rĕšāʿîm*] will perish.

Ps 1:1–2, 1:5–6

The proverbs of Solomon son of David, king of Israel . . .
The wise man [*ḥākām*] who hears them increases his grasp,
and the prudent one [*nābôn*] acquires intelligence
For understanding proverb and epigram,
the words of the wise and their riddles.
Reverence of Yahweh is the beginning of knowledge;
Fools [*ʾĕwîlîm*] despise wisdom and discipline.

Prov 1:1, 1:5–7

These editorial notices share three characteristics: first, they address the reader as one who is "wise" or seeks to obtain wisdom; second, they emphasize the importance of studying and understanding the text; and third, they classify the human race in two camps: on the one side are the righteous, the wise, and the prudent ones; on the other side the wicked, the sinners, the fools, and the insolent.[82]

Each of these three characteristics is related to the fact that the national heritage has become literature. Being literature, the religious tradition has to be read and to be studied; the reader "mutters" the text over and over (Ps 1:2) in order to penetrate its meaning (Hos 14:10, Prov 1:6). Righteousness comes from reading, and the very act of reading amounts almost to proof of righteousness. The new role of the written word turns intelligence into a moral virtue; the wise one belongs by definition to the righteous, just as the fools and the wicked are in the same pack. The stereotypical division between the righteous and the wicked—or the wise and the fools, the prudent and the insolent—is an expression of the rift between a growing class of readers and a nonliterate majority.

The very likeness of the scribal introductions and postscripts found in Psalms, Proverbs, and the Minor Prophets may be taken as an indication of the fact that the same scribal circles that prepared the edition of the Twelve were also involved in the edition of the Psalms and the Proverbs, which means that the edition of the three corpora took place at about the same time. What triggered such significant editorial activity? The dogma of the post-prophetic era was not its sole impetus, since the belief in the closure of the canonical era is perhaps a necessary but hardly a sufficient condition for publication. The decisive factor is more likely to have been the increasing demand for a national literature by an educated public.

The Hebrew scribes of the time were not alone in their effort to publish a national literature. The Hellenization of the Near East led to an increased production of national—and often nationalistic—historiography. The Babylonian priest Berossus wrote the history of Mesopotamia in the third century B.C.E.; Manetho wrote the history of Egypt in the second century B.C.E. (we still use his system of counting the Egyptian dynasties).[83] The publication of the Prophets, the Psalms, and the Proverbs by the temple scribes of Jerusalem can be viewed as a Jewish response to the cultural impact of Hellenism: this was the national library of the Jewish people ("the ancestral books," according to Ben Sira's grandson; "our books," in the words of Josephus).[84]

Hebrew scribes had been reading and transmitting literary works since the late pre-exilic era; in the early Hellenistic period, however, they took the initiative to edit large parts of their written heritage for the purpose of publication. Until then, the Psalms, the Proverbs, and the Prophets had circulated in writing only among the scribal elite; the new edition in the Hellenistic period was innovative and revolutionary in the sense that the scribes put the venerated texts at the disposal of a general audience. The effect was a democratization of the written tradition. There was no printing press, of course, but manuscripts began to be copied in increasing numbers. About a century later, around 150 B.C.E., the collections of Qumran attest to the existence of multiple copies of traditional literature. By the witness of Ben Sira, copies were available for study in schools.

The fact that the Jerusalem scribes prepared Psalms and Proverbs for publication at about the same time that they edited the Scroll of the Twelve means that the interpretation of the Masoretic sequence— Prophets (Neviim) and then Writings (Ketuvim)—as the chronological order of canonization is mistaken. The canonization of the Writings, if the anachronism be permitted, is in no way secondary to that of the Prophets. In fact, the repartition of the biblical books over the two sections is subject to fluctuations; Josephus reckons Ruth, Chronicles, Ezra-Nehemiah, Esther, Job, and Daniel among the Prophets, mentioning only four "remaining books" (*C. Ap.* 1.38).[85] And while there is ample evidence of an early tripartition of the Hebrew scriptures, the fundamental distinction is really between "the Law and the Prophets," as the expression goes in the Gospels and elsewhere (e.g., 4 Macc 18:10–19, first century C.E.), which implies that "Prophets" could be used to designate all the "ancestral books" outside the Torah.[86]

There is no reason to believe that the scribes of the early Hellenistic period had less veneration for Psalms and Proverbs than for the Prophets. On the contrary, they prepared the editions of Psalms and Proverbs in the same spirit in which they edited the Prophets; like the Prophets, Psalms and Proverbs were books from the era of the Holy Spirit, written by famous men who had the gift of prophecy.[87] When the scribes were publishing what might be called a national library, they naturally included Psalms and Proverbs in the collection. It was their intention to put the ancestral heritage in the hands of a lay readership; the selection criterion they used was primarily antiquity, on the assumption that antiquity equaled inspiration by the Spirit.

By publishing a "national library," the scribes were producing a kind of canon without closing it. It bears emphasizing once more that the early Hellenistic scribes did not close the canon but declared the era of revelation to be closed; they invented the idea of a canonical era. The dogma they enunciated allowed for the possibility of the discovery of other works not yet known but nevertheless from the canonical era; a successful forgery could thus become part of the national library as well. The case of Daniel offers the most remarkable illustration. Written just before the middle of the second century B.C.E., some one hundred years after the scribal doctrine of the canonical era had developed, the Book of Daniel was accepted into the ancestral literary heritage because the religious authorities gave credence to the fiction of its authorship by a prophet from the Babylonian Exile. God had told Daniel to keep his book sealed until the time of the end (Dan 12:4); readers could adduce this as an explanation for why the book had only recently come to light.

The earliest attestations of the Hebrew canon as a list come from the second half of the first century C.E. (Josephus, *C. Ap.* 1.38; 2 Esdras 14). Between 250 B.C.E. and 50 C.E., it seems that there was no canon in the sense of a *numerus fixus* of holy books. The widely accepted doctrine of the era of revelation permitted discussion about the authenticity, antiquity, and authorship of specific books. To judge by the evidence of the Old Greek translation of the Hebrew Bible (the so-called *kaige* edition), some circles did not regard Esther and Qohelet as genuine works of the canonical era.[88] The absence of Esther among the Dead Sea Scrolls supports this observation. On the other hand, the Qumran community did apparently accept the Enoch writings and Jubilees as genuinely ancient—an opinion that the scribal milieu of Jerusalem, from which Ben Sira came, did not share.[89]

The closure of the canon is the result of the eventual consensus among Pharisee scholars about the age and authenticity of the books of the Hebrew Bible. They accepted Qohelet and Song of Songs among the ancestral books because they held King Solomon to be their real author; they accepted Ruth and Esther because they identified the time frame of the compositions with the time of the authors. Later tradition attributes Job to Moses; its occurrence at Qumran in an archaic script shows that the idea predates the Common Era. By taking the reign of Artaxerxes as the *terminus ad quem* of the prophetic era (Josephus, *C. Ap.* 1.38), Chronicles, Ezra, and Nehemiah could also be viewed as inspired literature, assuming Ezra and Nehemiah had written them (so *b. B. Bat.* 14b). Content and ideas were not at issue where canonicity was at stake; the scholarly debate was about authorship and antiquity.[90]

In his defense of Judaism, Josephus acknowledges the existence of Jewish books written after the era of revelation, from Artaxerxes (ca. 400 B.C.E.) to his own day (ca. 80 C.E.). These, as he writes, "have not been deemed worthy of equal credit [*pistis*] with the earlier records, because of the failure of the exact succession [*diadochē*] of the prophets" (*C. Ap.* 1.41). The Greek translation of the Hebrew scriptures extant in the Septuagint includes a number of these later works. The broader selection of the Septuagint has at times been taken to imply that the Jews at Alexandria, where the translation originated, had a larger canon than the Palestinian Jews. The discussion is somewhat spurious, because the term "canon" is inappropriate in this context. There was no Septuagint as yet, only Greek translations and adaptations of various Hebrew books; the Greek Bible is an invention of a later time.[91]

Conclusion

The canonization of the Hebrew scriptures—which is the final act in the making of the Hebrew Bible—is an act of closure in the sense that the scribes of the Second Temple propagated the notion of the closure of the prophetic era, which might also be termed the canonical era; the closure of the canon is a derivative of that doctrine. The notion of closure underlies the edition of the Minor Prophets in the form of the Scroll of the Twelve; the artificial construction of a twelfth prophet springs from the wish of the scribes to present the succession of the prophets as completed and, therefore, closed. The Jewish scholars did not develop a doctrine about the closure of the Hebrew canon in parallel to the dogma of the closure of the prophetic era; the closure of the list is legitimized by the doctrine of the prophetic era, on the understanding that ancient books that were still hidden from the public were meant to remain secret (2 Esdras 14).

The criteria for establishing the Hebrew canon were authorship and antiquity; often the issue narrowed down to the authenticity of books claiming to be part of the heritage of the canonical era. In this respect, different Jewish communities professed different opinions and had, thus, different canons. Members of the Qumran community believed in the authenticity of the Enoch literature and Jubilees, which they studied alongside the Prophets. There is no evidence that people at Qumran rejected the doctrine of the prophetic era; on the contrary, the practice of scriptural commentary, extant in the so-called *pesharim*, implies that the community recognized the special character of the ancestral books. Unlike the scribal circles in Jerusalem, however, they credited a significant amount of pseudonymous literature with authenticity.

The canon of the Hebrew scriptures has come about on account of two decisions carried out by persons or institutions in a position of authority. One decision was the promulgation of the Torah as the law of the land, issued by God, legitimized by the king, and enforced by Ezra and Nehemiah; the political motive behind this decree is unmistakable. The second act of authority, occurring about two centuries later, was the enunciation of the dogma of the prophetic era. The edge of the doctrine lay in the rejection of claims of inspiration by people from the post-prophetic era. The scribal establishment of Jerusalem attempted to secure its moral leadership by disqualifying contemporaneous visionaries and ecstatics as empty chatterboxes; the real prophets were the Books of the Prophets, to whose interpretation the scribes held the keys.[92]

The coming about of the biblical canon is a triumph of scribal culture in the sense that the scribes succeeded in transforming the written traditions of a professional elite into a national library. The promulgation of the Torah as the law of the land turned part of the scribal tradition into a national work of reference; the codification of the law implied a transfer of authority from persons to a book. The publication of the Prophets and the other books turned the heritage of the Hebrew scribes into a national heritage; as a result, the scribal practices of study, memorization, and interpretation became part of the religious habits of a nation. Scrolls were the symbols of Hebrew scribal culture; as the Bible became the symbol of Jewish religion, Judaism assumed traits of the scribal culture.[93]

The canonization of the scriptures is the final act in the making of the

Hebrew Bible; what follows is the history of its reception. From its earliest scribblings to the closure of the canon, the Hebrew Bible was the work of the Hebrew scribes; to tell the story of its making is to enter their world. In this book I have explored the scribal culture of antiquity in an attempt to do justice to the anonymous men to whom we owe the Bible. Though they have obscured their presence in the text, it is their legacy to the world; once we recognize their role in its making we will read the Bible with different eyes.

Notes · Selected Bibliography · Index

Notes

Introduction

1. See, e.g., Richard Elliot Friedman, *Who Wrote the Bible?* 2nd ed. (San Francisco: Harper, 1997), for an immensely popular representative of the genre.

1. Books That Are Not Books

1. From *biblion,* derived from *biblos,* originally the Greek name for the papyrus plant; hence "papyrus roll," hence "book."

2. 1 Macc 12:9 uses the expression *ta biblia ta hagia;* 2 Macc 8:23 speaks about *hē hiera biblos,* "the holy book," presumably in reference to the Pentateuch. Note also the reference to "the ancestral books" *(tōn . . . patriōn bibliōn)* in the Prologue to Ben Sira (ca. 140 B.C.E.). Around 100 C.E., Josephus speaks about "our books [*biblia*]" (C. Ap. 1.38).

3. For an introduction to the subject, see Susan Niditch, *Oral World and Written Word: Ancient Israelite Literature,* Library of Ancient Israel (Louisville: Westminster John Knox Press, 1996). For a more general introduction to the history of scribes, writing, and books, see Leila Avrin, *Scribes, Script, and Books: The Book Arts from Antiquity to the Renais-*

sance (Chicago: American Library Association; London: The British Library, 1991).

4. Mogens T. Larsen, "What They Wrote on Clay," in Karen Schousboe and Mogens T. Larsen, eds., *Literacy and Society* (Copenhagen: Akademisk Forlag, 1989), 121–148, esp. 134. On fluctuations in the spread of literacy over time, see Mogens T. Larsen, "The Mesopotamian Lukewarm Mind: Reflections on Science, Divination and Literacy," in Francesca Rochberg-Halton, ed., *Language, Literature, and History: Philological and Historical Studies Presented to Erica Reiner,* American Oriental Series 67 (New Haven: American Oriental Society, 1987), 203–225, esp. 219–221. Larsen assumes "a fairly widespread literacy" in the first half of the second millennium B.C.E. (220).

5. John R. Baines, "Literacy and Ancient Egyptian Society," *Man* 18 (1983): 572–599; John R. Baines and Christopher Eyre, "Four Notes on Literacy," *Göttinger Miszellen* 61 (1983): 65–96, esp. 65–72; John R. Baines, "Schreiben," *LÄ* 5:693–698, esp. 695; Herman te Velde, "Scribes and Literacy in Ancient Egypt," in Herman L. J. Vanstiphout et al., eds., *Scripta signa vocis: Studies about Scripts, Scriptures, Scribes and Languages in the Near East Presented to J. H. Hospers* (Groningen: Forsten, 1986), 253–264; Leonard H. Lesko, "Some Comments on Ancient Egyptian Literacy and Literati," in Sarah Israelit-Groll, ed., *Studies in Egyptology Presented to Miriam Lichtheim,* 2 vols. (Jerusalem: Magnes, 1990), 2:656–659; Lesko, "Literacy," in Donald B. Redford, ed., *The Oxford Encyclopedia of Ancient Egypt* (Oxford: Oxford University Press, 2001), 2:297–299.

6. William V. Harris, *Ancient Literacy* (Cambridge, MA: Harvard University Press, 1989), 328. For a balanced view on the various shades of literacy in Greece, see also Rosalind Thomas, *Literacy and Orality in Ancient Greece,* Key Themes in Ancient History (Cambridge: Cambridge University Press, 1992).

7. Compare the judicious observations by Donald B. Redford, "Scribe and Speaker," in Ehud Ben Zvi and Michael H. Floyd, eds., *Writings and Speech in Israelite and Ancient Near Eastern Prophecy,* SBL Symposium Series 10 (Atlanta: Society of Biblical Literature, 2000), 145–218, esp. 145–159.

8. Compare the observation by Simo Parpola, according to whom "literacy in the Assyrian Empire was far more widespread than hitherto assumed. [. . . literacy] was within the reach of every affluent Assyrian family." See

Parpola, "The Man without a Scribe and the Question of Literacy in the Assyrian Empire," in Beate Pongratz-Leisten et al., eds., *Ana šadî Labnāni lū allik: Beiträge zu altorientalischen und mittelmeerischen Kulturen. Festschrift für Wolfgang Röllig,* AOAT 247 (Kevelaer: Butzon & Bercker; Neukirchen-Vluyn: Neukirchener Verlag, 1997), 315–324, esp. 320–321. For a similar conclusion about literacy at the end of the third and the beginning of the second millennia, see Claus Wilcke, *Wer las und schrieb in Babylonien und Assyrien: Überlegungen zur Literalität im Alten Zweistromland,* Bayerische Akademie der Wissenschaften, Phil.-Hist. Klasse, Sitzungsberichte Jahrgang 2000:6 (Munich: C. H. Beck, 2000).

9. See, e.g., André Lemaire, *Les écoles et la formation de la Bible dans l'ancien Israel,* OBO 39 (Fribourg: Editions Universitaires; Göttingen: Vandenhoeck & Ruprecht, 1981), 48; Joseph Naveh, *Early History of the Alphabet: An Introduction to West Semitic Epigraphy and Palaeography* (Jerusalem: Magnes; Leiden: Brill, 1982), 75–76; Aaron Demsky, "Writing in Ancient Israel: The Biblical Period," in Martin-Jan Mulder, ed., *Mikra: Text, Translation, Reading and Interpretation of the Hebrew Bible in Ancient Judaism and Early Christianity,* Compendia Rerum Iudaicarum ad Novum Testamentum 2/1 (Assen: Van Gorcum; Philadelphia: Fortress, 1988), 2–20, esp. 15 (popular literacy in Israel from 750 B.C.E. onward); Michael D. Coogan, "Literacy and the Formation of Biblical Literature," in Prescott H. Williams, Jr., and Theodore Hiebert, eds., *Realia Dei: Essays in Archaeology and Biblical Interpretation in Honor of Edward F. Campbell, Jr., at His Retirement* (Atlanta: Scholars Press, 1999), 47–61, esp. 47–49.

10. See, e.g., Sean Warner, "The Alphabet: An Innovation and Its Diffusion," *VT* 30 (1980): 81–90; Meir Bar-Ilan, "Illiteracy in the Land of Israel in the First Centuries C.E.," in Simcha Fishbane et al., eds., *Essays in the Social Scientific Study of Judaism and Jewish Society,* vol. 2 (New York: Ktav, 1992), 46–61; Ian M. Young, "Israelite Literacy: Interpreting the Evidence," *VT* 48 (1998): 239–253, 408–422.

11. A case in point are the publications on the subject by Alan R. Millard, whose belief in widespread literacy in ancient Israel goes in tandem with his defense of the antiquity and authenticity of the books of the Bible, including the New Testament Gospels. See, from a plethora of publications, Millard, "An Assessment of the Evidence of Writing in Ancient Israel," in Janet Amitai, ed., *Biblical Archaeology Today: Proceedings of the Inter-*

national Congress of Biblical Archaeology, Jerusalem, April 1984 (Jerusalem: Israel Exploration Society, 1985), 301–312; Millard, *Reading and Writing in the Time of Jesus,* The Biblical Seminar 69 (Sheffield: Sheffield Academic Press, 2000).

12. See Insup Taylor and Martin M. Taylor, *Writing and Literacy in Chinese, Korean and Japanese,* Studies in Written Language and Literacy 3 (Amsterdam: Benjamins, 1995).

13. Compare Larsen, "Lukewarm Mind," 219: "A text gave cues, so that for instance a literary text must be understood as an aid to an oral performance."

14. A. Leo Oppenheim's speculation ("The Archives of the Palace of Mari: A Review Article," *JNES* 11 [1952]: 129–139, esp. 133 note 3) that the expression *ina libbi dabābu* (based on a textual reconstruction) means "to read in silence," as opposed to *šasû,* "to read aloud," has not been borne out by the evidence.

15. For a balanced view on silent reading in antiquity, see Bernard M. W. Knox, "Silent Reading in Antiquity," *Greek, Roman and Byzantine Studies* 9 (1968): 421–435.

16. Lachish Letter 3, lines 10–13: *wgm kl spr 'šr yb' 'ly 'm qr'ty 'th w'ḥr 'tnnhw 'l m'wmh;* my translation follows the majority interpretation: see, e.g., André Lemaire, *Inscriptions Hébraiques: Les ostraca,* Littératures anciennes du Proche-Orient 9 (Paris: Cerf, 1977), 100–109; James M. Lindenberger, *Ancient Aramaic and Hebrew Letters,* ed. Kent Harold Richards, SBL Writings from the Ancient World 4 (Atlanta: Scholars Press, 1994), 111–112; Johannes Renz, *Die althebräische Inschriften,* Handbuch der Althebräischen Epigraphik 1 (Darmstadt: Wissenschaftliche Buchgesellschaft, 1995), 412–419. For a different interpretation see Frank Moore Cross, "A Literate Soldier: Lachish Letter III," in *Leaves from an Epigrapher's Notebook: Collected Papers in Hebrew and West Semitic Palaeography and Epigraphy,* Harvard Semitic Studies 51 (Winona Lake, IN: Eisenbrauns, 2003), 129–132, esp. 130; repr. from Ann Kort and Scott Morschauser, eds., *Biblical and Related Studies Presented to Samuel Iwry* (Winona Lake, IN: Eisenbrauns, 1985), 41–47.

17. See, for Egypt, Redford, "Scribe and Speaker," 161–162.

18. For the practice of displaying texts by affixing them to the city gate, see Lachish Letter 4, lines 3–4: "I have written on the [gate] door according to all [the instructions] which you sent to me" (*ktbty 'l hdlt kkl 'šr šlḥ[th ']ly*). I follow the interpretation of Cross, *Epigrapher's Notebook,*

133–134, originally published as "Lachish Letter IV," *Bulletin of the American Schools of Oriental Research* 144 (1956): 24–25. Admittedly, though, the translation "column [of a scroll]" for *dlt* is also possible; see Renz, *Die althebräische Inschriften*, 421 and note 2. For the practice in Mesopotamia of publishing texts by affixing them to the city gate, see *Chicago Assyrian Dictionary* Š/3, 195–196 under *šūdūtu*. The text of Deut 12:4–27 is the result of a conflation of two parallel announcements of the decree. Their formulation, as well as the liberty of the scribes in elaborating on the basic message, implies that they were to be read aloud.

19. Wilfred G. Lambert and Alan R. Millard, *Atra-ḫasīs: The Babylonian Story of the Flood* (Oxford: Clarendon, 1969), 104–105, col. viii, lines 16–19. For a translation see also Benjamin R. Foster, *Before the Muses: An Anthology of Akkadian Literature,* 2 vols. (Bethesda, MD: CDL Press, 1993), 1:183. For a study of the indications in the text for oral-musical performance, see Anne E. Kilmer, "Fugal Features of Atrahasis: The Birth Theme," in Marianna E. Vogelzang and Herman L. J. Vanstiphout, eds., *Mesopotamian Poetic Language: Sumerian and Akkadian,* CM 6 (Groningen: Styx, 1996), 127–136.

20. *Erra* V 49, 53–54 (Foster, *Before the Muses,* 2:804).

21. Andrew R. George, *The Babylonian Gilgamesh Epic: Introduction, Critical Edition and Cuneiform Texts,* 2 vols. (Oxford: Oxford University Press, 2003), 1:21–22. On the oral performance of written texts, see also Joan Goodnick Westenholz, "Oral Tradition and Written Texts in the Cycle of Akkade," in Marianna E. Vogelzang and Herman L. J. Vanstiphout, eds., *Mesopotamian Epic Literature: Oral or Aural?* (Lewiston, NY: The Edwin Mellen Press, 1992), 123–154, esp. 147–153. See also *Chicago Assyrian Dictionary* Z, 35–36, under *zamāru.*

22. The word *ḥāzôn,* literally "vision," developed the technical meaning "prophecy"; see 2 Sam 7:17 *(dĕbārîm)* // 1 Chron 17:15 *(ḥāzôn);* Isa 1:1; Ob 1; Nah 1:1; Francis Brown, Samuel R. Driver, and Charles A. Briggs, *A Hebrew and English Lexicon of the Old Testament* (Oxford: Oxford University Press, 1907), 302–303, under *ḥāzôn* and *ḥizzāyôn;* Ludwig Koehler, Walter Baumgartner, and Jakob J. Stamm, *Hebräisches und aramäisches Lexikon zum Alten Testament* (Leiden: Brill, 1967–1995), 289, under *ḥāzôn.* I take the conjunction of *ktb* and *b'r* as a hendiadys in analogy with Deut 27:8, "And on those stones you shall inscribe every word of this Teaching most distinctly" (NJPS). Following a suggestion by Joachim Schaper, I take *qôrē'* as a designation of the town crier; see

Schaper, "Exilic and Post-Exilic Prophecy and the Orality/Literacy Problem," *VT* 55 (2005): 324–342, esp. 333. The Hebrew *qôrē'* is functionally comparable to the Mesopotamian *nāgiru;* see the *Chicago Assyrian Dictionary* N/1, 115–117. The Mesopotamian herald "rounds up" the city and makes a proclamation *(šasû)* to the citizens on behalf of the authorities.

23. For a survey of the characteristics of "oral" texts, i.e., written texts in cultures that are predominantly nonliterate, see Walter J. Ong, *Orality and Literacy: The Technologizing of the Word* (London and New York: Methuen, 1982), esp. 31–77.

24. Compare Alger N. Doane, "The Ethnography of Scribal Writing and Anglo-Saxon Poetry: Scribe as Performer," *Oral Tradition* 9 (1994): 420–439, on the scribes as "performers."

25. The phrase is from Ong, *Orality and Literacy,* 37.

26. Ibid., 38.

27. For the text of the *Babylonian Theodicy,* see Wilfred G. Lambert, *Babylonian Wisdom Literature* (Oxford: Clarendon, 1960), 63–91; Foster, *Before the Muses,* 2:806–814.

28. *Ana tāmarti,* literally "for looking up"; for a study of this and similar expressions, see Laurie E. Pearce, "Statements of Purpose: Why Scribes Wrote," in Mark Cohen et al., eds., *The Tablet and the Scroll: Near Eastern Studies in Honor of William W. Hallo* (Bethesda, MD: CDL Press, 1993), 185–193, esp. 186–188.

29. *Laws of Hammurabi,* xlviii, 3–19 (Martha T. Roth, *Law Collections from Mesopotamia and Asia Minor,* SBL Writings from the Ancient World 6 [Atlanta: Scholars Press, 1995], 134).

30. Simo Parpola, *Letters from Assyrian and Babylonian Scholars,* SAA 10 (Helsinki: Helsinki University Press, 1993), no. 202:8–12.

31. Compare John Barton, "What Is a Book? Modern Exegesis and the Literary Conventions of Ancient Israel," in Johannes C. de Moor, ed., *Intertextuality in Ugarit and Israel,* Oudtestamentische Studien 40 (Leiden: Brill, 1998), 1–14.

32. See the monumental study by Richard A. Rousse and Mary A. Rousse, *Illiterati et uxorati: Manuscripts and Their Makers; Commercial Book Producers in Medieval Paris 1200–1500,* 2 vols. (London: Harvey Miller, 2000). For a useful introduction to the subject, see Louis Jacques Bataillon et al., eds., *La production du livre universitaire au Moyen Age: Exemplar et pecia. Actes du symposium tenu au Collegio San*

Bonaventura de Grottaferrata en mai 1983 (Paris: Editions du Centre National de la Recherche Scientifique, 1988).

33. See Hugues V. Shooner, "La production du livre par la pecia," in Bataillon et al., eds., *La production du livre*, 17–37, esp. 19–20.

34. See Lambert and Millard, *Atra-ḫasīs*, 31–32; Hermann Hunger, *Babylonische und assyrische Kolophone*, AOAT 2 (Kevelaer: Butzon & Bercker; Neukirchen-Vluyn: Neukirchener Verlag, 1968), nos. 13–15.

35. See Benno Landsberger, *Der kultische Kalender der Babylonier und der Assyrer*, Leipziger Semitistische Studien 6/1–2 (Leipzig: Hinrichs, 1915), 119–126.

36. Lambert and Millard, *Atra-ḫasīs*, 32.

37. Hunger, *Babylonische und assyrische Kolophone*, 2.

38. On the Assurbanipal library, see Giovanni Lanfranchi, "The Library at Nineveh," in Joan Goodnick Westenholz, ed., *Capital Cities: Urban Planning and Spiritual Dimensions. Proceedings of the Symposium Held on May 27–29, 1996, Jerusalem, Israel*, Bible Lands Museum Jerusalem Publications 2 (Jerusalem: Bible Lands Museum, 1998), 147–156; Jeanette C. Fincke, "The Babylonian Texts of Nineveh: Report on the British Museum's Ashurbanipal Library Project," *AfO* 50 (2003–2004): 111–149; Fincke, "The British Museum Ashurbanipal Library Project" (Papers of the XLIXe Rencontre Assyriologique Internationale, London, 7–11 July 2003, Part One; London: British School of Archaeology in Iraq), *Iraq* 66 (2004): 55–60; Grant Frame and Andrew R. George, "The Royal Libraries of Nineveh: New Evidence for King Ashurbanipal's Tablet Collecting" (Papers of the XLIXe Rencontre Assyriologique Internationale, London, 7–11 July 2003, Part Two; London: British School of Archaeology in Iraq), *Iraq* 67 (2005): 265–284.

39. Ludwig Blau, *Studien zum althebräischen Buchwesen und zur biblischen Literaturgeschichte* (Budapest: Landes-Rabbinerschule in Budapest, 1902), 188–194.

40. Dov Zlotnick, *The Tractate Mourning*, Yale Judaica Studies 17 (New Haven: Yale University Press, 1966), 70, lines 45–47.

41. Matt 20:2; *b. ʿAbod. Zar.* 62a. See Daniel Sperber, *Roman Palestine 200–400: Money and Prices*, 2nd ed. (Bar-Ilan: Bar-Ilan University Press, 1991), 101–102.

42. Cf. Jaroslav Černý, *Paper and Books in Ancient Egypt* (London: H. K. Lewis & Co., 1952), 23: "These frequent palimpsests can best be explained if we assume that papyrus was relatively expensive material."

43. Naphtali Lewis, *Papyrus in Classical Antiquity* (Oxford: Clarendon, 1974), 129–134, esp. p. 133. On the cost of papyrus, see also Hans-Joachim Drexhage, *Preise, Mieten-Pachten, Kosten und Löhne im römischen Ägypten bis zum Regierungsantritt Diokletians*, Vorarbeiten zu einer Wirtschaftsgeschichte des römischen Ägypten 1 (Sankt Katharinen: Scripta Mercaturae Verlag, 1991), 384–389; Naphtali Lewis, *Greeks in Ptolemaic Egypt: Case Studies in the Social History of the Hellenistic World* (Oxford: Clarendon, 1986), 51, 54–55; Catherine Hezser, *Jewish Literacy in Roman Palestine*, Texts and Studies in Ancient Judaism 81 (Tübingen: Mohr Siebeck, 2001), 132–133. Raffaella Cribiore, *Writing, Teachers, and Students in Graeco-Roman Egypt*, American Studies in Papyrology 36 (Atlanta: Scholars Press, 1996), 59, argues that papyrus was not very costly in Roman Egypt, citing the fact that writing exercises from the period often have blank areas.

44. Theodore C. Skeat, "The Length of the Standard Papyrus Roll and the Cost-Advantage of the Codex," *Zeitschrift für Papyrologie und Epigraphie* 45 (1982): 169–175, esp. 175.

45. Claire Préaux, *L'économie royale des Lagides* (Brussels: Edition de la Fondation égyptologique Reine Elisabeth, 1939), 187–196; Theophrastus, *Hist.Plant.* 4.8.4; Josephus, *Bell.Jud.* 1.130 = *Ant.* 14.33.

46. On private possession of scrolls among Jews in the Roman period, see also the insightful observations by Günter Stemberger, "Öffentlichkeit der Tora im Judentum: Anspruch und Wirklichkeit," *Jahrbuch für Biblische Theologie* 11 (1996): 91–101.

47. Theodore C. Skeat, "Early Christian Book-Production: Papyri and Manuscripts," in *The Cambridge History of the Bible*, vol. 2: *The West from the Fathers to the Reformation*, ed. Geoffrey W. H. Lampe (Cambridge: Cambridge University Press, 1969), 54–79, esp. 71.

48. Colin H. Roberts and Theodore C. Skeat, *The Birth of the Codex* (London: Published for the British Academy by Oxford University Press, 1983), 35–37.

49. Skeat, "Early Christian Book-Production," 69–72.

50. The earliest illustrations of a conventional order of the biblical books are extant in the canonical lists from the second century C.E. onward. Nahum M. Sarna, "The Order of the Books," in Charles Berlin, ed., *Studies in Jewish Bibliography, History and Literature in Honor of I. Edward Kiev* (New York: Ktav, 1971), 407–413, argues that the order of the biblical books in *b. Bab. Bat.* 15a mirrors the arrangement of the scrolls on the

shelves of a library. In fact the order follows the presumed chronology by author, as shown in Louis Jacobs, "Rabbinic Views on the Order and Authorship of the Biblical Books," in *Structure and Form in the Babylonian Talmud* (Cambridge: Cambridge University Press, 1991), 31–41, esp. 34.

51. See, e.g., Renz and Röllig, *Handbuch,* 1:57–59.

52. See Ernst F. Weidner, "Assyrische Beschreibungen der Kriegs-Reliefs Aššurbânaplis," *AfO* 8 (1932–33): 175–203, esp. 176; Thorkild Jacobsen, "Oral to Written," in M. A. Dandamayev et al., eds., *Societies and Languages of the Ancient Near East: Studies in Honor of I. M. Diakonoff* (Warminster: Aries & Phillips, 1982), 129–137, esp. 134; Mordechai Cogan, "A Plaidoyer on Behalf of the Royal Scribes," in Mordechai Cogan and Israel Eph'al, eds., *Ah Assyria . . . : Studies in Assyrian History and Ancient Near Eastern Historiography Presented to Hayim Tadmor,* Scripta Hierosolymitana 33 (Jerusalem: Magnes, 1991), 121–128, esp. 125–127.

53. Compare the oral creation of written texts in Egypt, on which see the illuminating observations by Redford, "Scribe and Speaker," 205.

54. See Skeat, "The Length of the Standard Papyrus Roll," esp. 170; see also R. Lansing Hicks, "*Delet* and *měgillāh:* A Fresh Approach to Jeremiah XXXVI," *VT* 33 (1983): 46–66, esp. 62–65.

55. Note the use of a catch-line in 2 Chron 36:22–23 = Ezra 1:1–2 to signal the fact that the separate scrolls belong to one work; see Blau, *Studien zum althebräischen Buchwesen,* 58; Menahem Haran, "Book-Size and the Device of Catch-Lines in the Biblical Canon," *Journal of Jewish Studies* 36 (1985): 1–11, esp. 5–11.

56. See Leighton D. Reynolds and Nigel G. Wilson, *Scribes and Scholars: A Guide to the Transmission of Greek and Latin Literature,* 2nd ed. (Oxford: Clarendon, 1974), 2: "It is not difficult to imagine that an ancient reader faced with the need to verify a quotation or check a reference would rely if possible on his memory of the passage rather than go to the trouble of unwinding the roll and perhaps thereby accelerating the process of wear and tear. This would certainly account for the fact that when one ancient author quotes another there is so often a substantial difference between the two versions."

57. See Martin P. Nilsson, *Die hellenistische Schule* (Munich: Beck, 1955), esp. 83–84; Henri-Irénée Marrou, *Histoire de l'éducation dans l'Antiquité* (Paris: Seuil, 1965), esp. 161–180. On the Hellenization of Jewish culture in general, see 2 Macc 4:9–15.

58. On libraries, and book culture more generally, see Henri Leclerq, "Bibliothèques," *Dictionnaire d'archéologie chrétienne et de liturgie,* ed. Fernand Cabrol et al. (Paris: Letouzey & Ané, 1907–1953), 2:842–904; Carl Wendel, "Bibliothek," *Reallexikon für Antike und Christentum,* ed. Theodor Klauser et al. (Stuttgart: Hiersemann, 1941–), 2:231–274; Rudolf Pfeiffer, *History of Classical Scholarship,* vol. 1: *From the Beginnings to the End of the Hellenistic Age* (Oxford: Clarendon, 1968). For studies focused on Palestine, see Martin Hengel, "'Schriftauslegung' und 'Schriftwerdung' in der Zeit des Zweiten Tempels," in Martin Hengel and Hermut Löhr, eds., *Schriftauslegung im antiken Judentum und im Urchristentum,* Wissenschaftliche Untersuchungen zum Neuen Testament 73 (Tübingen: Mohr Siebeck, 1994), 1–71, esp. 8–12; Hezser, *Jewish Literacy,* 160–168.

59. See Ben Zion Wacholder, "The Letter from Judas Maccabee to Aristobulus: Is 2 Maccabees 1:10b–2:18 Authentic?" *Hebrew Union College Annual* 49 (1978): 89–133.

60. Frank Moore Cross, *The Ancient Library of Qumran,* 3rd ed. (Sheffield: Sheffield Academic Press, 1995); Hartmut Stegemann, *The Library of Qumran: On the Essenes, Qumran, John the Baptist, and Jesus* (Leiden: Brill; Grand Rapids: Eerdmans, 1998), esp. 80–138.

61. Cross, *Ancient Library,* 43.

62. Theophrastus, *Hist.Plant.* 4.8.4; Josephus, *Bell.Jud.* 1.130 = *Ant.* 14.33.

63. Ulrich von Wilamowitz-Möllendorff, *Einleitung in die griechische Tragödie* (Berlin: Weidmannsche Buchhandlung, 1910), 121–128.

64. Černý, *Paper and Books,* 26–27.

65. Erica Reiner, "Plague Amulets and House Blessings," *JNES* 19 (1960): 148–155.

66. Compare the statement of Pfeiffer, *History of Classical Scholarship,* 1:102, "The book is one of the characteristic signs of the new, the Hellenistic world."

67. A. Leo Oppenheim, *Ancient Mesopotamia: Portrait of a Dead Civilization,* rev. ed. completed by Erica Reiner (Chicago: Chicago University Press, 1977), 13.

2. Authorship in Antiquity

1. So far as I have been able to ascertain, the first to enunciate the *e mente auctoris* principle was Baruch Spinoza (1632–1677) in the *Tractatus*

Theologico-Politicus (1670), here quoted from *Opera*, 4 vols., ed. Carl Gebhardt (Heidelberg: Carl Winter, 1925; repr. 1973), 3:1–249. According to Spinoza we have to be aware of the historical circumstances of the time of composition to be able to dwell on those matters "which the author may have had in mind" *(quas author in mente habere potuerit,* p. 96). Interpreters can use Spinoza's method, so the philosopher argues, "that we may understand the meaning of the author" *(ut mentem authoris percipiamus,* p. 97; see also pp. 84, 91). The hermeneutical principle soon found advocates among Reformed exegetes. Johann Heinrich May (1653–1719) writes in 1694, "Therefore, because everybody is the best interpreter of his own words, one has to ascertain first of all which meaning corresponds with the intention of the author" *(quis sensus auctoris menti conveniat),* "not that which is possible and appeals to us." (*Praefatio* to Matthew Poole, *Synopsis criticorum,* 4th ed., Frankfurt 1694, fol. **3 reverse, left column). The early modern emphasis on the *e mente auctoris* principle has some antecedents in late antiquity; see, e.g., Augustine, *De doctr. Christ.* 2.13.19, who argues that a translator must be familiar with the biblical languages because "an interpreter often departs from the meaning of the author *(a sensu auctoris . . . aberrat)* if he is not sufficiently knowledgeable." (References courtesy Henk-Jan de Jonge, Universiteit Leiden, and Peter van Rooden, Universiteit van Amsterdam.)

2. Charles Taylor, *Sources of the Self: The Making of the Modern Identity* (Cambridge: Cambridge University Press, 1989), esp. 368–390, quotation p. 376.

3. See, e.g., Thomas K. Cheyne, *Jeremiah: His Life and Times,* Men of the Bible (London: Nisbet, 1888); Samuel R. Driver, *Isaiah: His Life and Times,* Men of the Bible (London: Nisbet, 1888); Hugo Gressmann, *Mose und seine Zeit,* Forschungen zur Religion und Literatur des Alten und Neuen Testaments 18 (Göttingen: Vandenhoeck & Ruprecht, 1913); John Skinner, *Prophecy and Religion: Studies in the Life of Jeremiah* (Cambridge: Cambridge University Press, 1922); Elias Auerbach, *Moses* (Amsterdam: Ruys, 1953); Henri Cazelles, *A la recherche de Moïse* (Paris: Cerf, 1979). See also, from a different perspective, Sigmund Freud, *Der Mann Moses und die monotheistische Religion: Drei Abhandlungen* (Amsterdam: Allert de Lange, 1939).

4. For a translation and introduction of the *Vitae Prophetarum* see Douglas R. A. Hare, "The Lives of the Prophets," in James H. Charlesworth, ed.,

The Old Testament Pseudepigrapha, 2 vols. (Garden City: Doubleday, 1985), 2:379–399.

5. Roland Barthes, "The Death of the Author," *Aspen Magazine* 5–6 (1967) [inaccessible to me]. The first publication in French, under the title "La mort de l'auteur," was in *Manteia* 5 (1968): 12–17, reprinted in Barthes, *Oeuvres complètes: Tome II: 1966–1973,* ed. Eric Marty (Paris: Seuil, 1994), 491–495. For another English translation see Barthes, *Image— Music—Text: Essays Selected and Translated by Stephen Heath* (Glasgow: Fontana, 1977), 142–148. For modern views on authorship see, e.g., Maurice Biriotti and Nicola Miller, eds., *What Is an Author?* (Manchester: Manchester University Press, 1993).

6. Note the presence of a reference to Lysimachus, son of Ptolemy, as the translator of Esther, in the LXX translation of Esther. On the date of Lysimachus see Lewis B. Paton, *The Book of Esther,* International Critical Commentary (Edinburgh: T&T Clark, 1908), 30.

7. On Mesopotamian colophons see Erle Leichty, "The Colophon," in Robert D. Biggs and John A. Brinkman, eds., *Studies Presented to A. Leo Oppenheim* (Chicago: Oriental Institute, 1964), 147–154; Hermann Hunger, *Babylonische und assyrische Kolophone,* AOAT 2 (Kevelaer: Butzon & Bercker; Neukirchen-Vluyn: Neukirchener Verlag, 1968). See also the review of Hunger's study by Wilfred G. Lambert in *Welt des Orients* 5 (1970): 290–291.

8. See, for a representative illustration of the majority view, Karl Hecker, "Tradition und Originalität in der altorientalischen Literatur," *Archiv Orientalní* 45 (1977): 245–258, esp. 248, 256.

9. Irving L. Finkel, "Adad-apla-iddina, Esagil-kīn-apli, and the Series SA.GIG," in Erle Leichty et al., eds., *A Scientific Humanist: Studies in Memory of Abraham Sachs* (Philadelphia: The S. N. Kramer Fund, 1988), 143–159, esp. 148–150.

10. Mark J. Geller, "Astronomy and Authorship," *Bulletin of the School of Oriental and African Studies* 53 (1990): 209–213, is just one example of an important study with a misleading title.

11. For this motif see Leonidas Kalugila, *The Wise King: Studies in Royal Wisdom as Divine Revelation in the Old Testament and Its Environment,* Coniectanea Biblica, Old Testament Series 15 (Lund: Gleerup, 1980).

12. See, e.g., Benjamin R. Foster, *Before the Muses: An Anthology of Akkadian Literature,* 2 vols. (Bethesda, MD: CDL Press, 1993), 1:239–245.

13. *Gilgamesh* I 6, 24–28; see Christopher Walker, "The Second Tablet of *ṭupšenna pitēma*: An Old Babylonian Naram-Sin Legend?" *JCS* 33 (1981): 193–194.

14. For the Cuthean legend see Joan Goodnick Westenholz, *Legends of the Kings of Akkade* (Winona Lake, IN: Eisenbrauns, 1997), 263–368; Foster, *Before the Muses*, 1:257–269. For the Sargon legend see Brian Lewis, *The Sargon Legend: A Study of the Akkadian Text*, American Schools of Oriental Research Dissertation Series 4 (Cambridge, MA: American Schools of Oriental Research, 1980); Goodnick Westenholz, *Legends of the Kings of Akkade*, 36–49; Foster, *Before the Muses*, 2:819–820.

15. See Edmond Sollberger, "The Cruciform Monument," *Jaarbericht Ex Oriente Lux* 20 (1967–68): 50–70; Foster, *Before the Muses*, 1:273–277; Tremper Longman III, *Fictional Akkadian Autobiography: A Generic and Comparative Study* (Winona Lake, IN: Eisenbrauns, 1991), 83–88.

16. Rykle Borger, "Gott Marduk und Gott-König Šulgi als Propheten," *Bibliotheca Orientalis* 28 (1971): 3–24, esp. 14–15, 20–24; Foster, *Before the Muses*, 1:270–272.

17. For a fundamental and insightful study of the subject, see Josef A. Sint, *Pseudonymität im Altertum: Ihre Formen und ihre Gründe*, Commentationes Aenipontanae 15 (Innsbruck: Universitätsverlag Wagner, 1960). For a succinct but useful survey of opinions on the significance of pseudepigraphy in the biblical world, see David G. Meade, *Pseudonymity and Canon: An Investigation into the Relationship of Authorship and Authority in Jewish and Earliest Christian Tradition*, Wissenschaftliche Untersuchungen zum Neuen Testament 39 (Tübingen: Mohr, 1986), 4–12. For a more recent study focusing on biblical and parabiblical literature in the light of the Dead Sea Scrolls, see Esther G. Chazon and Michael Stone, eds., *Pseudepigraphic Perspectives: The Apocrypha and Pseudepigrapha in Light of the Dead Sea Scrolls*, Studies on the Texts of the Discoveries of Judah 31 (Leiden: Brill, 1999).

18. The classical demonstration has been offered by Wilhelm M. L. de Wette, *Dissertatio critica qua Deuteronomium a prioribus Pentateuchi libris diversum, alius cuiusdam recentioris actoris opus esse monstratur* (University of Jena, 1805). The identification of Josiah's "Book of the Law" with Deuteronomy already occurs in St. Jerome's (340–420 C.E.) *Commentary to Ezekiel*, 1:1; as well as in a scholium to 2 Kings 22 by Procopius of Gaza (465–529 C.E.); see Eberhard Nestle, "Miscellen," *ZAW* 22 (1902): 170–172, esp. 170–171.

19. Karl Marti, *Der Prophet Jeremia von Anatot* (Basel: Detloff, 1889), 18–20.
20. Pss 3–32, 34–41, 51–65, 68–71, 86, 101, 103, 108–110, 122, 124, 131, 133, 138–145.
21. See 4Q397 Frags. 14–21, line 10 // 4Q398, Frags. 14–17, col. i, lines 2–3 = 4QMMT C, 10 ("David" is mentioned alongside "the Book of Moses" and "the Books of the Prophets"); 2 Macc 2:13, *ta tou David;* Heb 4:7, where Ps 95 is referred to as being "in David," i.e., the Book of Psalms attributed to David.
22. For David as a musician, see 1 Sam 16:14–23; 2 Sam 1:17–27; Amos 6:5; LXX Ps 151:2; 11QPs = 11Q5, Col. XVIII, line 4. For David as the presumed author of Psalms see, e.g., Acts 4:25–26 (Ps 2).
23. For the interpretation of 2 Chron 35:25 see Robert H. Pfeiffer, *Introduction to the Old Testament,* 5th ed. (New York: Harper, 1941), 804. Compare also Josephus, *Ant.,* 10.78–79, where Josephus interprets the authorship of Jeremiah to mean that Lamentations is a prediction of the capture of Jerusalem by Titus.
24. For David as "prophet" see 11QPs 27.3–11; Acts 2:30; Josephus, *Ant.* 8.109–110; Philo, *Agr.* 50; *Rer. Div. Her.* 290; *Sifre Deut.* 1.1; for Solomon as "prophet" see Sir 24:33; *Tg. Ps.-J.* on 1 Kings 5:13; Philo, *De Ebr.* 31; *Sipre Deut.* 1.1.
25. Meade, *Pseudonymity and Canon,* 55, 91, 102, cf. 43, 53, 69, 72.
26. Compare the standard line for the insertion of the name and patronym of the user in Babylonian formulaic prayers; see Werner Mayer, *Untersuchungen zur Formensprache der babylonischen "Gebetsbeschwörungen,"* Studia Pohl, series maior 5 (Rome: Biblical Institute Press, 1976), 46–56.
27. Wilfred G. Lambert, "The Gula Hymn of Bulluṭsa-rabi," *Orientalia* 36 (1967): 105–132; Foster, *Before the Muses,* 2:491–499.
28. Another example of a prayer by an identified author is the Late Babylonian lament of Nabû-šuma-ukîn = Amel-Marduk = Evil-Merodach; see Irving L. Finkel, "The Lament of Nabû-šuma-ukîn," in Johannes Renger, ed., *Babylon: Focus mesopotamischer Geschichte, Wiege früher Gelehrsamkeit, Mythos in der Moderne. 2. Internationales Colloquium der Deutschen Orient-Gesellschaft 24.–26. März 1998 in Berlin,* Colloquien der Deutschen Orient Gesellschaft 2 (Saarbrücken: Saarbrücker Druckerei und Verlag, 1999), 323–342.
29. Lambert, *Babylonian Wisdom Literature,* 63–91; Foster, *Before the Muses,* 2:806–814.

30. See Wilfred G. Lambert, "A Catalogue of Texts and Authors," *JCS* 16 (1962): 59–77, esp. 66; see also Finkel, "Adad-apla-iddina," 144. For the *List of Sages and Scholars*, see Johannes van Dijk, in Heinrich J. Lenzen, *XVIII. Vorläufiger Bericht über die . . . Ausgrabungen in Uruk-Warka* (Berlin: Mann, 1962), 44–52, Pl. 27, lines 17–18; see also Finkel, "Adad-apla-iddina," 144.

31. Another acrostic prayer is in the name of Assurbanipal; see Alasdair Livingstone, *Court Poetry and Literary Miscellanea*, SAA 3 (Helsinki: Helsinki University Press, 1989), 6–10; Foster, *Before the Muses*, 2:720–724. The text was presumably commissioned by the king. The signature of the text is a combination of honorary authorship plus individual identification of the suppliant.

32. Wilfred G. Lambert, "Literary Style in First Millennium Mesopotamia," *JAOS* 88 (1968): 123–132, esp. 130–132; Ronald F. G. Sweet, "A Pair of Double Acrostics in Akkadian," *Orientalia* 38 (1969): 459–460; Foster, *Before the Muses*, 2:620–621.

33. Luigi Cagni, *L'Epopea di Erra*, Studi Semitici 34 (Rome: Istituto di studi del Vicino Oriente, 1969); Foster, *Before the Muses*, 2:771–805.

34. For this translation see Karlheinz Deller and Werner R. Mayer, "Akkadische Lexikographie: *CAD* M," *Orientalia* 53 (1984): 72–124, esp. 121–122.

35. *Erra* V 42–45 (Foster, *Before the Muses*, 2:804).

36. See the judicious remarks by Peter Machinist and Hayim Tadmor, "Heavenly Wisdom," in Mark E. Cohen et al., eds., *The Tablet and the Scroll: Near Eastern Studies in Honor of William W. Hallo* (Bethesda, MD: CDL Press, 1993), 146–151, esp. 147.

37. Erich Ebeling, "Der Mythos 'Herr aller Menschen' vom Pestgotte Ira," in Hugo Gressmann, ed., *Altorientalische Texte zum Alten Testament*, 2nd ed. (Berlin and Leipzig: De Gruyter, 1926), 212–230, esp. 229 note d; Rintje Frankena, "Untersuchungen zum Irra-Epos," *Bibliotheca Orientalis* 14 (1957): 2–10, esp. 6.

38. The *Catalogue of Texts and Authors* puts Kabti-ilāni-Marduk after Adapa but before King Enmerkar. The Seleucid *List of Sages and Scholars*, line 13, makes him a contemporary of King Ibbi-Sin (third dynasty of Ur, ca. 2050).

39. The term *ak-ka-du-ú* means "man of Akkad" rather than "[the land/city of] Akkad"; on this I agree with Stephanie Dalley (*Myths from Mesopotamia: Creation, The Flood, Gilgamesh, and Others* [Oxford: Oxford

University Press, 1989], 308) and Benjamin Foster (*Before the Muses,* 2:800), against Luigi Cagni (*Epopea,* 119, 242).

40. See also Dalley, *Myths from Mesopotamia,* 315 note 52: "This line indicates that there is an important element of pseudo-prophecy in the epic." Compare the Neo-Assyrian oracle collections that consistently give the name of the prophet or prophetess (*ša pî* NN); see Simo Parpola, *Assyrian Prophecies,* SAA 9 (Helsinki: Helsinki University Press, 1997). The practice in cuneiform literature corresponds with the biblical custom of assigning authors to the prophetical scrolls.

41. William W. Hallo and Johannes J. A. van Dijk, *The Exaltation of Inanna,* Yale Near Eastern Researches 3 (New Haven: Yale University Press, 1968), 1: "Cuneiform literature has long been stigmatized as anonymous."

42. Foster, *Before the Muses,* 1:20. See also Benjamin R. Foster, "On Authorship in Akkadian Literature," *Annali dell' Istituto Orientale di Napoli* 51 (1990): 17–32.

43. Wilfred G. Lambert, "A Catalogue of Texts and Authors," *JCS* 16 (1962): 59–77.

44. Fragment VI 15–17 (= K.9717+81-7-27,71 Rev. 15–17) is either an explanatory commentary to Fragment I 1(5)–7, or an explanation of the chain of tradition pertinent to all the works previously listed. The mention of Adapa in this section is therefore no indication of "the lack of a consistent chronological scheme," contrary to Lambert, "Catalogue," 76.

45. Citation from Lambert, "Catalogue," 59.

46. See, for the following, Louis Jacobs, "Rabbinic Views on the Order and Authorship of the Biblical Books," in *Structure and Form in the Babylonian Talmud* (Cambridge: Cambridge University Press, 1991), 31–41.

47. The presumed antiquity of Job is based on Job 19:24, which mentions stone as writing material. Note that at Qumran only the books of the Pentateuch and Job are attested in paleographical script (4QpaleoJob^c = 4Q101). The canon of Old Testament books preserved by Epiphanius (*De mensuris et ponderibus,* 23), independently surviving in a medieval manuscript of 2 Clemens and the Didache, puts Job between Joshua and Judges; see Jean-Paul Audet, "A Hebrew-Aramaic List of Books of the Old Testament in Greek Transcription," *Journal of Theological Studies* 1 (1950): 135–154, esp. 138. On the presumed antiquity of stone as writing material, see also the statement by Assurbanipal: "I have examined stone inscriptions (*abnī*) from before the Flood" (Maximilian Streck, *Assurbanipal und die letzten assyrischen Könige bis zum Untergang*

Nineveh's, 3 vols., Vorderasiatische Bibliothek 7 [Leipzig: Hinrichs, 1916], 2:256:17'–18', cf. Rykle Borger, *Beiträge zum Inschriftenwerk Assurbanipals* [Wiesbaden: Harrassowitz, 1996], 187).

48. Marcel Mauss, "Une Catégorie de l'Esprit Humain: La Notion de Personne, Celle de 'Moi,'" *The Journal of the Royal Anthropological Institute* 68 (1938): 263–281; Michael Carrithers et al., eds., *The Category of the Person: Anthropology, Philosophy, History* (Cambridge: Cambridge University Press, 1985). Compare also the interesting observations by Alasdair MacIntyre, *After Virtue: A Study in Moral Theory*, 2nd ed. (London: Duckworth, 1985), esp. 27–30, on the notion of "character" in nineteenth-century Germany and England, and in modern times.

49. See Martin Hengel, "Anonymität, Pseudepigraphie und 'Literarische Fälschung' in der jüdisch-hellenistischer Literatur," in Kurt von Fritz, ed., *Pseudepigrapha 1*, Entretiens sur l'Antiquité Classique 18 (Geneva: Fondation Hardt, 1972), 231–308, esp. 283, where Hengel argues that in Judaism "the consciousness of literary property and individuality of authorship was underdeveloped in comparison to the Greco-Roman world."

50. A case in point is the description of the underworld in *Gilgamesh*, Standard Version, VII 184–193 (Dalley, *Myths from Mesopotamia*, 89); Descent of Ishtar, lines 4–11 (Foster, *Before the Muses*, 1:404); and Nergal and Ereshkigal, Standard Version, column ii 59' to column iii 8' (Foster, *Before the Muses*, 1:420).

51. On the practice and perception of plagiarism in antiquity, see Eduard Stemplinger, *Das Plagiat in der griechischen Literatur* (Leipzig and Berlin: Teubner, 1912).

52. Hence the frequent references to the king at the end of Akkadian texts; see Brigitte R. M. Groneberg, *Lob der Ištar: Gebet und Ritual an die altbabylonische Venusgöttin*, CM 8 (Groningen: Styx, 1997), 87, col. V, lines 23–29; Lambert, *Babylonian Wisdom Literature*, 88–89, line 297; Finkel, "Adad-apla-iddina," 149–150, lines 19'–20', 31'–33'.

53. 11QPs = 11Q5, Col. XXVII, line 2. The text runs: "And David, son of Jesse, was a sage [*ḥākām*], and a light like the light of the sun, [and] a scribe . . . And he wrote psalms."

3. In Search of the Scribes, I

1. David Diringer, *Le iscrizioni antico-ebraiche palestinesi* (Florence: Le Monnier, 1934), 235–237, no. 75 *(lšlm, bn 'dnyh, h<s>pr);* Francesco Vattioni, "I sigilli ebraici," *Biblica* 50 (1969): 357–388, no. 74 *('mṣ*

hspr); Pierre Bordreuil, "Inscriptions sigillaires ouest-sémitiques, II: Un cachet hébreu récemment acquis par le Cabinet des Médailles de la Bibliothèque Nationale," *Syria* 52 (1975): 107–118: *lm'š, bn. mnḥ, hspr* (ca. 700 B.C.E.); Nahman Avigad, *Bullae and Seals from a Post-Exilic Judean Archive,* Qedem Monographs of the Institute of Archaeology 4 (Jerusalem: Hebrew University, Institute of Archaeology, 1976), 7–8, no. 6: *lyrmy hspr* (ca. 500 B.C.E.). Compare also the use of *spr'* following a personal name in colophons of the Aramaic letters from the chancery of the Persian satrap of Egypt; see George R. Driver, *Aramaic Documents of the Fifth Century B.C.,* abr. and rev. ed. (Oxford: Oxford University Press, 1957), nos. 4:4, 6:6, 7:10, 8:6, 9:3, 10:5. For the occurrence of the term on a Phoenician seal see André Lemaire, "Essai sur cinq sceaux phéniciens," *Semitica* 27 (1977): 29–40, esp. 33, no. 4, and comments on 38–39.

2. See, e.g., Tryggve N. D. Mettinger, *Solomonic State Officials: A Study of Civil Government Officials of the Israelite Monarchy,* Coniectanea Biblica, OT Series 5 (Lund: Gleerup, 1971), 146–156; Michael Fishbane, *Biblical Interpretation in Ancient Israel* (Oxford: Clarendon, 1985), 28–32; David M. Carr, *Writing on the Tablet of the Heart: Origins of Scripture and Literature* (New York: Oxford University Press, 2005), 47–61, 84–88.

3. Šulgi Hymn B, lines 13–20. For translations see Åke W. Sjöberg, "The Old Babylonian Eduba," in Stephen B. Lieberman, ed., *Sumerological Studies in Honor of Thorkild Jacobsen on His Seventieth Birthday, June 7, 1974,* Assyriological Studies 20 (Chicago: University of Chicago Press, 1975), 159–179, esp. 172–173; Samuel N. Kramer, *From the Poetry of Sumer: Creation, Glorification, Adoration* (Berkeley: University of California Press, 1979), 63; Niek Veldhuis, "The Cuneiform Tablet as an Educational Tool," *Dutch Studies Published by Near Eastern Languages and Literature* 2/1 (1996): 11–26, esp. 13. For similar claims by other early kings, see Herman L. J. Vanstiphout, "Lipit-Eštar's Praise in the Edubba," *JCS* 30 (1978): 33–61, esp. 36–37, lines 17–24a; Cyril John Gadd and Samuel Noah Kramer, *Literary and Religious Texts,* Ur Excavations, Texts 6/1 (London: British Museum; Philadelphia: University Museum of the University of Pennsylvania, 1963), no. 99, reverse, column V, lines 22–30; see Sjöberg, "Old Babylonian Eduba," 175 (Sin-iddinam).

4. Maximilian Streck, *Assurbanipal und die letzten assyrischen Könige bis*

zum Untergang Nineveh's, 3 vols., Vorderasiatische Bibliothek 7 (Leipzig: Hinrichs, 1916), 2:254:10'–256:18', cf. Rykle Borger, *Beiträge zum Inschriftenwerk Assurbanipals* (Wiesbaden: Harrassowitz, 1996), 187. For the interpretation of the last phrase, see Wilfred G. Lambert, "A Late Babylonian Copy of an Expository Text," *JNES* 48 (1989): 215–221, esp. 220–221. On this self-praise of Assurbanipal see also Piotr Michalowski, "The Doors of the Past," in Israel Eph'al et al., eds., *Hayim and Miriam Tadmor Volume,* Eretz-Israel 27 (Jerusalem: The Israel Exploration Society, 2003), 136*–152*, esp. 143*.

5. In the Old Babylonian period there were female scribes in Mari and Sippar, where they served mostly as secretaries to palace women (Mari) and female devotees of Šamaš (Sippar); see Brigitte Lion, "Dame Inanna-ama-mu, scribe à Sippar," *RA* 95 (2001): 7–32; Andrew R. George, *The Babylonian Gilgamesh Epic: Introduction, Critical Edition and Cuneiform Texts,* 2 vols. (Oxford: Oxford University Press, 2003), 1:483, esp. note 129. For a reference to the scribal education of a first-millennium princess, see Mikko Luukko and Greta Van Buylaere, *The Political Correspondence of Esarhaddon,* SAA 16 (Helsinki: Helsinki University Press, 2002), no. 28, lines 3–4, addressed to Libbāli-šarrat, the future wife of Assurbanipal, "Why don't you write your tablet and do your homework?"

6. See Dominique Charpin, *Le clergé d'Ur au siècle d'Hammurabi,* Hautes Etudes Orientales 22 (Geneva: Droz, 1986), 420–434; Eleanor Robson, "The Tablet House: A Scribal School in Old Babylonian Nippur," *RA* 95 (2001): 39–66, esp. 62; Andrew R. George, "In Search of the é.dub.ba.a: The Ancient Mesopotamian School in Literature and Reality," in Yitschak Sefati et al., eds., *"An Experienced Scribe Who Neglects Nothing": Ancient Near Eastern Studies in Honor of Jacob Klein* (Bethesda, MD: CDL Press, 2005), 127–137. At Ugarit in the late Bronze Age, scribal education took place in private houses as well; see Wilfred H. van Soldt, "Babylonian Lexical, Religious and Literary Texts and Scribal Education at Ugarit," in Manfried Dietrich and Oswald Loretz, eds., *Ugarit: Ein ostmediterranes Kulturzentrum im Alten Orient; Ergebnisse und Perspektiven der Forschung,* Abhandlungen zur Literatur Alt-Syriens-Palästinas 7 (Münster: Ugarit-Verlag, 1995), 171–212, esp. 180.

7. See Niek Veldhuis, *Religion, Literature, and Scholarship: The Sumerian Composition Nanše and the Birds,* CM 22 (Leiden: Brill/Styx, 2004), 58–66.

8. Wilfred G. Lambert, *Babylonian Wisdom Literature* (Oxford: Clarendon, 1960), 8.

9. Paul-Alain Beaulieu, "New Light on Secret Knowledge in Late Babylonian Culture," *ZA* 82 (1992): 98–111.

10. Antoine Cavigneaux, *Textes scolaires du temple de Nabû ša ḫarê* (Baghdad: Republic of Iraq, Ministry of Culture and Information, State Organization of Antiquities and Heritage, 1981).

11. An anonymous letter to King Esarhaddon denounces a goldsmith for having hired a Babylonian scholar to privately teach his son to read exorcism, extispicy omens, and astrology. Such behavior was reprehensible, obviously, because the instruction in these potentially dangerous crafts took place outside the institutional context of the temple workshop. For the text in question see Simo Parpola, "The Man without a Scribe and the Question of Literacy in the Assyrian Empire," in Beate Pongratz-Leisten et al., eds., *Ana šadî Labnāni lū allik: Beiträge zu altorientalischen und mittelmeerischen Kulturen. Festschrift für Wolfgang Röllig*, AOAT 247 (Kevelaer: Butzon & Bercker; Neukirchen-Vluyn: Neukirchener Verlag, 1997), 315–324, esp. 321, note 18; Martti Nissinen, *References to Prophecy in Neo-Assyrian Sources*, SAA Studies 7 (Helsinki: Helsinki University Press, 1998), 142 and note 541.

12. Akkadian *mār mummu*; see Hermann Hunger, *Babylonische und assyrische Kolophone*, AOAT 2 (Kevelaer: Butzon & Bercker; Neukirchen-Vluyn: Neukirchener Verlag, 1968), nos. 354, 402.

13. Petra D. Gesche, *Schulunterricht in Babylonien im ersten Jahrtausend v.Chr.*, AOAT 275 (Münster: Ugarit-Verlag, 2001), 153–166.

14. Note the reference to "Nabu who dwells in the temple workshop"; see Hunger, *Kolophone*, no. 234.

15. On the possibility of acquiring literacy without a formal education, for instance in the context of very specific tasks of bookkeeping, see Leonhard Sassmannshausen, "Zur babylonischen Schreiberausbildung," *Baghdader Mitteilungen* 33 (2002): 211–228.

16. Bendt Alster, *Proverbs of Ancient Sumer: The World's Earliest Proverb Collections*, 2 vols. (Bethesda, MD: CDL Press, 1997) 1:53, collection 2.40.

17. On the role of rote learning see Hartmut Waetzoldt, "Der Schreiber als Lehrer in Mesopotamien," in Johann Georg von Hohenzollern and Max Liedtke, eds., *Schreiber—Magister—Lehrer: Zur Geschichte und Funktion eines Berufsstandes* (Bad Heilbrunn: Julius Klinkhardt, 1989),

33–50, esp. 36. For the so-called lexical lists and the role of oral instruction see Miguel Civil, "Lexicography," in Stephen B. Lieberman, ed., *Sumerological Studies in Honor of Thorkild Jacobsen on His Seventieth Birthday, June 7, 1974,* Assyriological Studies 20 (Chicago: University of Chicago Press, 1975), 123–157.

18. Alster, *Proverbs of Ancient Sumer,* 1:54, collection 2.47.

19. Steve Tinney, "On the Curricular Setting of Sumerian Literature," *Iraq* 61 (1999): 159–172.

20. Lambert, *Babylonian Wisdom Literature,* 70, line 6.

21. The first copy of the text was published by Erich Ebeling, *Keilschrifttexte aus Assur religiösen Inhalts,* Wissenschaftliche Veröffentlichung der Deutschen Orient-Gesellschaft 28 (Leipzig: Hinrichs, 1915–1919), no. 44. The most recent edition, with a score transcription of four copies, is that by Mark J. Geller, "Incipits and Rubrics," in Andrew R. George and Irving L. Finkel, eds., *Wisdom, Gods and Literature: Studies in Assyriology in Honour of W. G. Lambert* (Winona Lake, IN: Eisenbrauns, 2000), 225–258, esp. 242–254. An additional copy has been published by Egbert von Weiher, *Spätbabylonische Texte aus Uruk* 5, Ausgrabungen der Deutschen Forschungsgemeinschaft in Uruk-Warka 13 (Mainz: Philipp von Zabern, 1998), no. 231.

22. See Jean Bottéro, "Le Manuel de l'Exorciste et son calendrier," *Annuaire de l'Ecole Pratique des Hautes Etudes, IVème section, 1974–75* (1975): 95–142, esp. 124–126; repr. in *Mythes et rites de Babylone* (Paris: Honoré Champion, 1985), 65–112.

23. Geller, "Incipits and Rubrics," 19–20, lines 36–40. Note that line 39 is an intrusion; see Bottéro, "Manuel de l'Exorciste," 90. For the interpretation of *kitpudu šutaddunu mitḫurti* (line 40 = Rev. 17) see Bottéro, "Manuel de l'Exorciste," 85.

24. Geller, "Incipits and Rubrics," 20, lines 1–42.

25. Wilfred G. Lambert, "A Catalogue of Texts and Authors," *JCS* 16 (1962): 59–77, esp. 64–65, no. I, lines 1–4. A minor myth of the first millennium tries to reconcile Ea's role as divine author with that of Nabû as patron deity of the scribes by saying that Ea's texts were eventually entrusted to Nabû, who thereby received the exorcistic corpus (*āšipūtu,* written *a-*GU.GU-*ta*) as his designated lot; see Wilfred G. Lambert, "Twenty-One 'Poultices,'" *Anatolian Studies* 30 (1980): 77–83, esp. 78.

26. Benno Landsberger, "Scribal Concepts of Education," in Carl H. Kraeling and Robert MacAdams, eds., *City Invincible: A Symposium on*

Urbanization and Cultural Development in the Ancient Near East (Chicago: University of Chicago Press, 1960), 94–123, esp. 119.

27. See Åke W. Sjöberg, "Der Examenstext A," *ZA* 64 (1975): 137–176, esp. 140, line 2. On the examination see also Waetzoldt, "Der Schreiber als Lehrer," 37; Gesche, *Schulunterricht,* 198.

28. See Wilfred G. Lambert, "The Qualifications of Babylonian Diviners," in Stefan Maul, ed., *Festschrift für Rykle Borger zu seinem 65. Geburtstag am 24. Mai 1994: tikip santakki mala bašmu . . .,* CM 10 (Groningen: Styx, 1998), 141–158, esp. 143. The text in question was published by Heinrich Zimmern, *Beiträge zur Kenntnis der babylonischen Religion, II: Ritualtafeln für den Wahrsager, Beschwörer und Sänger* (Leipzig: Hinrichs, 1901), no. 1–20, line 14; the term is *egirtu,* "certificate."

29. Ebeling, *Keilschrifttexte,* no. 44, line 30. For a transliteration see Geller, "Incipits and Rubrics," 248 *(kullat nagbi nēmeqi).*

30. A cuneiform letter from the Neo-Assyrian period refers to the scholars as men who have the complete corpus of scribal learning "stored in their mind"; see Grant Frame and Andrew R. George, "The Royal Libraries of Nineveh: New Evidence for King Ashurbanipal's Tablet Collecting" (Papers of the XLIXe Rencontre Assyriologique Internationale, London, 7–11 July 2003, Part 2; London: British School of Archaeology in Iraq), *Iraq* 67 (2005): 265–284, esp. 272.

31. Fritz Rudolf Kraus, *Vom mesopotamischen Menschen der altbabylonischen Zeit und seiner Welt* (Amsterdam: North-Holland Publishing Company, 1973), 18–32, esp. 23.

32. See Francesca Rochberg, "Scribes and Scholars: The ṭupšar Enūma Anu Enlil," in Joachim Marzahn and Hans Neumann, eds., *Assyriologica et Semitica: Festschrift für Joachim Oelsner,* AOAT 252 (Münster: Ugarit-Verlag, 2000), 359–375, esp. 365. Compare the "assembly of the exorcists [*āšipī*] of the Esagil-temple," mentioned in cuneiform texts from Hellenistic Babylonia; see Gilbert J. P. McEwan, *Priest and Temple in Hellenistic Babylonia,* Freiburger Altorientalische Studien 4 (Wiesbaden: Franz Steiner, 1981), 21–24. For the Neo-Assyrian period see Brigitte Menzel, *Assyrische Tempel,* 2 vols., Studia Pohl series maior 10/1–2 (Rome: Biblical Institute Press, 1981), 1:247. Compare the situation at Emar, where scholar-scribes were primarily connected with the temple; see Jun Ikeda, "Scribes in Emar," in Kazuko Watanabe, ed., *Priests and Officials in the Ancient Near East* (Heidelberg: Carl Winter, 1999), 163–185, esp. 177–178.

33. See, e.g., Marc J. H. Linssen, *The Cults of Uruk and Babylon: The Temple Ritual Texts as Evidence for Hellenistic Cult Practises,* CM 25 (Leiden: Brill & Styx, 2004), 5–6.

34. On the Babylonian priesthood see Johannes Renger, "Untersuchungen zur Priestertum in der altbabylonischen Zeit," *ZA* 58 (1967): 110–188; *ZA* 59 (1969): 104–230; Gilbert J. P. McEwan, *Priest and Temple in Hellenistic Babylonia,* Freiburger Altorientalische Studien 4 (Wiesbaden: Franz Steiner, 1981); Richard A. Henshaw, *Female and Male: The Cultic Personnel; The Bible and the Rest of the Ancient Near East,* Princeton Theological Monograph Series 31 (Allison Park, PA: Pickwick Publications, 1994), esp. 9–10. None of these studies discusses the internal hierarchy of the priesthood.

35. The observation is valid in particular for the Old Babylonian period; see Rivkah Harris, *Ancient Sippar: A Demographic Study of an Old-Babylonian City (1894–1595 B.C.),* Uitgaven van het Nederlands Historisch-Archaeologisch Instituut te Istanbul (Leiden: Nederlands Instituut voor het Nabije Oosten, 1975), 176–178; Rintje Frankena, *Kommentar zu den altbabylonischen Briefen aus Lagaba und anderen Orten,* Studia ad tabulas cuneiformes a F.M.Th. de Liagre Böhl collectas pertinentia 4 (Leiden: Nederlands Instituut voor het Nabije Oosten, 1978), 79–80.

36. See Heinrich Zimmern, "Der Schenkenliebeszauber," *ZA* 32 (1918–1919): 164–184, esp. 170.

37. On the scribal art as a source of income see "In Praise of the Scribal Art," lines 5–6: "Strive after the scribal art and it will surely enrich you, work hard at the scribal art and it will bring you wealth." Translated in Benjamin R. Foster, *Before the Muses,* 3rd ed. (Bethesda, MD: CDL Press, 2005), 1023.

38. See Simo Parpola, *Letters from Assyrian and Babylonian Scholars,* SAA 10 (Helsinki: Helsinki University Press, 1993). For the following, see especially Parpola's introduction (xiii–xxxv).

39. Ronald F. G. Sweet, "The Sage in Akkadian Literature: A Philological Study," in John G. Gammie and Leo G. Perdue, eds., *The Sage in Israel and the Ancient Near East* (Winona Lake, IN: Eisenbrauns, 1990), 45–65, esp. 51–57. See, as an example, the flattering comment of Marduk-šumu-uṣur, chief diviner of Assurbanipal: "Aššur, in a dream, called the grandfather of the king [= Sennacherib], my lord, a sage *(apkallu);* the king, lord of kings, is an offspring of a sage and Adapa: you have surpassed the wisdom of the Abyss *(nēmeqe apsî)* and all scholarship

(ummânūtu)," in Parpola, *Letters from Assyrian and Babylonian Scholars,* no. 174, lines 7–9.

40. See Simo Parpola, "The Forlorn Scholar," in Francesca Rochberg-Halton, ed., *Language, Literature, and History: Philological and Historical Studies Presented to Erica Reiner,* American Oriental Series 67 (New Haven: American Oriental Society, 1987), 257–278.

41. See Parpola, *Letters from Assyrian and Babylonian Scholars,* xxvi, table I: "The Inner Circle."

42. Åke W. Sjöberg, "Der Vater und sein missratener Sohn," *JCS* 25 (1973): 105–169, esp. 112, lines 115–116: "Enlil has decreed as the lot of humankind that the son should take the profession of his father."

43. See Parpola, *Letters from Assyrian and Babylonian Scholars,* no. 182, reverse 28, "I have learned [my craft] from my father" (written by a *bārû*); Hermann Hunger, *Astrological Reports to Assyrian Kings,* SAA 8 (Helsinki: Helsinki University Press, 1992), no. 454, reverse 6 (written by an astrologer); Alasdair Livingstone, *Mystical and Mythological Explanatory Works of Assyrian and Babylonian Scholars* (Oxford: Clarendon, 1986), 28–29, tablet K. 2670, lines 7–8.

44. See Paul-Alain Beaulieu, "The Descendants of Sîn-lēqi-unninni," in Joachim Marzahn and Hans Neumann, eds., *Assyriologica et Semitica: Festschrift für Joachim Oelsner,* AOAT 252 (Münster: Ugarit-Verlag, 2000), 1–16.

45. On the difference between the two see Edith F. Ritter, "Magical-expert *(āšipu)* and Physician *(asû):* Notes on Two Complementary Professions in Babylonian Medicine," in Hans G. Güterbock and Thorkild Jacobsen, eds., *Studies in Honor of Benno Landsberger on His Seventy-Fifth Birthday, April 21, 1965,* Assyriological Studies 16 (Chicago: University of Chicago Press, 1965), 299–322.

46. Parpola, *Letters from Assyrian and Babylonian Scholars,* no. 160, lines 36–42.

47. Compare Beaulieu, "The Descendants of Sîn-lēqi-unninni," 13. Note that the Curriculum of Exorcism, first published by Erich Ebeling as no. 44 of *Keilschrifttexte aus Assur religiösen Inhalts,* did include *Enūma Anu Enlil* and *Šumma ālu;* see Geller, "Incipits and Rubrics," 251, line 39.

48. On the temple as a center of scholarship see also Geert de Breucker, "Berossos and the Mesopotamian Temple as Centre of Knowledge during the Hellenistic Period," in Alasdair A. MacDonald et al., eds., *Learned*

Antiquity: Scholarship and Society, Groningen Studies in Cultural Change 5 (Leuven: Peeters, 2003), 13–23.

49. Ebeling, *Keilschrifttexte,* no. 31, reverse 4; see Hunger, *Kolophone,* no. 192.

50. Stephen Langdon, *Die Neubabylonischen Königsinschriften,* Vorderasiatische Bibliothek 4 (Leipzig: Hinrichs, 1912), 254–256, no. 6, lines 32–33. For this text see also Paul-Alain Beaulieu, *The Reign of Nabonidus King of Babylon 556–539 B.C.,* Yale Near Eastern Researches 10 (New Haven: Yale University Press, 1989), 7 inscription no. 5. For a new edition of the text see Hanspeter Schaudig, *Die Inschriften Nabonids von Babylon und Kyros' des Grossen,* AOAT 256 (Münster: Ugarit-Verlag, 2001), 384–394, no. 2.9. Note that the expression *ṭupšar mināti enqūtu* means "wise architects" (*Chicago Assyrian Dictionary,* M/2, 88), not "numerous wise scribes," against Beaulieu, *Reign of Nabonidus,* 7; and Rochberg, "Scribes and Scholars," 365.

51. So Alexander Heidel, "The Meaning of *mummu* in Akkadian Literature," *JNES* 7 (1948): 98–105, esp. 102–104; Beaulieu, *Reign of Nabonidus,* 8.

52. On *gerginakku* see the *Chicago Assyrian Dictionary,* G, 87.

53. See Hunger, *Kolophone,* nos. 106, 130, 137, 151, 166, 328, 369, 461.

54. Ibid., no. 12.

55. Ibid., no. 151.

56. Ibid., no. 106, lines 6–8: "The scholar who does not change a line and puts it [back] in the library—may Ishtar look upon him kindly; who makes it leave the Eanna temple—may Ishtar pursue him in anger." See also nos. 192:4–5, 193:5, and elsewhere in the colophons. The emphatic reference to divine retribution in case of nonreturn of the tablet suggests that theft was a serious problem for the libraries.

57. Stefan M. Maul, *Zukunfbewältigung: Eine Untersuchung altorientalischen Denkens anhand der babylonisch-assyrischen Löserituale (Namburbi),* Baghdader Forschungen 18 (Mainz: Philipp von Zabern, 1994), 161–162.

58. It is known that the Marduk temple in Babylon had a library on account of the reference to it in Hunger, *Kolophone,* no. 151.

59. For an overview of cuneiform libraries see Olof Pedersén, *Archives and Libraries in the Ancient Near East 1500–300 B.C.* (Bethesda, Md.: CDL Press, 1998), 129–213.

60. Ibid., 194.

61. W. al-Jadir, "Une bibliothèque et ses tablettes dans le quartier sacré de Sippar," *Archeologia* 224 (1987): 18–27; W. al-Jadir, "Le quartier de l'É.BABBAR de Sippar (Sommaire des fouilles de 1985–1989, 8–11èmes campagnes)," in Léon de Meyer and Hermann Gasche, eds., *Mésopotamie et Elam,* Proceedings of the Thirty-sixth Rencontre Assyriologique Internationale, Mesopotamian History and Environment, Occasional Publications 1 (Ghent: University of Ghent, 1991), 193–196.

62. Lambert, *Babylonian Wisdom Literature,* 259 line 19: "The scribal art is the mother of orators and the father of scholars."

63. *Enūma eliš* V 146: *enqu mūdû mithariš limtalku.* For a translation see Foster, *Before the Muses,* 1:400.

64. See *Erra* V 56 (Foster, *Before the Muses,* 2:804); Geller, "Incipits and Rubrics," 20 line 40. For the interpretation of this line see Bottéro, "Manuel de l'Exorciste," 115.

65. On the oral lore of the scholars see Yaakov Elman, "Authoritative Oral Tradition in Neo-Assyrian Scribal Circles," *Journal of Ancient Near Eastern Studies of Columbia University* 7 (1975): 19–32.

66. Veldhuis, *Religion, Literature, and Scholarship,* 66.

67. See Ernst F. Weidner, "Geheimschrift," *RlA* 3:185–188.

68. Andrew W. George observes that the excerpt tablet of *Gilgamesh* from a private library at Huzirina (modern Sultantepe) contains all kinds of orthographical errors reflecting Aramaic writing practice; see George, *Babylonian Gilgamesh Epic,* 1:369–373, esp. 370.

69. The scribal use of a cryptic pseudo-Sumerian in first-millennium texts is apparently meant to show off what the scribes considered supreme learning and profound erudition; see the observations by Thorkild Jacobsen, "Abstruse Sumerian," in Mordechai Cogan and Israel Eph'al, eds., *Ah Assyria . . .: Studies in Assyrian History and Ancient Near Eastern Historiography Presented to Hayim Tadmor,* Scripta Hierosolymitana 33 (Jerusalem: Magnes, 1991), 278–291.

70. See Ebeling, *Keilschrifttexte,* no. 230, reverse 9–15: "Secret of the exorcists. The initiate may show it to [another] initiate, but to a noninitiate he may not show it. Make your son whom you love take an oath by Asalluhi and [DN] and show it to him." See also, in connection with *bārûtu,* Lambert, "Qualifications of Babylonian Diviners," 149, lines 19–22.

71. Beaulieu, "New Light on Secret Knowledge," 101.

72. See, e.g., Wilfred G. Lambert, "An Address of Marduk to the Demons," *AfO* 17 (1954–56): 310–321, esp. 313, commentary to line 6; Adam Falkenstein, "Zwei Rituale aus seleukidischer Zeit," in Heinrich Lenzen,

XV. Vorläufiger Bericht Uruk-Warka, Abhandlungen der Deutschen Orient-Gesellschaft 4 (Berlin: Mann, 1959), 36–44, esp. 40, lines 10'–11'; Parpola, *Letters from Assyrian and Babylonian Scholars,* no. 96, reverse.

73. For a survey of secrecy colophons see Rykle Borger, "Geheimwissen," *RlA* 3:188–191; Borger, *Handbuch der Keilschriftliteratur,* 3 vols. (Berlin: W. de Gruyter, 1967–1975), 3:119 #108; Paul-Alain Beaulieu, "New Light on Secret Knowledge in Late Babylonian Culture," *ZA* 82 (1992): 98–111, esp. 110–111. See also Oliver R. Gurney et al., *The Sultantepe Tablets,* 2 vols. (London: The British Institute of Archaeology at Ankara, 1957–1964), 2.300, reverse, line 19: . . . *mu-du-ú mu-da-a li-ka[l-li]m la mu-du-u la* (nu) *immar* (igiⁱ); Wilfred G. Lambert, "Processions to the Akitu House," *Revue d'Assyriologie* 91 (1997): 49–80, esp. 73, BM 77028, reverse, line 6': "secret of the scholars [written: sag érin-*ni* = *niṣirti ummânī*], property of Nabu, king of [the world]."

74. *Ludlul* II 29–31 (Lambert, *Babylonian Wisdom Literature,* 40–41).

75. See Parpola, "The Forlorn Scholar," 260–261, lines 29–30.

76. Foster, *Before the Muses,* 2:825 (the so-called *aluzinnu-*text); 2:832–833, lines 120–134 (Poor Man of Nippur); Andrew R. George, "Ninurta-pāqidāt's Dog Bite, and Notes on Other Comic Tales," *Iraq* 55 (1993): 63–75.

77. See Rosalind M. Janssen and Jacobus J. Janssen, *Growing Up in Ancient Egypt* (London: The Rubicon Press, 1990), 67–68, on the prestige associated with literacy.

78. For an example of an Egyptian scribal family see the description of the scholar-scribe Amenwahsu in David M. Carr, *Writing on the Tablet of the Heart: Origins of Scripture and Literature* (New York: Oxford University Press, 2005), 66.

79. Pascal Vernus, "Quelques exemples du type du "parvenu" dans l'Egypte Ancienne," *Bulletin de la Société Francaise d'Egyptologie* 59 (1970): 31–47, esp. 41–44; Adelheid Schlott, *Schrift und Schreiber im Alten Ägypten* (Munich: C. H. Beck, 1989), 182.

80. Against Hellmut Brunner, *Altägyptische Erziehung* (Wiesbaden: Harrassowitz, 1957), 41–42.

81. See Ronald J. Williams, "The Sage in Egyptian Literature," in John G. Gammie and Leo G. Perdue, eds., *The Sage in Israel and the Ancient Near East* (Winona Lake, IN: Eisenbrauns, 1990), 19–30, esp. 22.

82. For a useful and charming introduction to the subject see Janssen and Janssen, *Growing Up in Ancient Egypt,* 67–89.

83. Winfried Barta, "Das Schulbuch Kemit," *Zeitschrift für Ägyptische Sprache und Altertumskunde* 105 (1978): 6–14.

84. See Alan H. Gardiner, *Ancient Egyptian Onomastica*, 3 vols. (London: Oxford University Press, 1947).

85. Ronald J. Williams, "Scribal Training in Ancient Egypt," *JAOS* 92 (1972): 214–221, esp. 215; John D. Ray, "Egyptian Wisdom Literature," in John Day et al., eds., *Wisdom in Ancient Israel: Essays in Honour of J. A. Emerton* (Cambridge: Cambridge University Press, 1995), 17–29, esp. 18.

86. Günter Burkard, *Textkritische Untersuchungen zu ägyptischen Weisheit-slehren des alten und mittleren Reiches*, Ägyptologische Abhandlungen 34 (Wiesbaden: Harrassowitz, 1977).

87. Williams, "Scribal Training," 216.

88. See Janssen and Janssen, *Growing Up in Ancient Egypt*, 80.

89. On the House of Life see Alan H. Gardiner, "The House of Life," *Journal of Egyptian Archaeology* 24 (1938): 157–179; Aksel Volten, *Demotische Traumdeutung*, Analecta Aegyptiaca 3 (Copenhagen: Munksgaard, 1942), 17–44; Michail Alexandrovic Korostovcev, *Pistsy Drevnevo Egipta* [*The Scribes of Ancient Egypt*] (Moscow: Editions of Oriental Literature, 1962), 50–73, for which see the summary in French by Dimitri Meeks in *Revue d'Egyptologie* 19 (1967): 189–193; Jean-Claude Goyon, *Confirmation du pouvoir royal au nouvel an*, Bibliothèque d'Etude 52 (Cairo: Institut Français d'Archéologie Orientale; Brooklyn: Brooklyn Museum, 1972), 104–105, note 207; Manfred Weber, "Lebenshaus I.," *LÄ* 3:954–957.

90. Volten, *Traumdeutung*, 36, speaks of the *pr-ꜥnḫ* as "ein Kollegium." Donald B. Redford, *Pharaonic King-Lists, Annals, and Day-Books: A Contribution to the Study of the Egyptian Sense of History*, Society for the Study of Egyptian Antiquities 4 (Mississauga, Ont.: Benben, 1986), 91 note 72, argues for an interpretation of *pr-ꜥnḫ* as "an abstraction, a cult organization rather than a physical building." Both the term *house (pr)* and the topographical references to *pr-ꜥnḫ* render it unlikely that the term denotes primarily a corporation rather than a locality.

91. Volten, *Traumdeutung*, 38.

92. Gardiner, "House of Life," 176; Serge Sauneron, *Les prêtres de l'ancienne Egypte*, 2nd ed. (Paris: Perséa, 1988), 142–145, esp. 143.

93. For the term *workshop* see Gardiner, "House of Life," 176.

94. For the expression see Brunner, *Altägyptische Erziehung*, 32 note 82.

95. On the equivalence between *pr-ʿnḫ* and *pr-mdꜣt* in Edfu see Goyon, *Confirmation du pouvoir royal,* 105.

96. On Egyptian libraries see Günter Burkard, "Bibliotheken im alten Ägypten: Überlegungen zum Methodik ihres Nachweises und Übersicht zum Stand der Forschung," *Bibliothek: Forschung und Praxis* 4 (1980): 79–115; Vilmos Wessetzky, "Bibliothek," *LÄ* 1:783–785.

97. Compare the trilingual Canopus decree from Tanis that equates "the scribes of the House of Life" with the hieroglyphic *rḫw-(ï)ḫt,* "the ones that know things," and Greek *hierogrammateis;* see Wilhelm Spiegelberg, *Der demotische Text der Priesterdekrete von Kanopus und Memphis (Rosettana), mit hieroglyphischen und griechischen Fassungen* (Heidelberg: Carl Winter, 1922), 4.

98. For studies of the Egyptian priesthood see Gustave Lefebvre, *Histoire des grands prêtres d'Amun de Karnak jusqu'à la XXIe dynastie* (Paris: Geuthner, 1929); Hermann A. J. Kees, *Das Priestertum im Ägyptischen Staat vom Neuen Reich bis zur Spätzeit,* Probleme der Ägyptologie 1 (Leiden: Brill, 1953); Frédérique von Kaenel, *Les prêtres-ouâb de Sekhmet et les conjurateurs de Serket,* Bibliothèque de l'Ecole des Hautes Etudes, Sciences Religieuses 87 (Paris: Presses Universitaires de France, 1984); Charles Maystre, *Les grands prêtres de Ptah de Memphis,* OBO 113 (Fribourg: Universitätsverlag; Göttingen: Vandenhoeck & Ruprecht, 1992). For a general survey see Sauneron, *Les prêtres;* published in English as *The Priests of Ancient Egypt,* trans. David Lorton (Ithaca: Cornell University Press, 2000).

99. The Hebrew word *ḥarṭōm* derives from Egyptian *ḥry-tp;* see Joseph Vergote, *Joseph en Egypte: Genèse chap. 37–50 à la lumière des études égyptologiques récentes,* Orientalia et Biblica Lovaniensia 3 (Louvain: Publications Universitaires, 1959), 67–73. Note that Assyrian texts also refer to *ḥarṭibī* in the service of the king; see, e.g., Frederick Mario Fales and John Nicholas Postgate, *Imperial Administrative Records, Part I: Palace and Temple Administration,* SAA 7 (Helsinki: Helsinki University Press, 1992), no. 1, reverse, col. ii, line 2.

100. See Kees, *Priestertum,* 19–29.

101. See Miriam Lichtheim, *Ancient Egyptian Literature,* 3 vols. (Berkeley: University of California Press, 1973–80) 1:140, where Neferti is called "a great lector-priest of Bastet . . ., a citizen with capable arm, a scribe with excellent fingers."

102. Examples of products from the House of Life include the *Teachings of*

Ani, written by a temple scribe (Lichtheim, *Ancient Egyptian Literature,* 2:135–146), and the *Teaching of Amennakhte,* whose author was a scribe of the House of Life; see Georges Posener, "L'exordre de l'Instruction éducative d'Amennakhte," *Revue d'Egyptologie* 10 (1955): 61–72, esp. 64.

4. In Search of the Scribes, II

1. See Edward Lipiński, "Royal and State Scribes in Ancient Jerusalem," in John A. Emerton, ed., *Congress Volume Jerusalem 1986,* Supplements VT 40 (Leiden: Brill, 1988), 157–164, esp. 157, which I paraphrase here.
2. For surveys and translations see Graham I. Davies, *Ancient Hebrew Inscriptions: Corpus and Concordance* (Cambridge: Cambridge University Press, 1991); Klaas A. D. Smelik, *Writings from Ancient Israel: A Handbook of Historical and Religious Documents,* trans. Graham I. Davies (Edinburgh: T&T Clark, 1991); Johannes Renz and Wolfgang Röllig, *Handbuch der althebräische Epigraphik,* 4 vols. (Darmstadt: Wissenschaftliche Buchgesellschaft, 1995).
3. Even if we reckon that there are a considerable number of forgeries among the so-called bullae, their number remains impressive. For publications of clay tags and seals see Nahman Avigad and Benjamin Sass, *Corpus of West Semitic Stamp Seals* (Jerusalem: The Israel Academy of Sciences and Humanities, 1997); Renz and Röllig, *Handbuch,* 2/2:79–433.
4. On scribal practices at Qumran see Emanuel Tov, *Scribal Practices and Approaches Reflected in the Texts Found in the Judean Desert,* Studies on the Texts of the Desert of Judah 54 (Leiden: Brill, 2004).
5. For God as writer see Exod 24:12, 31:18, 32:15–16, 32:32, 34:1; Deut 4:13, 5:22 (19), 9:10, 10:2, 10:4; 2 Kings 17:37 (the unidentified "he" is either God or Moses); Hos 8:12. For prophets and other inspired human writers see Exod 17:14, 24:4, 34:27–28; Num 33:2; Deut 31:9, 31:22, 31:24; Josh 8:32 (Moses); Josh 24:26 (Joshua); 1 Sam 10:25 (Samuel); Isa 8:1, 30:8; 2 Chron 26:22 (Isaiah); Jer 30:2 (Jeremiah); Ezek 24:2, 37:16, 37:20, 43:11 (Ezekiel); Hab 2:2 (Habakkuk); Dan 7:1 (Daniel).
6. Ludwig Koehler, Walter Baumgartner, and Jakob J. Stamm, *Hebräisches und aramäisches Lexikon zum Alten Testament,* 4 vols. (Leiden: Brill, 1967–1995), 724 under *sōpēr.*
7. On the implements used by Hebrew scribes see J. Philip Hyatt, "The Writing of an Old Testament Book," *The Biblical Archaeologist* 6

(1943): 71–80, esp. 78–79; Hans Peter Rüger, "Schreibmaterial, Buch und Schrift," in Kurt Galling, ed., *Biblisches Reallexikon*, 2nd ed. (Tübingen: Mohr, 1977), 289–292, esp. 290.

8. Compare R. Lansing Hicks, "*Delet* and *měgillāh*: A Fresh Approach to Jeremiah XXXVI," *VT* 33 (1983): 46–66.

9. Note that *šěyā'* (2 Sam 20:25), *šîšā'* (1 Kings 4:3), and *šawšā'* (1 Chron 18:16) are not proper names but corruptions of the Egyptian scribal title *sš š'.t* or *sḫ š'.t*, "scribe of letters"; see Aelred Cody, "Le titre égyptien et le nom propre du scribe de David," *Revue Biblique* 72 (1965): 381–393; Tryggve N. D. Mettinger, *Solomonic State Officials: A Study of the Civil Government Officials of the Israelite Monarchy*, Coniectanea Biblica, Old Testament Series 5 (Lund: Gleerup, 1971), 25–30.

10. See T. Ray Hobbs, "Shebna," *ABD* 5:1172–1173.

11. Mettinger, *Solomonic State Officials*, 45–48.

12. See also, in addition to the reference in the previous note, Johannes Begrich, "Sōfēr und Mazkīr: Eine Beitrag zur inneren Geschichte des davidisch-solomonischen Grossreiches und des Königreiches Juda," *ZAW* 58 (1940): 1–29.

13. Hans Heinrich Schaeder, *Esra der Schreiber*, Beiträge zur historischen Theologie 5 (Tübingen: Mohr Siebeck, 1930), 39–51.

14. *Ahiqar*, column I, line 1, see Arthur Cowley, *Aramaic Papyri of the Fifth Century B.C.* (Oxford: Clarendon, 1923), 212. Compare the designation of the god Nabu as "the wise scribe" *(spr' ḥkym')* in one of the Arebsun inscriptions; see Mark Lidzbarski, *Ephemeris für semitische Epigraphik*, 3 vols. (Giessen: Töpelman, 1902–1915), 1:325. Mandaic texts also speak about *nbu sapra (u)hakima*, "Nabu, the wise scribe"; see Ethel S. Drower and Rudolf Macuch, *A Mandaic Dictionary* (Oxford: Clarendon, 1963), 287 under *nbu, 'nbu*.

15. Instead of reading "and the Levites," it is preferable to take "the Levites" as an apposition to the thirteen names mentioned just before (so with 1 Esd 9:48 and the Vulgate, against the Masoretic Text).

16. 11QPs = 11Q5, Col. XXVII, line 2. The text runs: "And David, son of Jesse, was a Sage [*ḥākām*], and a light like the light of the sun, [and] a scribe . . . And he wrote psalms."

17. See Elias J. Bickerman, *The Jews in the Greek Age* (Cambridge, MA: Harvard University Press, 1988), 163.

18. Christine Schams, *Jewish Scribes in the Second-Temple Period*, JSOT Supplement Series 291 (Sheffield: Sheffield Academic Press, 1998).

19. Compare A. Leo Oppenheim, "The Position of the Intellectual in Mesopotamian Society," *Daedalus* 104 (1975): 37–46, on the various types of Mesopotamian scribes (bureaucrat, poet, and scholar).

20. See Martin D. Goodman, "Texts, Scribes and Power in Roman Judaea," in Alan K. Bowman and Greg Woolf, eds., *Literacy and Power in the Ancient World* (Cambridge: Cambridge University Press, 1994), 99–108, esp. 102.

21. Against Schaeder, *Esra der Schreiber,* 41; Joseph Blenkinsopp, *Sage, Priest, Prophet: Religious and Intellectual Leadership in Ancient Israel,* Library of Ancient Israel (Louisville, KY: Westminster John Knox Press, 1995), 31.

22. Lipiński, "Royal and State Scribes," 159–161.

23. Moshe Weinfeld, *Deuteronomy and the Deuteronomic School* (Oxford: Oxford University Press, 1972; repr. Winona Lake, IN: Eisenbrauns, 1992), 158–171.

24. William M. Schniedewind, *How the Bible Became a Book* (New York: Cambridge University Press, 2004), esp. 84–90.

25. For a discussion of the Hebrew term see Michael Fishbane, *Biblical Interpretation in Ancient Israel* (Oxford: Clarendon, 1985), 33; James L. Crenshaw, *Education in Ancient Israel: Across the Deadening Silence,* The Anchor Bible Reference Library (New York: Doubleday, 1998), 107–108. For the interpretation "to bring in," understood as the depositing of written texts in a library, see H. Louis Ginsberg, *The Israelian Heritage of Judaism,* Texts and Studies 24 (New York: The Jewish Theological Seminary of America, 1982), 37 note 53.

26. Schniedewind, *How the Bible Became a Book,* 90.

27. Lipiński, "Royal and State Scribes," 160.

28. Schniedewind, *How the Bible Became a Book,* 84–85.

29. Lipiński, "Royal and State Scribes," 160.

30. See James Muilenburg, "Baruch the Scribe," in John I. Durham and Joshua R. Porter, eds., *Proclamation and Presence: Old Testament Essays in Honour of Gwynne Henton Davies* (London: SCM Press, 1970), 215–238, esp. 227–231. See also Jack R. Lundblom, "Baruch," *ABD* 1:617.

31. Nahman Avigad, *Hebrew Bullae from the Time of Jeremiah: Remnants of a Burnt Archive* (Jerusalem: Israel Exploration Society, 1986), 28–29, 125–130.

32. Robert Deutsch and Michael Heltzer, *Forty New Ancient West Semitic Inscriptions* (Tel Aviv and Jaffa: Archaeological Center Publications,

1994), 37–38, no. 11; Hershel Shanks, "Fingerprint of Jeremiah's Scribe," *Biblical Archaeology Review* 22/2 (1996): 36–38.

33. See, e.g., Christopher A. Rollston, "Non-Provenanced Epigraphs, I: Pillaged Antiquities, Northwest Semitic Forgeries, and Protocol for Laboratory Tests," *Maarav* 10 (2003): 135–193, esp. 160–162.

34. According to the official indictment of the Israel Antiquities Authority, a scholar and an antiquities dealer collaborated in the production and sold the piece for $100,000 to the London-based collector Shlomo Moussaieff.

35. Note the account of the discovery of the bullae by Avigad, *Hebrew Bullae,* 12–13, which should suffice to throw serious doubt on the authenticity of the artifacts.

36. Sigmund Mowinckel, "Psalms and Wisdom," in Martin Noth and D. Winton Thomas, eds., *Wisdom in Israel and in the Ancient Near East,* Festschrift H. H. Rowley, Supplements VT 3 (Leiden: Brill, 1955), 205–224, esp. 206, implies that Baruch was in fact a temple scribe.

37. In view of the role of Baruch in Jer 36, the reference to Jeremiah's "writing" *(ktb)* a deed of purchase in Jer 32:10 may be taken to mean that Jeremiah commissioned Baruch to prepare a deed of purchase.

38. A. Leo Oppenheim, *Ancient Mesopotamia: Portrait of a Dead Civilization,* rev. ed. completed by Erica Reiner (Chicago: University of Chicago Press, 1977), 95–109.

39. Schniedewind, *How the Bible Became a Book,* 85: "writing . . . was an activity of royal scribes. The temple would also have had scribes, but there is no reason to assume that temple scribes were suddenly interested in writing for public consumption."

40. Note the explicit designation of the temple of Bethel as a "royal sanctuary" *(miqdaš-melek)* and a "state temple" *(bêt mamlākâ)* in Amos 7:13. For the royal authority over temples see 1 Kings 12:31; 2 Kings 23:19; Jer 20:1–3.

41. See the survey of opinions in Thomas A. Busink, *Der Tempel von Jerusalem von Salomo bis Herodes: Eine archäologisch-historische Studie unter Berücksichtigung des westsemitischen Tempelbaus,* 2 vols. (Leiden: Brill, 1970), 1:618–637. Busink rejects the idea that the temple was planned as a royal chapel but acknowledges its dependency on the palace.

42. See W. Boyd Barrick, "Dynastic Politics, Priestly Succession, and Josiah's Eighth Year," *ZAW* 112 (2000): 564–582.

43. For the royal appointment of priests see 1 Kings 12:31; Gösta W.

Ahlström, *Royal Administration and National Religion in Ancient Palestine,* Studies in the History of the Ancient Near East 1 (Leiden: Brill, 1982), 29–30 and note 152. For royal disposal of the temple funds see 1 Kings 15:18; 2 Kings 16:8; Matthias Delcor, "Le trésor de la maison de Yahweh des origines à l'Exil," *VT* 12 (1962): 353–377.

44. See Karel van der Toorn, "The Babylonian New Year Festival: New Insights from the Cuneiform Texts and Their Bearing on Old Testament Study," in John A. Emerton, ed., *Congress Volume Leuven,* Supplements VT 43 (Leiden: Brill, 1991), 331–344.

45. Compare 1 Sam 21:2–7, 22:11–19; Ahlström, *Royal Administration,* 44–74.

46. See Erhard S. Gerstenberger, *Der bittende Mensch: Bittritual und Klagelied des Einzelnen im Alten Testament,* Wissenschaftliche Monographien zum Alten und Neuen Testament 51 (Neukirchen-Vluyn: Neukirchener Verlag, 1980), esp. 137–139. For the practice of dedicating written prayers as votive gifts see Harold L. Ginsberg, "Psalms and Inscriptions of Petition and Acknowledgement," in Saul Lieberman et al., eds., *Louis Ginsberg Jubilee Volume on the Occasion of His Seventieth Birthday* (New York: The American Academy of Jewish Research, 1945), 159–171; Günther Bornkamm, "Lobpreis, Bekenntnis und Opfer," in Walther Eltester and Franz Heinrich Kettler, eds., *Apophoreta: Festschrift Ernst Hänchen zu seinem 70. Geburtstag,* Beihefte zur Zeitschrift für die neutestamentliche Wissenschaft 30 (Berlin: Töpelmann, 1964), 46–63, esp. 56–58.

47. Manfried Dietrich et al., *The Cuneiform Alphabetic Texts from Ugarit, Ras Ibn Hani and Other Places,* Die Keilschrifttexte aus Ugarit (KTU), 2nd ed., Abhandlungen zur Literatur Alt-Syriens-Palästinas und Mesopotamiens 8 (Münster: Ugarit-Verlag, 1995), 28, no. 1.6 VI:54–58, trans. after Mark S. Smith, "The Baal Cycle," in Simon B. Parker, ed., *Ugaritic Narrative Poetry,* SBL Writings from the Ancient World 9 (Atlanta: Scholars Press, 1997), 81–180, esp. 164. For the interpretation of the passage and the use of *ťy* in the meaning of "secretary" see Wilfred H. van Soldt, "'atn prln, 'attā/ēnu the Diviner," *Ugarit-Forschungen* 21 (1989): 365–368.

48. See Hans-Walter Wolff, *Dodekapropheton I: Hosea,* 2nd ed., Biblischer Kommentar zum Alten Testament 14/1 (Neukirchen-Vluyn: Neukirchener Verlag, 1965), 186; James L. Mays, *Hosea: A Commentary* (London: SCM Press, 1969), 122; Andrew A. Macintosh, *Hosea* (Edin-

burgh: T&T Clark, 1997), 325–327. Contrast the view of Francis I. Andersen and David Noel Freedman, *Hosea,* Anchor Bible 24 (Garden City, NY: Doubleday, 1980), 509, who argue that Hosea is not referring to the written Torah.

49. See Jacob Hoftijzer and Gerrit van der Kooij, eds., *The Balaam Text from Deir 'Alla Re-evaluated: Proceedings of the International Symposium held at Leiden 21–24 August 1989* (Leiden: Brill, 1991), and more especially the contributions by André Lemaire (33–57) and Manfred Weippert (151–184).

50. See Sigmund Mowinckel, "The Prophetic Word in the Psalms and the Prophetic Psalms," in *The Psalms in Israel's Worship,* 2 vols., trans. D. R. Ap-Thomas (Oxford: Basil Blackwell, 1962) 2:53–73.

51. Mowinckel, "Psalms and Wisdom," 207.

52. Claude F. A. Schaeffer, *The Cuneiform Texts of Ras Shamra-Ugarit,* The Schweich Lectures of the British Academy 1936 (London: Oxford University Press, 1939), 34–35. The library in question is also known as the house of the high priest; see Marguerite Yon, *La cité d'Ougarit sur le tell de Ras Shamra* (Paris: Editions Recherche sur les Civilisations, 1997), 116.

53. On the Shilonite background of Samuel see Martin A. Cohen, "The Role of the Shilonite Priesthood in the United Monarchy of Ancient Israel," *Hebrew Union College Annual* 36 (1965): 59–98, esp. 66. The Levitical background of the House of Eli may be inferred from the fact that Moses is alluded to as the ancestor of the Shilonite priesthood in 1 Sam 2:27. See also Joseph Blenkinsopp, *Sage, Priest, Prophet: Religious and Intellectual Leadership in Ancient Israel,* Library of Ancient Israel (Louisville, KY: Westminster John Knox Press, 1995), 75.

54. See James L. Crenshaw, *Education in Ancient Israel: Across the Deadening Silence* (New York: Doubleday, 1998), 106; Rollston, "Pillaged Antiquities," 155 and note 53.

55. On the basis of socio-archaeological arguments, David W. Jamieson-Drake, *Scribes and Schools in Monarchic Judah,* JSOT Supplement Series 109 (Sheffield: Sheffield Academic Press, 1991), reaches the conclusion that there was room for only one school in monarchic Judah, located in Jerusalem. It is inherently unlikely that both the temple and the palace offered programs in scribal training.

56. There are grounds to make a case for an authorship of Levitical scribes; see, e.g., Hugh G. M. Williamson, *1 and 2 Chronicles,* The New Cen-

tury Bible Commentary (London: Marshall Morgan & Scott, 1982), 17; Joachim Schaper, *Priester und Leviten im achämenidischen Juda: Studien zur Kult- und Sozialgeschichte Israels in persischer Zeit*, Forschungen zum Alten Testament 31 (Tübingen: Mohr Siebeck, 2000), 298; note the pro-Levitical bias in 2 Chron 29, especially verse 34.

57. See, respectively, Neh 8; 2 Chron 17:7–9; Mal 2:7; 1 Chron 15:2; 2 Chron 5:3–6.

58. See, respectively, Neh 9; 2 Chron 30:21–27; Ezra 3:10; Neh 11:17, 12:24–25, 27–29; 1 Chron 9:33–34, 15:16–22, 16; 2 Chron 7:6, 29:26–30, 20:14–19.

59. See, respectively, 1 Chron 23:4; 2 Chron 19:8; Neh 10:38; 2 Chron 24:5–6, 34:9; 1 Chron 24:6, 26:29–32; 2 Chron 34:13.

60. See 1 Chron 9:17–27; 2 Chron 8:14, 34:12–13; Ezra 3:8.

61. For the role of writing in the practice of law see, in addition to the various law collections in the Bible, Ps 149:9, "written verdict" *(mišpāṭ kātûb)*; Job 31:35, "O that Shaddai would reply to my writ [*tāwî*], or my adversary in court draw up a bill [*wĕsēper kātab ʾîš rîbî*]."

62. On the Aramaic *Levi Document* and its connection with the *Testament of Levi* see Robert A. Kugler, *From Patriarch to Priest: The Levi-Priestly Tradition from* Aramaic Levi *to* Testament of Levi, Early Judaism and Its Literature 9 (Atlanta: Scholars Press, 1996).

63. The Cairo Geniza *Testament of Levi* 88–90 (CTLevi ar, Cambridge Col. e 17–19; 4Q213 fragment 1, i 9–10; fragment 1 ii + 2, 12–13). See Michael E. Stone and Jonas C. Greenfield, "Remarks on the Aramaic Testament of Levi from the Geniza," *Revue Biblique* 86 (1979): 214–230, esp. 226–227; Henryk Drawnel, *An Aramaic Wisdom Text from Qumran: A New Interpretation of the Levi Document*, Supplements to the Journal for the Study of Judaism 86 (Leiden: Brill, 2004), 155–172. Compare *T. Levi* 13.2: "Teach your children reading and writing too, so that they might have understanding throughout all their lives, as they ceaselessly read the Law of God." On the verb *ʾlp* see Michael David Coogan, " **ʾLP*, 'To Be an Abecedarian,'" *JAOS* 110 (1990): 322.

64. See the survey of opinions by Drawnel, *Aramaic Wisdom Text*, 63–75. Drawnel himself argues for a date in the early Hellenistic period.

65. See Julius Wellhausen, *Prolegomena zur Geschichte Israels,* 6th ed. (Berlin, Leipzig: W. de Gruyter, 1905, repr. 1927; 1st ed. 1878), esp. 115–145; W. Robertson Smith, "Levites," *Encyclopaedia Britannica*, 10th ed. (= 9th ed.), 24 vols. with 11 supplementary vols., ed. Sir Donald Mac-

kenzie Wallace et al., 1902–1903, 3:2770–2776; Gustav Hölscher, "Levi," *Paulys Realencyclopädie der classischen Altertumswissenschaft,* 49 vols., new ed. Georg Wissowa (Munich: Druckenmüller; Stuttgart: Metzler, 1984–1997), 12/2:2155–2208; Kurt Möhlenbrinck, "Die levitischen Überlieferungen des Alten Testaments," ZAW 52 (1934): 184–231; Anton H. J. Gunneweg, *Leviten und Priester: Hauptlinien der Traditionsbildung und Geschichte des israelitisch-jüdischen Kultpersonals,* Forschungen zur Religion und Literatur des Alten und Neuen Testaments 89 (Göttingen: Vandenhoeck & Ruprecht, 1965); Aelred Cody, *A History of Old Testament Priesthood,* Analecta Biblica 35 (Rome: Pontifical Biblical Institute, 1969), esp. 146–174; Frank Moore Cross, "The Priestly Houses of Early Israel," in *Canaanite Myth and Hebrew Epic* (Cambridge, MA: Harvard University Press, 1973), 195–215; Götz Schmitt, "Der Ursprung des Levitentums," ZAW 94 (1982): 575–599; Diether Kellermann, "lēwî," *Theologisches Wörterbuch zum Alten Testaments,* 8 vols., ed. G. Johannes Botterweck and Helmer Ringgren (Stuttgart: Kohlhammer, 1970–1995), 4:499–521 (with extensive bibliography on the question); Kugler, *From Patriarch to Priest;* Mark S. Smith, *The Pilgrimage Pattern in Exodus,* JSOT Supplement Series 239 (Sheffield: Sheffield Academic Press, 1997), 257–261; Merlin D. Rehm, "Levites and Priests," ABD 4:297–310; Joachim Schaper, *Priester und Leviten im achämenidischen Juda: Studien zur Kult- und Sozialgeschichte Israels in persischer Zeit,* Forschungen zum Alten Testament 31 (Tübingen: Mohr Siebeck, 2000).

66. For the Deuteronomic expression see Deut 17:9, 17:18, 18:1, 24:8, 27:9; see also the expression "the priests, sons of Levi" *(hakkōhănîm běnê lēwî),* in Deut 21:5, 31:9. The evidence from Chronicles is found in 1 Chron 9:2, 13:2, 15:11, 15:14, 23:2, 24:6; 2 Chron 7:6, 8:14, 8:15, 11:13, 17:8, 19:8, 23:4, 23:6, 24:5, 29:4, 29:16, 29:26, 29:34, 30:15, 30:17, 30:21, 30:25, 31:2, 31:9, 31:17, 34:30, 35:8, 35:10, 35:11, 35:18; see also the pair of "the sons of Aaron and the Levites," 1 Chron 15:4; 2 Chron 13:9, 13:10, 31:19, 35:14.

67. On the northern roots of the Levites see Menahem Haran, *Temples and Temple-Service in Ancient Israel: An Inquiry into Biblical Cult Phenomena and the Historical Setting of the Priestly School* (Oxford: Clarendon, 1978; repr. Winona Lake, IN: Eisenbrauns, 1985), 110.

68. See, e.g., Matt 16:21, 20:18, 21:15; Mark 10:33, 11:18, 11:27, 14:1, 14:43, 14:53; Luke 9:22, 19:47; and elsewhere in the synoptic Gospels.

69. The text of the Seleucid Charter is extant in Jos., *Ant.* 12.138–144. On the authenticity of the Charter see Elias Bickerman, "La charte séleucide de Jérusalem," *Revue des Etudes Juives* 100 (1935): 4–35.

70. Compare Ezra 2:36–42//Neh 7:39–45, 10:18–24. The Hebrew designations are *lĕwiyyim, mĕšōrĕrîm, šō'ărîm,* and *kōhănîm.* Customarily, the priests precede the Levites in the lists.

71. Jos., *Ant.* 12.142: *hē gerousia kai hoi hiereis kai hoi grammateis tou hierou kai hoi hieropsaltai.* Note that the occurrence of "Levites" alongside "the scribes of the temple" *(grammateusi tou hierou)* in *Ant.* 11.128 goes back, ultimately, to Ezra 7:24 and does not contradict the identification of Levites and scribes; see Bickerman, "La charte séleucide," 19.

72. The "elders" *(presbyteroi)* are at times referred to as "the principal men" (Luke 19:47, *hoi prōtoi tou laou*). They apparently correspond with the *gerousia* mentioned in the Seleucid Charter. The council of elders developed under the Ptolemies. From the time of Herod onward it was known as the Sanhedrin. See Martin Hengel, *Judentum und Hellenismus: Studien zu ihrer Begegnung unter besonderer Berücksichtigung Palästinas bis zur Mitte des 2. Jh.s v.Chr.,* 2nd ed., Wissenschaftliche Untersuchungen zum Neuen Testament 10 (Tübingen: Mohr, 1973), 48–51.

73. Compare Joseph Blenkinsopp, *Prophecy and Canon: A Contribution to the Study of Jewish Origins* (Notre Dame, IN: University of Notre Dame Press, 1970), 31.

74. Those who believe in the existence of schools include André Lemaire, *Les écoles et la formation de la Bible dans l'ancien Israel,* OBO 39 (Fribourg: Editions Universitaires; Göttingen: Vandenhoeck & Ruprecht, 1981); Eric W. Heaton, *The School Tradition of the Old Testament,* The Bampton Lectures for 1994 (Oxford: Oxford University Press, 1994). For a critical assessment see, e.g., James Barr, review of Lemaire, *Les écoles,* in *Bibliotheca Orientalis* 40 (1983): 137–142; Jamieson-Drake, *Scribes and Schools.* For a balanced view on scribal education and schools in Roman Palestine see Catherine Hezser, *Jewish Literacy in Roman Palestine,* Texts and Studies in Ancient Judaism 81 (Tübingen: Mohr Siebeck, 2001), esp. 39–109, 124.

75. For evidence on nonformal scribal training see especially the Kadesh-Barnea inscriptions discussed by Graham I. Davies, "Were There Schools in Ancient Israel?" in John Day et al., eds., *Wisdom in Ancient Israel: Essays in Honour of J. A. Emerton* (Cambridge: Cambridge University Press, 1995), 199–211, esp. 210.

76. Compare *b. B. Bat.* 15a: "The Holy One, blessed be He, dictated; Moses repeated; and Moses wrote down." A biblical reference to dictation has been claimed at Prov 22:20, provided it be emendated as *hălō' kātabtā'* (MT: *kātabtî,* cf. LXX *apograpsai*) *lĕkā millĕšônî* (MT: *šlšmw*) *rōb mô'ĕṣôt* (MT: *bĕmô'ĕṣôt*) *wādā'at,* "Didn't you write down for yourself from my tongue a multitude of counsels and knowledge?" The emendation comes from August Klostermann, *Schulwesen im alten Israel* (Leipzig: Deichert, 1908), 35–37. It has been superseded by the discovery of the Egyptian background of the verse, for which see Adolf Erman, "Eine ägyptische Quelle der 'Sprüche Salomos,'" *Sitzungsberichte der preussischen Akademie der Wissenschaften, phil.-hist. Klasse* 15 (1924): 86–93, esp. 89–90; Glendon E. Bryce, *A Legacy of Wisdom: The Egyptian Contribution to the Wisdom of Israel* (Lewisburg: Bucknell University Press; London: Associated University Presses, 1979), 18, 81–87.

77. Menahem Haran, "On the Diffusion of Literacy and Schools in Ancient Israel," in John A. Emerton, ed., *Congress Volume Jerusalem 1986,* Supplements VT 40 (Leiden: Brill, 1988), 81–95, esp. 91.

78. On acrostics see Max Löhr, "Alphabetische und alphabetisierende Lieder im AT," *ZAW* 25 (1905): 173–198; Peter Andreas Munch, "Die alphabetische Akrostichie in der judischen Psalmendichtung," *Zeitschrift der deutschen morgenländischen Gesellschaft* 90 (1936): 703–710; Will M. Soll, "Babylonian and Biblical Acrostics," *Biblica* 69 (1988): 305–323; Hanan Eshel and John Strugnell, "Alphabetical Acrostics in Pre-Tannaitic Hebrew," *Catholic Biblical Quarterly* 62 (2000): 441–458.

79. But note that in Ps 25, verse 5 is to suffice for the *he* and the *yod* together, and that verse 22 is a scribal postscript not belonging to the acrostic as such.

80. Prov 31:10–31 being part of the Book of Proverbs, its use in the process of acquiring *ḥokmâ* in the sense of "education" is more than likely. The reference to the fear of Yahweh being the beginning of *ḥokmâ* in Ps 111:10 points to a use of the text in the classroom as well. The presence of an acrostic in Sir 51:13–30 confirms the connection between the genre of acrostics and the school (compare Sir 51:23).

81. On the genre of lists in the Bible see Wolfgang Richter, *Exegese als Literaturwissenschaft: Entwurf einer alttestamentlichen Literaturtheorie und Methodologie* (Göttingen: Vandenhoeck & Ruprecht, 1971), 143–144.

82. See Michael E. Stone, "Lists of Revealed Things in the Apocalyptic Literature," in Frank Moore Cross et al., eds., *Magnalia Dei: The Mighty Acts*

of God; Essays on the Bible and Archaeology in Memory of G. Ernest Wright (Garden City, NY: Doubleday, 1976), 414–452, esp. 414–435.

83. See Gerhard von Rad, "Hiob XXXVIII und die altägyptische Weisheit," in Martin Noth and D. Winton Thomas, eds., *Wisdom in Israel and in the Ancient Near East,* Festschrift H. H. Rowley, Supplements VT 3 (Leiden: Brill, 1955), 293–301, who offers the interesting suggestion that the rhetorical questions in Job 38 echo the questions of a teacher in the classroom.

84. On the correspondences between Deut 28 and the Neo-Assyrian treaty texts see especially Hans Ulrich Steymans, *Deuteronomium 28 und die adê zur Thronfolgeregelung Asarhaddons: Segen und Fluch im Alten Orient und in Israel,* OBO 145 (Fribourg: Universitätsverlag; Göttingen: Vandenhoeck & Ruprecht, 1995).

85. See, e.g., Nili Shupak, "The Sitz im Leben of the Book of Proverbs in the Light of Comparison of Biblical and Egyptian Wisdom Literature," *Revue Biblique* 94 (1987): 98–119.

86. Lemaire, *Les écoles,* 72–83.

87. Crenshaw, *Education in Ancient Israel,* 107.

88. Eugene Ulrich, *The Dead Sea Scrolls and the Origins of the Bible,* Studies in the Dead Sea Scrolls and Related Literature (Grand Rapids: Eerdmans; Leiden: Brill, 1999), 19.

89. See Mark S. Smith, "The Levitical Compilation of the Psalter," ZAW 103 (1991): 258–263.

90. The term *enculturation* is borrowed from David M. Carr, whose monograph *Writing on the Tablet of the Heart: Origins of Scripture and Literature* (New York: Oxford University Press, 2005) emphasizes throughout the importance of immersion in the written tradition as a means to internalize the "Cultural Memory."

91. For *pišru* see the *Chicago Assyrian Dictionary* P, 429–430.

92. Tamara C. Eskenazi, *In an Age of Prose: A Literary Approach to Ezra-Nehemiah,* SBL Monograph Series 36 (Atlanta: Scholars Press, 1988).

93. The expression is from John W. Miller, *The Origins of the Bible: Rethinking Canon History* (New York and Mahwah, NJ: Paulist Press, 1994), 138, where he is commenting on 2 Chron 31:4.

94. Neh 10:38–39, 12:37, 13:10–14. See also Morton Smith, *Palestinian Parties and Politics That Shaped the Old Testament,* 2nd ed. (London: SCM Press, 1987), 102.

95. Joseph Naveh, *Early History of the Alphabet: An Introduction to West*

Semitic Epigraphy and Palaeography (Jerusalem: Magnes; Leiden: Brill, 1982), 78.

96. Compare the well-known opening phrase of *Pirqe Aboth:* "Moses received the Law from Sinai and handed it down to Joshua, and Joshua to the elders, and the elders to the Prophets; and the Prophets handed it down to the men of the Great Synagogue" (*M. Ab.* 1.1).

97. See Frederick E. Greenspahn, "Why Prophecy Ceased," *JBL* 108 (1989): 37–47.

98. According to 2 Chron 26:5, the otherwise unknown prophet Zechariah was "instructor *(mēbîn)* in the visions of God." In the Dead Sea Scrolls, David is referred to as a *sôpēr;* see 11QPs = 11Q5, Col. XXVII, line 2. The Babylonian Talmud qualifies Enoch, Moses, and Elijah as "the great scribes of Israel" (*b. Soṭah* 13b; compare *Seder Olam Rabbah* 17).

99. In Job 4:12–16, Eliphaz the Temanite, a wisdom teacher, claims prophetic inspiration for his views. Ben Sira "pours out teaching like prophecy" (Sir 24:33).

100. For a literary reflection of the tension, bordering on open conflict, between Aaronides and Levites see Num 16:1–35.

5. Making Books

1. For the interpretation of "making books" as "copying scrolls" see Viktor Burr, *Bibliothekarische Notizen zum Alten Testament* (Bonn: Bouvier, 1969), 30 note 83.

2. The reduction of the role of the scribe to that of copyist is apparent in such remarks as, "The anonymous author of edition II [of Jeremiah] was not a scribe, as we are not dealing with scribal phenomena, but he was an editor who produced one of the stages of the literary growth of the book"; see Emanuel Tov, "The Literary History of the Book of Jeremiah in the Light of Its Textual History," in Jeffrey H. Tigay, ed., *Empirical Models for Biblical Criticism* (Philadelphia: University of Pennsylvania Press, 1985), 211–237, citation from 216. In his more recent study, *Scribal Practices and Approaches Reflected in the Texts Found in the Judean Desert* (Leiden: Brill, 2004), esp. 7–10, Tov offers a more nuanced appreciation of scribal activity in ancient Israel. For a defense of the view that the scribes were first and foremost copyists see John Van Seters, "The Redactor in Biblical Studies: A Nineteenth-Century Anachronism," *Journal of Northwest Semitic Languages* 29 (2003): 1–19.

3. James Muilenburg, "Baruch the Scribe," in John I. Durham and Joshua R. Porter, eds., *Proclamation and Presence: Old Testament Essays in Honour of Gwynne Henton Davies* (London: SCM Press, 1970), 215–238, quotation from 219.

4. See 11QPs = 11Q5, Col. XXVII, line 2. The text runs: "And David, son of Jesse, was a Sage [ḥākām], and a light like the light of the sun, [and] a scribe . . . And he wrote psalms."

5. For the prohibition against adding or subtracting as part of scribal ethics concerning scrupulous adherence to an original text, see the observations by Michael Fishbane, "Varia Deuteronomica," ZAW 84 (1972): 349–352, esp. 350, and the reference to the *Song of Erra,* tablet V, lines 43–44 (Benjamin R. Foster, *Before the Muses: An Anthology of Akkadian Literature,* 2 vols. (Bethesda, MD: CDL Press, 1993] 2:804).

6. Jean-Marie Durand, *Archives épistolaires de Mari,* Archives Royales de Mari 26 (Paris: Recherche sur les Civilisations, 1988), no. 414:29–35. An English translation is conveniently available in Wolfgang Heimpel, *Letters to the King of Mari: A New Translation, with Historical Introduction, Notes, and Commentary,* Mesopotamian Civilizations 12 (Winona Lake, IN: Eisenbrauns, 2003), 356. My translation departs slightly from the one Heimpel offers in accordance with the interpretation I advance in "Old Babylonian Prophecy between the Oral and the Written," *Journal of Northwest Semitic Languages* 24 (1998): 55–70, esp. 64.

7. See Karel van der Toorn, "Cuneiform Documents from Syria-Palestine: Texts, Scribes, and Schools," *Zeitschrift des Deutschen Palästina-Vereins* 116 (2000): 97–113, esp. 107.

8. See, e.g., Hermann Gunkel, "Die Propheten als Schriftsteller und Dichter," in Hans Schmidt, *Die grossen Propheten* (Göttingen: Vandenhoeck & Ruprecht, 1915), xxxvi–lxxii, esp. xxxviii: "Die Propheten sind ursprünglich nicht Schriftsteller, sondern Redner gewesen." So, too, John J. Schmitt, "Prophecy: Preexilic Hebrew Prophecy," ABD 5:482–489, esp. 483: "The preexilic prophets themselves did not write down the words they spoke. Prophets are speakers."

9. On the background of the three reports see Dominique Charpin, "Le contexte historique et géographique des prophéties dans les textes retrouvés à Mari," *Bulletin of the Canadian Society for Mesopotamian Studies* 23 (1992): 21–31, esp. 23–24; Jack Sasson, "Water beneath Straw: Adventures of a Prophetic Phrase in the Mari Archives," in Ziony Zevit et al., eds., *Solving Riddles and Untying Knots: Biblical,*

Epigraphic, and Semitic Studies in Honor of Jonas C. Greenfield (Winona Lake, IN: Eisenbrauns, 1995), 598–608.

10. Heimpel, *Letters,* 252 note 3 to no. 197, translates "shock-head" on the basis of a derivation of *qammatum* from the verb *qamāmu,* "to stand up (of hair), to be unkempt." The interpretation agrees with the ecstatic aspect of prophecy in the Mari letters, as evidenced in the use of the verb *maḫû,* in the N-stem, "to enter into a trance, to be frenzied."

11. Durand, *Archives épistolaires,* no. 199, lines 41–54; Heimpel, *Letters,* 253–254.

12. Durand, *Archives épistolaires,* no. 197, lines 6–24; Heimpel, *Letters,* 251. Durand and Heimpel translate lines 22–24 as "Do not enter the city without extispicy!" My interpretation reads the pertinent lines as *ba-lum te-er-tim, a-na li-ib-bi a-d[e-e], la te-er-ru-u[b].* For the idiom *ina* [var.: *ana*] *libbi adê erēbu* compare Simo Parpola, *Letters from Assyrian and Babylonian Scholars,* SAA 10 (Helsinki: Helsinki University Press, 1993), nos. 6:19; 7:13–14.

13. Durand, *Archives épistolaires,* no. 202, lines 5–20; Heimpel, *Letters,* 255.

14. So with Sasson, "Water," 605, against Heimpel, *Letters,* 255, note to no. 202.

15. See Friedrich Giesebrecht, *Das Buch Jeremia,* Handkommentar zum Alten Testament III.2/1 (Göttingen: Vandenhoeck & Ruprecht, 1907), 45, 143; Wilhelm Rudolph, *Jeremia,* 3rd ed., Handbuch zum Alten Testament 1/12 (Tübingen: Mohr Siebeck, 1968), 53; Henning Graf Reventlow, "Gattung und Überlieferung in der 'Tempelrede Jeremias,'" *ZAW* 81 (1969): 315–352, esp. 325–326; William L. Holladay, *Jeremiah 2: A Commentary on the Book of the Prophet Jeremiah Chapters 26–52,* Hermeneia (Minneapolis: Fortress Press, 1989), 103; Jack R. Lundblom, *Jeremiah 1–20: A New Translation with Introduction and Commentary,* Anchor Bible 21A (New York: Doubleday, 1999), 471; Lundblom, *Jeremiah 21–36: A New Translation with Introduction and Commentary,* Anchor Bible 21B (New York: Doubleday, 2004), 285–286.

16. See Giesebrecht, *Jeremia,* 45; Reventlow, "Gattung und Überlieferung," 339; Helga Weippert, *Die Prosareden des Jeremiabuches,* Beihefte ZAW 132 (Berlin: De Gruyter, 1973), 29; Holladay, *Jeremiah 1: A Commentary on the Book of the Prophet Jeremiah Chapters 1–25,* Hermeneia (Philadelphia: Fortress Press, 1986), 248.

17. On the notion of Jerusalem as the successor of Shiloh in the

Deuteronomistic theology see John Day, "The Destruction of the Shiloh Sanctuary and Jeremiah VII 12, 14," in John A. Emerton, ed., *Studies in the Historical Books of the Old Testament,* Supplements VT 30 (Leiden: Brill, 1979), 87–94, esp. 89 and note 13.

18. On the subject of folktales see the classic studies by Hermann Gunkel, *The Folktale in the Old Testament,* Historic Texts and Interpreters in Biblical Scholarship 5 (Sheffield: Academic Press, 1987), translation of *Das Märchen im Alten Testament* (Tübingen: Mohr, 1917); and Gunkel, *Legends of Genesis* (New York: Schocken Books, 1987), translation of "Die Sagen der Genesis," preface to *Genesis,* 3rd ed., Göttinger Handkommentar zum Alten Testament 1/1 (Göttingen: Vandenhoeck & Ruprecht, 1910), VII–C. See also Pierre Gibert, *Une théorie de la légende: Hermann Gunkel (1862–1932) et les légendes de la Bible* (Paris: Flammarion, 1979), which also contains a French translation of the first four chapters of "Die Sagen."

19. For a fundamental study of the texts see Klaus Koch, *Was ist Formgeschichte? Methoden der Bibelexegese,* 3rd ed. (Neukirchen: Neukirchener Verlag, 1974), 135–162; in English, *The Growth of the Biblical Tradition: The Form-Critical Method,* trans. S. M. Cupitt (New York: Charles Scribner's, 1969), 111–132. The reference to Hurrian customs as a way to explain the wife-sister motif is unnecessary in view of its folkloristic background, against Ephraim Avigdor Speiser, "The Wife-Sister Motif in the Patriarchal Narratives," in *Oriental and Biblical Studies: Collected Writings of E. A. Speiser,* ed. Jacob J. Finkelstein and Moshe Greenberg (Philadelphia: University of Pennsylvania Press, 1969), 62–82.

20. In the source-critical analysis, Gen 12:10–20 and 26:6–11 are traditionally assigned to J; Gen 20:1–18 to E; see Gunkel, *Genesis,* 168–169.

21. Benno Landsberger, "Die babylonische Theodizee," *ZA* 43 (1936): 32–76; Wilfred G. Lambert, *Babylonian Wisdom Literature* (Oxford: Clarendon, 1960), 63–91; Foster, *Before the Muses,* 2:806–814.

22. See Johannes van Dijk in Heinrich J. Lenzen, *XVIII. Vorläufiger Bericht über die . . . Ausgrabungen in Uruk-Warka* (Berlin: Mann, 1962), 44–52, Tafel 27. See also Irving L. Finkel, "Adad-apla-iddina, Esagil-kīn-apli, and the Series SA.GIG," in Erle Leichty et al., eds., *A Scientific Humanist: Studies in Memory of Abraham Sachs* (Philadelphia: The S. N. Kramer Fund, 1988), 143–159, esp. 144.

23. The acrostic calls the author a *mašmaššu,* "exorcist, ritual specialist." For the dialogue as a debate between scholars see lines 1, 5, 6, 7, 35, 45,

57, 78, 147, 199, 200, 213, 254, and 289 of the *Theodicy*. On the Mesopotamian school dialogues, mostly in Sumerian, see Dietz Otto Edzard, "Literatur," *RlA* 7: 35–48, esp. 44–45, ¶¶ 3.6.2 and 3.6.3; Konrad Volk, "Edubba'a und Edubba'a-Literatur: Rätsel und Lösungen," *ZA* 90 (2000): 1–30.

24. Note lines 205–207: "My stylus, . . . its cuneiform writing he explained to me, but he did not disclose to me [the meaning of] the incomprehensible cuneiform tablets." For the reading of line 207 see the *Chicago Assyrian Dictionary* E, 34.

25. On acrostics see Max Löhr, "Alphabetische und alphabetisierende Lieder im AT," *ZAW* 25 (1905): 173–198; Peter Andreas Munch, "Die alphabetische Akrostichie in der judischen Psalmendichtung," *Zeitschrift der deutschen morgenländischen Gesellschaft* 90 (1936): 703–710; Will M. Soll, "Babylonian and Biblical Acrostics," *Biblica* 69 (1988): 305–323; Hanan Eshel and John Strugnell, "Alphabetical Acrostics in Pre-Tannaitic Hebrew," *Catholic Biblical Quarterly* 62 (2000): 441–458.

26. See Gerhard von Rad, "Hiob XXXVIII und die altägyptische Weisheit," in Martin Noth and D. Winton Thomas, eds., *Wisdom in Israel and in the Ancient Near East,* Festschrift H. H. Rowley, Supplements VT 3 (Leiden: Brill, 1955), 293–301.

27. For the use of proverb quotations in Qohelet see Robert Gordis, *Koheleth—The Man and His World: A Study of Ecclesiastes,* 3rd ed. (New York: Schocken Books, 1973), 95–108.

28. Wilfred G. Lambert, "The Gula Hymn of Bulluṭsa-rabi," *Orientalia* 36 (1967): 105–132; Foster, *Before the Muses,* 2:491–499.

29. According to the *Catalogue of Texts and Authors,* Bulluṭsa-rabi was an exorcist *(mašmaššu)* and a scholar *(ummânu)* from Babylon; see Wilfred G. Lambert, "A Catalogue of Texts and Authors," *JCS* 16 (1962): 59–77, esp. 66. On the nature of the Gula hymn see Lambert, "Gula Hymn," 108–114. On the phenomenon of citation and paraphrase from memory see the observations by David M. Carr, *Writing on the Tablet of the Heart: Origins of Scripture and Literature* (New York: Oxford University Press, 2005), 36.

30. Note the suggestion by Robert H. Pfeiffer, *Introduction to the Old Testament,* 5th ed. (New York and London: Harper, 1941), 804, that the various "works" mentioned by the Chronicler refer in fact to sections of a putative Midrash of the Books of Kings. On the practice of referring to a section by its name see Bruce M. Metzger, *Historical and Literary*

Studies: Pagan, Jewish, and Christian, New Testament Tools and Studies 8 (Leiden: Brill, 1968), esp. 59–60.

31. The words "mere show" are from Charles C. Torrey, "The Chronicler as Editor and as Independent Narrator," *American Journal of Semitic Languages and Literature* 25 (1909): 157–173, quotation on 173. In some cases the existence of the sources the Chronicler mentions is doubtful; in others, there can be little doubt about the existence of the source, but the reference itself is invalid. See also the notion of "ghost source" used by Pfeiffer, *Introduction,* 805.

32. See Sara Japhet, *I & II Chronicles: A Commentary* (London: SCM Press, 1993), 14–19, for the sources used in Chronicles (and see 19–23 for a discussion of the sources mentioned in Chronicles). On the sources of the Chronicler see also Pfeiffer, *Introduction,* 801–808.

33. As observed by Sigmund Mowinckel, "Psalms and Wisdom," in Martin Noth and D. Winton Thomas, eds., *Wisdom in Israel and in the Ancient Near East,* Festschrift H. H. Rowley, Supplements VT 3 (Leiden: Brill, 1955), 205–224, esp. 207.

34. See the illuminating treatment of the authorship of the Psalms by Sigmund Mowinckel, *The Psalms in Israel's Worship,* 2 vols., trans. D. R. Ap-Thomas (Oxford: Basil Blackwell, 1962), 2:85–103. Note the following quotations: "It is among the temple singers that we must look for the authors of the psalms" (85); "In other words the singers also had to be 'scribes' or 'sages' and the 'wise scribes' were actually at that time the real 'literary men' and poets" (94).

35. For a discussion of the meaning of the verb *heʿetîqû* ('tq, hipʿil), here translated as "transcribe," see H. Louis Ginsberg, *The Israelian Heritage of Judaism,* Texts and Studies 24 (New York: The Jewish Theological Seminary of America, 1982), 37 note 53; Michael Fishbane, *Biblical Interpretation in Ancient Israel* (Oxford: Clarendon, 1985), 33; James L. Crenshaw, *Education in Ancient Israel: Across the Deadening Silence,* The Anchor Bible Reference Library (New York: Doubleday, 1998), 107–108.

36. Quotation from Mogens T. Larsen, "The Babylonian Lukewarm Mind: Reflections on Science, Divination and Literacy," in Francesca Rochberg-Halton, ed., *Language, Literature, and History: Philological and Historical Studies Presented to Erica Reiner,* American Oriental Series 67 (New Haven: American Oriental Society, 1987), 211, tributary to Walter J. Ong, *Orality and Literacy: The Technologizing of the Word* (London: Methuen, 1982), 37–38.

37. See Edzard, "Literatur," 45 ¶ 3.7.1.d; Wolfgang Röllig, "Überblick über die akkadische Literatur," *RlA* 7:48–66, esp. 59 ¶ 4.7.2.a; Bendt Alster, *The Instructions of Suruppak: A Sumerian Proverb Collection,* Mesopotamia 2 (Copenhagen: Akademisk forlag, 1974).

38. On *Listenwissenschaft,* see Wolfram von Soden, "Leistung und Grenze sumerischer und babylonischer Wissenschaft," *Die Welt als Geschichte* 2 (1936): 411–464 and 509–557; repr., with Benno Landsberger, *Die Eigenbegrifflichkeit der babylonischen Welt* (Darmstadt: Wissenschaftliche Buchgesellschaft, 1965), 21–133; see esp. 35–74; see also Von Soden, *Sprache, Denken und Begriffsbildung im alten Orient* (Mainz: Akademie der Wissenschaften und der Literatur; Wiesbaden: Steiner, 1974), esp. 12–16; Larsen, "The Babylonian Lukewarm Mind," 203–225, esp. 208–211.

39. Citation from Miguel Civil et al., *The Series lú = ša and Related Texts,* Materials for the Sumerian Lexicon 12 (Rome: Pontifical Biblical Institute, 1969), 102–103, lines 204–216. On *kurgarrû* and *assinnu* see Stefan M. Maul, "*Kurgarrû* und *assinnu* und ihr Stand in der babylonischen Gesellschaft," in Volkert Haas, ed., *Ausserseiter und Randgruppen: Beiträge zu einer Sozialgeschichte des alten Orients* (Konstanz: Universitätsverlag, 1992), 159–171.

40. On the intellectual significance of *Listenwissenschaft,* see Jack Goody, *The Domestication of the Savage Mind* (Cambridge: Cambridge University Press, 1977), 74–111.

41. See, e.g., Alan H. Gardiner, *Ancient Egyptian Onomastica,* 3 vols. (London: Oxford University Press, 1947).

42. On lists in the Bible see Wolfgang Richter, *Exegese als Literaturwissenschaft: Entwurf einer alttestamentlichen Literaturtheorie und Methodologie* (Göttingen: Vandenhoeck & Ruprecht, 1971), 143–144. See also the list of female jewelry in Isa 3:18–23, and the list of imported and exported ware in Ezek 27:12–24.

43. The list of the fifty names starts on tablet VI and runs through tablet VII. For the traditional god lists see Wilfred G. Lambert, "Götterliste," *RlA* 3:473–479. For a study of the fifty names of Marduk and their exegesis by the scribes see Jean Bottéro, "Les noms de Marduk, l'écriture et la 'logique' en Mésopotamie ancienne," in Maria DeJong Ellis, ed., *Essays on the Ancient Near East in Memory of Jacob Joel Finkelstein,* Memoirs of the Connecticut Academy of Arts and Sciences 19 (Hamden, CT: Archon Books, 1977), 5–28.

44. See Gerhard von Rad, "Hiob XXXVIII und die altägyptische Weisheit,"

in Martin Noth and D. Winton Thomas, eds., *Wisdom in Israel and in the Ancient Near East,* Festschrift H. H. Rowley, Supplements VT 3 (Leiden: Brill, 1955), 293–301.

45. Ulla Jeyes, *Old Babylonian Extispicy: Omen Texts in the British Museum,* Uitgaven van het Nederlands Historisch-Archaeologisch Instituut te Istanbul 64 (Leiden: Nederlands Instituut voor het Nabije Oosten, 1989), 160, lines 4–9.

46. See Ernst F. Weidner, "Historisches Material in der babylonischen Omen-Literatur," *Mitteilungen der Altorientalischen Gesellschaft* 4 (1928–29): 226–240, esp. 226; Jean Bottéro, *Mesopotamia: Writing, Reasoning, and the Gods,* trans. Zainab Bahrani and Marc Van de Mieroop (Chicago: University of Chicago Press, 1992), 130–131; Larsen, "The Lukewarm Mind," 212. For a critique of the consensus view see Frederick H. Cryer, *Divination in Ancient Israel and Its Near Eastern Environment: A Socio-Historical Investigation,* Journal for the Study of the Old Testament, Supplement Series 142 (Sheffield: Sheffield Academic Press, 1994), 150–156; Ulla Koch-Westenholz, *Mesopotamian Astrology: An Introduction to Babylonian and Assyrian Celestial Divination,* Carsten Niebuhr Institute Publications 19 (Copenhagen: Museum Tusculanum Press, 1995), 13–19.

47. See Jean Bottéro, "Symptômes, signes, écritures," in Jean-Pierre Vernant et al., *Divination et Rationalité* (Paris: Seuil, 1974), 70–197, esp. 153–167. The *Myth of Enmeduranki* calls the liver "the tablet of the gods"; see Wilfred G. Lambert, "Enmeduranki and Related Matters," *JCS* 21 (1967): 126–138, esp. 132.

48. See William S. Morrow, "Mesopotamian Scribal Techniques and Deuteronomic Composition: Notes on *Deuteronomy and the Hermeneutics of Legal Innovation*," *Zeitschrift für die altorientalische Rechtsgeschichte* 6 (2000): 302–313, esp. 308, who discusses the expansionary tendencies in omen literature and law books. The scribes used deductive reasoning to generate new hypothetical cases from existing material and known situations.

49. The name "Covenant Code" derives from Exod 24:7, according to which Moses read "the Book of the Covenant" *(sēper habbĕrît)* to the people. The Covenant Code is widely held to begin in Exod 20:22 and end in Exod 23:33. For a discussion see, e.g., Georg Fohrer, *Einleitung in das Alte Testament,* 12th ed. (Heidelberg: Quelle & Meyer, 1979), 146–150. I take Exod 21:1–22:16 to be the early core of the Code.

50. Citation from the series *If a City Is Set on a Height (Šumma ālu)*, tablet
    12, lines 28–29, in the translation by Sally M. Freedman, *If a City Is Set
    on a Height: The Akkadian Omen Series Šumma Alu in Mēlê Šakin, Vol-
    ume 1: Tablets 1–21*, Occasional Publications of the Samuel Noah
    Kramer Fund 17 (Philadelphia: The University of Pennsylvania Museum,
    1998), 195.
51. On the scribal use of subscriptions in Leviticus see Michael Fishbane,
    "Accusations of Adultery: A Study of Law and Scribal Practice in Num-
    bers 5:11–31," *Hebrew Union College Annual* 45 (1974): 25–45,
    esp. 32–33.
52. The following observations are based on Simo Parpola, *Assyrian Proph-
    ecies*, SAA 9 (Helsinki: Helsinki University Press, 1997), LIII–LV. See also
    on the subject Martti Nissinen, "Spoken, Written, Quoted, and Invented:
    Orality and Writtenness in Ancient Near Eastern Prophecy," in Ehud Ben
    Zvi and Michael H. Floyd, eds., *Writings and Speech in Israelite and An-
    cient Near Eastern Prophecy*, SBL Symposium Series 10 (Atlanta: Society
    of Biblical Literature, 2000), 235–271, esp. 248–254.
53. Compare, e.g., Jack R. Lundblom, *Jeremiah 1–20: A New Translation
    with Introduction and Commentary*, Anchor Bible 21A (New York:
    Doubleday, 1999), 249–297 (eleven oracles, extant in vv. 2:1–3, 4–9, 10–
    13, 14–19, 20–22, 23–25a, 25b–27a,b, 27c–28, 29–30, 31–32, 33–37);
    Robert P. Carroll, *Jeremiah: A Commentary*, Old Testament Library
    (London: SCM, 1986), 115–140 (nine units, extant in 2:1–3, 4–9, 10–13,
    14–19, 20–22, 23–25, 26–28, 29–32, 33–37). For a discussion of the
    connection between the separate oracles and the secondarily crafted pro-
    phetic speech see Siegfried Herrmann, *Jeremia*, Biblisches Kommentar
    zum Alten Testament 12/2 (Neukirchen: Neukirchener Verlag, 1990),
    104.
54. See Hunger, *Kolophone*, 6–8, under "Vorlage."
55. See the Standard Babylonian colophon, which says "copied from broken
    tablets; the reader should not treat it callously but restore the breaks,"
    see Hunger, *Kolophone*, no. 498, line 3.
56. After the opening line of the epic known from the Old Babylonian Penn-
    sylvania tablet, see Stephen Langdon, *The Epic of Gilgamesh*, Publica-
    tions of the Babylonian Section 10/3 (Philadelphia: University of Pennsyl-
    vania, 1917), rev. iii 35.
57. By presenting the epic as a *narû*-inscription (I i 24–28), the editor of the
    standard version put the text "in the key of wisdom," as William L.

Moran observes in "The Epic of Gilgamesh: A Document of Ancient Humanism," *Bulletin of the Canadian Society for Mesopotamian Studies* 22 (1991): 15–22, quotation on 19; repr. in *The Most Magic Word,* ed. Ronald S. Hendel, The Catholic Biblical Quarterly Monograph Series 35 (Washington, DC: The Catholic Biblical Association of America, 2002), 5–20.

58. See Andrew F. George, *The Babylonian Gilgamesh Epic: Introduction, Critical Edition and Cuneiform Texts,* 2 vols. (Oxford: Oxford University Press, 2003) 1:538–539.

59. See the pertinent observations in the realm of biblical literature by Norbert Lohfink, "Fortschreibung? Zur Technik von Rechtsrevisionen im deuteronomischen Bereich, erörtert an Deuteronomium 12, Ex 21,2–11 und Dtn 15,12–18," in Timo Veijola, ed., *Das Deuteronomium und seine Querbeziehungen,* Schriften der Finnischen Exegetischen Gesellschaft 62 (Helsinki: Finnische Exegetische Gesellschaft; Göttingen: Vandenhoeck & Ruprecht, 1996), 127–171, esp. 143–144.

60. See Tzvi Abusch, "The Development and Meaning of the Epic of Gilgamesh: An Interpretive Essay," *JAOS* 121 (2001): 614–622. According to Abusch, "In an early form, this Gilgamesh tale [i.e., the Old Babylonian version] did not include the Utnapishtim episode . . . But already, the Old Babylonian tale hints at the presence of an embryonic form of the Utnapishtim episode" (617). See also Jeffrey Tigay, *The Evolution of the Gilgamesh Epic* (Philadelphia: University of Pennsylvania Press, 1982), 214–240.

61. According to George, *Gilgamesh Epic,* 1:32–33, the Sin-leqe-unninni version added a prologue and an epilogue, as well as the Flood narrative and the homily by Uta-napishti.

62. See Yaakov Elman, "Authoritative Oral Tradition in Neo-Assyrian Scribal Circles," *Journal of the Ancient Near Eastern Society of Columbia University* 7 (1975): 19–32.

63. For the following see especially David Brown, *Mesopotamian Planetary Astronomy-Astrology,* CM 18 (Groningen: Styx, 2000), 156–160.

64. Brown, *Astronomy-Astrology,* 158.

65. For *Utukkū lemnūtu* see Markham J. Geller, *Forerunners to Udug-Ḫul: Sumerian Exorcistic Incantations,* Freiburger Altorientalische Studien 12 (Stuttgart: Franz Steiner, 1985); for *Maqlû* see I. Tzvi Abusch, *Babylonian Witchcraft Literature: Case Studies,* Brown Judaic Studies 132 (Atlanta: Scholars Press, 1987), 3–4, 13–44. The term "forerunners" can be

used only in retrospect because it understands the earlier texts as stages moving toward a final edition. The scribes who wrote the texts did not write forerunners; they were contributing to a textual tradition whose ultimate destiny they did not know.

66. On these two aspects of tradition see Wolfgang Schenke, "Texttradierung, -kritik," *LÄ* 6:459–462. For a brief discussion and references to further literature see David M. Carr, *Writing on the Tablet of the Heart: Origins of Scripture and Literature* (New York: Oxford University Press, 2005), 78 note 93.

67. David P. Silverman, "Textual Criticism in the Coffin Texts," in James P. Allen et al., *Religion and Philosophy in Ancient Egypt,* Yale Egyptological Studies 3 (New Haven: Yale Egyptological Seminar, 1989), 29–53, quotation on 32–33.

68. See Matthieu Heerma van Voss, "Totenbuch," *LÄ* 6:641–643.

69. See Curt Kuhl, "Die 'Wiederaufnahme'—ein literarkritisches Prinzip?" *ZAW* 64 (1952): 1–11.

70. See Michael Fishbane, "Accusations of Adultery: A Study of Law and Scribal Practice in Numbers 5:11–31," *Hebrew Union College Annual* 45 (1974): 25–45, esp. 26–27.

71. For a discussion of the evidence see Emanuel Tov, "The Literary History of the Book of Jeremiah in the Light of Its Textual History," in Jeffrey H. Tigay, ed., *Empirical Models for Biblical Criticism* (Philadelphia: University of Pennsylvania Press, 1985), 211–237; Pierre-Maurice Bogaert, "Le livre de Jérémie en perspective: Les deux rédactions selon les travaux en cours," *Revue Biblique* 101 (1994): 363–406.

72. See especially Pierre-Maurice Bogaert, "Urtext, texte court et relecture: Jérémie xxxiii 14–26 TM et ses préparations," in John A. Emerton, ed., *Congress Volume Leuven 1989,* VT Supplements 43 (Leiden: Brill, 1991), 236–247; Yohanan Goldman, *Prophétie et royauté au retour de l'exil: Les origines littéraires de la forme massorétique du livre de Jérémie,* OBO 118 (Fribourg: Universitätsverlag; Göttingen: Vandenhoeck & Ruprecht, 1992), 9–37, 38–64.

73. Compare Goldman, *Prophétie et royauté,* 31 and note 59.

74. See Samuel Noah Kramer, "The Epic of Gilgameš and Its Sumerian Sources: A Study in Literary Evolution," *JAOS* 64 (1944): 7–23, esp. 19–23.

75. See Jeffrey H. Tigay, *The Evolution of the Gilgamesh Epic* (Philadelphia: University of Pennsylvania Press, 1982), 111–119.

76. Adolf Erman, "Eine ägyptische Quelle der 'Sprüche Salomos,'" *Sitzungsberichte der preussischen Akademie der Wissenschaften, phil.-hist. Klasse* 15 (1924): 86–93 and Taf. VI–VII.

77. Erman, "Eine ägyptische Quelle," 89–90; Glendon E. Bryce, *A Legacy of Wisdom: The Egyptian Contribution to the Wisdom of Israel* (Lewisburg: Bucknell University Press; London: Associated University Presses, 1979), 18, 81–87.

78. Gary A. Rendsburg, "Hebrew Philological Notes (II)," *Hebrew Studies* 42 (2001): 187–195, esp. 192–195.

79. Sven P. Vleeming and Jan Wim Wesselius, "An Aramaic Hymn of the Fifth Century B.C.," *Bibliotheca Orientalis* 39 (1982): 501–509, esp. 502, 509; Charles F. Nims and Richard C. Steiner, "A Paganized Version of Psalm 20:2–6 from the Aramaic Text in Demotic Script," *JAOS* 103 (1983): 261–274.

80. See Moshe Weinfeld, "The Pagan Version of Psalm 20:2–6: Vicissitudes of a Psalmodic Creation in Israel and Its Neighbors," in Benjamin Mazar et al., eds., *Nahman Avigad Volume,* Eretz-Israel 18 (Jerusalem: The Israel Exploration Society, 1985), 130–140 (in Hebrew with English summary); Mathias Delcor, "Remarques sur la datation de Ps 20 comparée à celle du psaume araméen apparenté dans le papyrus Amherst 63," in Manfried Dietrich and Oswald Loretz, eds., *Mesopotamica—Ugaritica—Biblica: Festschrift für Kurt Bergerhof zur Vollendung seines 70. Lebensjahres am 7. Mai 1992,* AOAT 232 (Kevelaer: Butzon & Bercker; Neukirchen-Vluyn: Neukirchener Verlag, 1993), 25–43.

81. So with Nims and Steiner, "Paganized Version," 266, against Karl-Theodor Zauzich, "Der Gott des aramäisch-demotischen Papyrus Amherst 63," *Göttinger Miszellen* 85 (1985): 89–90 ("Yaho"); and Ingo Kottsieper, "Anmerkungen zu Pap. Amherst 63 I: 12,11–19: Eine aramäische Version von Ps 20," *ZAW* 100 (1988): 217–244, esp. 224–226 ("El").

82. On the presumed identification of Baal Zaphon with Horus see Peter Dils, "Horus," *Dictionnaire de la civilisation phénicienne et punique,* ed. Edouard Lipiński (Turnhout: Brepols, 1992), 220. In Pelusium, the statue of Zeus Kasios was actually an image of Harpocrates or Horus-the-Child; see Otto Eissfeldt, *Baal Zaphon, Zeus Kasios und der Durchzug der Israeliten durchs Meer* (Halle: Niemeyer, 1932), 41–42.

83. So Nims and Steiner, "Paganized Version," 271–272.

84. For a convenient survey of the differences between the Babylonian original and the Assyrian version see Stephanie Dalley, *Myths from Mesopota-*

mia: Creation, The Flood, Gilgamesh and Others (Oxford: Oxford University Press, 1989), 228–277, esp. 228–229, and notes 3–4 (274) and 21 (275).

85. For a study of the phenomenon see Mordechai Cogan, "A Plaidoyer on Behalf of the Royal Scribes," in Mordechai Cogan and Israel Eph'al, eds., *Ah, Assyria . . .: Studies in Assyrian History and Ancient Near Eastern Historiography Presented to Hayim Tadmor,* Scripta Hierosolymitana 33 (Jerusalem: Magnes, 1991), 121–128.

86. Martha T. Roth, *Law Collections from Mesopotamia and Asia Minor,* SBL Writings from the Ancient World 6 (Atlanta: Scholars Press, 1995), 26–27.

87. Ibid., 43.

88. Ibid., 122–123, ¶¶ 209–214.

89. Ibid., 160, ¶ 21; 173–174, ¶¶ 50–53.

90. Jacob. J. Finkelstein, *The Ox That Gored,* Transactions of the American Philosophical Society 71/2 (Philadelphia: The American Philosophical Society, 1981), 19 note 11.

91. For a discussion of the scribal tradition behind the cuneiform laws (including the law on striking a pregnant woman) see Pamela Barmash, *Homicide in the Biblical World* (Cambridge: Cambridge University Press, 2005), 132–140.

92. I owe this example to Bernard M. Levinson, "The Manumission of Hermeneutics: The Slave Laws of the Pentateuch as a Challenge to Contemporary Pentateuchal Theory," in André Lemaire, ed., *Congress Volume Leiden 2004,* Supplements VT 109 (Leiden: Brill, 2006), 281–321. See also Levinson, "The Birth of the Lemma: The Restrictive Reinterpretation of the Covenant Code's Manumission Law by the Holiness Code (Leviticus 25:44–46)," *JBL* 124 (2005): 617–639.

93. The series was edited by René Labat, *Traité akkadien de diagnostics et pronostics médicaux* (Paris: Académie internationale d'histoire des sciences; Leiden: Brill, 1951).

94. See Irving L. Finkel, "Adad-apla-iddina, Esagil-kīn-apli, and the Series SA.GIG," in Erle Leichty et al., eds., *A Scientific Humanist: Studies in Memory of Abraham Sachs* (Philadelphia: The S. N. Kramer Fund, 1988), 143–159; Nils P. Heessel, *Babylonisch-assyrische Diagnostik,* AOAT 43 (Münster: Ugarit-Verlag, 2000), 104–110.

95. For the interpretation of *sur gibil* as "new text" I am indebted to a study by Marten Stol to be published in the Festschrift for Robert D. Biggs.

96. Finkel, "Adad-apla-iddina," 148–149, lines 18, 20, 24–26.

97. See Egbert von Weiher, *Spätbabylonische Texte aus Uruk 2,* Ausgrabungen der Deutschen Forschungsgemeinschaft in Uruk-Warka 10 (Berlin: Mann, 1983), no. 2, II, lines 75–76: "Let a menopausal woman spin [Sum *sur,* Akk *ṭamû*] with the right hand"; Wolfgang Heimpel, *Tierbilder in der sumerischen Literatur* (Rome: Pontifical Biblical Institute, 1968), 506: the demon "twists the man as into a rope" (Sum *sur,* Akk *zâru*); compare Bendt Alster and Herman Vanstiphout, "Lahar and Ashnan: Presentation and Analysis of a Sumerian Disputation," *Acta Sumerologica* 9 (1987): 1–43, esp. 20, line 100. For the interpretation of Sum *éš.síg.sur.ra* as "a leash of spun wool" see Bendt Alster, "The Proverbs of Ancient Sumer: An Update," *NABU* 1999: 86–89, esp. 87; Barry L. Eichler, "On Weaving Etymological and Semantic Threads: The Semitic Root QL'," in Tzvi Abusch et al., eds., *Lingering over Words: Studies in Ancient Near Eastern Literature in Honor of William L. Moran* (Atlanta: Scholars Press, 1990), 163–169, esp. 166–167.

98. See Gene B. Gragg, "The Keš Temple Hymn," in Åke W. Sjöberg et al., *The Collection of the Sumerian Temple Hymns,* Texts from Cuneiform Sources 3 (Locust Valley, NY: Augustin, 1969), 155–188, esp. 167 line 11: "Its words she wove [*sur*] intricately like a net [*sa*]."

99. See Thorkild Jacobsen, "Oral to Written," in Muhammad A. Dandamayev et al., eds., *Societies and Languages of the Ancient Near East: Studies in Honor of I. M. Diakonoff* (Warminster: Aries & Phillips, 1982), 129–137, esp. 131–132.

100. See the observations by Nils P. Heessel, "'Wenn ein Mann zum Haus des Kranken geht. . .': Intertextuelle Bezüge zwischen der Serie *šumma ālu* und der zweite Tafel der Serie SA.GIG," *AfO* 48–49 (2001–2002): 24–49; Barbara Böck, *Die babylonisch-assyrische Morphoskopie,* AfO Beiheft 27 (Vienna: Institut für Orientalistik der Universität Wien; Horn: Ferdinand Berger & Söhne, 2000), esp. 55.

101. Finkel, "Adad-apla-iddina," 148–149, line 24'. See the observations by Heessel, *Diagnostik,* 106 note 40.

102. Mark J. Geller speculates that Esagil-kīn-apli also acted as the editor of a host of other works, such as *Lugale, Angim,* and *Enūma Anu Enlil;* see Geller, "Astronomy and Authorship," *Bulletin of the School of Oriental and African Studies* 53 (1990): 209–213, esp. 210–213. The crucial piece of evidence Geller adduces is the second part of the *Curriculum for Exorcists,* for which see Geller, "Incipits and Rubrics," in Andrew R. George and Irving L. Finkel, eds., *Wisdom, Gods and Literature: Studies*

in Assyriology in Honour of W. G. Lambert (Winona Lake, IN: Eisenbrauns, 2000), 225–258, esp. 242–254. Lines 27–42 of the *Curriculum* list "incipits of the *ašipūtu* series of Esagil-kīn-apli," which Geller understands to indicate that the texts that follow all go back to Esagil-kīn-apli as their editor. While this interpretation cannot be excluded, the *Curriculum* more likely refers to Esagil-kīn-apli as being responsible for establishing an advanced curriculum.

103. See Jeffrey H. Tigay, "Conflation as a Redactional Technique," in Jeffrey H. Tigay, ed., *Empirical Models for Biblical Criticism* (Philadelphia: University of Pennsylvania Press, 1985), 53–95.

104. See the classic and lucid demonstration by Hermann Gunkel, *Genesis*, 3rd ed., Göttinger Handkommentar zum Alten Testament I/I (Göttingen: Vandenhoeck & Ruprecht, 1910), 59–77, 137–152, esp. 137–140. Gunkel qualifies the story as a textbook case of source criticism for beginners (137).

105. See John A. Emerton, "An Examination of Some Attempts to Defend the Unity of the Flood Narrative in Genesis," *VT* 37 (1987): 401–420; *VT* 38 (1988): 1–21.

106. Gen 6:5–8, 7:1–5, and 8:20–22 belong to J; Gen 6:9–22, 8:1–5, and 9:1–17 are from P. In the analysis of some modern authors, P acted as the editor of J, which means that P does not stand for a document but for a scribe who added his comments to the J narrative; see, e.g., Lutz Schrader, "Kommentierende Redaktion im Noah-Sintflutt-Komplex der Genesis," *ZAW* 110 (1998): 489–502.

107. Susan Niditch, *Oral World and Written Word: Ancient Israelite Literature,* Library of Ancient Israel (Louisville, KY: Westminster John Knox Press, 1996), 113.

6. The Teaching of Moses

1. Karl Marti, *Der Prophet Jeremia von Anatot* (Basel: Detloff, 1889), 18–20.

2. For the classical demonstration see Wilhelm M. L. de Wette, *Dissertatio critica qua Deuteronomium a prioribus Pentateuchi libris diversum, alius cuiusdam recentioris actoris opus esse monstratur* (University of Jena, 1805). The identification of Josiah's "Book of the Law" with Deuteronomy occurs as early as St. Jerome's (340–420 C.E.) *Commentary to Ezekiel,* 1:1; as well as in a scholium to 2 Kings 22 by Procopius of Gaza

(465–529 C.E.); see Eberhard Nestle, "Miscellen," *ZAW* 22 (1902): 170–172, esp. 170–171.

3. Calum M. Carmichael, *The Laws of Deuteronomy* (Ithaca, NY: Cornell University Press, 1974), esp. 17–33, privileges the genre of the valedictory address; his only reference to treaty language is on 259, note 8. Other authors focus exclusively on the treaty aspect of Deuteronomy; see, e.g., Dennis J. McCarthy, *Treaty and Covenant,* Analecta Biblica 21a (Rome: Biblical Institute Press, 1981), 157–205; Eckhart Otto, *Das Deuteronomium: Politische Theologie und Rechtsreform in Juda und Assyrien,* Beihefte ZAW 284 (Berlin: De Gruyter, 1999). Moshe Weinfeld emphasizes that Deuteronomy "is presented in its entirety as a valedictory oration delivered by Moses shortly before his death." At the same time, though, he notes that "the structure of the state treaty . . . has . . . been preserved in its original form in Deuteronomy." Weinfeld makes no attempt to explain how the two perspectives relate to each other; see Weinfeld, *Deuteronomy and the Deuteronomic School* (Oxford: Oxford University Press, 1972; repr. Winona Lake, IN: Eisenbrauns, 1992), quotations on 10 and 65.

4. See, e.g., Robert H. Pfeiffer, *Introduction to the Old Testament,* 5th ed. (New York: Harper, 1941), 182: "The canonical book of Deuteronomy represents the last stage of the long process of editing and supplementing the book of Josiah, and it attained its present form about 400 B.C., more than two centuries after Deuteronomy was found in the temple."

5. For a survey of the discussion in recent research see Horst Dietrich Preuss, *Deuteronomium,* Erträge der Forschung 164 (Darmstadt: Wissenschaftliche Buchgesellschaft, 1982); Norbert Lohfink, ed., *Das Deuteronomium: Entstehung, Gestalt und Botschaft,* Bibliotheca Ephemeridum Theologicarum Lovaniensium 68 (Leuven: Peeters, 1985); Georg Braulik, ed., *Bundesdokument und Gesetz: Studien zum Deuteronomium,* Herders Biblische Studien 4 (Freiburg: Herder, 1995); Timo Veijola, ed., *Das Deuteronomium und seine Querbeziehungen,* Schriften der Finnischen Exegetischen Gesellschaft 62 (Helsinki: Finnische Exegetische Gesellschaft; Göttingen: Vandenhoeck & Ruprecht, 1996); Georg Braulik, ed., *Das Deuteronomium,* Österreichische Biblische Studien 23 (Frankfurt: Peter Lang, 2003).

6. See, e.g., Gottfried Seitz, *Redaktionsgeschichtliche Studien zum Deuteronomium,* Beiträge zur Wissenschaft vom Alten und Neuen Testament 93 (Stuttgart: Kohlhammer, 1971); Norbert Lohfink, "Gab es eine

deuteronomistische Bewegung?," in Walter Gross, ed., *Jeremia und die "deuteronomistische Bewegung,"* Bonner Biblische Beiträge 98 (Weinheim: Beltz Athenäum, 1995), 313–382, esp. 347 and note 114; repr. *Studien zum Deuteronomium und zur deuteronomistischen Literatur,* 4 vols., Stuttgarter Biblische Aufsatzbände, Altes Testament 8, 12, 20, 31 (Stuttgart: Katholisches Bibelwerk, 1990–2000), 3:65–142; English trans., "Was There a Deuteronomistic Movement?" in Linda S. Schearing and Steven L. MacKenzie, eds., *Those Elusive Deuteronomists: The Phenomenon of Pan-Deuteronomism,* JSOT Supplement Series 268 (Sheffield: Sheffield Academic Press, 1999), 36–66; Georg Braulik, *Die deuteronomischen Gesetze und der Dekalog: Studien zum Aufbau von Deuteronomium 12–26,* Stuttgarter Bibelstudien 145 (Stuttgart: Katholisches Bibelwerk, 1991), esp. 115–118; see also Braulik's analysis in Erich Zenger et al., *Einleitung,* Kohlhammer Studienbücher Theologie 1/1 (Stuttgart: Kohlhammer, 2004), 136–155, esp. 140–149.

7. Thus the so-called Göttingen School, represented by such scholars as Rudolf Smend, Walter Dietrich, and Timo Veijola, on which see Otto Kaiser, *Einleitung in das Alte Testament: Eine Einführung in ihre Ergebnisse und Probleme,* 5th ed. (Gütersloh: Gerd Mohn, 1984), 167–168, 176. Examples of their analysis include Smend, "Das Gesetz und die Völker: Ein Beitrag zur deuteronomistischen Redaktionsgeschichte," in Hans Walter Wolff, ed., *Probleme biblischer Theologie: Gerhard von Rad zum 70. Geburtstag* (Munich: Chr. Kaiser, 1971), 494–509, repr. in *Gesammelte Studien,* 3 vols., Beiträge zur evangelischen Theologie 99, 100, 109 (Munich: Chr. Kaiser, 1986–1991), 1:124–137; *Die Entstehung des Alten Testaments,* 2nd ed. (Stuttgart: Kohlhammer, 1981), 111–125, #19; Dietrich, *Prophetie und Geschichte: Eine redaktionsgeschichtliche Untersuchung zum deuteronomistischen Geschichtswerk,* Forschungen zur Religion und Literatur des Alten und Neuen Testaments 108 (Göttingen: Vandenhoeck & Ruprecht, 1972); Dietrich, "Niedergang und Neuanfang: Die Haltung der Schlussredaktion des deuteronomistischen Geschichtswerkes zu den wichtigsten Fragen ihrer Zeit," in Bob Becking and Marjo C. A. Korpel, eds., *The Crisis of Israelite Religion: Transformation of Religious Tradition in Exilic and Post-Exilic Times,* Oudtestamentische Studien 42 (Leiden: Brill, 1999), 45–70; Veijola, *Das Königtum in der Beurteilung der deuteronomistischen Historiographie: Eine redaktionsgeschichtliche Untersuchung,* Annales Academiae Scientiarium Fennicae, Series B, 198 (Helsinki: Suomalainen

Tiedeakatemia, 1977). See also Preuss, *Deuteronomium,* 46–61; Eckhart Otto, "Von der Programmschrift einer Rechtsreform zum Verfassungsentwurf des Neuen Israel: Die Stellung des Deuteronomiums in der Rechtsgeschichte Israels," in Georg Braulik, ed., *Bundesdokument und Gesetz: Studien zum Deuteronomium,* Herders Biblische Studien 4 (Freiburg: Herder, 1995), 93–104; Otto, "Biblische Rechtsgeschichte als Fortschreibungsgeschichte," *Bibliotheca Orientalis* 56 (1999): 5–14.

8. The "canon formula" is not specifically linked to treaty texts. Many royal inscriptions from Mesopotamia insist that the text is to be preserved unaltered; see, e.g., the epilogue of the so-called Code of Hammurabi, xlix 18–44, as translated by Martha T. Roth, *Law Collections from Mesopotamia and Asia Minor,* SBL Writings from the Ancient World 6 (Atlanta: Scholars Press, 1995), 136. For other examples see the *Chicago Assyrian Dictionary* E, 175 under *enû* 1d1'; *Chicago Assyrian Dictionary* N/1, 167 under *nakāru* 8b; *Chicago Assyrian Dictionary* Š/1, 406–407 under *šanû* 4c. The injunctions demonstrate both the importance attached to the original formulation of the text and the occurrence of corrections and revisions.

9. The genealogy of Ezra in Ezra 7:1–5 traces his ancestry back to "Aaron the chief priest" (Ezra 7:5). The commentaries are ill at ease with the reference to the prophetic gifts of the high priest in John 11:51. Reference is sometimes made to Jos., *Ant.* 11.327; 13.282–283.299–300, where Josephus speaks about the gift of foresight of John Hyrcanus. The point of the Gospel passage, however, is that the gift is linked to the office rather than the person.

10. In this reconstruction I basically follow the one proposed by Lohfink, "Gab es eine deuteronomistische Bewegung?" 335–349. See also Norbert Lohfink, "Fortschreibung? Zur Technik von Rechtsrevisionen im deuteronomischen Bereich, erörtert an Deuteronomium 12, Ex 21,2–11 und Dtn 15,12–18," in Timo Veijola, ed., *Das Deuteronomium und seine Querbeziehungen,* Schriften der Finnischen Exegetischen Gesellschaft 62 (Helsinki: Finnische Exegetische Gesellschaft; Göttingen: Vandenhoeck & Ruprecht, 1996), 127–171, esp. 146–147.

11. Since Deut 17:18 is from the early exilic period, the "double" of the Torah in the possession of the king is a purely hypothetical copy.

12. For a reference to the preparation of a new copy of a text because the papyrus of the original had grown mold, see the so-called Shabaka Stone from Egypt; Richard Parkinson and Stephen Quirke, *Papyrus* (London:

British Museum Press, 1995), 74–75. For an English translation of the Egyptian text see James P. Allen, *COS* 1.16:23–26.

13. For an elaboration of the comparison see Karel van der Toorn, "The Iconic Book: Analogies between the Babylonian Cult of Images and the Veneration of the Torah," in van der Toorn, ed., *The Image and the Book: Iconic Cults, Aniconism, and the Rise of Book Religion in Israel and the Ancient Near East,* Contributions to Biblical Exegesis and Theology 21 (Leuven: Peeters, 1997), 229–248, esp. 232–239.

14. On the production, consecration, and theology of cult images in Mesopotamia see Angelika Berlejung, *Die Theologie der Bilder: Herstellung und Einweihung von Kultbildern in Mesopotamien und die alttestamentliche Bilderpolemik,* OBO 162 (Fribourg: Universitätsverlag; Göttingen: Vandenhoeck & Ruprecht, 1998); Michael B. Dick, *Born in Heaven, Made on Earth: The Making of the Cult Image in the Ancient Near East* (Winona Lake, IN: Eisenbrauns, 1999); Michael B. Dick and Christopher B. F. Walker, *The Induction of the Cult Image in Ancient Mesopotamia: The Mesopotamian* mīs pî *Ritual,* SAA Literary Texts 1 (Helsinki: The Neo-Assyrian Text Corpus Project, 2001).

15. Indirect support for this reconstruction of the process of revision and expansion may be found in the biblical story of the Scroll of Baruch; after the first scroll had been lost to the fire, a second one was prepared that contained several additions (Jer 36:32 "and more of the like was added").

16. The scribes added the historical summary in Deut 1–3 as well as the presentation of Joshua as the successor of Moses (Deut 31) as a means to link Deuteronomy to the Deuteronomistic History. The notice of Deut 1:5, in conjunction with the postscript in Num 36:13, served as a link with the preceding books of the Pentateuch; see the pertinent observations by Eckhart Otto, "Vom biblischen Hebraismus der persischen Zeit zum rabbinischen Judaismus in römischer Zeit: Zur Geschichte der spätbiblischen und frühjüdischen Schriftgelehrsamkeit," *Zeitschrift für altorientalische und biblische Rechtsgeschichte* 10 (2004): 1–49, esp. 28–29.

17. See Jeffrey H. Tigay, *The Evolution of the Gilgamesh Epic* (Philadelphia: University of Pennsylvania Press, 1982); Andrew F. George, *The Babylonian Gilgamesh Epic: Introduction, Critical Edition and Cuneiform Texts,* 2 vols. (Oxford: Oxford University Press, 2003).

18. See H. G. Mitchell, "The Use of the Second Person in Deuteronomy, *JBL*

18 (1899): 61–109; Carl Steuernagel, *Das Deuteronomium*, 2nd ed., Handkommentar zum Alten Testament 1/3.1 (Göttingen: Vandenhoeck & Ruprecht, 1923); Willy Staerk, *Das Problem des Deuteronomiums: Ein Beitrag zur neuesten Pentateuchkritik*, Beiträge zur Forderung christlicher Theologie, Reihe 2, Sammlung wissenschaftlicher Monographien 29/2 (Gütersloh: Bertelsmann, 1924); Georges Minette de Tillesse, "Sections 'tu' et sections 'vous' dans le Deutéronome," *VT* 12 (1962): 29–87, revised and summarized under the name Gaetan Minette de Tillesse, "TU & VOUS dans le Deutéronome," in Reinhart G. Kratz and Hermann Spieckermann, eds., *Liebe und Gebot: Studien zum Deuteronomium*, Festschrift zum 70. Geburtstag von Lothar Perlitt, Forschungen zur Religion und Literatur des Alten und Neuen Testaments 190 (Göttingen: Vandenhoeck & Ruprecht, 2000), 156–163.

19. See Tigay, *Evolution*, 214–240; Tzvi Abusch, "The Development and Meaning of the Epic of Gilgamesh: An Interpretive Essay," *JAOS* 121 (2001), 614–622; George, *Babylonian Gilgamesh Epic*, 1.32–33.

20. Robert H. Pfeiffer does not discuss the mechanics of textual growth in connection with Deuteronomy but proposes an editorial history very similar to the one I follow. He distinguishes four editions, beginning with the reform document (621), followed by an expanded edition written between 600–550, a History Edition written ca. 550, and a Wisdom Edition written between 500 and 450; Pfeiffer, *Introduction*, 187.

21. The repetitive resumption of Deut 26:19 in 28:1 demonstrates that Deut 27 is an insertion.

22. The term *'ēdōt*, here translated as "treaty stipulations," is originally a *plurale tantum*, later vocalized as *'ēdūt/'ēdût*; compare Akkadian *adû* and Aramaic *'dy*. See Bruno Volkwein, "Masoretisches *'ēdūt, 'ēdwōt, 'ēdōt*: "Zeugnis" oder 'Bundesbestimmungen'?" *Biblische Zeitschrift* 13 (1969): 18–40; Choon-Leong Seow, "The Designation of the Ark in Priestly Theology," *Hebrew Annual Review* 8 (1985): 185–198, esp. 192–193; Manfred Krebernik, "M. Weinfelds Deuteronomiumskommentar aus assyriologischer Sicht," in Georg Braulik, ed., *Bundesdokument und Gesetz: Studien zum Deuteronomium*, Herders Biblische Studien 4 (Freiburg: Herder, 1995), 27–36, esp. 30; Eckart Otto, *Das Deuteronomium im Pentateuch und Hexateuch*, Forschungen zum Alten Testament 30 (Tübingen: Mohr Siebeck, 2000), 117 and note 40; David Talshir, "*'āḥôt* and *'ēdôt* in Ancient Hebrew," *Zeitschrift für Althebraistik* 15–16 (2002–03): 108–123. For a different view see Ber-

nard Couroyer, "'EDŪT; Stipulation de traité ou enseignement?" *Revue Biblique* 95 (1988): 321–331, who draws a semantic parallel with Egyptian *meter,* "instruction, education."

23. On the correspondence between Deut 4:45 and 28:68 see Eckart Otto, *Das Deuteronomium im Pentateuch und Hexateuch,* 129, who attributes the rubric and the colophon to an exilic editor.

24. The comparison with Hittite treaties has been based, in large measure, on the publications by Johannes Friedrich, *Staatsverträge des Ḫatti-Reiches in hethitischer Sprache,* Mitteilungen der Vorderasiatisch-ägyptischen Gesellschaft 31/1 and 34/1 (Leipzig: J. C. Hinrichs, 1926 and 1930); Viktor Korošec, *Hethitische Staatsverträge,* Leipziger rechtswissenschaftliche Studien 60 (Leipzig: T. Weicher, 1931). For an English translation of the main texts see Itamar Singer and Harry A. Hoffner, Jr., *COS* 2.17–18:93–106. The comparison with the Neo-Assyrian texts has focused on the so-called vassal treaties of Esarhaddon, in which the Assyrian king had his vassals swear allegiance to Assurbanipal as his successor. The first reliable publication of these texts was by Donald J. Wiseman, "The Vassal Treaties of Esarhaddon," *Iraq* 20 (1958): 1–99. The text is now available in Simo Parpola and Kazuko Watanabe, *Neo-Assyrian Treaties and Loyalty Oaths,* SAA 2 (Helsinki: Helsinki University Press, 1988), 28–58. Literature on the comparison of Deuteronomy with the Neo-Assyrian treaties includes Rintje Frankena, "The Vassal-Treaties of Esarhaddon and the Dating of Deuteronomy," in Jacobus Hoftijzer, ed., *Kaf hē 1940–1965,* Oudtestamentische Studien 14 (Leiden: Brill, 1965), 122–154; Hans Ulrich Steymans, *Deuteronomium 28 und die adê zur Thronfolgeregelung Asarhaddons: Segen und Fluch im Alten Orient und in Israel,* OBO 145 (Fribourg: Universitätsverlag; Göttingen: Vandenhoeck & Ruprecht, 1995). For a balanced and illuminating assessment of the parallels between Deuteronomy and the Neo-Assyrian treaty texts see Krebernik, "M. Weinfelds Deuteronomiumskommentar."

25. William L. Moran, "The Ancient Near Eastern Background of the Love of God in Deuteronomy," *Catholic Biblical Quarterly* 25 (1963): 77–87; repr. *The Most Magic Word,* ed. Ronald S. Hendel, The Catholic Biblical Quarterly Monograph Series 35 (Washington, DC: The Catholic Biblical Association of America, 2002), 170–181; Weinfeld, *Deuteronomy and the Deuteronomic School,* 81–91.

26. In view of the continued sacrificial practice at the Arad shrine, it is possible that the success of Josiah's reform was limited to a religious purge in

Jerusalem; see Christoph Uehlinger, "Gab es eine joschianische Kultreform? Plädoyer für ein begründetes Minimum," in Walter Gross, ed., *Jeremia und die "deuteronomistische Bewegung,"* Bonner Biblische Beiträge 98 (Weinheim: Beltz Athenäum, 1995), 57–89; English trans., "Was There a Cult Reform under King Josiah? The Case for a Well-Grounded Minimum," in Lester Grabbe, ed., *Good Kings and Bad Kings,* Library of Hebrew Bible/Old Testament Studies 393, European Seminar in Historical Methodology 5 (London and New York: T&T Clark, 2005), 279–316. The triumphalism of the Jerusalem temple-goers depicted in the temple sermon of Jeremiah (Jer 7:4), as well as the prophet's characterization of the temple as a "den of thieves" (Jer 7:11), presumably an effect of the rule that tithes might be converted into money to be spent in the sanctuary (Deut 14:24–26), both suggest that the notion of a centralized cult in Jerusalem had become common coinage in 608 (for the date of the temple sermon see Jer 26:1).

27. Albrecht Alt, "Die Heimat des Deuteronomiums," *Kleine Schriften zur Geschichte des Volkes Israel,* 3 vols., ed. Martin Noth (Munich: C. H. Beck, 1953–1959), 2:250–275, esp. 253 note 3. See also Preuss, *Deuteronomium,* 100–101; Otto, *Das Deuteronomium: Politische Theologie,* 360–364; Timo Veijola, *Moses Erben: Studien zum Dekalog, zum Deuteronomismus und zum Schriftgelehrtentum,* Beiträge zur Wissenschaft vom Alten und Neuen Testament 149 (Stuttgart: Kohlhammer, 2000), 77 and note 10.

28. Compare Joseph Blenkinsopp, *Sage, Priest, Prophet: Religious and Intellectual Leadership in Ancient Israel,* Library of Ancient Israel (Louisville, KY: Westminster John Knox Press, 1995), 159.

29. Conflation is a redactional technique whereby scribes, in the presence of two versions of the text, do not choose either one but fuse the two into one (see Chapter 5); see also Jeffrey H. Tigay, "Conflation as a Redactional Technique," in Tigay, ed., *Empirical Models for Biblical Criticism* (Philadelphia: University of Pennsylvania Press, 1985), 53–95.

30. On the role of written messages to proclaim a reform decree see Nadav Na'aman, "The Distribution of Messages in the Kingdom of Judah in the Light of the Lachish Ostraca," *VT* 53 (2003): 169–180.

31. This reconstruction assumes a pre-exilic origin of Deuteronomy, as argued by Hugo Gressmann, "Josia und das Deuteronomium," *ZAW* 42 (1924): 313–337; Karl Budde, "Das Deuteronomium und die Reform König Josias," *ZAW* 44 (1926): 177–224; Walter Baumgartner, "Der

Kampf um das Deuteronomium," *Theologische Rundschau* 1 (1929): 7–25, esp. 22–25; Lewis B. Paton, "The Case for the Post-Exilic Origin of Deuteronomy," *JBL* 47 (1928): 322–357. A minority of scholars propose a post-exilic date for Deuteronomy; see Gustav Hölscher, "Komposition und Ursprung des Deuteronomiums," *ZAW* 40 (1922): 161–255, esp. 227–255; Robert H. Kennett, *The Church of Israel: Studies and Essays*, ed. Stanley A. Cook (Cambridge: Cambridge University Press, 1933), 73–98, esp. 90; Sigmund Mowinckel, *Erwägungen zur Pentateuch Quellenfrage* (Trondheim: Universitetsforlaget, 1964), 22; Kaiser, *Einleitung*, 131–134.

32. See, e.g., Preuss, *Deuteronomium*, 104–106; Bernard M. Levinson, *Deuteronomy and the Hermeneutics of Legal Innovation* (New York: Oxford University Press, 1998), 3–13; Eckhart Otto, "Biblische Rechtsgeschichte als Fortschreibungsgeschichte," *Bibliotheca Orientalis* 56 (1999): 5–14. H. Wheeler Robinson, *Inspiration and Revelation in the Old Testament* (Oxford: Clarendon, 1946), 213, refers to the Deuteronomic Code as "an expanded edition of the Book of the Covenant." Groundbreaking work in the area of intrabiblical legal exegesis and legal innovation in Deuteronomy has been done by Jacob Weingreen; see for instance his "The Deuteronomic Legislator: A Proto-Rabbinic Type," in John I. Durham and John R. Porter, eds., *Proclamation and Presence: Old Testament Essays in Honour of Gwynne Henton Davies* (London: SCM Press, 1970), 76–89.

33. See, e.g., Frankena, "Vassal Treaties"; Otto, *Das Deuteronomium: Politische Theologie.*

34. See especially Steymans, *Deuteronomium 28.*

35. The term "Ten Commandments," or "Decalogue" (Hebrew *'aśeret haddĕbārîm*, Exod 34:28; Deut 4:13, 10:4), is something of a misnomer when it comes to Deut 5:6–18. In the Deuteronomic version of the Commandments, the Sabbath Commandment takes a central position (5:12–15); it is preceded by commandments concerning the worship of Yahweh (5:6–10) and the use of his name (5:11), and followed by commandments about parents (5:16) and moral injunctions (5:17–21). See Norbert Lohfink, "Zur Dekalogfassung von Dt 5," *Biblische Zeitschrift* 9 (1965): 17–32.

36. Hebrew *wĕlō' yāsāp*, "and he did not continue" (*scil.* speaking; Hebr *lĕdabbēr*). Compare *'îm-yōsĕpîm 'ănaḥnû lišmōa'*, "If we continue to listen," in 5:22.

37. See Otto, *Das Deuteronomium im Pentateuch und Hexateuch,* 115–126, esp. 117.

38. In the compositional logic of the Torah Edition, the laws in the central section of Deuteronomy (12–26) represent oral lore transmitted by Moses; hence their introduction with the words, "These are the decrees and the verdicts" (12:1; cf. 26:16). Stephen Kaufman has argued that the sequence of the laws of Deut 12–26 mirrors the order of the Ten Commandments; see "The Structure of the Deuteronomic Law," *Maarav* 1/2 (1978–79): 105–158; see also Georg Braulik, "Die Abfolge der Gesetze in Deuteronomium 12–26 und der Dekalog," in Norbert Lohfink, ed., *Das Deuteronomium: Entstehung, Gestalt und Botschaft,* Bibliotheca Ephemeridum Theologicarum Lovaniensium 68 (Leuven: Peeters, 1985), 252–272; Braulik, *Die deuteronomischen Gesetze und der Dekalog: Studien zum Aufbau von Deuteronomium 12–26,* Stuttgarter Bibelstudien 145 (Stuttgart: Katholisches Bibelwerk, 1991); and the review by Eckhart Otto in *Theologische Literaturzeitung* 119 (1994): 15–17. If Kaufman's argument is accepted, the disposition of the laws in Deut 12–26 would signal that the "decrees and verdicts" revealed to Moses orally are contained, virtually, in the written Torah. Contradictions between the two are therefore impossible.

39. On oral lore in Mesopotamia see Yaakov Elman, "Authoritative Oral Tradition in Neo-Assyrian Scribal Circles," *Journal of Ancient Near Eastern Studies of Columbia University* 7 (1975): 19–32.

40. Norbert Lohfink argues that the prominence of the Sabbath commandment in the Deuteronomic version of the Decalogue (Deut 5:12–15) excludes a pre-exilic dating; see Lohfink, "Zur Dekalogfassung," 27, 30–31. While Lohfink advocates an exilic date for the Deuteronomic Decalogue, he posits a pre-exilic date for chapter 5 as a whole. He is thus forced to assume that the pre-exilic version of the chapter—a chimera, in my opinion—contained a different version of the Decalogue (see esp. 27–29).

41. If Jeremiah's Letter to the exiles (Jer 29) provides reliable information, the first years of the Judean Exile in Babylonia were permeated by expectations of a national restoration. The aborted insurgence of 594 B.C.E. may be taken as another manifestation of nationalistic aspirations.

42. See, in addition to the commentaries, Norbert Lohfink, "Die Sicherung der Wirksamkeit des Gotteswortes durch das Prinzip der Schriftlichkeit der Tora und durch das Prinzip der Gewaltenteilung nach den

Ämtergesetzen des Buches Deuteronomium (Dtn 16,18–18,21)," in Hans Wolter, ed., *Testimonium veritati: Philosophische und theologische Studien zu kirchlichen Fragen der Gegenwart*, Festschrift Wilhelm Kempf, Frankfurter theologische Studien 7 (Frankfurt: Knecht, 1971), 143–155; repr. *Studien zum Deuteronomium*, 1:305–323; Georg Braulik, "Zur Abfolge der Gesetze in Deuteronomium 16,18–21,23: Weitere Beobachtungen," *Biblica* 69 (1988): 63–92.

43. Deut 16:21–17:1 are generally held to be intrusions originally at home in Deut 12; see Preuss, *Deuteronomium*, 134.

44. On the judicial role of the king see, e.g., 2 Sam 15:4; 1 Kings 3; Ps 72:1–4.

45. For a refutation of this argument see Frank Crüsemann, *Die Tora: Theologie und Sozialgeschichte des alttestamentlichen Gesetzes* (Munich: Kaiser, 1992), 242–248, who stresses the Utopian character of much of ancient Near Eastern law.

46. Norbert Lohfink glosses over the distinction between the terms *sēper hattôrâ* and *sēper habbĕrît* by implicitly adopting the perspective of the History Edition; see Lohfink, "Zur Fabel des Deuteronomiums," in Georg Braulik, ed., *Bundesdokument und Gesetz: Studien zum Deuteronomium*, Herders Biblische Studien 4 (Freiburg: Herder, 1995), 65–78, esp. 72 and note 19.

47. Many scholars have advocated an interpretation of Deut 34:10–12 as an editorial conclusion to the Pentateuch. For a survey see Stephen B. Chapman, *The Law and the Prophets: A Study in Old Testament Canon Formation*, Forschungen zum Alten Testament 27 (Tübingen: Mohr Siebeck, 2000), 113–131. Though the text can certainly be read as such a conclusion, it was originally designed to close the Book of Deuteronomy.

48. The contradiction between Deut 34:10–12 and Deut 18:15–18 eventually led to an interpretation of Deut 18:15–18 as a Messianic prophecy, because if (a) Moses cannot have lied, and (b) never again did there arise a prophet like Moses, then (c) the prophet like Moses is yet to come. The Messianic reading of Deut 18:15–18 is reflected in Mal 3:22–24, which identifies the "prophet like Moses" with Elijah.

49. Martin Noth, *Überlieferungsgeschichtliche Studien, 1: Die sammelnden und bearbeitenden Geschichtswerke im Alten Testament*, Schriften der Königsberger Gelehrten Gesellschaft, Geisteswissenschaftliche Klasse 18/2 (Halle: Niemeyer, 1943; repr. Tübingen: Niemeyer, 1957), esp. 12–18 (54–60); English trans., *The Deuteronomistic History*, JSOT Supplement Series 15 (Sheffield: JSOT Press, 1981).

50. The repetitive resumption of Deut 26:19 in Deut 28:1 shows that Deut 27 is an insertion. The chapter is at least slightly at odds with the notion of cult centralization, since the altar at Mt. Ebal is to serve for sacrifices (27:6–7). It is usually assumed that the episode is at home in a tradition about a covenant renewal at Shechem (compare Josh 24).

51. In the opinion of Preuss, *Deuteronomium,* 102, the piece is *eindeutig spät,* under reference to much secondary literature.

52. Citation from Pfeiffer, *Introduction,* 185.

53. The points of correspondence between Deut 4:1–40 and 30:1–20 are numerous and substantial; they demonstrate that the chapters are the two brackets of one editorial frame. For a perceptive study of the correspondences between the two chapters, see Moshe Weinfeld, *Deuteronomy 1–11,* The Anchor Bible 5 (New York: Doubleday, 1991), 215–216. On their common ideological ring see Hans Walther Wolff, "Das Kerygma des deuteronomistischen Geschichtswerk," *ZAW* 73 (1961): 171–186, esp. 182–183.

54. Most notably in their reference to the classic Mesopotamian saying about the impossibility of humans going up to the heavens or down to the underworld. It is possible that the so-called canon formula in Deut 4:2 was borrowed from Mesopotamian scribal tradition as well; see Michael Fishbane, "Varia Deuteronomica," *ZAW* 84 (1972): 349–352, esp. 350.

55. Wilfred G. Lambert, *Babylonian Wisdom Literature* (Oxford: Clarendon, 1960), 148–149, lines 83–84.

56. See, e.g., Thorkild Jacobsen, *The Harps That Once . . . : Sumerian Poetry in Translation* (New Haven: Yale University Press, 1987), 399 (Gudea Cylinder A ix 2–4); Samuel Noah Kramer, "Gilgamesh and the Land of the Living," *JCS* 1 (1947): 3–46, esp. 10:28–29; Gilgamesh Y (the Yale tablet) 140–143, on which see George, *The Babylonian Gilgamesh Epic,* 1:200–201; Tigay, *Evolution,* 164–165; Lambert, *Babylonian Wisdom Literature,* 76:82–83, 86:256–257 *(Babylonian Theodicy);* ibid., 40:33–38 *(Ludlul).* A study on the theme has been published by Frederick E. Greenspahn, "A Mesopotamian Proverb and Its Biblical Reverberations," *JAOS* 114 (1994): 33–38, esp. 33–35.

57. Prov 30:3–4; Job 11:7–8.

58. The date of Deut 19–25 is debated. Georg Braulik argues for a post-exilic origin of Deut 19–25 on the grounds that the chapters betray dependence on the Holiness Code; see Braulik, "Weitere Beobachtungen zur Beziehung zwischen dem Heiligkeitsgesetz und Deuteronomium 19–25,"

in Timo Veijola, ed., *Das Deuteronomium und seine Querbeziehungen,* Schriften der Finnischen Exegetischen Gesellschaft 62 (Helsinki: Finnische Exegetische Gesellschaft; Göttingen: Vandenhoeck & Ruprecht, 1996), 23–55.

59. On the link between Deut 4 and other parts of Deuteronomy see Preuss, *Deuteronomium,* 86–89.

60. Compare Joseph Blenkinsopp, *Prophecy and Canon: A Contribution to the Study of Jewish Origins* (Notre Dame: University of Notre Dame Press, 1970), 31: "Much of the material in [Deuteronomy] could perhaps be explained quite plausibly on the hypothesis of levitical authorship."

61. On the northern background of the Deuteronomic scribes see Karel van der Toorn, *Family Religion in Babylonia, Syria, and Israel: Continuity and Change in the Forms of Religious Life,* Studies in the History and Culture of the Ancient Near East 7 (Leiden: Brill, 1996), 352–355, with references to the relevant literature.

62. See, e.g., Otto, *Das Deuteronomium im Pentateuch und Hexateuch,* 117–118.

63. Norbert Lohfink suggests that the passage means that the priests were to consult the written Torah preserved in the sanctuary, i.e., the Deuteronomic Code, and read the relevant section (Lohfink, "Die Sicherung," 152–153). If this were the case, however, one would expect a reference to "this" Torah, or "[this] Book" of the Torah. It is not clear whether Deut 24:8 implies that the Levitical priests are to consult the written Torah of Moses before they give instructions for dealing with a skin infection.

64. On the Torah *šebbe'al-peh* see Ephraim E. Urbach, *The Sages: Their Concepts and Beliefs,* trans. Israel Abrahams, Publications of the Perry Foundation (Jerusalem: Magnes Press, 1979), 290–292.

65. For the interpretation of the passage see Lothar Perlitt, "Mose als Prophet," *Evangelische Theologie* 31 (1971): 588–608, esp. 597; Robert R. Wilson, *Prophet and Society in Ancient Israel* (Philadelphia: Fortress Press, 1980), 162 and note 52; Matthias Köckert, "Zum literargeschichtlichen Ort des Prophetengesetzes Dtn 18 zwischen dem Jeremiabuch und Dtn 13," in Reinhart G. Kratz and Hermann Spieckermann, eds., *Liebe und Gebot: Studien zum Deuteronomium,* Festschrift zum 70. Geburtstag von Lothar Perlitt, Forschungen zur Religion und Literatur des Alten und Neuen Testaments 190 (Göttingen: Vandenhoeck & Ruprecht, 2000), 80–100.

66. On the "sermons" of Deuteronomy see Preuss, *Deuteronomium*, 95–96.

67. In accordance with the Mesopotamian dictum that "the scribal art is the mother of orators"; see Lambert, *Babylonian Wisdom Literature*, 259 line 19. For an example of a Deuteronomic oration put into the mouth of the priest see Deut 20:1–4.

68. See Braulik, "Die Abfolge der Gesetze," 252; Eckart Otto, "Deuteronomium 4: Die Pentateuchredaktion im Deuteronomiumsrahmen," in Timo Veijola, ed., *Das Deuteronomium und seine Querbeziehungen*, Schriften der Finnischen Exegetischen Gesellschaft 62 (Helsinki: Finnische Exegetische Gesellschaft; Göttingen: Vandenhoeck & Ruprecht, 1996), 196–222, esp. 211.

69. My interpretation of Deut 1:5 is indebted to the perceptive observations by Timo Veijola, "Die Deuteronomisten als Vorgänger der Schriftgelehrten: Ein Beitrag zur Entstehung des Judentums," in *Moses Erben*, 192–240, esp. 215–216.

7. Manufacturing the Prophets

1. See Walther Zimmerli, "Vom Prophetenwort zum Prophetenbuch," *Theologische Literaturzeitung* 104 (1979): 481–496, esp. 488.

2. See Jacobus Hoftijzer and Gerrit van der Kooij, eds., *The Balaam Text from Deir 'Alla Re-Evaluated: Proceedings of the International Symposium Held at Leiden, 21–24 August 1989* (Leiden: Brill, 1991), especially the contributions by André Lemaire (33–57) and Manfred Weippert (151–184).

3. See Gen 33:17; Josh 13:27; Judg 8:4–17; Pss 60:8, 108:8.

4. See Manfred Weippert, "The Balaam Text from Deir 'Alla and the Study of the Old Testament," in Hoftijzer and van der Kooij, eds., *Balaam Text*, 151–184; Othmar Keel and Christoph Uehlinger, *Göttinnen, Götter und Gottessymbole: neue Erkenntnisse zur Religionsgeschichte Kanaans und Israels aufgrund bislang unerschlossener ikonographischer Quellen*, Quaestiones Disputatae 134 (Freiburg: Herder, 1992), 234–237; in English, *Gods, Goddesses, and Images of God in Ancient Israel*, trans. Thomas H. Trapp (Minneapolis: Fortress, 1998), 207–210.

5. See Georges Posener, "Sur l'emploi de l'encre rouge dans les manuscrits égyptiens," *Journal of Egyptian Archaeology* 37 (1951): 75–80; Jaroslav Černý, *Paper and Books in Ancient Egypt* (London: H. K. Lewis, 1952), 24.

6. See, e.g., John M. P. Smith et al., *A Critical and Exegetical Commentary in Micah, Zephaniah, Nahum, Habakkuk, Obadiah and Joel* (Edinburgh: T&T Clark, 1911), 8–16; Robert R. Wilson, *Prophet and Society in Ancient Israel* (Philadelphia: Fortress Press, 1980), 274.

7. William McKane, "Prophecy and the Prophetic Literature," in George W. Anderson, ed., *Tradition and Interpretation: Essays by Members of the Society for Old Testament Study* (Oxford: Clarendon, 1979), 163–188, quotation on 181.

8. The following observations are based on Simo Parpola, *Assyrian Prophecies*, SAA 9 (Helsinki: Helsinki University Press, 1997), LIII–LV. See also Martti Nissinen, "Spoken, Written, Quoted, and Invented: Orality and Writtenness in Ancient Near Eastern Prophecy," in Ehud Ben Zvi and Michael H. Floyd, eds., *Writings and Speech in Israelite and Ancient Near Eastern Prophecy,* SBL Symposium Series 10 (Atlanta: Society of Biblical Literature, 2000), 235–271, esp. 248–254.

9. See, e.g., Hermann Gunkel, "Die Propheten als Schriftsteller und Dichter," in Hans Schmidt, *Die grossen Propheten* (Göttingen: Vandenhoeck & Ruprecht, 1915), xxxvi–lxxii, esp. xxxviii.

10. The reference to writing in Isa 30:8 reflects later speculation about the purpose of written prophecy; the text does not go back to Isaiah but flowed from the pen of later scribes. The scribes responsible for the transmission of the Isaiah collection interpreted the text as an "everlasting witness" (*lĕ'ēd 'ad-'ôlām,* according to the revocalized text of Isa 30:8) by analogy with the Book of the Torah (Deut 31:26, *lĕ'ēd*). Jer 30:1–4, which refers to Jeremiah as a writer, is designed to authenticate the so-called Book of Consolation (Jer 30–31), secondarily inserted in the Jeremiah scroll.

11. The word *ḥāzôn,* literally "vision," developed the technical meaning "prophecy"; see 2 Sam 7:17 *(dĕbārîm)*//1 Chron 17:15 *(ḥāzôn)*; Isa 1:1; Obad 1; Nah 1:1; Francis Brown, Samuel R. Driver, and Charles A. Briggs, *A Hebrew and English Lexicon of the Old Testament* (Oxford: Oxford University Press, 1907), 302–303 under *ḥāzôn* and *ḥizzāyôn;* Ludwig Koehler, Walter Baumgartner, and Jakob J. Stamm, *Hebräisches und aramäisches Lexikon zum Alten Testament* (Leiden: Brill, 1967–1995), 289 under *ḥāzôn.* I take the conjunction of *ktb* and *b'r* as a hendiadys in analogy with Deut 27:8, "And on those stones you shall inscribe every word of this Teaching most distinctly" (NJPS). Following a suggestion by Joachim Schaper, I take *qôrē'* as a designation of the town

crier; see Schaper, "Exilic and Post-Exilic Prophecy and the Orality/Literacy Problem," *VT* 55 (2005): 324–342, esp. 333. The Hebrew *qôrē'* is functionally comparable to the Mesopotamian *nāgiru*, for which see the *Chicago Assyrian Dictionary* N/1, 115–117. The Mesopotamian herald "rounds up" the city and makes a proclamation *(šasû)* to the citizens on behalf of the authorities.

12. On the Habakkuk passage see also Michael H. Floyd, "Prophecy and Writing in Habakkuk 2,1–5," *ZAW* 105 (1993): 462–481, who argues that Habakkuk used writing primarily as a means of disseminating an oracle (477).

13. The expression for "brush" is *ḥereṭ 'ĕnôš: ḥereṭ* means "stylus," *'ĕnôš* stands for "weak, soft"; taken together, the expression refers to a brush of the type used on occasion by Egyptian scribes.

14. For the text see Rykle Borger, *Beiträge zum Inschriftenwerk Assurbanipals* (Wiesbaden: Otto Harrassowitz, 1996), 40–41, lines 118–127 (Assurbanipal Prism A, par. 34). For a translation and discussion see A. Leo Oppenheim, *The Interpretation of Dreams in the Ancient Near East,* Transactions of the American Philosophical Society 46/3 (Philadelphia: The American Philosophical Society, 1956), 201–202, 249–250.

15. See Borger, *Beiträge,* 41, line 121*.

16. See Gösta W. Ahlström, *The History of Ancient Palestine from the Palaeolithic Period to Alexander's Conquest,* JSOT Supplement Series 146 (Sheffield: Sheffield Academic Press, 1993), 792; Rainer Albertz, "Die Zerstörung des Jerusalemer Tempels 587 v.Chr.: Historische Einordnung und religionspolitische Bedeutung," in Johannes Haan, ed., *Zerstörung des Jerusalemer Tempels: Geschehen—Wahrnehmung—Bewältigung,* Wissenschaftliche Untersuchungen zum Neuen Testament 147 (Tübingen: Mohr Siebeck, 2002), 23–39, esp. 26.

17. See Menahem Haran, "On the Diffusion of Literacy and Schools in Ancient Israel," in John A. Emerton, ed., *Congress Volume Jerusalem 1986,* Supplements VT 40 (Leiden: Brill, 1988), 81–95, esp. 90–91 note 21.

18. Lachish Letter 3:20–21. For a study of this letter see Frank Moore Cross, "A Literate Soldier: Lachish Letter III," in Ann Kort and Scott Morschauser, eds., *Biblical and Related Studies Presented to Samuel Iwry* (Winona Lake, IN: Eisenbrauns, 1985), 41–47; repr. in *Leaves from an Epigrapher's Notebook: Collected Papers in Hebrew and West Semitic Palaeography and Epigraphy,* Harvard Semitic Studies 51 (Winona Lake, IN: Eisenbrauns, 2003), 129–132.

19. Most of the "prophetic letters" from Mari are actually reports on prophecy by royal officials. For letters written by prophets themselves see Jean-Marie Durand et al., *Archives épistolaires de Mari,* 2 vols., Archives royales de Mari 26 (Paris: Editions Recherche sur les Civilizations, 1988), 1 nos. 192–194; 2 no. 414:29–35. For a possible prophetic letter from Ishchali see Maria DeJong Ellis, "The Goddess Kititum Speaks to King Ibal-pi-el: Oracle Texts from Ishchali," *MARI* 5 (1987): 235–266, but note the discussion by William Moran, who argues that the text is an oracle report for filing purposes; see Moran, "An Ancient Prophetic Oracle," in *The Most Magic Word,* ed. Ronald S. Hendel, The Catholic Biblical Quarterly Monograph Series 35 (Washington, DC: The Catholic Biblical Association of America, 2002), 140–147, esp. 142; repr. from Georg Braulik et al., eds., *Biblische Theologie und gesellschaftlicher Wandel: Festschrift Norbert Lohfink* (Freiburg: Herder, 1993), 252–259.

20. See, e.g., Jer 7, 26, 28; Ezek 26:1, 29:17, 30:20, 31:1, 32:1, 32:17; Hag 1:1, 2:1.

21. See David A. Glatt-Gilad, "The Personal Names in Jeremiah as a Source for the History of the Period," *Hebrew Studies* 41 (2000): 31–45.

22. Ahikam son of Shaphan, Jer 26:24; Elasah son of Shaphan, Jer 29:3; Gemariah son of Shaphan, Jer 36:10; Gedaliah son of Ahikam son of Shaphan, Jer 39:14, 39:40, 39:41, 43:6.

23. Shaphan was a palace scribe; 2 Kings 22:3. Gemariah son of Shaphan was probably a scribe as well, unless the title refers back to the father, Jer 36:10.

24. See, e.g., Timothy Polk, *The Prophetic Persona: Jeremiah and the Language of the Self,* JSOT Supplement Series 32 (Sheffield: JSOT Press, 1984); Henry Mottu, *Les 'confessions' de Jérémie: Une protestation contre la souffrance,* Le monde de la Bible 14 (Geneva: Labor et Fides, 1985); A. R. Pete Diamond, *The Confessions of Jeremiah in Context: Scenes of Prophetic Drama,* JSOT Supplement Series 45 (Sheffield: JSOT Press, 1987); Kathleen M. O'Connor, *The Confessions of Jeremiah: Their Interpretation and Role in Chapters 1–25,* SBL Dissertation Series 94 (Atlanta: Scholars Press, 1988); Karl-Friedrich Pohlmann, *Die Ferne Gottes—Studien zum Jeremiabuch: Beiträge zu den 'Konfessionen' im Jeremiabuch und ein Versuch zur Frage nach den Anfängen der Jeremiatradition,* Beihefte ZAW 179 (Berlin: De Gruyter, 1989), 1–111; Mark S. Smith, *The Laments of Jeremiah and Their Contexts: A Literary and Redactional Study of Jeremiah 11–20,* SBL Monograph Series 42

(Atlanta: Scholars Press, 1990). The classic study is by Walter Baumgartner, *Die Klagegedichte des Jeremia,* Beihefte ZAW 32 (Giessen: Töpelmann, 1917); in English, *Jeremiah's Poems of Lament,* trans. David E. Orton, Historic Texts and Interpreters in Biblical Scholarship 7 (Sheffield: JSOT Press, 1987).

25. The so-called autobiographies from Mesopotamia are pseudo-autobiographies; see Tremper Longman III, *Fictional Akkadian Autobiography: A Generic and Comparative Study* (Winona Lake, IN: Eisenbrauns, 1991). The possible exceptions, such as the apology of Adad-Guppi (see COS 1.147:477–478), are more concerned with social role and reputation than with the psychology of the individual.

26. Pierre E. Bonnard, *Le Psautier selon Jérémie: Influence littéraire et spirituelle de Jérémie sur trente-trois psaumes,* Lectio Divina 26 (Paris: Cerf, 1960), studies the connections between Jeremiah's Confessions and Psalms but fails to pay due attention to the dependence of the Confessions on the Psalms.

27. Compare Jer 20:14–18 with Job 3:3–26: the curse on the day of birth.

28. See Wilfred G. Lambert, "A Further Attempt at the Babylonian 'Man and His God,'" in Francesca Rochberg-Halton, ed., *Language, Literature, and History: Philological and Historical Studies Presented to Erica Reiner,* American Oriental Series 67 (New Haven: American Oriental Society, 1987), 187–202.

29. See Wilfred G. Lambert, *Babylonian Wisdom Literature* (Oxford: Clarendon, 1960), 21–62, 283–302, 343–345.

30. In Jer 1:18 read *ḥōmat,* "wall," instead of *ḥōmôt,* "walls," and strike *ûlĕʿammûd barzel,* "and an iron pillar," absent from the LXX and presumably added by the edition preserved in the MT.

31. For a study of the correspondences between the Books of Micah and Jeremiah see Jun-Hee Cha, *Micha und Jeremia,* Bonner biblische Beiträge 107 (Weinheim: Beltz Athenaeum, 1996).

32. Since the correspondences between the Confessions of Jeremiah and the Book of Micah are confined to Mic 1–3 and 7:1–6, the other parts of Micah (i.e., Mic 4–6, 7:7–20) could be exilic or post-exilic expansions.

33. On the role of memorized citations in the production of new texts see the insightful observations by David M. Carr, *Writing on the Tablet of the Heart: Origins of Scripture and Literature* (New York: Oxford University Press, 2005).

34. Sigmund Mowinckel, *Zur Komposition des Buches Jeremia,* Skrifter

utgitt av Videnskapsselskapet i Kristiania II, Historisk-filosofisk Klasse 1913:5 (Kristiana: Dybwad, 1914), 7–10.

35. See also Alexander Rofé, *Introduction to the Prophetic Literature* (Sheffield: Sheffield Academic Press, 1997), 20–23.

36. Against Alexander Rofé, *The Prophetical Stories* (Jerusalem: Magnes, 1988), 118.

37. Henrik Samuel Nyberg, "Das textkritische Problem des Alten Testaments am Hoseabuch demonstriert," *ZAW* 52 (1934): 241–254, esp. 243–244; Nyberg, *Studien zum Hoseabuche,* Uppsala Universitets Årsskrift 1935:6 (Uppsala: Lundequistska Bokhandeln, 1935); Harris Birkeland, *Zum hebräischen Traditionswesen: Die Komposition der prophetischen Bücher des Alten Testaments,* Avhandlinger utgitt av Det Norske Videnskaps-Akademie i Oslo, II. Hist.-Filos. Klasse 1938:1 (Oslo: Jacob Dybwad, 1938); Sigmund Mowinkel, *Prophecy and Tradition: The Prophetic Books in the Light of the Study of the Growth and History of the Tradition,* Avhandlinger utgitt av Det Norske Videnskaps-Akademie i Oslo, II. Hist.-Filos. Klasse 1946:3 (Oslo: Jacob Dybwad, 1946 [1947]).

38. See, as an example of a trend, Anton H. J. Gunneweg, *Mündliche und schriftliche Tradition der vorexilischen Prophetenbücher als Problem der neueren Prophetenforschung,* Forschungen zur Religion und Literatur des Alten und Neuen Testaments 73 (Göttingen: Vandenhoeck & Ruprecht, 1959).

39. See, for a discussion, Walter J. Ong, *Orality and Literacy: The Technologizing of the Word* (London: Methuen, 1982), 57–68.

40. J. Andrew Dearman, "My Servants the Scribes: Composition and Context in Jeremiah 36," *JBL* 109 (1990): 403–421, quotation on 419, note 43.

41. For a discussion of the evidence see Emanuel Tov, "The Literary History of the Book of Jeremiah in the Light of Its Textual History," in Jeffrey H. Tigay, ed., *Empirical Models for Biblical Criticism* (Philadelphia: University of Pennsylvania Press, 1985), 211–237; Pierre-Maurice Bogaert, "Le livre de Jérémie en perspective: Les deux rédactions selon les travaux en cours," *Revue Biblique* 101 (1994): 363–406. According to a minority view, the edition underlying the Masoretic text is chronologically prior to the edition underlying the LXX; see Georg Fischer, "Jer 25 und die Fremdvölkersprüche: Unterschiede zwischen hebräischem und griechischem Text," *Biblica* 72 (1991): 474–499; Arie van der Kooij, "Jeremiah 27:5–15: How Do MT and LXX Relate to Each Other?" *Jour-*

nal of Northwest Semitic Languages 20 (1994): 59–78. Konrad Schmid, *Buchgestalten des Jeremiabuches: Untersuchungen zur Redaktions- und Rezeptionsgeschichte von Jer 30–33 im Kontext des Buches,* Wissenschaftliche Monographien zum Alten und Neuen Testament 72 (Neukirchen: Neukirchener Verlag, 1996), 15–23, argues that Jer^{MT} and Jer^{LXX} should be regarded as two independent editions existing side by side; in many cases he gives chronological priority to the MT.

42. See, e.g. Bernhard Duhm, *Das Buch Jeremia,* Kurzer Hand-Commentar zum Alten Testament 9 (Tübingen and Leipzig: Mohr, 1901), 270.

43. See especially Pierre-Maurice Bogaert, "Urtext, texte court et relecture: Jérémie xxxiii 14–26 TM et ses préparations," in John A. Emerton, ed., *Congress Volume Leuven 1989,* VT Supplements 43 (Leiden: Brill, 1991), 236–247; Yohanan Goldman, *Prophétie et royauté au retour de l'exil: Les origines littéraires de la forme massorétique du livre de Jérémie,* OBO 118 (Fribourg: Universitätsverlag; Göttingen: Vandenhoeck & Ruprecht, 1992), 9–37, 38–64.

44. Compare Goldman, *Prophétie et royauté,* 31 and note 59.

45. On the significance of the seventy-years prophecy see Schmid, *Buch-gestalten,* 223–227.

46. More precisely, Jer 2:1–3:5 and Jer 3:19–4:2, since Jer 3:6–12 and Jer 3:14–18 have been inserted.

47. The MT introduces the oracle of vv. 2–3 by a standard formula implying that it was addressed to Jerusalem; this part is missing in the LXX and is obviously secondary. Another introduction in v. 4 applies the rest of the chapter to "the house of Jacob/Israel," i.e., the Northern Kingdom. Commentators agree that in fact all the oracles of chapter 2 are addressed to Israel. The one reference to Judah in 2:27 is a repeated passage, the proper place of which is 11:12–13.

8. Inventing Revelation

1. According to Eusebius, *Hist. Eccl.* 3.10, Josephus qualified the books of the Jews as "divine" *(theia).* Eusebius is citing from *C. Ap.* 1.38–40, where the Josephus manuscripts omit the word "divine."

2. For an early observation of the parallel between the notion of revelation in the Bible and in Babylonia see Friedrich Delitzsch, *Zweiter Vortrag über Babel und Bibel,* 2nd ed. (Stuttgart: Deutsche Verlags-Anstalt, 1904), 50–51, note 9.

3. This definition of religion is a free variation on the famous definition proposed by Melford E. Spiro, according to whom religion is "an institution consisting of culturally patterned interactions with culturally postulated superhuman beings." See Spiro, "Religion: Problems of Definition and Explanation," in Michael Banton, ed., *Anthropological Approaches to the Study of Religion,* Association of Social Anthropologists Monographs 3 (London: Tavistock Publications, 1966), 85–126, quotation on 96.

4. Wilfred G. Lambert, "A Catalogue of Texts and Authors," *JCS* 16 (1962): 59–77.

5. Fragment VI 15–17 (= K.9717+81-7-27,71, rev. 15–17) is either an explanatory commentary to Fragment I 1(5)-7 or an explanation of the chain of tradition pertinent to all the works previously listed. The mention of Adapa in this section is therefore not an indication of "the lack of a consistent chronological scheme," contrary to Lambert, "Catalogue," 76.

6. See the judicious observations by William W. Hallo, "On the Antiquity of Sumerian Literature," *JAOS* 83 (1963): 167–176, esp. 175.

7. Lambert, "Catalogue," 64–65, fragment I, line 4. The myths in question are *Lugale,* for which see Johannes J. A. van Dijk, *Lugal ud me-lám-bi nir-gál: Le récit épique et didactique des travaux de Ninurta, du Déluge, et de la Nouvelle Création* (Leiden: Brill, 1983); and *Angim,* for which see Jerrold S. Cooper, *The Return of Ninurta to Nippur: an-gim dím-ma,* Analecta Orientalia 52 (Rome: Pontifical Biblical Institute, 1978). The scholarly use of the texts took its cue from the list of stones in *Lugale,* and of slain enemies in *Angim.* On Ninurta as the scribe and secretary of the gods see Amar Annus, *The God Ninurta in the Mythology and Royal Ideology of Ancient Mesopotamia,* SAA Studies 14 (Helsinki: The Neo-Assyrian Text Corpus Project, 2002), 81–90.

8. Lambert, "Catalogue," 66–67, fragment VI, line 16. For another reference to Adapa in the role of transcriber and editor see the Persian Verse Account of Nabonidus, which speaks about the series *Enūma Anu Enlil* (deliberately distorted into the title *Uskaru Anu Enlil*), "which Adapa compiled [*ikṣuru*]"; see Peter Machinist and Hayim Tadmor, "Heavenly Wisdom," in Mark E. Cohen et al., eds., *The Tablet and the Scroll: Near Eastern Studies in Honor of William W. Hallo* (Bethesda, MD: CDL Press, 1993), 146–151, esp. 146–147.

9. For the *lām abūbu* reference see Lambert, "Catalogue," 66–67, fragment

VI, line 15. The mention of Anšekurra in Lambert, "Catalogue," 66–67, fragment VI, line 17, suggests that the passage is referring to the chain of tradition, in which the successive *apkallus* inherit the lore of their predecessors. I propose the following reconstruction of lines 15–17: "[Texts and recipes] from before the Flood [which Ea spoke and Ada]pa wrote at his dictation [and which NN] wrote down from the mouth of Anšekura." In this reconstruction Anšekura ("He-who-entered-heaven," interpreting *anše-kur-ra* as Sumerian *an-šè ku₄-ra*) is another name of Adapa.

10. The *terminus post quem* is furnished by the reference to the *Song of Erra*, presumably composed after 800 B.C.E., and the *terminus ante quem* is the end of the reign of Assurbanipal (668–627), since all the copies of the *Catalogue* are from the libraries of Assurbanipal. For the date of *Erra* see Luigi Cagni, *L'Epopea di Erra*, Studi Semitici 34 (Rome: Istituto di studi di Vicino Oriente, 1969), 37–45; Wolfram von Soden, "Etemenanki vor Asarhaddon nach der Erzählung vom Turmbau zu Babel und dem Erra-Mythos," *Ugarit-Forschungen* 3 (1971): 253–263, esp. 255–256 (ca. 764 B.C.E.) and note his supplementary observations in *AfO* 34 (1987): 67–69.

11. Walter Mayer, "Sargons Feldzug gegen Urartu 714 v.Chr.: Text und Übersetzung," *Mitteilungen der Deutschen Orient-Gesellschaft* 115 (1983): 65–132, esp. 68, lines 7–6: *ša . . . ina ṭuppi maḫrî išṭurušu bēl [nē]meqi ᵈNiššiku.* Compare Arthur G. Lie, *The Inscriptions of Sargon II King of Assyria* (Paris: Geuthner, 1929), Plate 9, lines 57–59: "In the month of Simanu, which by decree of Anu, Enlil, and Ea-Ninšiku has been proclaimed as the month of the brick-god in view of making bricks and building cities and houses."

12. Wilfred G. Lambert, "Three Literary Prayers of the Babylonians," *AfO* 19 (1959–60): 47–66, esp. 59, line 146. Note the parallel with "his prayer" *(tēmeqišu)* in the following line.

13. Wilfred G. Lambert, "The Twenty-One 'Poultices,'" *Anatolian Studies* 30 (1980): 77–83. The "poultices" *(mēlū)* are said to be "from the mouth of Ea," p. 78, text "LKA 146" reverse, line 16; cf. p. 80, text "BM 33999," line 11.

14. See Lambert, "Poultices," 80, for the passage in which Nabu, the god of writing, is said to have brought up the texts from the Apsû. For Apsû as the "house of wisdom" *(bīt nēmeqi)* see Erica Reiner, *Šurpu: A Collection of Sumerian and Akkadian Incantations,* AfO Beiheft 11 (Graz: Ernst Weidner, 1958), 17, tablet II, line 149. For other references to texts from the Apsû see the *Chicago Assyrian Dictionary* A/2, 195–196. Note also

the unpublished text K. 3311+, line 15, *niṣirti apsî*, "secret from the Abyss," quoted in the *Chicago Assyrian Dictionary* A/2, 196.

15. The notion of a heavenly revelation might be viewed as a reinterpretation of the Sumerian concept of the arts of human civilization as having "come down from heaven"; see Shulgi Hymn B, line 273, *nam-lù-ùlu an-ta sì-ga-ta*, "humanity descended from heaven"; Jacob Klein, *The Royal Hymns of Shulgi King of Ur: Man's Quest for Immortal Fame,* Transactions of the American Philosophical Society 71/7 (Philadelphia: The American Philosophical Society, 1981), 20 note 86.

16. A bilingual praise of Nebuchadnezzar I (1125–1104) refers to the Babylonian king as "offspring of [Enmeduranki] . . . who sat in the presence of Šamaš and Adad." See Wilfred G. Lambert, "Enmeduranki and Related Matters," *JCS* 21 (1967): 126–138, esp. 128, lines 8–10.

17. For the myth see Lambert, "Enmeduranki," 132; Lambert, "The Qualifications of Babylonian Diviners," in Stefan Maul, ed., *Festschrift für Rykle Borger zu seinem 65. Geburtstag am 24. Mai 1994: tikip santakki mala bašmu . . .*, CM 10 (Groningen: Styx, 1998), 141–158, esp. 148–149.

18. See the Old Babylonian prayer of the diviner published by Ivan Starr, *The Rituals of the Diviner,* Bibliotheca Mesopotamica 12 (Malibu: Undena, 1983), lines 9 and 18: "O Shamash, you have opened the locks of the gates of heaven; you went up a staircase of pure lapis lazuli . . . Let the judges, the great gods, who sit on golden thrones, who eat at a table of lapis lazuli, sit before you" (see p. 30 for the Akkadian, p. 37 for English translation). Starr rightly notes the interplay between the celestial and the terrestrial spheres, as the divination ceremony on earth mirrors the proceedings in heaven; see Starr, *Rituals of the Diviner,* 57–58. Note that the "assembly" of Shamash and Adad is replicated, so to speak, in the close connection between the sanctuaries of the gods in Sippar; see Daniel Schwemer, *Die Wettergottgestalten Mesopotamiens und Nordsyriens im Zeitalter der Keilschriftkulturen: Materialien und Studien nach den schriftlichen Quellen* (Wiesbaden: Harrassowitz, 2001), 321–324.

19. See lines 16–18, apparently an expansion of the text; see Lambert, "Enmeduranki," 127.

20. See Hermann Hunger, *Babylonische und Assyrische Kolophone,* AOAT 2 (Kevelaer: Butzon & Bercker; Neukirchen-Vluyn: Neukirchener Verlag, 1968), no. 325: *bārûtu* [nam-azu] *pirišti* [ad-ḫal] *šamê u erṣeti nēmeqi* ᵈ*Šamaš u* ᵈ*Adad*, "*bārûtu,* secret of heaven and underworld, wisdom of Shamash and Adad."

21. See Piotr Michalowski, "Adapa and the Ritual Process," *Rocznik Orientalistyczny* 41 (1980): 77–82.

22. Sergio A. Picchioni, *Il poemetto di Adapa* (Budapest; Eötvös Loránd Tudományegyetem, 1981); Shlomo Izre'el, *Adapa and the South Wind: Language Has the Power of Life and Death*, Mesopotamian Civilizations 10 (Winona Lake, IN: Eisenbrauns, 2001).

23. Picchioni, *Adapa*, 122. For the restoration see especially Wolfram von Soden, "Bemerkungen zum Adapa-Mythos," in Barry L. Eichler et al., eds., *Kramer Anniversary Volume: Cuneiform Studies in Honor of Samuel Noah Kramer*, AOAT 25 (Kevelaer: Butzon & Bercker; Neukirchen-Vluyn: Neukirchener Verlag, 1976), 427–433, esp. 432–433. Note also the restorations and translation by Izre'el, *Adapa*, 96–99.

24. For a survey see Picchioni, *Adapa*, 82–101.

25. A reference to heavenly revelations is also implied in the personal name Anšekura found in the *Catalogue of Texts and Authors;* see Lambert, "Catalogue," 66–67, fragment VI, line 17, assuming that the name should be interpreted as an.šè ku₄.ra, "Who Entered Heaven," instead of anše.kur.ra, "Horse." For other references to *apkallu*s having access to heaven see Erica Reiner, "The Etiological Myth of the 'Seven Sages,'" *Orientalia* 30 (1961): 1–11.

26. See Heinrich Zimmern, *Beiträge zur Kenntnis der Babylonischen Religion* (Leipzig: J. C. Hinrichs, 1901), 96–97, no. 1–21, lines 11–12: *niṣirti bārûti ša* ᵈ*Ea imbû*, "secret art of extispicy, which Ea proclaimed." An alternative interpretation reads [*mūdû nāṣir*] *niṣirti bārûti ša* ᵈ*Ea imbû*, "[the expert who keeps] the secret art of extispicy, whom Ea has called."

27. See, e.g., Thorkild Jacobsen, *The Harps That Once . . . : Sumerian Poetry in Translation* (New Haven: Yale University Press, 1987), 399 (Gudea Cylinder A ix 2–4); Samuel Noah Kramer, "Gilgamesh and the Land of the Living," *JCS* 1 (1947): 3–46, esp. 10:28–29; Gilgamesh Y (the Yale tablet) 140–143, for which see Andrew F. George, *The Babylonian Gilgamesh Epic: Introduction, Critical Edition and Cuneiform Texts*, 2 vols. (Oxford: Oxford University Press, 2003), 1:200–201; Tigay, *Evolution*, 164–165; Wilfred G. Lambert, *Babylonian Wisdom Literature* (Oxford: Clarendon, 1960), 76:82–83; 86:256–257 *(Babylonian Theodicy);* ibid., 40:33–38 *(Ludlul)*. A study on the theme has been published by Frederick E. Greenspahn, "A Mesopotamian Proverb and Its Biblical Reverberations," *JAOS* 114 (1994): 33–38, esp. 33–35.

28. For the expression, *niṣirti šamê u erṣeti*, see Hunger, *Kolophone*, nos. 325 and 519; Robert D. Biggs, "An Esoteric Babylonian Commentary," *RA*

62 (1968): 51–58, esp. 53, Obverse 4: *niṣirti šamê u erṣeti uṣur,* "Preserve the secret of heaven and the underworld." See also the Enmeduranki text discussed above. Compare the more poetic variant *kanak uṣurāti šamê u erṣeti pirišti lalgar,* "Seal of the designs of heaven and underworld, secret of the Abyss," in the curriculum list for exorcism; see Erich Ebeling, *Keilschrifttexte aus Assur religiösen Inhalts,* 2 vols., Wissenschaftliche Veröffentlichungen der Deutschen Orient-Gesellschaft 28 and 34 (Leipzig: Hinrichs, 1919–1923), 1:44, line 31.

29. See Hunger, *Kolophone,* no. 533, line 2: *ša pî apkallī labīrūti ša lām abūbi;* the colophon says that the ointments and bandages are "from the mouth of the Ancient Sages from before the Flood, which in Šuruppak in the second year of Enlil-bāni, King of Isin [from the First Dynasty of Isin, 1859 B.C.E.], Enlil-uballiṭ, the sage of Nippur, left behind." The colophon implies the existence of a chain of tradition going back to the antediluvian sages. Compare the expression *niṣirti apkallī* in Hunger, *Kolophone,* no. 328, line 13. Note also the unusual *niṣirti Lu-Nanna apkal Ur,* "secret of Lu-Nanna the apkallu from Ur," colophon of a medical text, K. 8080, cited by Wilfred G. Lambert, "Ancestors, Authors, and Canonicity," *JCS* 11 (1957): 1–14.112, esp. 7 note 27.

30. Text published by Ebeling, *Keilschrifttexte,* 2.177, Obv. IV 25–33, Rev. IV 1–3; for a transliteration and translation see Hunger, *Kolophone,* no. 292.

31. Compare the observations by Lambert, "Ancestors, Authors, and Canonicity," 8–9.

32. See Hunger, *Kolophone,* no. 328, line 13.

33. According to the Babylonian priest Berossus (ca. 300 B.C.E.), the writings of the *apkallu*s had been hidden in Sippar, where they were found after the Flood. See Stanley M. Burstein, *The Babyloniaca of Berossus,* Sources from the Ancient Near East 1/5 (Malibu: Undena, 1978), 20.

34. For another example see Erich Ebeling, *Literarische Keilschrifttexte aus Assur* (Berlin: Akademie-Verlag, 1953), no. 36, Obv. 4–7, Rev. 1, for which see A. Leo Oppenheim, *The Interpretation of Dreams in the Ancient Near East,* Transactions of the American Philosophical Society, 46/3 (Philadelphia: American Philosophical Society, 1956), 354; Hunger, *Kolophone,* no. 290.

35. For this translation see Karlheinz Deller and Werner R. Mayer, "Akkadische Lexikographie: *CAD M,*" *Orientalia* 53 (1984): 72–124, esp. 121–122.

36. *Erra,* tablet V, lines 42–45 (Benjamin R. Foster, *Before the Muses: An An-*

thology of Akkadian Literature, 2 vols. [Bethesda, MD: CDL Press, 1993], 2:804).

37. *Enūma eliš,* tablet VII, lines 157–158: *taklimti maḫrû idbubu pānuššu, išṭurma ištakan ana šimê arkûti.* The translation is freely after Herman Vanstiphout, "Enuma Elish as a Systematic Creed: An Essay," *Orientalia Lovaniensia Periodica* 23 (1992): 37–61, esp. 37. See also Jean Bottéro and Samuel Noah Kramer, *Lorsque les dieux faisaient l'homme: Mythologie mésopotamienne* (Paris: Gallimard, 1989), 653: "Telle est la révélation qu'un Ancien, devant qui on l'avait exposée, mit et disposa par écrit pour l'enseigner à la postérité." This understanding of the text is already implied in the observation on *taklimtu* by Delitzsch, *Zweiter Vortrag,* 50–51, note 9.

38. Compare *Erra,* V, line 43, which uses the verb *šabrû,* "to show," for the act of revelation. In the prophetic books of the Hebrew Bible, the reception of a verbal message from God is often referred to with the verb *ḥāzâ,* "to see," a prophecy being a *ḥāzôn,* literally "vision." See the observations by Delitzsch, *Zweiter Vortrag,* 50–51, note 9, on *taklimtu, šubrû,* and Hebrew *ḥāzôn.*

39. On the verb *šakānu* in the sense of "to put on the curriculum," see Simo Parpola, *Letters from Assyrian Scholars to the Kings Esarhaddon and Assurbanipal, Part II: Commentary and Appendices,* AOAT 5/2 (Kevelaer: Butzon & Bercker; Neukirchen-Vluyn: Neukirchener Verlag, 1983), 99–100. Note also the *Song of Erra,* tablet V, line 59: *zamaru šâšu ana matīma liššakinma,* "May this song be established forever."

40. See especially Wilfred G. Lambert, "The Reign of Nebuchadnezzar I: A Turning Point in the History of Ancient Mesopotamian Religion," in William S. McCullough, ed., *The Seed of Wisdom: Essays in Honour of Th. J. Meek* (Toronto: University of Toronto Press, 1964), 3–13.

41. See Christopher Walker, "The Second Tablet of *ṭupšenna pitema:* An Old Babylonian Naram-Sin Legend?" *JCS* 33 (1981): 191–195, esp. 194.

42. In earlier publications I have pursued this line of explanation; see, e.g., Karel van der Toorn, "Sources in Heaven: Revelation as a Scholarly Construct in Second Temple Judaism," in Ulrich Hübner and Ernst Axel Knauf, eds., *Kein Land für sich allein: Studien zum Kulturkontakt in Kanaan, Israel/Palästina und Ebirnâri für Manfred Weippert zum 65. Geburtstag,* OBO 186 (Fribourg: Universitätsverlag; Göttingen: Vandenhoeck & Ruprecht, 2002), 265–277, esp. 272–273.

43. See Peter L. Berger, *The Sacred Canopy: Elements of a Sociological Theory of Religion* (Garden City, NY: Doubleday, 1967), 126–153; Berger, *A*

Rumor of Angels: Modern Society and the Rediscovery of the Supernatural (Garden City, NY: Doubleday, 1969), 42–56.

44. For a history of the post-Kassite era see John A. Brinkman, *A Political History of Post-Kassite Babylonia* (Analecta Orientalia 43; Rome: Pontifical Biblical Institute, 1968).

45. The author Saggil-kinam-ubbib is mentioned in the *List of Sages and Scholars* for having been the chief scholar during the reigns of Nebuchadnezzar I (1125–1104) and Adad-apla-iddina (1068–1047). For this list see Jacobus van Dijk in Heinrich J. Lenzen, *XVIII. Vorläufiger Bericht über die . . . Ausgrabungen in Uruk-Warka* (Berlin: Mann, 1962), 44–52, Tafel 27; see also Irving L. Finkel, "Adad-apla-iddina, Esagil-kīn-apli, and the Series SA.GIG," in Erle Leichty et al., eds., *A Scientific Humanist: Studies in Memory of Abraham Sachs* (Philadelphia: The S. N. Kramer Fund, 1988), 143–159, esp. 144.

46. Lambert, *Babylonian Wisdom Literature,* 74, line 58.

47. For the interpretation of *ṭēnšina* as "their destiny," "the divine decree about them," see Marten Stol, "The Reversibility of Human Fate in *Ludlul* II," in Önhan Tunca and Danielle Deheselle, eds., *Tablettes et images aux pays de Sumer et d'Akkad: Mélanges offerts à Monsieur H. Limet* (Liège: Université de Liège, 1996), 179–183. Stol bases his interpretation on *Ludlul* II 43.

48. *Theodicy,* lines 82–86. For the interpretation of lines 83–84 see *Chicago Assyrian Dictionary* Q, 248a, and *Chicago Assyrian Dictionary* S, 27b, both of which quote the unpublished duplicate, British Museum no. 47745 (for which see also *Chicago Assyrian Dictionary* K, 386a).

49. *Theodicy,* lines 256–257, 264.

50. Lambert, *Babylonian Wisdom Literature,* 26; Foster, *Before the Muses,* 1.308–325 ("Mature Period, 1500–1000 B.C."); Wolfram von Soden, "Der leidende Gerechte," in *Texte aus der Umwelt des Alten Testaments,* ed. Otto Kaiser, 3 vols. with suppl. (Gütersloh: Gerd Mohn, 1982–2001), 3:110–135, esp. 112. If *Ludlul* is from the late Kassite period, as most scholars think, it is slightly older than the *Theodicy.*

51. One Shubshi-mashre-Shakkan is known to have been a deputy of the Kassite king Nazimaruttash (c. 1307–1282 B.C.E.); see Wilfred G. Lambert, "Ancestors, Authors, and Canonicity," *JCS* 11 (1957): 1–14, 112, esp. 6; Von Soden, "Der leidende Gerechte," 111.

52. Anzanunzû, a name of Ea, god of wisdom, whose dwelling is in the waters underneath the earth; cf. Von Soden, "Der leidende Gerechte," 112.

53. Against Hermann Spieckermann, "*Ludlul bēl nēmeqi* und die Frage nach

der Gerechtigkeit Gottes," in Stefan Maul, ed., *Festschrift für Rykle Borger zu seinem 65. Geburtstag am 24. Mai 1994: tikip santakki mala bašmu . . .*, CM 10 (Groningen: Styx, 1998), 329–341, esp. 336.

54. Rainer Albertz, "Der sozialgeschichtliche Hintergrund des Hiobbuches und der 'Babylonischen Theodizee,'" in Jörg Jeremias and Lothar Perlitt, eds., *Die Botschaft und die Boten: Festschrift für Hans Walter Wolff zum 70. Geburtstag* (Neukirchen-Vluyn: Neukirchener Verlag, 1981), 349–372, esp. 351–357.

55. Brinkman, *Post-Kassite Babylonia*, 129–144.

56. See Karel van der Toorn, "Theodicy in Akkadian Literature," in Antti Laato and Johannes C. de Moor, eds., *Theodicy in the World of the Bible* (Leiden: Brill, 2003), 57–89, esp. 67–69.

57. See Jean Nougayrol, "(Juste) souffrant (R. S. 25.460)," *Ugaritica* 5 (1968): 265–273, 435; Wolfram von Soden, "Bemerkungen zu einigen literarischen Texten in akkadischer Sprache aus Ugarit," *Ugarit-Forschungen* 1 (1969): 189–195, esp. 191–193; Wolfram von Soden, "Klage eines Dulders mit Gebet an Marduk," in Kaiser, ed., *Texte aus der Umwelt des Alten Testaments,* 3/1:140–143; Foster, *Before the Muses,* 1:326–327.

58. For a very similar approach to these matters see Jack Goody, "Canonization in Oral and Literate Cultures," in Arie van der Kooij and Karel van der Toorn, eds., *Canonization and Decanonization: Papers Presented to the International Conference of the Leiden Institute for the Study of Religions (LISOR) held at Leiden 9–10 January 1997,* Studies in the History of Religions 82 (Leiden: Brill, 1997), 3–16.

59. Compare the observation by Ulla Koch-Westenholz, *Babylonian Liver Omens,* Carsten Niebuhr Institute Publications 25 (Copenhagen: Museum Tusculanum Press, 2000), 15: "For many centuries . . . the written tradition of extispicy was apparently a side branch to the oral main stream."

60. A perusal of Simo Parpola, *Letters from Assyrian and Babylonian Scholars,* SAA 10 (Helsinki: Helsinki University Press, 1993), yields many examples, such as no. 276 r. 11–13, "I sent the king exactly as it is written on the tablet." Compare the comments by A. Leo Oppenheim, "Divination and Celestial Observation in the Late Assyrian Empire," *Centaurus* 14 (1969): 97–135, esp. 123.

61. See Miguel Civil, "Lexicography," in Stephen Lieberman, ed., *Sumerological Studies in Honor of Thorkild Jacobsen on His Seventieth*

Birthday, June 7, 1974, Assyriological Studies 20 (Chicago: University of Chicago Press, 1975), 123–157, esp. 128, 130–131.

62. Irving L. Finkel, "Adad-apla-iddina, Esagil-kīn-apli, and the Series SA.GIG," in Erle Leichty et al., eds., *A Scientific Humanist: Studies in Memory of Abraham Sachs* (Philadelphia: The S. N. Kramer Fund, 1988), 143–159.

63. George, *The Babylonian Gilgamesh Epic,* 1:28–33.

64. Koch-Westenholz, *Mesopotamian Astrology,* 42–43.

65. See the observations by Francesca Rochberg, *The Heavenly Writing: Divination, Horoscopy, and Astronomy in Mesopotamian Culture* (New York: Cambridge University Press, 2004), 212–219.

66. For a survey of secrecy colophons see Rykle Borger, "Geheimwissen," *RlA* 3:188–191; Borger, *Handbuch der Keilschriftliteratur,* 3 vols. (Berlin: W. de Gruyter, 1967–1975), 3:119 #108; Paul-Alain Beaulieu, "New Light on Secret Knowledge in Late Babylonian Culture," *ZA* 82 (1992): 98–111, esp. 110–111. See also Oliver R. Gurney et al., *The Sultantepe Tablets,* 2 vols. (London: The British Institute of Archaeology at Ankara, 1957–1964), 2:300, reverse, line 19: . . . *mu-du-ú mu-da-a li-ka[l-li]m la mu-du-u la* [nu] *immar* [igiⁱ]; Wilfred G. Lambert, "Processions to the Akitu House," *Revue d'Assyriologie* 91 (1997): 49–80, esp. 73, BM 77028, reverse, line 6': "secret of the scholars [written: sag érin-*ni* = *nişirti ummânī*], property of Nabu, king of [the world]."

67. See Hunger, *Kolophone,* nos. 40 and 50; compare the observations by Beaulieu, "New Light on Secrecy," 98. See also the Tukulti-Ninurta Epic, in which the texts of exorcism, liturgical prayers, divination, and medicine are qualified as *nişir[ti . . .*]; Wilfred G. Lambert, "Three Unpublished Fragments of the Tukulti-Ninurta Epic," *AfO* 18 (1957–58): 44.

68. Plato, *Epistula* B, 314B-C: "The greatest safeguard is to avoid writing and to learn by heart, for it is not possible that what is written down should not get divulged."

69. See Jan N. Bremmer, "Religious Secrets and Secrecy in Classical Greece," in Hans G. Kippenberg and Guy G. Stroumsa, eds., *Secrecy and Concealment: Studies in the History of Mediterranean and Near Eastern Religions,* Numen Supplements 65 (Leiden: Brill, 1995), 61–78.

70. On this aspect of secrecy see Sissela Bok, *Secrets: On the Ethics of Concealment and Revelation* (New York: Pantheon Books, 1982), 45–48. On secrets and secret societies see also the groundbreaking work of Georg Simmel, "Das Geheimnis und die geheime Gesellschaft," in *Soziologie:*

Untersuchungen über die Formen der Vergesellschaftung, Georg Simmel Gesamtausgabe (Frankfurt: Suhrkamp, 1992), 383–455.

71. See Christoph Uehlinger, "Gab es eine joschianische Kultreform? Plädoyer für ein begründetes Minimum," in Walter Gross, ed., *Jeremia und die "deuteronomistische Bewegung,"* Bonner Biblische Beiträge 98 (Weinheim: Beltz Athenäum, 1995), 57–89; in English, "Was There a Cult Reform under King Josiah? The Case for a Well-Grounded Minimum," in Lester Grabbe, ed., *Good Kings and Bad Kings,* Library of Hebrew Bible/Old Testament Studies 393, European Seminar in Historical Methodology 5 (London: T&T Clark International, 2005), 279–316.

72. On the date of the oracle see Wilhelm Rudolph, *Jeremia,* 3rd ed., Handbuch zum Alten Testament 1/12 (Tübingen: Mohr Siebeck, 1968), XIX–XX; William L. Holladay, *Jeremiah 1: A Commentary on the Book of the Prophet Jeremiah Chapters 1–25,* Hermeneia (Philadelphia: Fortress Press, 1986), 282; Jack R. Lundblom, *Jeremiah 1–20: A New Translation with Introduction and Commentary,* Anchor Bible 21A (New York: Doubleday, 1999), 516.

73. Wilhelm M. L. de Wette, *Dissertatio critica qua Deuteronomium a prioribus Pentateuchi libris diversum, alius cuiusdam recentioris actoris opus esse monstratur* (University of Jena, 1805).

74. The interpretation of Jer 8:8–9 as a reference to Deuteronomy goes back to Karl Marti, *Der Prophet Jeremia von Anatot* (Basel: Detloff, 1889), 18–20. See also Bernhard Duhm, *Das Buch Jeremia,* Kurzer Hand-Commentar zum Alten Testament 9 (Tübingen and Leipzig: J. C. B. Mohr, 1901), 88–89; Robert Hatch Kennett, "Origin of the Aaronite Priesthood," *Journal of Theological Studies* 6 (1905): 161–186, esp. 183–184; Moshe Weinfeld, *Deuteronomy and the Deuteronomic School* (Oxford: Oxford University Press, 1972), 158–161.

75. See Bernard M. Levinson, *Deuteronomy and the Hermeneutics of Legal Innovation* (New York: Oxford University Press, 1998). H. Wheeler Robinson, *Inspiration and Revelation in the Old Testament* (Oxford: Clarendon Press, 1946), 213, refers to the Deuteronomic Code as "an expanded edition of the Book of the Covenant."

76. The equation of wisdom and Torah is also found at Sir 1:26, 6:37, 15:1, 19:20, 21:11. In Sir 14:20, Ben Sira paraphrases Ps 1:2 ("Happy is the man . . . who studies His Torah"; compare Josh 1:8) by saying, "Happy is the man who studies wisdom" *('šry 'nwš bḥkmh yhgh).*

77. *m. 'Abot* 3.14: *kĕlî šebbô nibrā' hā'ôlām.* Compare the *Pesiqta de Rav*

Kahana, which says that "the Torah was a creature in My presence when the world was not created yet, for two thousand years." Bernard Mandelbaum, *Pesikta de Rav Kahana according to an Oxford Manuscript* (New York: Jewish Theological Seminary of America, 1962), 222, lines 16–17.

78. On Ezekiel as a writing prophet see, e.g., Robert R. Wilson, *Prophet and Society in Ancient Israel* (Philadelphia: Fortress Press, 1980), 283.

79. See, e.g., Christopher Rowland, *The Open Heaven: A Study of Apocalyptic in Judaism and Early Christianity* (London: SPCK, 1982), 9–72; John J. Collins, *The Apocalyptic Imagination: An Introduction to Jewish Apocalyptic Literature,* 2nd ed. (Grand Rapids, MI: Eerdmans, 1998), 1–42; Collins, "From Prophecy to Apocalypticism: The Expectation of the End," in Collins, ed., *The Origins of Apocalypticism in Judaism and Christianity* (The Encyclopaedia of Apocalypticism 1; New York: Continuum, 1998), 129–161.

80. See the observations by John Barton, *Oracles of God: Perceptions of Ancient Prophecy in Israel after the Exile* (London: Darton, Longman, & Todd, 1986), esp. 8, 200–201.

81. See Ina Willi-Plein, "Das Geheimnis der Apokalyptik," *VT* 27 (1977): 62–81, esp. 68–74.

82. See also 1 Enoch 14:1; 81:1–2.

83. For a typology of the rubrics see Gene M. Tucker, "Prophetic Superscriptions and the Growth of a Canon," in George W. Coats and Burke O. Long, eds., *Canon and Authority: Essays in Old Testament Religion and Theology* (Philadelphia: Fortress, 1977), 56–70. Note his observation on 70: "The collectors and redactors of the prophetic tradition—early and late—began to interpret the words attributed to the prophets as a written form of revelation. With the superscriptions to these books they advanced ideas of authority which would eventually surface in the form of the biblical canon."

9. Constructing the Canon

1. On canons and canonicity see the annotated bibliography by Jan A. M. Snoek in Arie van der Kooij and Karel van der Toorn, eds., *Canonization and Decanonization: Papers Presented to the International Conference of the Leiden Institute for the Study of Religions (LISOR) held at Leiden 9–10 January 1997,* Studies in the History of Religions 82 (Leiden: Brill,

1997), 435–506. The literature on canons and canonicity is still steadily growing. Among the more recent publications see esp. Jean-Marie Auwels and Henk Jan de Jonge, eds., *The Biblical Canons,* Bibliotheca ephemeridum theologicarum lovaniensium 163 (Leuven: Peeters, 2003). For a convenient introduction to the subject from a broad perspective see Robert von Hallberg, ed., *Canons* (Chicago: University of Chicago Press, 1984).

2. The earliest list is by Melito, bishop of Sardis (ca. 170 C.E.), quoted by Eusebius, *Hist. Eccl.* 4.26.14. The list given by Epiphanius of Salamis (315–403) in *De mensuris et ponderibus,* 23, reflects a bilingual list that may be from the second century C.E. as well; see Jean-Paul Audet, "A Hebrew-Aramaic List of Books of the Old Testament in Greek Transcription," *Journal of Theological Studies* 1 (1950): 135–154; David Goodblatt, "Audet's 'Hebrew-Aramaic' List of the Books of the OT Revisited," *JBL* 101 (1982): 75–84, and 75 note 2 for references to the earlier secondary literature. For a survey of the various lists from the Eastern and Western church see Henry B. Swete, *An Introduction to the Old Testament in Greek,* 2nd ed., rev. Richard R. Ottley (Cambridge: Cambridge University Press, 1914), 203–214.

3. Eusebius, *Hist. Eccl.* 3.25.6, 4.26.12, 6.25.1–6. On *kanōn, endiathēkos,* and *katalogos* in the work of Eusebius see Gregory A. Robbins, "Eusebius' Lexicon of 'Canonicity,'" *Studia Patristica* 25 (1993): 134–141.

4. See Eusebius, *Hist. Eccl.* 4.26.13, where he quotes Melito of Sardis, on the number *(arithmos)* and the order *(taxis)* of the books.

5. See the discussion by Arie van der Kooij, "The Canonization of Ancient Books Kept in the Temple of Jerusalem," in Van der Kooij and Van der Toorn, eds., *Canonization and Decanonization,* 17–40, esp. 20–21.

6. The Codex Alexandrinus, containing both the Old Testament and the New, is from the fifth century C.E.

7. Heinrich Graetz, "Der alttestamentliche Kanon und sein Abschluss," in *Kohelet oder der Salomonische Prediger übersetzt und kritisch erläutert* (Leipzig: C. F. Winter, 1871), 147–173; Frants Buhl, *Kanon und Text des Alten Testaments* (Leipzig: Faber, 1891); Gerrit Wildeboer, *Die Entstehung des Alttestamentlichen Kanons: Historisch-kritische Untersuchung* (Gotha: Perthes, 1891); Herbert E. Ryle, *The Canon of the Old Testament* (London: Macmillan, 1892).

8. See Jack P. Lewis, "What Do We Mean By Jabneh?" *Journal of Bible and*

Religion 32 (1964): 125–132; Peter Schäfer, "Der sogenannte Synode von Jabne, II: Der Abschluss des Kanons," *Judaica* 31 (1975): 116–124; Günter Stemberger, "Die sogenannte "Synode von Jabne" und das frühe Christentum," *Kairos* 19 (1977): 14–21; Giuseppe Veltri, "Zur traditionsgeschichtlichen Entwicklung des Bewusstseins von einem Kanon: Die Yavneh-Frage," *Journal for the Study of Judaism* 21 (1990): 210–226, esp. 215–219; David E. Aune, "On the Origins of the 'Council of Javneh,'" *JBL* 110 (1991): 491–493; Jack P. Lewis, "Jamnia (Jabneh), Council of," *ABD* 3:634–637; Lewis, "Jamnia after Forty Years," *Hebrew Union College Annual* 70–71 (1999–2000): 233–259.

9. Baruch J. Schwartz, "Bible," in R. J. Zwi Werblowsky and Geoffrey Wigoder, eds., *The Oxford Dictionary of the Jewish Religion* (New York: Oxford University Press, 1997), 121–125, quotation on 121–122.

10. See, e.g., the conclusion of Gunther Wanke, "Bibel I. Die Entstehung des Alten Testaments als Kanon," *Theologische Realenzyklopädie*, 36 vols., ed. Gerhard Krause and Gerhard Müller (Berlin: De Gruyter, 1977–2004), 6:1–8: "Das Alte Testament ist nicht entstanden aufgrund einer Reihe autoritativer Entscheidungen, sondern es hat sich selbst in seinen Teilen unabhängig von Institutionen in solchen Kreisen als Autorität durchgesetzt, die in Krisensituationen die Identität des Volkes Israel durch die Tradition bewahren wollten" (7).

11. See the *Belgic Confession*, article 5, and the *Westminster Confession of Faith*, 1.5.

12. See Jerome, *Epistula* 5 *("sacra bibliotheca")*; *De viribus illustribus*, 75 *("bibliotheca divina")*.

13. See, e.g., Nahum M. Sarna, "The Order of the Books," in Charles Berlin, ed., *Studies in Jewish Bibliography, History and Literature in Honor of I. Edward Kiev* (New York: Ktav, 1971), 407–413, esp. 411; Roger Beckwith, *The Old Testament Canon of the New Testament Church and Its Background in Early Judaism* (London: SPCK, 1985); John W. Miller, *The Origins of the Bible: Rethinking Canon History* (New York: Paulist Press, 1994); Arie van der Kooij, "The Canonization of Ancient Books"; Jan Assmann, "Fünf Stufen auf dem Wege zum Kanon: Tradition und Schriftkultur im alten Israel und frühen Judentum," in *Religion und kulturelles Gedächtnis* (Munich: Beck, 2000), 81–100, esp. 91–96.

14. On the Jerusalem temple library see, in addition to the literature mentioned previously, Viktor Burr, *Bibliothekarische Notizen zum Alten Testament* (Bonn: Bouvier, 1969), esp. 18–35.

15. On the date of the letter see Elias J. Bickermann, "Ein jüdischer Festbrief vom Jahre 124 v.Chr. (II Macc 1:1–9)," *Zeitschrift für die neutestamentliche Wissenschaft* 32 (1933): 233–254, esp. 234; on the authenticity of the letter to the Alexandrian Jews see Ben Zion Wacholder, "The Letter from Judas Maccabee to Aristobulus: Is 2 Maccabees 1:10b–2:18 Authentic?" *Hebrew Union College Annual* 49 (1978): 89–133. On the significance of the word *bibliothēkē* in Esth 2:23 LXX, Ezra 6:1 LXX, and 2 Macc 2:13 see Mechthild Kellermann, "'Wenn ihr nun eines von diesen Büchern braucht, so lasst es euch holen.' (2 Makk. 2,15): Eine antike Aufforderung zur Fernleihe," *Zeitschrift des Deutschen Palästina-Vereins* 98 (1982): 104–109.

16. Moshe Greenberg, "The Stabilization of the Text of the Hebrew Bible Reviewed in the Light of the Biblical Materials from the Judean Desert," *JAOS* 76 (1956): 157–167, quotation on 160. Contrast Menahem Haran, "Archives, Libraries, and the Order of the Biblical Books," *Journal of the Ancient Near Eastern Society at Columbia University* 22 (1993): 51–61, who argues that "the relative size of the reading public was no smaller among Jews than in Greece and Rome, but their few books were not enough to make up libraries" (57).

17. For the classical world see Jenoe Platthy, *Sources on the Earliest Greek Libraries* (Amsterdam: Adolf M. Hakkert, 1968). The first public library in Athens was established in the second century B.C.E. The library of Alexandria, founded by Ptolemy I Soter, preceded the library in Athens. Contrast the opinion of Archibald Henry Sayce, "The Libraries of David and Solomon," *Journal of the Royal Asiatic Society* 1931 (1931): 783–790, esp. 788: "In the Mosaic period the Oriental world was as well stocked with books and what we should call public libraries as it was in the Greek epoch."

18. For a survey of secrecy colophons see Rykle Borger, "Geheimwissen," *RlA* 3:188–191; Borger, *Handbuch der Keilschriftliteratur*, 3 vols. (Berlin: W. de Gruyter, 1975), 3:119, #108; Paul-Alain Beaulieu, "New Light on Secret Knowledge in Late Babylonian Culture," *ZA* 82 (1992): 98–111, esp. 110–111.

19. Josephus, *Ant.* 10.57–58. A similar course of events is implied by 2 Chron 34:14, "While they were bringing out the money that had been brought into the house of the Lord, Hilkiah the priest found the Book of the Law of the Lord given through Moses."

20. For a cuneiform parallel see the letter by Assurbanipal in which he com-

missions copies of all the texts that are in the "treasures" (the Akkadian term is *makkūru*) of Nabu of Borsippa, where "treasures" stands for the temple library; see Grant Frame and Andrew R. George, "The Royal Libraries of Nineveh: New Evidence for King Ashurbanipal's Tablet Collecting" (Papers of the Forty-ninth Rencontre Assyriologique Internationale, London, 7–11 July 2003, Part Two; London: British School of Archaeology in Iraq), *Iraq* 67 (2005): 265–284, esp. 267.

21. Beckwith, *Old Testament Canon*, 85.

22. Josephus, *Ant.* 5.61; cf. 3.38, 4.303.

23. Beckwith, *Old Testament Canon*, 82–83; see also Arie van der Kooij, *Die alten Textzeugen des Jesajabuches*, OBO 35 (Fribourg: University of Fribourg; Göttingen: Vandenhoeck & Ruprecht, 1981), 333.

24. See, from a wealth of literature, Heinrich Otten, "Bibliotheken im Alten Orient," *Das Altertum* 1 (1955): 67–81; Jeremy A. Black and William J. Tait, "Archives and Libraries in the Ancient Near East," *Civilizations of the Ancient Near East*, 4 vols., ed. Jack M. Sasson et al. (New York: Charles Scribner's Sons, 1995), 4:2197–2209. On libraries in Mesopotamia see Mogens Weitemeyer, "Archive and Library Technique in Ancient Mesopotamia," *Libri* 6/3 (1956): 217–238, esp. 224–234; Klaas R. Veenhof, ed., *Cuneiform Archives and Libraries: Papers Read at the Thirtieth Recontre Assyriologique Internationale, Leiden 4–8 July 1983* (Istanbul: Nederlands Historisch-Archaeologisch Instituut; Leiden: Nederlands Instituut voor het Nabije Oosten, 1986); Olof Pedersén, *Archives and Libraries in the Ancient Near East 1500–300 B.C.* (Bethesda, MD: CDL Press, 1998); Piotr Michalowski, "The Libraries of Babel: Text, Authority, and Tradition in Ancient Mesopotamia," in Gillis J. Dorleijn and Herman L. J. Vanstiphout, eds., *Cultural Repertoires: Structure, Functions and Dynamics*, Groningen Studies in Cultural Change 3 (Leuven: Peeters, 2003), 105–129. On Egyptian libraries see Vilmos Wessetzky, "Bibliothek," *LÄ* 1:783–785; Günter Burkard, "Bibliotheken im alten Ägypten: Überlegungen zum Methodik ihres Nachweises und Übersicht zum Stand der Forschung," *Bibliothek: Forschung und Praxis* 4 (1980): 79–115.

25. See, for this fundamental distinction, Assmann, "Fünf Stufen," 92.

26. For an overview of cuneiform libraries see Pedersén, *Archives and Libraries*, 129–213.

27. For a slightly different view see Donald B. Redford, *Pharaonic King-Lists, Annals, and Day-Books: A Contribution to the Study of the Egyp-*

tian Sense of History, Society for the Study of Egyptian Antiquities 4 (Mississauga, Ont.: Benben, 1986), whose reconstruction of a hypothetical Egyptian temple library (pp. 215–228) is based on the conviction that "by the 5th Cent. B.C. the temple considered itself to be, and in fact was, a repository of all the texts preserving Egyptian civilization" (223).

28. See Vilmos Wessetzky, "Die Bücherliste des Tempels von Edfu und Imhotep," *Göttinger Miszellen* 83 (1984): 85–89.

29. On the Assurbanipal library see Giovanni Lanfranchi, "The Library at Nineveh," in Joan Goodnick Westenholz, ed., *Capital Cities: Urban Planning and Spiritual Dimensions; Proceedings of the Symposium Held on May 27–29, 1996, Jerusalem, Israel*, Bible Lands Museum Jerusalem Publications 2 (Jerusalem: Bible Lands Museum, 1998), 147–156; Jeanette C. Fincke, "The Babylonian Texts of Nineveh: Report on the British Museum's Ashurbanipal Library Project," *AfO* 50 (2003–2004): 111–149; Fincke, "The British Museum Ashurbanipal Library Project" (Papers of the Forty-ninth Rencontre Assyriologique Internationale, London, 7–11 July 2003, Part One; London: British School of Archaeology in Iraq), *Iraq* 66 (2004): 55–60; Frame and George, "Royal Libraries."

30. See Simo Parpola, *Letters from Assyrian Scholars to the Kings Esarhaddon and Assurbanipal*, AOAT 5/1 (Kevelaer: Butzon & Bercker; Neukirchen-Vluyn: Neukirchener Verlag, 1970), nos. 318 and 331; Parpola, *Letters from Assyrian and Babylonian Scholars*, SAA 10 (Helsinki: Helsinki University Press, 1993), nos. 101 and 102; Frederick Mario Fales and John Nicholas Postgate, *Imperial Administrative Records, Part II: Provincial and Military Administration*, SAA 11 (Helsinki: Helsinki University Press, 1995), no. 156.

31. See Frame and George, "Royal Libraries," 276–277.

32. For records of tablet acquisitions see Simo Parpola, "Assyrian Library Records," *JNES* 42 (1983): 1–29; Wilfred G. Lambert, "A Late Assyrian Catalogue of Literary and Scholarly Texts," in Barry L. Eichler, ed., *Kramer Anniversary Volume: Cuneiform Studies in Honor of Samuel Noah Kramer*, AOAT 25 (Kevelaer: Butzon & Bercker; Neukirchen-Vluyn: Neukirchener Verlag, 1976), 313–318. For estimates of the holdings of the Assurbanipal libraries see Parpola, "Assyrian Library Records," 6; Pedersén, *Archives and Libraries*, 164. The number of tablets and fragments is about 30,000; the total is reduced to one-third of that number when one counts only complete tablets. The numerous writing boards in the library's collection have not been preserved.

33. Reginald C. Thompson, *Cuneiform Tablets from the British Museum,* 22 (London: British Museum, 1906), no. 1. The expression here quoted is found at line 37: *ana ekalliya ṭābu.*

34. The translation is by Frame and George, "Royal Libraries," 281. In its defense, one might quote lines 27–28 of the letter: "and any texts that might be needed in the palace [*mimma ḫišiḫti ina ekalli*], as many as there are."

35. Frame and George, "Royal Libraries," 267, line 9; 273–274, lines 8–10.

36. Quotation from Frame and George, "Royal Libraries," 281.

37. See Stephen J. Lieberman, "Canonical and Official Cuneiform Texts: Towards an Understanding of Assurbanipal's Personal Tablet Collection," in Tzvi Abusch et al., eds., *Lingering over Words: Studies in Ancient Near Eastern Literature in Honor of William L. Moran* (Atlanta: Scholars Press, 1990), 305–336.

38. On the polemical overtones of these works see Benjamin G. Wright III, "Putting the Puzzle Together: Some Suggestions Concerning the Social Location of the Wisdom of Ben Sira," *SBL 1996 Seminar Papers,* Seminar Papers Series 35 (Atlanta: Scholars Press, 1996), 133–149.

39. For an interpretation of some catalogues as library catalogues see Claus Wilcke, *Kollationen zu den Sumerischen literarischen Texten aus Nippur in der Hilprecht-Sammlung Jena,* Abhandlungen der Sächsischen Akademie der Wissenschaften zu Leipzig, Phil.-hist. Kl. 65/4 (Berlin: Akademie Verlag, 1976), 41; Mark J. Geller, "Incipits and Rubrics," in Andrew R. George and Irving L. Finkel, eds., *Wisdom, Gods and Literature: Studies in Assyriology in Honour of W. G. Lambert* (Winona Lake, IN: Eisenbrauns, 2000), 225–258, esp. 225. For a survey of the evidence and possible interpretations see Joachim Krecher, "Kataloge, literarische," *RlA* 5:478–485; Piotr Michalowski, "A New Sumerian 'Catalogue' from Nippur," *Oriens Antiquus* 19 (1980): 265–268; Michalowski, "Observations on a Sumerian Literary Catalogue from Ur," *JCS* 36 (1984): 89–92; Aron Shaffer, "A New Look at Some Old Catalogues," in George and Finkel, eds., *Wisdom, Gods and Literature,* 429–436.

40. See especially Miguel Civil, "Lexicography," in Stephen J. Lieberman, ed., *Sumerological Studies in Honor of Thorkild Jacobsen on His Seventieth Birthday, June 7, 1974,* Assyriological Studies 20 (Chicago: University of Chicago, 1975), 123–157, esp. 145 note 36; Eleanor Robson, "The Tablet House: A Scribal School in Old Babylonian Nippur," *RA* 95

(2001): 39–66, esp. 55–59; Herman L. J. Vanstiphout, "The Old Babylonian Literary Canon: Structure, Function and Intention," in Dorleijn and Vanstiphout, eds., *Cultural Repertoires*, 1–28, esp. 6–28.

41. For Egyptian inventories of written texts see Maurice Alliot, *Le culte d'Horus à Edfou au temps des Ptolémées*, Bibliothèque d'Etudes 20/1 (Cairo: Imprimerie de l'Institut Français d'Archéologie Orientale, 1949), 146–150; Wessetzky, "Bücherliste"; Serge Sauneron, *Les prêtres de l'ancienne Egypte*, 2nd ed. (Paris: Perséa, 1988), 144–145.

42. See Louis Jacobs, "Rabbinic Views on the Order and Authorship of the Biblical Books," in *Structure and Form in the Babylonian Talmud* (Cambridge: Cambridge University Press, 1991), 31–41; against Sarna, "Order of the Books," 411. Sarna speculates that the scrolls were kept on wooden shelves. On the basis of a rather implausible interpretation of Eccl 12:11, Viktor Burr proposes that the scrolls were kept in wooden chests; see Burr, *Bibliothekarische Notizen*, 27–29. In the absence of pertinent data, we do not know the physical organization of the temple library.

43. See Carl Wendel, *Die Griechisch-Römische Buchbeschreibung verglichen mit der des Vorderen Orients*, Hallische Monographien 3 (Halle: Niemeyer, 1949), 69–75; Otto Regenbogen, "Pinax," *Paulys Realencyclopädie der classischen Altertumswissenschaft*, 49 vols., new ed. Georg Wissowa (Munich: Druckenmüller; Stuttgart: Metzler, 1984–1997), 20/2:1408–1482, esp. 1455–1462; Rudolf Pfeiffer, *History of Classical Scholarship: From the Beginnings to the End of the Hellenistic Age* (Oxford: Clarendon, 1968), 205–208.

44. Compare the existence of the twelve-volume work *About the Acquisition and the Selection of Books (Peri ktēseōs kai eklogēs bibliōn)* by Philo of Byblos (second century C.E.).

45. See Dieter Georgi, "Die Aristoteles- und Theophrastausgabe des Andronikus von Rhodus: Ein Beitrag zur Kanonsproblematik," in Rüdiger Bartelmus et al., eds., *Konsequente Traditionsgeschichte: Festschrift für Klaus Baltzer zum 65. Geburtstag*, OBO 126 (Fribourg: Universitätsverlag; Göttingen: Vandenhoeck & Ruprecht, 1993), 45–78, esp. 71–72; James C. Vanderkam, "Revealed Literature in the Second Temple Period," in *Studies in the Hebrew Bible and Second Temple Literature*, Supplements to the Journal for the Study of Judaism 62 (Leiden: Brill, 2000), 1–30, esp. 30.

46. See the observations by Reynolds and Wilson, *Scribes and Scholars*, 8. Compare also Black and Tait, "Archives and Libraries," 2208: "Libraries

were crucial for the transmission of literate culture, and their mere existence led to the emergence of scholarly—or even scholastic—approaches to written texts."

47. For an argument exploring the notion of the Hebrew scriptures as a "countercurriculum" see David M. Carr, *Writing on the Tablet of the Heart: Origins of Scripture and Literature* (New York: Oxford University Press, 2005), 10, 141–156. For most authors, the curriculum hypothesis does not imply that the books of the Bible were originally designed as textbooks. This cautionary note is not entirely superfluous, since proponents of the curriculum model have sometimes implied that most of the biblical literature was composed with an educational perspective in mind. For an example see André Lemaire, who argues that there is "a strong connection between the Bible and education in ancient Israel. Biblical texts were essentially written with a didactic and educational aim." Quotation from Lemaire, "Education in Ancient Israel," *ABD* 2:305–312, quotation on 311.

48. So Simo Parpola, *Letters from Assyrian Scholars to the Kings Esarhaddon and Assurbanipal, Part II: Commentary and Appendices,* AOAT 5/2 (Kevelaer: Butzon & Bercker; Neukirchen-Vluyn: Neukirchener Verlag, 1983), 99–100, on the basis of a letter by a senior scholar suggesting that two tablets be removed from the divination corpus and two others be "established" in their stead. For this letter see Simo Parpola, *Letters from Assyrian and Babylonian Scholars,* SAA 10 (Helsinki: Helsinki University Press, 1993), no. 177. In the catalogue of the medical series *Sakikkû,* as well as in the *Curriculum of the Exorcist,* the verb used for establishing a text as part of the curriculum is *kunnu,* also meaning "to establish"; see Irving L. Finkel, "Adad-apla-iddina, Esagil-kīn-apli, and the Series SA.GIG," in Erle Leichty, ed., *A Scientific Humanist: Studies in Memory of Abraham Sachs* (Philadelphia: The S. N. Kramer Fund, 1988), 143–159, esp. 148, line A 62//B 26': *ana aḫāzi* [níg.zu] *ukīn* [du-in]; Geller, "Incipits and Rubrics," 242, line 1: *ana aḫāzi* [níg.du] *u tāmarti* [igi.du₈] *kunnu.* Note the combination of the verbs in the *Song of Erra,* tablet V, line 59: *zamaru šâšu ana matima liššakinma likūn gadu ulla,* "May this song be established forever, that it endure for eternity."

49. Royal patronage of the scribal curriculum is implied, too, by the reference to the king in the notice on the editorial activities of Esagil-kīn-apli; see Finkel, "Adad-apla-iddina," 150, line 33'.

50. The terms "shepherd" *(re'û)* and "herdsman" *(nāqidu)* in line 148 refer

to the king, as is clear from line 150; see Benjamin R. Foster, *Before the Muses: An Anthology of Akkadian Literature,* 2 vols. (Bethesda, MD: CDL Press, 1993), 1:400 and note 6; contrast Alexander Heidel, *The Babylonian Genesis: The Story of Creation,* 2nd ed. (Chicago: University of Chicago Press, 1951), 60 and note 153; Stephany Dalley, *Myths from Mesopotamia: Creation, The Flood, Gilgamesh and Others* (Oxford: Oxford University Press, 1989), 273.

51. For another example of a text that looks to the school as the channel of transmission and the way into the stream of tradition see the *Song of Erra,* tablet V, lines 49–61, esp. 55–56, 59 (Foster, *Before the Muses,* 2:804).

52. Vanstiphout, "Old Babylonian Literary Canon," 6–28.

53. Ibid., 10–11.

54. See, for the following, Peter Frei, "Zentralgewalt und Lokalautonomie im Achämenidenreich," in Peter Frei and Klaus Koch, *Reichsidee und Reichsorganisation im Perserreich,* OBO 55 (Fribourg: Universitätsverlag; Göttingen: Vandenhoeck & Ruprecht, 1984), 7–43; Reinhard G. Kratz, *Translatio imperii: Untersuchungen zu den aramäischen Danielerzählungen und ihrem theologiegeschichtlichen Umfeld,* Wissenschaftliche Monographien zum Alten und Neuen Testament 63 (Neukirchen-Vluyn: Neukirchener Verlag, 1991), 246–255; Kenneth G. Hoglund, *Achaemenid Imperial Administration in Syria-Palestine and the Missions of Ezra and Nehemiah,* SBL Dissertation Series 125 (Atlanta: Scholars Press, 1992), esp. 207–240; Jan Assmann, "Fünf Stufen auf dem Weg zum Kanon: Tradition und Schriftkultur im alten Israel und frühen Judentum," in *Religion und kulturelles Gedächtnis: Zehn Studien* (Munich: Beck, 2000), 81–100, esp. 89–91.

55. Wilhelm Spiegelberg, *Die sogenannte Demotische Chronik des Pap. 215 der Bibliothèque Nationale zu Paris,* Demotische Studien 7 (Leipzig: J. C. Hinrichs, 1915), esp. 30–32; Nathaniel Julius Reich, "The Codification of the Egyptian Laws by Darius and the Origin of the 'Demotic Chronicle,'" *Mizraim: Journal of Papyrology, Egyptology, History of Ancient Law and Their Relations to the Civilizations of Bible Lands* 1 (1933): 178–185. See also Kratz, *Translatio imperii,* 250–251. The code was to be written in Demotic as well as Aramaic.

56. Eberhard Otto, *Die biographischen Inschriften der ägyptischen Spätzeit: Ihre geistesgeschichtliche und literarische Bedeutung,* Probleme der Ägyptologie 2 (Leiden: Brill, 1954), 169–173, nr. 30, esp. 172–173; Mir-

iam Lichtheim, *Ancient Egyptian Literature,* 3 vols. (Berkeley: University of California Press, 1973–1980), 3:36–41; Alan B. Lloyd, "The Inscription of Udjahorresnet: A Collaborator's Testament," *Journal of Egyptian Antiquities* 68 (1982): 166–180; Joseph Blenkinsopp, "The Mission of Udjahorresnet and Those of Ezra and Nehemiah," *JBL* 106 (1987): 409–421.

57. For the origins of the synagogue see Shmuel Safrai, "The Synagogue," in Shmuel Safrai and Menahem Stern, eds., *The Jewish People in the First Century,* Compendia Rerum Iudaicarum ad Novum Testamentum 1/2 (Assen: Van Gorcum, 1976), 908–944, esp. 909–913.

58. See, e.g., Ulrich Kellermann, "Erwägungen zum Esragesetz," *ZAW* 80 (1968): 373–385; Ralph W. Klein, "Ezra and Nehemiah in Recent Studies," in Frank Moore Cross et al., eds., *Magnalia Dei: The Mighty Acts of God; Essays on the Bible and Archaeology in Memory of G. Ernest Wright* (Garden City, NY: Doubleday, 1976), 361–376, esp. 366–368; Cees Houtman, "Ezra and the Law: Observations on the Supposed Relation between Ezra and the Pentateuch," in Bertil Albrektson et al., eds., *Remembering All the Way . . . : A Collection of Old Testament Studies Published on the Occasion of the Fortieth Anniversary of the Oudtestamentisch Werkgezelschap in Nederland,* Oudtestamentische Studiën 21 (Leiden: Brill, 1981), 91–115.

59. See Julius Wellhausen, *Prolegomena zur Geschichte Israels,* 3rd ed. (Berlin: Georg Reimer, 1886; first published as *Geschichte Israels* in 1878), 407. On the connection between the law of Ezra and the Pentateuch see Sigmund Mowinckel, *Studien zu dem Buche Ezra-Nehemia,* III: *Die Ezrageschichte und das Gesetz Moses,* Skrifter utgitt av det Norske Videnskapsakademi i Oslo II Historisk-filosofisk Klasse, nova series, 7 (Oslo: Universitetsvorlaget, 1965), 124–141; Frank Crüsemann, "Israel in der Perserzeit: Eine Skizze in Auseinandersetzung mit Max Weber," in Wolfgang Schluchter, ed., *Max Webers Sicht des antiken Christentums: Interpretation und Kritik,* Suhrkamp Taschenbuch Wissenschaft 548 (Frankfurt: Suhrkamp, 1985), 205–232, esp. 216–217; Hugh G. M. Williamson, *Ezra, Nehemiah,* World Bible Commentary 16 (Waco: Word Books, 1985), xxxvii–xxxix; Williamson, "The Concept of Israel in Transition," in Ronald E. Clements, *The World of Ancient Israel: Sociological, Anthropological, and Political Perspectives* (Cambridge: Cambridge University Press, 1989), 141–161, esp. 154.

60. The definitive schism between Samaritans and Jews is generally dated in

the mid-fourth century B.C.E., since Alexander the Great authorized the erection of the Gerizim temple, according to Josephus, *Ant.* 11.315–324.

61. See Gunnar Östborn, *Cult and Canon: A Study in the Canonization of the Old Testament,* Acta Universitatis Upsaliensis 1950:10 (Uppsala: Almqvist & Wiksell, 1950), 92.

62. Finkel, "Adad-apla-iddina," 148–149, lines 18'–19', 25'.

63. Joseph Blenkinsopp, *Prophecy and Canon: A Contribution to the Study of Jewish Origins* (Notre Dame, IN: University of Notre Dame Press, 1970), 81; Odil Hannes Steck, *Der Abschluss der Prophetie im Alten Testament: Ein Versuch zur Frage der Vorgeschichte des Kanons,* Biblisch-Theologische Studien 17 (Neukirchen-Vluyn: Neukirchener Verlag, 1991), 15.

64. See the observations by Raymond Westbrook, "Codification and Canonization," in Edmond Lévy, ed., *La codification des lois dans l'Antiquité: Actes du Colloque de Strasbourg, 27–29 novembre 1997* (Paris: Boccard, 2000), 33–47.

65. For a study of especially this facet of canonization see Gerard L. Bruns, "Canon and Power in the Hebrew Scriptures," in Von Hallberg, ed., *Canons,* 65–83. Bruns is much indebted to Ellis Rivkin, *The Shaping of Jewish History: A Radical New Interpretation* (New York: Scribner, 1971).

66. On Amos see Volkmar Fritz, "Amosbuch, Amos-Schule und historischer Amos," in Fritz et al., eds., *Prophet und Prophetenbuch: Festschrift Otto Kaiser,* Beihefte ZAW 185 (Berlin: W. de Gruyter, 1989), 29–43.

67. The reconstruction goes back to Heinrich Ewald, *Die Propheten des Alten Bundes,* 3 vols., 2nd ed. (Göttingen: Vandenhoeck & Ruprecht, 1867–1868), 1:80–81. The hypothesis has found its way into several classic introductions to the Hebrew Bible; see, e.g., Robert H. Pfeiffer, *Introduction to the Old Testament,* 5th ed. (New York: Harper, 1941), 612; Otto Eissfeldt, *Einleitung in das Alte Testament,* 3rd ed. (Tübingen: J. C. B. Mohr, 1964), 595–596; Georg Fohrer, *Einleitung in das Alte Testament,* 12th ed. (Heidelberg: Quelle & Meyer, 1979), 511.

68. The position of Malachi in the scroll of the Minor Prophets, as well as the original number of Minor Prophets, is not unproblematic in view of the Qumran evidence. As reconstructed by Russell E. Fuller in Eugene Ulrich et al., *Qumran Cave 4.X: The Prophets,* Discoveries from the Judaean Desert 15 (Oxford: Clarendon, 1997), 221–231, pls. XL–XLII, Jonah followed Malachi in 4QXII[a]. Based on this reconstruction of the mid-

second-century B.C.E. text, several authors have speculated that the Minor Prophets originally numbered only nine prophets. In a first expansion, Joel and Obadiah were added; Jonah was the final addition. See Barry A. Jones, *The Formation of the Book of the Twelve: A Study in Text and Canon,* SBL Dissertation Series 149 (Atlanta: Scholars Press, 1995), 222–228, for references to earlier literature. For a defense of the Masoretic order as the original one see Odil Hannes Steck, "Zur Abfolge Maleachi-Jona in 4Q76 (4QXII^a)," *ZAW* 108 (1996): 249–253; Arndt Meinhold, *Maleachi,* Biblischer Kommentar zum Alten Testament 14/8.1 (Neukirchen: Neukirchener Verlag, 2000), 7.

69. For a study of Mal 3:22–24 and a case for its interpretation as a canon-conscious summary of the Prophets, see Stephen B. Chapman, *The Law and the Prophets: A Study in Old Testament Canon Formation,* Forschungen zum Alten Testament 27 (Tübingen: Mohr Siebeck, 2000), 131–146.

70. James A. Montgomery, *The Samaritans: The Earliest Jewish Sect, Their History, Theology and Literature* (Philadelphia: Winston, 1907; repr. New York: Ktav, 1968); Ferdinand Dexinger, *Der Taheb: Ein "messianischer" Heilsbringer der Samaritaner,* Kairos Religionswissenschaftliche Studien 3 (Salzburg: Müller, 1986); Dexinger, "Samaritan Eschatology," in Alan D. Crown, ed., *The Samaritans* (Tübingen: Mohr, 1989), 266–292, esp. 267–272 (review of the secondary literature) and 272–276 (theology of the Taheb).

71. The first Western scholar to point out the etymological link between Taheb and the verb *šûb,* "to return, to restore," was Wilhelm Gesenius in *De Samaritanorum Theologia ex fontibus ineditis commentatio* (Halle: Niemeyer, 1822), as noted by Dexinger, "Samaritan Eschatology," 268.

72. See Deut 34:5–6; 2 Kings 2:1–18; Sir 48:9. For popular views on the ascension of Moses see Cees Houtman, "Moses," in Karel van der Toorn et al., eds., *Dictionary of Deities and Demons in the Bible,* 2nd ed. (Leiden: Brill; Grand Rapids, MI: Eerdmans, 1999), 593–598, esp. 595–596. On the basis of this and other parallels between Elijah and Moses, Georg Fohrer concludes that the biblical sources present Elijah as "a second and new Moses"; Fohrer, *Elia,* 2nd ed. (Zurich: Zwingli Verlag, 1968), 57.

73. Many authors have noted the bracketing; see, e.g., Steck, *Abschluss der Prophetie,* 134–136; Frank Crüsemann, "Das 'portative Vaterland': Struktur und Genese des alttestamentlichen Kanons," in Aleida Assmann and Jan Assmann, eds., *Kanon und Zensur: Beiträge zur Archäologie der*

literarischen Kommunikation, II (Munich: Wilhelm Fink, 1987), 63–79, esp. 72.

74. See, e.g., Isa 66:19; Zech 9:13. For a detailed study of the Hellenistic layers in the Prophets see Steck, *Abschluss der Prophetie*, 25–126.

75. See, e.g., Peter Schäfer, *The History of the Jews in Antiquity: The Jews of Palestine from Alexander the Great to the Arab Conquest* (Luxembourg: Harwood Academic Publishers, 1995), esp. 20–21; trans. of *Geschichte der Juden in der Antike* (Stuttgart: Katholisches Bibelwerk, 1983).

76. See also *b. Yoma* 9b; *b. Sanh.* 11a; *y. Soṭah* 9,13.

77. For studies of the rabbinical doctrine see Rudolf Meyer, "Prophetentum und Propheten im Judentum der hellenistischen-römischen Zeit," *Theologisches Wörterbuch zum Neuen Testament*, 10 vols., ed. Gerhard Kittel et al. (Stuttgart: Kohlhammer, 1953–1979), 6:813–828, esp. 817–820; Ragnar Leivestad, "Das Dogma von der prophetenlosen Zeit," *New Testament Studies* 19 (1972–73): 288–299.

78. According to Josephus, *C. Ap.* 1.37, only prophets had authority to write records; they obtained their knowledge of the most remote and ancient history through the inspiration God gave them. For David as "prophet" see 11QPs^a 27.3–11; Acts 2:30; Josephus, *Ant.* 8.109–110; Philo, *Agr.* 50; *Rer. Div. Her.* 290; *Sipre Deut.* 1.1. For Solomon as "prophet" see Sir 24:33; *Tg. Ps.-J.* on 1 Kings 5:13; Philo, *De Ebr.* 31; *Sipre Deut.* 1.1.

79. On the notion of "ancestral" (*patrōios* or *patrios*) as applied to the Jewish "books" or "laws" see Hans G. Kippenberg, "Die jüdischen Überlieferungen als *patrioi nomoi*," in Richard Faber and Renate Schlesier, eds., *Die Restauration der Götter: Antike Religion und Neo-Paganismus* (Würzburg: Königshausen und Neumann, 1986), 45–60.

80. For a similar line of reasoning see Robert H. Charles, *A Critical History of the Doctrine of a Future Life in Israel, in Judaism, and in Christianity or Hebrew, Jewish, and Christian Eschatology from Pre-Prophetic Times Till the Close of the New Testament Canon*, 2nd ed. (London: Adam & Charles Black, 1913), 202–204; repr. as *Eschatology: The Doctrine of a Future Life in Israel, Judaism and Christianity: A Critical History*, with an introduction by George Wesley Buchanan (New York: Schocken Books, 1963); id., *The Apocrypha and Pseudepigrapha of the Old Testament in English* (Oxford: Clarendon, 1913), 2:viii–ix.

81. On the practice and perception of literary forgery in antiquity see the landmark study by Wolfgang Speyer, *Die literarische Fälschung im Altertum* (Munich: Beck, 1971).

82. For the "sapientializing" tendency of the scribal notices see Gerald T. Sheppard, *Wisdom as a Hermeneutical Construct: A Study in the Sapientializing of the Old Testament,* Beihefte ZAW 151 (Berlin: W. de Gruyter, 1980). According to Sheppard, "At a certain period in the development of Old Testament literature, wisdom became a theological category associated with an understanding of canon which formed a perspective from which to interpret Torah and prophetic traditions" (13).

83. On Berossus see Stanley M. Burstein, *The Babyloniaca of Berossus,* Sources from the Ancient Near East 1/5 (Malibu: Undena, 1978); on Manetho see Redford, *Pharaonic King-Lists,* 203–317.

84. Compare Kippenberg, "Die jüdischen Überlieferungen als *patrioi nomoi.*"

85. See the discussion by Van der Kooij, "Canonization of Ancient Books," 19–21.

86. This point has been made by many other authors; see, e.g., John Barton, *Oracles of God: Perceptions of Ancient Prophecy in Israel after the Exile* (London: Darton, Longman & Todd, 1986), 91–93; David M. Carr, "Canonization in the Context of Community: An Outline of the Formation of the Tanakh and the Christian Bible," in Richard D. Weis and David M. Carr, eds., *A Gift of God in Due Season: Essays on Scripture and Community in Honor of James A. Sanders,* JSOT Supplement Series 225 (Sheffield: Sheffield Academic Press, 1996), 22–64, esp. 40–41. For evidence of a tripartition see the Prologue to Ben Sira (ca. 130 B.C.E.), lines 8–10: "the Law, the Prophets, and the other ancestral books"; Josephus, *C. Ap.* 1.38: "the five books of Moses . . ., thirteen books of the prophets . . ., and four remaining books"; Halakhic Letter from Qumran (4Q397 Frags. 14–21, line 10 // 4Q398, Frags. 14–17, col. i, lines 2–3 = 4QMMT C, 10, from ca. 150 B.C.E.): "the book of Moses, the books of the prophets, and David"; Luke 24:44: "the Law of Moses, the Prophets, and the Psalms"; cf. 2 Macc 2:13; Philo, *De vita contemplativa,* 25. The earliest mention of "the Law, the Prophets, and the Writings" is by Gamaliel II (ca. 100 C.E.), quoted in *b. Sanh.* 90b. The significance of the Halakhic Letter from Qumran for the tripartite canon is disputed; see Eugene Ulrich, "The Non-Attestation of a Tripartite Canon in 4QMMT," *Catholic Biblical Quarterly* 65 (2003): 202–214.

87. For David as "prophet" see 11QPs^a 27.3–11; Acts 2:30; Josephus, *Ant.* 8.109–110; Philo, *Agr.* 50; *Rer. Div. Her.* 290; *Sipre Deut.* 1.1. For Solomon as "prophet" see Sir 24:33; *Tg. Ps.- J.* on 1 Kings 5:13; Philo, *De Ebr.* 31; *Sipre Deut.* 1.1.

88. Dominique Barthélemy, "L'état de la Bible juive depuis le début de notre ère jusqu'à la deuxième révolte contre Rome (131–135)," in Jean-Daniel Kaestli and Otto Wermelinger, eds., *Le canon de l'Ancien Testament: Sa formation et son histoire* (Geneva: Labor et Fides, 1984), 9–45, esp. 20–21.

89. For the social and ideological background of Ben Sira see Wright, "Putting the Puzzle Together." For an echo of the discussion about the authorship of 1 Enoch see Tertullian, *On Female Dress*, 1.3, who argues that Noah might have restored the book if it had not survived the deluge.

90. This goes against many modern authors; see, e.g., David G. Meade, *Pseudonimity and Canon: An Investigation into the Relationship of Authorship and Authority in Jewish and Earliest Christian Tradition*, Wissenschaftliche Untersuchungen zum Neuen Testament 39 (Tübingen: Mohr, 1986), who asserts that "the criterion for judgment was *content*, not authorship" (102). Meade bases his observation on a comparison between Daniel (included in the canon) and 1 Enoch (excluded from the canon). It is true that 1 Enoch contains doctrines deemed heretical by the Jerusalem authorities; that fact presumably confirmed the authorities in their conviction that the books simply could not have been written by Enoch.

91. See the illuminating observations by Arie van der Kooij, "The Septuagint: The First Translation of the Hebrew Bible?" *Bulletin of Judaeo-Greek Studies* 34 (2004): 27–28.

92. See Frederick E. Greenspahn, "Why Prophecy Ceased," *JBL* 108 (1989): 37–47.

93. Bernhard Lang qualifies the development as an "intellectualization" of religion; see Lang, "Das tanzende Wort: Intellektuelle Rituale im Fruhjüdentum, im Christentum und in östlichen Religionen," in Lang, ed., *Das tanzende Wort: Intellektuelle Rituale im Religionsvergleich* (Munich: Kösel, 1984), 15–48.

Selected Bibliography

Abusch, I. Tzvi, *Babylonian Witchcraft Literature: Case Studies,* Brown Judaic Studies 132 (Atlanta: Scholars Press, 1987).

Albertz, Rainer, "Der sozialgeschichtliche Hintergrund des Hiobbuches und der 'Babylonischen Theodizee,'" in Jörg Jeremias and Lothar Perlitt, eds., *Die Botschaft und die Boten: Festschrift für Hans Walter Wolff zum 70. Geburtstag* (Neukirchen-Vluyn: Neukirchener Verlag, 1981), 349–372.

Alt, Albrecht, "Die Heimat des Deuteronomiums," *Kleine Schriften zur Geschichte des Volkes Israel,* 3 vols., ed. Martin Noth (Munich: C. H. Beck, 1953–1959), 2:250–275.

Assmann, Jan, "Fünf Stufen auf dem Weg zum Kanon: Tradition und Schriftkultur im alten Israel und frühen Judentum," in *Religion und kulturelles Gedächtnis: Zehn Studien* (Munich: Beck, 2000), 81–100.

Audet, Jean-Paul, "A Hebrew-Aramaic List of Books of the Old Testament in Greek Transcription," *Journal of Theological Studies* 1 (1950): 135–154.

Aune, David E., "On the Origins of the 'Council of Javneh,'" *JBL* 110 (1991): 491–493.

Avigad, Nahman, *Bullae and Seals from a Post-Exilic Judean Archive,* Qedem Monographs of the Institute of Archaeology 4 (Jerusalem: Hebrew University, Institute of Archaeology, 1976).

———, *Hebrew Bullae from the Time of Jeremiah: Remnants of a Burnt Archive* (Jerusalem: Israel Exploration Society, 1986).

Avrin, Leila, *Scribes, Script, and Books: The Book Arts from Antiquity to the*

Renaissance (Chicago: American Library Association; London: The British Library, 1991).

Auwels, Jean-Marie, and Henk Jan de Jonge, eds., *The Biblical Canons,* Bibliotheca ephemeridum theologicarum lovaniensium 163 (Leuven: Peeters, 2003).

Baines, John R., "Literacy and Ancient Egyptian Society," *Man* 18 (1983): 572–599.

———, "Schreiben," *LÄ*, 5:693–698.

Baines, John R., and Christopher Eyre, "Four Notes on Literacy," *Göttinger Miszellen* 61 (1983): 65–96.

Bar-Ilan, Meir, "Illiteracy in the Land of Israel in the First Centuries C.E.," in Simcha Fishbane et al., eds., *Essays in the Social Scientific Study of Judaism and Jewish Society,* II (New York: Ktav, 1992), 46–61.

Barrick, W. Boyd, "Dynastic Politics, Priestly Succession, and Josiah's Eighth Year," *ZAW* 112 (2000): 564–582.

Barta, Winfried, "Das Schulbuch Kemit," *Zeitschrift für Ägyptische Sprache und Altertumskunde* 105 (1978): 6–14.

Barthélemy, Dominique, "L'état de la Bible juive depuis le début de notre ère jusqu'à la deuxième révolte contre Rome (131–135)," in Jean-Daniel Kaestli and Otto Wermelinger, eds., *Le canon de l'Ancien Testament: Sa formation et son histoire* (Geneva: Labor et Fides, 1984), 9–45.

Barton, John, *Oracles of God: Perceptions of Ancient Prophecy in Israel after the Exile* (London: Darton, Longman & Todd, 1986).

———, "What Is a Book? Modern Exegesis and the Literary Conventions of Ancient Israel," in Johannes C. de Moor, ed., *Intertextuality in Ugarit and Israel,* Oudtestamentische Studien 40 (Leiden: Brill, 1998), 1–14.

Bataillon, Louis Jacques, et al., eds., *La production du livre universitaire au Moyen Age: Exemplar et pecia. Actes du symposium tenu au Collegio San Bonaventura de Grottaferrata en mai 1983* (Paris: Editions du Centre National de la Recherche Scientifique, 1988).

Beaulieu, Paul-Alain, "The Descendants of Sîn-lēqi-unninni," in Joachim Marzahn and Hans Neumann, eds., *Assyriologica et Semitica: Festschrift für Joachim Oelsner,* AOAT 252 (Münster: Ugarit-Verlag, 2000), 1–16.

———, "New Light on Secret Knowledge in Late Babylonian Culture," *ZA* 82 (1992): 98–111.

Beckwith, Roger, *The Old Testament Canon of the New Testament Church and Its Background in Early Judaism* (London: SPCK, 1985).

Bickermann, Elias J., "La charte séleucide de Jérusalem," *Revue des Etudes Juives* 100 (1935): 4–35.

————, *The Jews in the Greek Age* (Cambridge, MA: Harvard University Press, 1988).

————, "Ein jüdischer Festbrief vom Jahre 124 v.Chr. (II Macc 1:1–9)," *Zeitschrift für die neutestamentliche Wissenschaft* 32 (1933): 233–254.

Black, Jeremy A., and William J. Tait, "Archives and Libraries in the Ancient Near East," in Jack M. Sasson et al., eds., *Civilizations of the Ancient Near East,* 4 vols. (New York: Charles Scribner's Sons, 1995), 4:2197–2209.

Blau, Ludwig, *Studien zum althebräischen Buchwesen und zur biblischen Literaturgeschichte* (Budapest: Landes-Rabbinerschule in Budapest, 1902).

Blenkinsopp, Joseph, "The Mission of Udjahorresnet and Those of Ezra and Nehemiah," *JBL* 106 (1987): 409–421.

————, *Prophecy and Canon: A Contribution to the Study of Jewish Origins* (Notre Dame, IN: University of Notre Dame Press, 1970).

Bogaert, Pierre-Maurice, "Le livre de Jérémie en perspective: les deux rédactions selon les travaux en cours," *Revue Biblique* 101 (1994): 363–406.

————, "Urtext, texte court et relecture: Jérémie xxxiii 14–26 TM et ses préparations," in John A. Emerton, ed., *Congress Volume Leuven 1989,* Supplements VT 43 (Leiden: Brill, 1991), 236–247.

Borger, Rykle, "Geheimwissen," *RlA* 3:188–191.

Bottéro, Jean, "Le Manuel de l'Exorciste et son calendrier," *Annuaire de l'Ecole Pratique des Hautes Etudes, IVeme section, 1974–75* (1975): 95–142.

————, "Symptômes, signes, écritures," in Jean-Pierre Vernant et al., *Divination et Rationalité* (Paris: Seuil, 1974), 70–197.

Braulik, Georg, ed., *Bundesdokument und Gesetz: Studien zum Deuteronomium* (Herders Biblische Studien 4; Freiburg: Herder, 1995).

————, ed., *Das Deuteronomium,* Österreichische Biblische Studien 23 (Frankfurt: Peter Lang, 2003).

————, *Die deuteronomischen Gesetze und der Dekalog: Studien zum Aufbau von Deuteronomium 12–26,* Stuttgarter Bibelstudien 145 (Stuttgart: Katholisches Bibelwerk, 1991).

————, "Zur Abfolge der Gesetze in Deuteronomium 16,18–21,23: Weitere Beobachtungen," *Biblica* 69 (1988): 63–92.

Brunner, Hellmut, *Altägyptische Erziehung* (Wiesbaden: Harrassowitz, 1957).

Burkard, Günter, "Bibliotheken im alten Ägypten: Überlegungen zum Methodik ihres Nachweises und Übersicht zum Stand der Forschung," *Bibliothek: Forschung und Praxis* 4 (1980): 79–115.

Burr, Viktor, *Bibliothekarische Notizen zum Alten Testament* (Bonn: Bouvier, 1969).

Carr, David M., "Canonization in the Context of Community: An Outline of the Formation of the Tanakh and the Christian Bible," in Richard D. Weis and David M. Carr, eds., *A Gift of God in Due Season: Essays on Scripture and Community in Honor of James A. Sanders,* JSOT Supplement Series 225 (Sheffield: Sheffield Academic Press, 1996), 22–64.

———, *Writing on the Tablet of the Heart: Origins of Scripture and Literature* (New York: Oxford University Press, 2005).

Černý, Jaroslav, *Paper and Books in Ancient Egypt* (London: H. K. Lewis & Co., 1952).

Chapman, Stephen B., *The Law and the Prophets: A Study in Old Testament Canon Formation,* Forschungen zum Alten Testament 27 (Tübingen: Mohr Siebeck, 2000).

Chazon, Esther G., and Michael Stone, eds., *Pseudepigraphic Perspectives: The Apocrypha and Pseudepigrapha in Light of the Dead Sea Scrolls,* Studies on the Texts of the Discoveries of Judah 31 (Leiden: Brill, 1999).

Civil, Miguel, "Lexicography," in Stephen B. Lieberman, ed., *Sumerological Studies in Honor of Thorkild Jacobsen on His Seventieth Birthday, June 7, 1974,* Assyriological Studies 20 (Chicago: University of Chicago Press, 1975), 123–157.

Cody, Aelred, "Le titre égyptien et le nom propre du scribe de David," *Revue Biblique* 72 (1965): 381–393.

Cogan, Mordechai, "A Plaidoyer on Behalf of the Royal Scribes," in Mordechai Cogan and Israel Eph'al, eds., *Ah Assyria . . . : Studies in Assyrian History and Ancient Near Eastern Historiography Presented to Hayim Tadmor,* Scripta Hierosolymitana 33 (Jerusalem: Magnes, 1991), 121–128.

Coogan, Michael David, "*'LP, 'To Be an Abecedarian,'" *JAOS* 110 (1990): 322.

———, "Literacy and the Formation of Biblical Literature," in Prescott H. Williams, Jr., and Theodore Hiebert, eds., *Realia Dei: Essays in Archaeology and Biblical Interpretation in Honor of Edward F. Campbell, Jr. at His Retirement* (Atlanta: Scholars Press, 1999), 47–61.

Crenshaw, James L., *Education in Ancient Israel: Across the Deadening Silence* (New York: Doubleday, 1998).

Cribiore, Raffaella, *Writing, Teachers, and Students in Graeco-Roman Egypt,* American Studies in Papyrology 36 (Atlanta: Scholars Press, 1996).

Cross, Frank Moore, *The Ancient Library of Qumran,* 3rd ed. (Sheffield: Sheffield Academic Press, 1995).

———, "A Literate Soldier: Lachish Letter III," in *Leaves from an Epigrapher's Notebook: Collected Papers in Hebrew and West Semitic Palaeography and Epigraphy,* Harvard Semitic Studies 51 (Winona Lake, IN: Eisenbrauns, 2003), 129–132; repr. from Ann Kort and Scott Morschauser, eds., *Biblical and Related Studies Presented to Samuel Iwry* (Winona Lake, IN: Eisenbrauns, 1985), 41–47.

———, "The Priestly Houses of Early Israel," in *Canaanite Myth and Hebrew Epic* (Cambridge, MA: Harvard University Press, 1973), 195–215.

Crüsemann, Frank, "Das 'portative Vaterland': Struktur und Genese des alttestamentlichen Kanons," in Aleida Assmann and Jan Assmann, eds., *Kanon und Zensur: Beiträge zur Archäologie der literarischen Kommunikation, II* (Munich: Wilhelm Fink, 1987), 63–79.

———, *Die Tora: Theologie und Sozialgeschichte des alttestamentlichen Gesetzes* (Munich: Kaiser, 1992), 242–248.

———, "Israel in der Perserzeit: Eine Skizze in Auseinandersetzung mit Max Weber," in Wolfgang Schluchter, ed., *Max Webers Sicht des antiken Christentums: Interpretation und Kritik,* Suhrkamp Taschenbuch Wissenschaft 548 (Frankfurt: Suhrkamp, 1985), 205–232.

Davies, Graham I., "Were There Schools in Ancient Israel?" in John Day et al., eds., *Wisdom in Ancient Israel: Essays in Honour of J. A. Emerton* (Cambridge: Cambridge University Press, 1995), 199–211.

Dearman, J. Andrew, "My Servants the Scribes: Composition and Context in Jeremiah 36," *JBL* 109 (1990): 403–421.

Demsky, Aaron, "Writing in Ancient Israel: The Biblical Period," in Martin-Jan Mulder, ed., *Mikra: Text, Translation, Reading and Interpretation of the Hebrew Bible in Ancient Judaism and Early Christianity,* Compendia Rerum Iudaicarum ad Novum Testamentum 2/1 (Assen: Van Gorcum; Philadelphia: Fortress, 1988), 2–20.

Edzard, Dietz Otto, "Literatur," *RlA* 7:35–48.

Elman, Yaakov, "Authoritative Oral Tradition in Neo-Assyrian Scribal Circles," *Journal of Ancient Near Eastern Studies of Columbia University* 7 (1975): 19–32.

Eshel, Hanan, and John Strugnell, "Alphabetical Acrostics in Pre-Tannaitic Hebrew," *Catholic Biblical Quarterly* 62 (2000): 441–458.

Eskenazi, Tamara C., *In an Age of Prose: A Literary Approach to Ezra-Nehemiah,* SBL Monograph Series 36 (Atlanta: Scholars Press, 1988).

Fincke, Jeanette C., "The Babylonian Texts of Nineveh: Report on the British Museum's Ashurbanipal Library Project," *AfO* 50 (2003–2004): 111–149.

———, "The British Museum Ashurbanipal Library Project" (Papers of the XLIXe Rencontre Assyriologique Internationale, London, 7–11 July 2003, Part One; London: British School of Archaeology in Iraq), *Iraq* 66 (2004): 55–60.

Finkel, Irving L., "Adad-apla-iddina, Esagil-kīn-apli, and the Series SA.GIG," in Erle Leichty et al., eds., *A Scientific Humanist: Studies in Memory of Abraham Sachs* (Philadelphia: The S. N. Kramer Fund, 1988), 143–159.

Finkelstein, Jacob. J., *The Ox That Gored,* Transactions of the American Philosophical Society 71/2 (Philadelphia: American Philosophical Society, 1981).

Fischer, Georg, "Jer 25 und die Fremdvölkersprüche: Unterschiede zwischen hebräischem und griechischem Text," *Biblica* 72 (1991): 474–499.

Fishbane, Michael, "Accusations of Adultery: A Study of Law and Scribal Practice in Numbers 5:11–31," *Hebrew Union College Annual* 45 (1974): 25–45.

———, "Biblical Colophons," *Catholic Biblical Quarterly* 42 (1980): 438–449.

———, *Biblical Interpretation in Ancient Israel* (Oxford: Clarendon, 1985).

———, "Varia Deuteronomica," *ZAW* 84 (1972): 349–352.

Floyd, Michael H., "Prophecy and Writing in Habakkuk 2,1–5," *ZAW* 105 (1993): 462–481.

Foster, Benjamin R., "On Authorship in Akkadian Literature," *Annali dell' Istituto Orientale di Napoli* 51 (1990): 17–32.

Frame, Grant, and Andrew R. George, "The Royal Libraries of Nineveh: New Evidence for King Ashurbanipal's Tablet Collecting" (Papers of the XLIXe Rencontre Assyriologique Internationale, London, 7–11 July 2003, Part Two; London: British School of Archaeology in Iraq), *Iraq* 67 (2005): 265–284.

Frankena, Rintje, "Untersuchungen zum Irra-Epos," *Bibliotheca Orientalis* 14 (1957): 2–10.

———, "The Vassal-Treaties of Esarhaddon and the Dating of Deuteronomy," in Jacobus Hoftijzer, ed., *Kaf hē 1940–1965,* Oudtestamentische Studien 14 (Leiden: Brill, 1965), 122–154.

Frei, Peter, "Zentralgewalt und Lokalautonomie im Achämenidenreich," in

Peter Frei and Klaus Koch, *Reichsidee und Reichsorganisation im Perserreich*, OBO 55 (Fribourg: Universitätsverlag; Göttingen: Vandenhoeck & Ruprecht, 1984), 7–43.

Fritz, Volkmar, "Amosbuch, Amos-Schule und historischer Amos," in Fritz et al., eds., *Prophet und Prophetenbuch: Festschrift Otto Kaiser*, Beihefte ZAW 185 (Berlin: W. de Gruyter, 1989), 29–43.

Gardiner, Alan H., *Ancient Egyptian Onomastica*, 3 vols. (London: Oxford University Press, 1947).

———, "The House of Life," *Journal of Egyptian Archaeology* 24 (1938): 157–179.

Geller, Mark J., "Astronomy and Authorship," *Bulletin of the School of Oriental and African Studies* 53 (1990): 209–213.

———, "Incipits and Rubrics," in Andrew R. George and Irving L. Finkel, eds., *Wisdom, Gods and Literature: Studies in Assyriology in Honour of W. G. Lambert* (Winona Lake, IN: Eisenbrauns, 2000), 225–258.

George, Andrew R., *The Babylonian Gilgamesh Epic: Introduction, Critical Edition and Cuneiform Texts*, 2 vols. (Oxford: Oxford University Press, 2003).

———, "In Search of the é.dub.ba.a: The Ancient Mesopotamian School in Literature and Reality," in Yitschak Sefati et al., eds., *"An Experienced Scribe Who Neglects Nothing": Ancient Near Eastern Studies in Honor of Jacob Klein* (Bethesda, MD: CDL Press, 2005), 127–137.

Georgi, Dieter, "Die Aristoteles- und Theophrastausgabe des Andronikus von Rhodus: Ein Beitrag zur Kanonsproblematik," in Rüdiger Bartelmus et al., eds., *Konsequente Traditionsgeschichte: Festschrift für Klaus Baltzer zum 65. Geburtstag*, OBO 126 (Fribourg: Universitätsverlag; Göttingen: Vandenhoeck & Ruprecht, 1993), 45–78.

Gesche, Petra D., *Schulunterricht in Babylonien im ersten Jahrtausend v.Chr.*, AOAT 275 (Münster: Ugarit-Verlag, 2001).

Ginsberg, Harold L., "Psalms and Inscriptions of Petition and Acknowledgement," in Saul Lieberman et al., eds., *Louis Ginsberg Jubilee Volume on the Occasion of His Seventieth Birthday* (New York: The American Academy of Jewish Research, 1945), 159–171.

Ginsberg, H. Louis, *The Israelian Heritage of Judaism*, Texts and Studies 24 (New York: The Jewish Theological Seminary of America, 1982).

Glatt-Gilad, David A., "The Personal Names in Jeremiah as a Source for the History of the Period," *Hebrew Studies* 41 (2000): 31–45.

Goldman, Yohanan, *Prophétie et royauté au retour de l'exil: Les origines littéraires de la forme massorétique du livre de Jérémie,* OBO 118 (Fribourg: Universitätsverlag; Göttingen: Vandenhoeck & Ruprecht, 1992).

Goodblatt, David, "Audet's "Hebrew-Aramaic" List of the Books of the OT Revisited," *JBL* 101 (1982): 75–84.

Goodman, Martin D., "Texts, Scribes and Power in Roman Judaea," in Alan K. Bowman and Greg Woolf, eds., *Literacy and Power in the Ancient World* (Cambridge: Cambridge University Press, 1994), 99–108.

Goody, Jack, "Canonization in Oral and Literate Cultures," in Arie van der Kooij and Karel van der Toorn, eds., *Canonization and Decanonization: Papers Presented to the International Conference of the Leiden Institute for the Study of Religions (LISOR) held at Leiden 9–10 January 1997,* Studies in the History of Religions 82 (Leiden: Brill, 1997), 3–16.

———, *The Domestication of the Savage Mind* (Cambridge: Cambridge University Press, 1977).

———, *The Logic of Writing and the Organisation of Society* (Cambridge: Cambridge University Press, 1986).

Graetz, Heinrich, "Der alttestamentliche Kanon und sein Abschluss," in *Kohelet oder der Salomonische Prediger übersetzt und kritisch erläutert* (Leipzig: C. F. Winter, 1871), 147–173.

Greenberg, Moshe, "The Stabilization of the Text of the Hebrew Bible Reviewed in the Light of the Biblical Materials from the Judean Desert," *JAOS* 76 (1956): 157–167.

Greenspahn, Frederick E., "A Mesopotamian Proverb and Its Biblical Reverberations," *JAOS* 114 (1994): 33–38.

———, "Why Prophecy Ceased," *JBL* 108 (1989): 37–47.

Gunkel, Hermann, "Die Propheten als Schriftsteller und Dichter," in Hans Schmidt, *Die grossen Propheten* (Göttingen: Vandenhoeck & Ruprecht, 1915), xxxvi–lxxii.

Gunneweg, Anton H. J., *Leviten und Priester: Hauptlinien der Traditionsbildung und Geschichte des israelitisch-jüdischen Kultpersonals,* Forschungen zur Religion und Literatur des Alten und Neuen Testaments 89 (Göttingen: Vandenhoeck & Ruprecht, 1965).

Hallberg, Robert von, ed., *Canons* (Chicago: University of Chicago Press, 1984).

Hallo, William W., "On the Antiquity of Sumerian Literature," *JAOS* 83 (1963): 167–176.

Haran, Menahem, "Archives, Libraries, and the Order of the Biblical Books,"

Journal of the Ancient Near Eastern Society at Columbia University 22 (1993): 51–61.

———, "Book-Size and the Device of Catch-Lines in the Biblical Canon," *Journal of Jewish Studies* 36 (1985): 1–11.

———, "On the Diffusion of Literacy and Schools in Ancient Israel," in John A. Emerton, ed., *Congress Volume Jerusalem 1986*, Supplements VT 40 (Leiden: Brill, 1988), 81–95.

Harris, William V., *Ancient Literacy* (Cambridge, MA: Harvard University Press, 1989).

Heaton, Eric W., *The School Tradition of the Old Testament*, The Bampton Lectures for 1994 (Oxford: Oxford University Press, 1994).

Hecker, Karl, "Tradition und Originalität in der altorientalischen Literatur," *Archiv Orientalní* 45 (1977): 245–258.

Heidel, Alexander, "The Meaning of *mummu* in Akkadian Literature," *JNES* 7 (1948): 98–105.

Hengel, Martin, "Anonymität, Pseudepigraphie und 'Literarische Fälschung' in der jüdisch-hellenistischer Literatur," in Kurt von Fritz, ed., *Pseudepigrapha 1*, Entretiens sur l'Antiquité Classique 18 (Geneva: Fondation Hardt, 1972), 231–308.

———, *Judentum und Hellenismus: Studien zu ihrer Begegnung unter besonderer Berücksichtigung Palästinas bis zur Mitte des 2. Jh.s v.Chr.*, 2nd ed., Wissenschaftliche Untersuchungen zum Neuen Testament 10 (Tübingen: Mohr, 1973).

———, "'Schriftauslegung' und 'Schriftwerdung' in der Zeit des Zweiten Tempels," in Martin Hengel and Hermut Löhr, eds., *Schriftauslegung im antiken Judentum und im Urchristentum*, Wissenschaftliche Untersuchungen zum Neuen Testament 73 (Tübingen: Mohr Siebeck, 1994), 1–71.

Hezser, Catherine, *Jewish Literacy in Roman Palestine*, Texts and Studies in Ancient Judaism 81 (Tübingen: Mohr Siebeck, 2001).

Hicks, R. Lansing, "*Delet* and *měgillāh*: A Fresh Approach to Jeremiah XXXVI," *VT* 33 (1983): 46–66.

Hoftijzer, Jacob, and Gerrit van der Kooij, eds., *The Balaam Text from Deir 'Alla Re-evaluated: Proceedings of the International Symposium held at Leiden 21–24 August 1989* (Leiden: Brill, 1991).

Hoglund, Kenneth G., *Achaemenid Imperial Administration in Syria-Palestine and the Missions of Ezra and Nehemiah*, SBL Dissertation Series 125 (Atlanta: Scholars Press, 1992).

Houtman, Cees, "Ezra and the Law: Observations on the Supposed Relation between Ezra and the Pentateuch," in Bertil Albrektson et al., *Remembering All the Way . . . : A Collection of Old Testament Studies Published on the Occasion of the Fortieth Anniversary of the Oudtestamentisch Werkgezelschap in Nederland,* Oudtestamentische Studiën 21 (Leiden: Brill, 1981), 91–115.

Hunger, Hermann, *Babylonische und assyrische Kolophone,* AOAT 2 (Kevelaer: Butzon & Bercker; Neukirchen-Vluyn: Neukirchener Verlag, 1968).

Ikeda, Jun, "Scribes in Emar," in Kazuko Watanabe, ed., *Priests and Officials in the Ancient Near East* (Heidelberg: Carl Winter, 1999), 163–185.

Jacobs, Louis, "Rabbinic Views on the Order and Authorship of the Biblical Books," in *Structure and Form in the Babylonian Talmud* (Cambridge: Cambridge University Press, 1991), 31–41.

Jacobsen, Thorkild, "Oral to Written," in Muhammad A. Dandamayev et al., eds., *Societies and Languages of the Ancient Near East: Studies in Honor of I. M. Diakonoff* (Warminster: Aries & Phillips, 1982), 129–137.

Jadir, W. al-, "Une bibliothèque et ses tablettes dans le quartier sacré de Sippar," *Archeologia* 224 (1987): 18–27.

———, "Le quartier de l'É.BABBAR de Sippar (Sommaire des fouilles de 1985–1989, 8–11èmes campagnes)," in Léon de Meyer and Hermann Gasche, eds., *Mésopotamie et Elam,* Proceedings of the 36th Rencontre Assyriologique Internationale; Mesopotamian History and Environment, Occasional Publications 1 (Ghent: University of Ghent, 1991), 193–196.

Jamieson-Drake, David W., *Scribes and Schools in Monarchic Judah,* JSOT Supplement Series 109 (Sheffield: Sheffield Academic Press, 1991).

Janssen, Rosalind M., and Jacobus J. Janssen, *Growing Up in Ancient Egypt* (London: The Rubicon Press, 1990).

Jones, Barry A., *The Formation of the Book of the Twelve: A Study in Text and Canon,* SBL Dissertation Series 149 (Atlanta: Scholars Press, 1995).

Kaufman, Stephen, "The Structure of the Deuteronomic Law," *Maarav* 1/2 (1978–79): 105–158.

Kees, Hermann A. J., *Das Priestertum im Ägyptischen Staat vom Neuen Reich bis zur Spätzeit,* Probleme der Ägyptologie 1 (Leiden: Brill, 1953).

Kellermann, Mechthild, "'Wenn ihr nun eines von diesen Büchern braucht, so lasst es euch holen' (2 Makk. 2,15): Eine antike Aufforderung zur Fernleihe," *Zeitschrift des Deutschen Palästina-Vereins* 98 (1982): 104–109.

Kellermann, Ulrich, "Erwägungen zum Esragesetz," *ZAW* 80 (1968): 373–385.

Kennett, Robert Hatch, "Origin of the Aaronite Priesthood," *Journal of Theological Studies* 6 (1905): 161–186.

Kippenberg, Hans G., "Die jüdischen Überlieferungen als *patrioi nomoi*," in Richard Faber and Renate Schlesier, eds., *Die Restauration der Götter: Antike Religion und Neo-Paganismus* (Würzburg: Königshausen und Neumann, 1986), 45–60.

Klostermann, August, *Schulwesen im alten Israel* (Leipzig: Deichert, 1908).

Knox, Bernard M. W., "Silent Reading in Antiquity," *Greek, Roman and Byzantine Studies* 9 (1968): 421–435.

Koch-Westenholz, Ulla, *Mesopotamian Astrology: An Introduction to Babylonian and Assyrian Celestial Divination*, Carsten Niebuhr Institute Publications 19 (Copenhagen: Museum Tusculanum Press, 1995).

Kooij, Arie van der, "The Canonization of Ancient Books Kept in the Temple of Jerusalem," in Arie van der Kooij and Karel van der Toorn, eds., *Canonization and Decanonization: Papers Presented to the International Conference of the Leiden Institute for the Study of Religions (LISOR) held at Leiden 9–10 January 1997*, Studies in the History of Religions 82 (Leiden: Brill, 1997), 17–40.

———, *Die alten Textzeugen des Jesajabuches*, OBO 35 (Fribourg: University of Fribourg; Göttingen: Vandenhoeck & Ruprecht, 1981).

———, "Jeremiah 27:5–15: How Do MT and LXX Relate to Each Other?" *Journal of Northwest Semitic Languages* 20 (1994): 59–78.

———, "The Septuagint: The First Translation of the Hebrew Bible?" *Bulletin of Judaeo-Greek Studies* 34 (2004): 27–28.

Korostovcev, Michail Alexandrovic, *Pistsy Drevnevo Egipta* [*The Scribes of Ancient Egypt*] (Moscow: Editions of Oriental Literature, 1962).

Kramer, Samuel Noah, "The Epic of Gilgameš and Its Sumerian Sources: A Study in Literary Evolution," *JAOS* 64 (1944): 7–23.

Kratz, Reinhard G., *Translatio imperii: Untersuchungen zu den aramäischen Danielerzählungen und ihrem theologiegeschichtlichen Umfeld*, Wissenschaftliche Monographien zum Alten und Neuen Testament 63 (Neukirchen-Vluyn: Neukirchener Verlag, 1991).

Kraus, Fritz Rudolf, *Vom mesopotamischen Menschen der altbabylonischen Zeit und seiner Welt* (Amsterdam: North-Holland Publishing Company, 1973).

Krebernik, Manfred, "M. Weinfelds Deuteronomiumskommentar aus assyriologischer Sicht," in Georg Braulik, ed., *Bundesdokument und Gesetz: Studien zum Deuteronomium,* Herders Biblische Studien 4 (Freiburg: Herder, 1995), 27–36.

Krecher, Joachim, "Kataloge, literarische," *RlA* 5:478–485.

Kugler, Robert A., *From Patriarch to Priest: The Levi-Priestly Tradition from Aramaic Levi to Testament of Levi,* Early Judaism and Its Literature 9 (Atlanta: Scholars Press, 1996).

Kuhl, Curt, "Die 'Wiederaufnahme'—ein literarkritisches Prinzip?" *ZAW* 64 (1952): 1–11.

Lambert, Wilfred G., "Ancestors, Authors, and Canonicity," *JCS* 11 (1957): 1–14, 112.

———, "A Catalogue of Texts and Authors," *JCS* 16 (1962): 59–77.

———, "Enmeduranki and Related Matters," *JCS* 21 (1967): 126–138.

———, "The Gula Hymn of Bullutsa-rabi," *Orientalia* 36 (1967): 105–132.

———, "A Late Assyrian Catalogue of Literary and Scholarly Texts," in Barry L. Eichler, ed., *Kramer Anniversary Volume: Cuneiform Studies in Honor of Samuel Noah Kramer,* AOAT 25 (Kevelaer: Butzon & Bercker; Neukirchen-Vluyn: Neukirchener Verlag, 1976), 313–318.

———, "The Qualifications of Babylonian Diviners," in Stefan Maul, ed., *Festschrift für Rykle Borger zu seinem 65. Geburtstag am 24. Mai 1994: tikip santakki mala bašmu . . .,* CM 10 (Groningen: Styx, 1998), 141–158.

———, "The Reign of Nebuchadnezzar I: A Turning Point in the History of Ancient Mesopotamian Religion," in William S. McCullough, ed., *The Seed of Wisdom: Essays in Honour of Th. J. Meek* (Toronto: University of Toronto Press, 1964), 3–13.

———, Review of Hermann Hunger, *Babylonische und assyrische Kolophone, Welt des Orients* 5 (1970): 290–291.

———, "Twenty-One 'Poultices,'" *Anatolian Studies* 30 (1980): 77–83.

Landsberger, Benno, "Die babylonische Theodizee," *ZA* 43 (1936): 32–76.

———, "Scribal Concepts of Education," in Carl H. Kraeling and Robert MacAdams, eds., *City Invincible: A Symposium on Urbanization and Cultural Development in the Ancient Near East* (Chicago: University of Chicago Press, 1960), 94–123.

Lanfranchi, Giovanni, "The Library at Nineveh," in Joan Goodnick Westenholz, ed., *Capital Cities: Urban Planning and Spiritual Dimensions, Proceedings of the Symposium Held on May 27–29, 1996, Jerusalem, Israel,* Bible Lands Museum Jerusalem Publications 2 (Jerusalem: Bible Lands Museum, 1998), 147–156.

Lang, Bernhard, "Das tanzende Wort: Intellektuelle Rituale im Fruhjüdentum, im Christentum und in östlichen Religionen," in Lang, ed., *Das tanzende Wort: Intellektuelle Rituale im Religionsvergleich* (Munich: Kösel, 1984), 15–48.

Larsen, Mogens T., "The Mesopotamian Lukewarm Mind: Reflections on Science, Divination and Literacy," in Francesca Rochberg-Halton, ed., *Language, Literature, and History: Philological and Historical Studies Presented to Erica Reiner*, American Oriental Series 67 (New Haven: American Oriental Society, 1987), 203–225.

———, "What They Wrote on Clay," in Karen Schousboe and Mogens T. Larsen, eds., *Literacy and Society* (Copenhagen: Akademisk Forlag, 1989), 121–148.

Leclerq, Henri, "Bibliothèques," *Dictionnaire d'archéologie chrétienne et de liturgie*, ed. Fernand Cabrol et al. (Paris: Letouzey & Ané, 1907–1953), 2:842–904.

Leichty, Erle, "The Colophon," in Robert D. Biggs and John A. Brinkman, eds., *Studies Presented to A. Leo Oppenheim* (Chicago: Oriental Institute, 1964), 147–154.

Leivestad, Ragnar, "Das Dogma von der prophetenlosen Zeit," *New Testament Studies* 19 (1972–73): 288–299.

Lemaire, André, *Les écoles et la formation de la Bible dans l'ancien Israel*, OBO 39 (Fribourg: Editions Universitaires; Göttingen: Vandenhoeck & Ruprecht, 1981).

———, "Education in Ancient Israel," *ABD* 2:305–312.

Lesko, Leonard H., "Literacy," in Donald B. Redford, ed., *The Oxford Encyclopedia of Ancient Egypt* (Oxford: Oxford University Press, 2001), 2:297–299.

———, "Some Comments on Ancient Egyptian Literacy and Literati," in Sarah Israelit-Groll, ed., *Studies in Egyptology Presented to Miriam Lichtheim*, 2 vols. (Jerusalem: Magnes, 1990), 2:656–659.

Levinson, Bernard M., "The Birth of the Lemma: The Restrictive Reinterpretation of the Covenant Code's Manumission Law by the Holiness Code (Leviticus 25:44–46)," *JBL* 124 (2005): 617–639.

———, *Deuteronomy and the Hermeneutics of Legal Innovation* (New York: Oxford University Press, 1998).

———, "The Manumission of Hermeneutics: The Slave Laws of the Pentateuch as a Challenge to Contemporary Pentateuchal Theory," in André Lemaire, ed., *Congress Volume Leiden 2004*, Supplements VT 109 (Leiden: Brill, 2006), 281–321.

Lewis, Jack P., "Jamnia after Forty Years," *Hebrew Union College Annual* 70–71 (1999–2000): 233–259.

Lewis, Naphtali, *Greeks in Ptolemaic Egypt: Case Studies in the Social History of the Hellenistic World* (Oxford: Clarendon, 1986).

———, *Papyrus in Classical Antiquity* (Oxford: Clarendon, 1974).

Lieberman, Stephen J., "Canonical and Official Cuneiform Texts: Towards an Understanding of Assurbanipal's Personal Tablet Collection," in Tzvi Abusch et al., eds., *Lingering over Words: Studies in Ancient Near Eastern Literature in Honor of William L. Moran* (Atlanta: Scholars Press, 1990), 305–336.

Lion, Brigitte, "Dame Inanna-ama-mu, scribe à Sippar," *RA* 95 (2001): 7–32.

Lipiński, Edward, "Royal and State Scribes in Ancient Jerusalem," in John A. Emerton, ed., *Congress Volume Jerusalem 1986,* Supplements VT 40 (Leiden: Brill, 1988), 157–164.

Lloyd, Alan B., "The Inscription of Udjahorresnet: A Collaborator's Testament," *Journal of Egyptian Antiquities* 68 (1982): 166–180.

Löhr, Max, "Alphabetische und alphabetisierende Lieder im AT," *ZAW* 25 (1905): 173–198.

Lohfink, Norbert, *Das Deuteronomium: Entstehung, Gestalt und Botschaft,* Bibliotheca Ephemeridum Theologicarum Lovaniensium 68 (Leuven: Peeters, 1985).

———, "Die Sicherung der Wirksamkeit des Gotteswortes durch das Prinzip der Schriftlichkeit der Tora und durch das Prinzip der Gewaltenteilung nach den Ämtergesetzen des Buches Deuteronomium (Dtn 16,18–18,21)," in Hans Wolter, ed., *Testimonium veritati: Philosophische und theologische Studien zu kirchlichen Fragen der Gegenwart,* Festschrift Wilhelm Kempf, Frankfurter theologische Studien 7 (Frankfurt: Knecht, 1971), 143–155; repr. *Studien zum Deuteronomium und zur deuteronomistischen Literatur,* 4 vols., Stuttgarter Biblische Aufsatzbände, Altes Testament 8, 12, 20, 31 (Stuttgart: Katholisches Bibelwerk, 1990–2000) 1:305–323.

———, "Fortschreibung? Zur Technik von Rechtsrevisionen im deuteronomischen Bereich, erörtert an Deuteronomium 12, Ex 21,2–11 und Dtn 15,12–18," in Timo Veijola, ed., *Das Deuteronomium und seine Querbeziehungen,* Schriften der Finnischen Exegetischen Gesellschaft 62 (Helsinki: Finnische Exegetische Gesellschaft; Göttingen: Vandenhoeck & Ruprecht, 1996), 127–171.

———, "Gab es eine deuteronomistische Bewegung?" in Walter Gross, ed.,

Jeremia und die "deuteronomistische Bewegung," Bonner Biblische Beiträge 98 (Weinheim: Beltz Athenäum, 1995), 313–382.

———, *Studien zum Deuteronomium und zur deuteronomistischen Literatur,* 4 vols., Stuttgarter Biblische Aufsatzbände, Altes Testament 8, 12, 20, 31 (Stuttgart: Katholisches Bibelwerk, 1990–2000).

———, "Zur Dekalogfassung von Dt 5," *Biblische Zeitschrift* 9 (1965): 17–32.

———, "Zur Fabel des Deuteronomiums," in Georg Braulik, ed., *Bundesdokument und Gesetz: Studien zum Deuteronomium,* Herders Biblische Studien 4 (Freiburg: Herder, 1995), 65–78.

Longman, Tremper, III, *Fictional Akkadian Autobiography: A Generic and Comparative Study* (Winona Lake, IN: Eisenbrauns, 1991).

Lundblom, Jack R., "Baruch," *ABD* 1:617.

Machinist, Peter, and Hayim Tadmor, "Heavenly Wisdom," in Mark E. Cohen et al., eds., *The Tablet and the Scroll: Near Eastern Studies in Honor of William W. Hallo* (Bethesda, MD: CDL Press, 1993), 146–151.

Marrou, Henri-Irénée, *Histoire de l'éducation dans l'Antiquité* (Paris: Seuil, 1965).

Marti, Karl, *Der Prophet Jeremia von Anatot* (Basel: Detloff, 1889).

McEwan, Gilbert J. P., *Priest and Temple in Hellenistic Babylonia,* Freiburger Altorientalische Studien 4 (Wiesbaden: Franz Steiner, 1981).

Meade, David G., *Pseudonymity and Canon: An Investigation into the Relationship of Authorship and Authority in Jewish and Earliest Christian Tradition,* Wissenschaftliche Untersuchungen zum Neuen Testament 39 (Tübingen: Mohr, 1986).

Meeks, Dimitri, Review of Korostovcev, *The Scribes of Ancient Egypt, Revue d'Egyptologie* 19 (1967): 189–193.

Mettinger, Tryggve N. D., *Solomonic State Officials: A Study of Civil Government Officials of the Israelite Monarchy,* Coniectanea Biblica, OT Series 5 (Lund: Gleerup, 1971).

Meyer, Rudolf, "Prophetentum und Propheten im Judentum der hellenistischen-römischen Zeit," *Theologisches Wörterbuch zum Neuen Testament,* 10 vols., ed. Gerhard Kittel et al. (Stuttgart: Kohlhammer, 1953–1979), 6:813–828.

Michalowski, Piotr, "Adapa and the Ritual Process," *Rocznik Orientalistyczny* 41 (1980): 77–82.

———, "The Libraries of Babel: Text, Authority, and Tradition in Ancient Mesopotamia," in Gillis J. Dorleijn and Herman L. J. Vanstiphout, eds.,

Cultural Repertoires: Structure, Functions and Dynamics, Groningen Studies in Cultural Change 3 (Leuven: Peeters, 2003), 105–129.

———, "A New Sumerian 'Catalogue' from Nippur," *Oriens Antiquus* 19 (1980): 265–268.

———, "Observations on a Sumerian Literary Catalogue from Ur," *JCS* 36 (1984): 89–92.

Millard, Alan R., "An Assessment of the Evidence of Writing in Ancient Israel," in Janet Amitai, ed., *Biblical Archaeology Today: Proceedings of the International Congress of Biblical Archaeology, Jerusalem, April 1984* (Jerusalem: Israel Exploration Society, 1985), 301–312.

———, "La prophétie et l'écriture: Israel, Aram, Assyrie," *Revue d'Histoire des Religions* 202 (1985): 125–145.

Miller, John W., *The Origins of the Bible: Rethinking Canon History* (New York and Mahwah, NJ: Paulist Press, 1994).

Moran, William L., "The Epic of Gilgamesh: A Document of Ancient Humanism," *Bulletin of the Canadian Society for Mesopotamian Studies* 22 (1991): 15–22; repr. in *The Most Magic Word,* ed. Ronald S. Hendel, The Catholic Biblical Quarterly Monograph Series 35 (Washington, DC: Catholic Biblical Association of America, 2002), 5–20.

Morrow, William S., "Mesopotamian Scribal Techniques and Deuteronomic Composition: Notes on *Deuteronomy and the Hermeneutics of Legal Innovation,*" *Zeitschrift für die altorientalische Rechtsgeschichte* 6 (2000): 302–313.

Mowinckel, Sigmund, *Erwägungen zur Pentateuch Quellenfrage* (Trondheim: Universitetsforlaget, 1964).

———, *Prophecy and Tradition: The Prophetic Books in the Light of the Study of the Growth and History of the Tradition,* Avhandlinger utgitt av det Norske Videnskaps-Akademie i Oslo, II. Hist.-Filos. Klasse 1946:3 (Oslo: Jacob Dybwad, 1946 [1947]).

———, "Psalms and Wisdom," in Martin Noth and D. Winton Thomas, eds., *Wisdom in Israel and in the Ancient Near East,* Festschrift H. H. Rowley, Supplements VT 3 (Leiden: Brill, 1955), 205–224.

———, *The Psalms in Israel's Worship,* 2 vols., trans. D. R. Ap-Thomas (Oxford: Basil Blackwell, 1962).

———, *Studien zu dem Buche Ezra-Nehemia,* III: *Die Ezrageschichte und das Gesetz Moses,* Skrifter utgitt av det Norske Videnskapsakademi i Oslo II Historisk-filosofisk Klasse, nova series, 7 (Oslo: Universitetsvorlaget, 1965).

———, *Zur Komposition des Buches Jeremia,* Skrifter utgitt av

Videnskapsselskapet i Kristiania II, Historisk-filosofisk Klasse 1913:5 (Kristiana: Dybwad, 1914).

Muilenburg, James, "Baruch the Scribe," in John I. Durham and Joshua R. Porter, eds., *Proclamation and Presence: Old Testament Essays in Honour of Gwynne Henton Davies* (London: SCM Press, 1970), 215–238.

Na'aman, Nadav, "The Distribution of Messages in the Kingdom of Judah in the Light of the Lachish Ostraca," *VT* 53 (2003): 169–180.

Niditch, Susan, *Oral World and Written Word: Ancient Israelite Literature*, Library of Ancient Israel (Louisville, KY: Westminster John Knox Press, 1996).

Nilsson, Martin P., *Die hellenistische Schule* (Munich: Beck, 1955).

Nissinen, Martti, *References to Prophecy in Neo-Assyrian Sources*, SAA Studies 7 (Helsinki: Helsinki University Press, 1998).

———, "Spoken, Written, Quoted, and Invented: Orality and Writtenness in Ancient Near Eastern Prophecy," in Ehud Ben Zvi and Michael H. Floyd, eds., *Writings and Speech in Israelite and Ancient Near Eastern Prophecy*, SBL Symposium Series 10 (Atlanta: Society of Biblical Literature, 2000), 235–271.

Ong, Walter J., *Orality and Literacy: The Technologizing of the Word* (London and New York: Methuen, 1982).

Oppenheim, A. Leo, "Divination and Celestial Observation in the Late Assyrian Empire," *Centaurus* 14 (1969): 97–135.

———, "The Position of the Intellectual in Mesopotamian Society," *Daedalus* 104 (1975): 37–46.

Otten, Heinrich, "Bibliotheken im Alten Orient," *Das Altertum* 1 (1955): 67–81.

Otto, Eckhart, "Biblische Rechtsgeschichte als Fortschreibungsgeschichte," *Bibliotheca Orientalis* 56 (1999): 5–14.

———, *Das Deuteronomium im Pentateuch und Hexateuch*, Forschungen zum Alten Testament 30 (Tübingen: Mohr Siebeck, 2000).

———, *Das Deuteronomium: Politische Theologie und Rechtsreform in Juda und Assyrien*, Beihefte ZAW 284 (Berlin: De Gruyter, 1999).

———, "Vom biblischen Hebraismus der persischen Zeit zum rabbinischen Judaismus in römischer Zeit: Zur Geschichte der spätbiblischen und frühjüdischen Schriftgelehrsamkeit," *Zeitschrift für die Altorientalische Rechtsgeschichte* 10 (2004): 1–49.

Parkinson, Richard, and Stephen Quirke, *Papyrus* (London: British Museum Press, 1995).

Parpola, Simo, "Assyrian Library Records," *JNES* 42 (1983): 1–29.

———, "The Forlorn Scholar," in Francesca Rochberg-Halton, ed., *Language, Literature, and History: Philological and Historical Studies Presented to Erica Reiner*, American Oriental Series 67 (New Haven: American Oriental Society, 1987), 257–278.

———, *Letters from Assyrian and Babylonian Scholars*, SAA 10 (Helsinki: Helsinki University Press, 1993).

———, *Letters from Assyrian Scholars to the Kings Esarhaddon and Assurbanipal, Part II: Commentary and Appendices*, AOAT 5/2 (Kevelaer: Butzon & Bercker; Neukirchen-Vluyn: Neukirchener Verlag, 1983).

———, "The Man without a Scribe and the Question of Literacy in the Assyrian Empire," in Beate Pongratz-Leisten et al., eds., *Ana šadî Labnāni lū allik: Beiträge zu altorientalischen und mittelmeerischen Kulturen. Festschrift für Wolfgang Röllig*, AOAT 247 (Kevelaer: Butzon & Bercker; Neukirchen-Vluyn: Neukirchener Verlag, 1997), 315–324.

Pearce, Laurie E., "Statements of Purpose: Why Scribes Wrote," in Mark Cohen et al., eds., *The Tablet and the Scroll: Near Eastern Studies in Honor of William W. Hallo* (Bethesda, MD: CDL Press, 1993), 185–193.

Pedersén, Olof, *Archives and Libraries in the Ancient Near East 1500–300 B.C.* (Bethesda, MD: CDL Press, 1998).

Pfeiffer, Rudolf, *History of Classical Scholarship, I: From the Beginnings to the End of the Hellenistic Age* (Oxford: Clarendon, 1968).

Platthy, Jenoe, *Sources on the Earliest Greek Libraries* (Amsterdam: Adolf M. Hakkert, 1968).

Posener, Georges, "Sur l'emploi de l'encre rouge dans les manuscrits égyptiens," *Journal of Egyptian Archaeology* 37 (1951): 75–80.

Rad, Gerhard von, "Hiob XXXVIII und die altägyptische Weisheit," in Martin Noth and D. Winton Thomas, eds., *Wisdom in Israel and in the Ancient Near East*, Festschrift H. H. Rowley, Supplements VT 3 (Leiden: Brill, 1955), 293–301.

Redford, Donald B., *Pharaonic King-Lists, Annals, and Day-Books: A Contribution to the Study of the Egyptian Sense of History*, Society for the Study of Egyptian Antiquities 4 (Mississauga, Ont.: Benben, 1986).

———, "Scribe and Speaker," in Ehud Ben Zvi and Michael H. Floyd, eds., *Writings and Speech in Israelite and Ancient Near Eastern Prophecy*, SBL Symposium Series 10 (Atlanta: Society of Biblical Literature, 2000), 145–218.

Regenbogen, Otto, "Pinax," *Paulys Realencyclopädie der classischen*

Altertumswissenschaft, 49 vols., ed. Georg Wissowa (Munich: Druckenmüller; Stuttgart: Metzler, 1984–1997), 20/2:1408–1482.

Reiner, Erica, "The Etiological Myth of the 'Seven Sages,'" *Orientalia* 30 (1961): 1–11.

———, "Plague Amulets and House Blessings," *JNES* 19 (1960): 148–155.

Renger, Johannes, "Untersuchungen zur Priestertum in der altbabylonischen Zeit," *ZA* 58 (1967): 110–188; *ZA* 59 (1969): 104–230.

Reynolds, Leighton D., and Nigel G. Wilson, *Scribes and Scholars: A Guide to the Transmission of Greek and Latin Literature*, 2nd ed. (Oxford: Clarendon, 1974).

Ritter, Edith F., "Magical-Expert *(āšipu)* and Physician *(asû)*: Notes on Two Complementary Professions in Babylonian Medicine," in Hans G. Güterbock and Thorkild Jacobsen, eds., *Studies in Honor of Benno Landsberger on His Seventy-fifth Birthday, April 21, 1965*, Assyriological Studies 16 (Chicago: University of Chicago Press, 1965), 299–322.

Roberts, Colin H., and Theodore C. Skeat, *The Birth of the Codex* (London: Published for the British Academy by Oxford University Press, 1983).

Robson, Eleanor, "The Tablet House: A Scribal School in Old Babylonian Nippur," *RA* 95 (2001): 39–66.

Rochberg, Francesca, *The Heavenly Writing: Divination, Horoscopy, and Astronomy in Mesopotamian Culture* (New York: Cambridge University Press, 2004).

———, "Scribes and Scholars: The ṭupšar Enūma Anu Enlil," in Joachim Marzahn and Hans Neumann, eds., *Assyriologica et Semitica: Festschrift für Joachim Oelsner*, AOAT 252 (Münster: Ugarit-Verlag, 2000), 359–375.

Rollston, Christopher A., "Non-Provenanced Epigraphs, I: Pillaged Antiquities, Northwest Semitic Forgeries, and Protocol for Laboratory Tests," *Maarav* 10 (2003): 135–193.

Rousse, Richard A., and Mary A. Rousse, *Illiterati et uxorati: Manuscripts and Their Makers; Commercial Book Producers in Medieval Paris 1200–1500*, 2 vols. (London: Harvey Miller, 2000).

Ryle, Herbert E., *The Canon of the Old Testament* (London: Macmillan, 1892).

Sarna, Nahum M., "The Order of the Books," in Charles Berlin, ed., *Studies in Jewish Bibliography, History and Literature in Honor of I. Edward Kiev* (New York: Ktav, 1971), 407–413.

Sassmannshausen, Leonhard, "Zur babylonischen Schreiberausbildung," *Baghdader Mitteilungen* 33 (2002): 211–228.

Sasson, Jack, "Water beneath Straw: Adventures of a Prophetic Phrase in the Mari Archives," in Ziony Zevit et al., eds., *Solving Riddles and Untying Knots: Biblical, Epigraphic, and Semitic Studies in Honor of Jonas C. Greenfield* (Winona Lake, IN: Eisenbrauns, 1995), 598–608.

Sauneron, Serge, *Les prêtres de l'ancienne Egypte,* 2nd ed. (Paris: Perséa, 1988); in English, *The Priests of Ancient Egypt,* trans. David Lorton (Ithaca: Cornell University Press, 2000).

Schaeder, Hans Heinrich, *Esra der Schreiber,* Beiträge zur historischen Theologie 5 (Tübingen: Mohr Siebeck, 1930).

Schäfer, Peter, "Der sogenannte Synode von Jabne, II: Der Abschluss des Kanons," *Judaica* 31 (1975): 116–124.

Schams, Christine, *Jewish Scribes in the Second-Temple Period,* JSOT Supplement Series 291 (Sheffield: Sheffield Academic Press, 1998).

Schaper, Joachim, "Exilic and Post-Exilic Prophecy and the Orality/Literacy Problem," *VT* 55 (2005): 324–342.

———, *Priester und Leviten im achämenidischen Juda: Studien zur Kult- und Sozialgeschichte Israels in persischer Zeit,* Forschungen zum Alten Testament 31 (Tübingen: Mohr Siebeck, 2000).

Schearing, Linda S., and Steven L. MacKenzie, eds., *Those Elusive Deuteronomists: The Phenomenon of Pan-Deuteronomism,* JSOT Supplement Series 268 (Sheffield: Sheffield Academic Press, 1999).

Schenke, Wolfgang, "Texttradierung, -kritik," *LÄ,* 6:459–462.

Schlott, Adelheid, *Schrift und Schreiber im Alten Ägypten* (Munich: C. H. Beck, 1989).

Schmid, Konrad, *Buchgestalten des Jeremiabuches: Untersuchungen zur Redaktions- und Rezeptionsgeschichte von Jer 30–33 im Kontext des Buches,* Wissenschaftliche Monographien zum Alten und Neuen Testament 72 (Neukirchen: Neukirchener Verlag, 1996).

Schniedewind, William M., *How the Bible Became a Book* (New York: Cambridge University Press, 2004).

Schousboe, Karen, and Mogens T. Larsen, eds., *Literacy and Society* (Copenhagen: Akademisk Forlag, 1989).

Shaffer, Aron, "A New Look at Some Old Catalogues," in Andrew R. George and Irving L. Finkel, eds., *Wisdom, Gods and Literature: Studies in Assyriology in Honour of W. G. Lambert* (Winona Lake, IN: Eisenbrauns, 2000), 429–436.

Sheppard, Gerald T., *Wisdom as a Hermeneutical Construct: A Study in the Sapientializing of the Old Testament,* Beihefte ZAW 151 (Berlin: W. de Gruyter, 1980).

Shooner, Hugues V., "La production du livre par la pecia," in Louis Jacques Bataillon et al., eds., *La production du livre universitaire au Moyen Age: Exemplar et pecia, Actes du symposium tenu au Collegio San Bonaventura de Grottaferrata en mai 1983* (Paris: Editions du Centre National de la Recherche Scientifique, 1988), 17–37.

Silverman, David P., "Textual Criticism in the Coffin Texts," in James P. Allen et al., *Religion and Philosophy in Ancient Egypt,* Yale Egyptological Studies 3 (New Haven: Yale Egyptological Seminar, 1989), 29–53.

Sint, Josef A., *Pseudonymität im Altertum: Ihre Formen und ihre Gründe,* Commentationes Aenipontanae 15 (Innsbruck: Universitätsverlag Wagner, 1960).

Sjöberg, Åke W., "Der Examenstext A," *ZA* 64 (1975): 137–176.

———, "Der Vater und sein missratener Sohn," *JCS* 25 (1973): 105–169.

———, "The Old Babylonian Eduba," in Stephen B. Lieberman, ed., *Sumerological Studies in Honor of Thorkild Jacobsen on His Seventieth Birthday, June 7, 1974,* Assyriological Studies 20 (Chicago: University of Chicago Press, 1975), 159–179.

Skeat, Theodore C., "Early Christian Book-Production: Papyri and Manuscripts," in *The Cambridge History of the Bible,* vol. 2: *The West from the Fathers to the Reformation,* ed. Geoffrey W. H. Lampe (Cambridge: Cambridge University Press, 1969), 54–79.

———, "The Length of the Standard Papyrus Roll and the Cost-Advantage of the Codex," *Zeitschrift für Papyrologie und Epigraphie* 45 (1982): 169–175.

Smith, Mark S., "The Levitical Compilation of the Psalter," *ZAW* 103 (1991): 258–263.

Smith, Morton, *Palestinian Parties and Politics That Shaped the Old Testament,* 2nd ed. (London: SCM Press, 1987).

Soden, Wolfram von, "Leistung und Grenze sumerischer und babylonischer Wissenschaft," *Die Welt als Geschichte* 2 (1936): 411–464 and 509–557; repr., with Benno Landsberger, *Die Eigenbegrifflichkeit der babylonischen Welt* (Darmstadt: Wissenschaftliche Buchgesellschaft, 1965), 21–133.

———, *Sprache, Denken und Begriffsbildung im alten Orient* (Mainz: Akademie der Wissenschaften und der Literatur; Wiesbaden: Steiner, 1974).

Soldt, Wilfred H. van, "'atn prln, ''attā/ēnu the Diviner,'" *Ugarit-Forschungen* 21 (1989): 365–368.

———, "Babylonian Lexical, Religious and Literary Texts and Scribal Education at Ugarit," in Manfried Dietrich and Oswald Loretz, eds., *Ugarit: Ein ostmediterranes Kulturzentrum im Alten Orient; Ergebnisse und*

Perspektiven der Forschung, Abhandlungen zur Literatur Alt-Syriens-Palästinas 7 (Münster: Ugarit-Verlag, 1995), 171–212.

Soll, Will M., "Babylonian and Biblical Acrostics," *Biblica* 69 (1988): 305–323.

Speyer, Wolfgang, *Die literarische Fälschung im Altertum* (Munich: Beck, 1971).

Steck, Odil Hannes, *Der Abschluss der Prophetie im Alten Testament: Ein Versuch zur Frage der Vorgeschichte des Kanons,* Biblisch-Theologische Studien 17 (Neukirchen-Vluyn: Neukirchener Verlag, 1991).

———, "Zur Abfolge Maleachi-Jona in 4Q76 (4QXII^a)," *ZAW* 108 (1996): 249–253.

Stegemann, Hartmut, *The Library of Qumran: On the Essenes, Qumran, John the Baptist, and Jesus* (Leiden: Brill; Grand Rapids: Eerdmans, 1998).

Stemberger, Günter, "Die sogenannte "Synode von Jabne" und das frühe Christentum," *Kairos* 19 (1977): 14–21.

———, "Öffentlichkeit der Tora im Judentum: Anspruch und Wirklichkeit," *Jahrbuch für Biblische Theologie* 11 (1996): 91–101.

Stemplinger, Eduard, *Das Plagiat in der griechischen Literatur* (Leipzig and Berlin: Teubner, 1912).

Steymans, Hans Ulrich, *Deuteronomium 28 und die adê zur Thronfolgeregelung Asarhaddons: Segen und Fluch im Alten Orient und in Israel,* OBO 145 (Fribourg: Universitätsverlag; Göttingen: Vandenhoeck & Ruprecht, 1995).

Stone, Michael E., and Jonas C. Greenfield, "Remarks on the Aramaic Testament of Levi from the Geniza," *Revue Biblique* 86 (1979): 214–230.

Sweet, Ronald F. G., "A Pair of Double Acrostics in Akkadian," *Orientalia* 38 (1969): 459–460.

———, "The Sage in Akkadian Literature: A Philological Study," in John G. Gammie and Leo G. Perdue, eds., *The Sage in Israel and the Ancient Near East* (Winona Lake, IN: Eisenbrauns, 1990), 45–65.

Thomas, Rosalind, *Literacy and Orality in Ancient Greece,* Key Themes in Ancient History (Cambridge: Cambridge University Press, 1992).

Tigay, Jeffrey, ed., *Empirical Models for Biblical Criticism* (Philadelphia: University of Pennsylvania Press, 1985).

———, *The Evolution of the Gilgamesh Epic* (Philadelphia: University of Pennsylvania Press, 1982).

Tinney, Steve, "On the Curricular Setting of Sumerian Literature," *Iraq* 61 (1999): 159–172.

Toorn, Karel van der, "Cuneiform Documents from Syria-Palestine: Texts, Scribes, and Schools," *Zeitschrift des Deutschen Palästina-Vereins* 116 (2000): 97–113.

———, "Sources in Heaven: Revelation as a Scholarly Construct in Second Temple Judaism," in Ulrich Hübner and Ernst Axel Knauf, eds., *Kein Land für sich allein: Studien zum Kulturkontakt in Kanaan, Israel/Palästina und Ebirnâri für Manfred Weippert zum 65. Geburtstag*, OBO 186 (Fribourg: Universitätsverlag; Göttingen: Vandenhoeck & Ruprecht, 2002), 265–277.

Tov, Emanuel, "The Literary History of the Book of Jeremiah in the Light of Its Textual History," in Jeffrey H. Tigay, ed., *Empirical Models for Biblical Criticism* (Philadelphia: University of Pennsylvania Press, 1985), 211–237.

———, *Scribal Practices and Approaches Reflected in the Texts Found in the Judean Desert*, Studies on the Texts of the Desert of Judah 54 (Leiden: Brill, 2004).

Tucker, Gene M., "Prophetic Superscriptions and the Growth of a Canon," in George W. Coats and Burke O. Long, eds., *Canon and Authority: Essays in Old Testament Religion and Theology* (Philadelphia: Fortress, 1977), 56–70.

Uehlinger, Christoph, "Gab es eine joschianische Kultreform? Plädoyer für ein begründetes Minimum," in Walter Gross, ed., *Jeremia und die "deuteronomistische Bewegung,"* Bonner Biblische Beiträge 98 (Weinheim: Beltz Athenäum, 1995), 57–89; in English, "Was There a Cult Reform under King Josiah? The Case for a Well-Grounded Minimum," in Lester Grabbe, ed., *Good Kings and Bad Kings*, Library of Hebrew Bible/Old Testament Studies 393, European Seminar in Historical Methodology 5 (London, New York: T&T Clark, 2005), 279–316.

Ulrich, Eugene, *The Dead Sea Scrolls and the Origins of the Bible*, Studies in the Dead Sea Scrolls and Related Literature (Grand Rapids: Eerdmans; Leiden: Brill, 1999).

———, "The Non-Attestation of a Tripartite Canon in 4QMMT," *Catholic Biblical Quarterly* 65 (2003): 202–214.

Vanderkam, James C., "Revealed Literature in the Second Temple Period," in *Studies in the Hebrew Bible and Second Temple Literature*, Supplements to the Journal for the Study of Judaism 62 (Leiden: Brill, 2000), 1–30.

Van Seters, John, "The Redactor in Biblical Studies: A Nineteenth-Century Anachronism," *Journal of Northwest Semitic Languages* 29 (2003): 1–19.

Vanstiphout, Herman L. J., "Lipit-Eštar's Praise in the Edubba," *JCS* 30 (1978): 33–61.

———, "The Old Babylonian Literary Canon: Structure, Function and Intention," in Gillis J. Dorleijn and Herman L. J. Vanstiphout, eds., *Cultural Repertoires: Structure, Functions and Dynamics,* Groningen Studies in Cultural Change 3 (Leuven: Peeters, 2003), 1–28.

Veenhof, Klaas R., ed., *Cuneiform Archives and Libraries: Papers Read at the 30e Recontre Assyriologique Internationale, Leiden 4–8 July 1983* (Istanbul: Nederlands Historisch-Archaeologisch Instituut; Leiden: Nederlands Instituut voor het Nabije Oosten, 1986).

Veijola, Timo, ed., *Das Deuteronomium und seine Querbeziehungen,* Schriften der Finnischen Exegetischen Gesellschaft 62 (Helsinki: Finnische Exegetische Gesellschaft; Göttingen: Vandenhoeck & Ruprecht, 1996).

———, *Moses Erben: Studien zum Dekalog, zum Deuteronomismus und zum Schriftgelehrtentum,* Beiträge zur Wissenschaft vom Alten und Neuen Testament 149 (Stuttgart: Kohlhammer, 2000).

Velde, Herman te, "Scribes and Literacy in Ancient Egypt," in Herman L. J. Vanstiphout et al., eds., *Scripta signa vocis: Studies about Scripts, Scriptures, Scribes and Languages in the Near East Presented to J. H. Hospers* (Groningen: Forsten, 1986), 253–264.

Veldhuis, Niek, "The Cuneiform Tablet as an Educational Tool," *Dutch Studies Published by Near Eastern Languages and Literature* 2/1 (1996): 11–26.

———, *Religion, Literature, and Scholarship: The Sumerian Composition Nanše and the Birds,* CM 22 (Leiden: Brill/Styx, 2004).

Vernus, Pascal, "Quelques exemples du type du "parvenu" dans l'Egypte Ancienne," *Bulletin de la Société Française d'Egyptologie* 59 (1970): 31–47.

Volk, Konrad, "Edubba'a und Edubba'a-Literatur: Rätsel und Lösungen," *ZA* 90 (2000): 1–30.

Wacholder, Ben Zion, "The Letter from Judas Maccabee to Aristobulus: Is 2 Maccabees 1:10b–2:18 Authentic?" *Hebrew Union College Annual* 49 (1978): 89–133.

Waetzoldt, Hartmut, "Der Schreiber als Lehrer in Mesopotamien," in Johann Georg von Hohenzollern and Max Liedtke, eds., *Schreiber—Magister—Lehrer: Zur Geschichte und Funktion eines Berufsstandes* (Bad Heilbrunn: Julius Klinkhardt, 1989), 33–50.

Warner, Sean, "The Alphabet: An Innovation and Its Diffusion," *VT* 30 (1980): 81–90.

Weber, Manfred, "Lebenshaus I.," *LÄ*, 3:954–957.

Weidner, Ernst F., "Geheimschrift," *RlA* 3:185–188.

Weinfeld, Moshe, *Deuteronomy and the Deuteronomic School* (Oxford: Oxford University Press, 1972; repr. Winona Lake, IN: Eisenbrauns, 1992).

Weingreen, Jacob, "The Deuteronomic Legislator: A Proto-Rabbinic Type," in John I. Durham and John R. Porter, eds., *Proclamation and Presence: Old Testament Essays in Honour of Gwynne Henton Davies* (London: SCM Press, 1970), 76–89.

Weippert, Manfred, "The Balaam Text from Deir 'Alla and the Study of the Old Testament," in Jacobus Hoftijzer and Gerrit van der Kooij, eds., *The Balaam Text from Deir 'Alla Re-Evaluated: Proceedings of the International Symposium Held at Leiden, 21–24 August 1989* (Leiden: Brill, 1991), 151–184.

Weitemeyer, Mogens, "Archive and Library Technique in Ancient Mesopotamia," *Libri* 6/3 (1956): 217–238.

Wendel, Carl, "Bibliothek," *Reallexikon für Antike und Christentum*, ed. Theodor Klauser et al. (Stuttgart: Hiersemann, 1941–), 2:231–274.

———, *Die Griechisch-Römische Buchbeschreibung verglichen mit der des Vorderen Orients*, Hallische Monographien 3 (Halle: Niemeyer, 1949).

Wessetzky, Vilmos, "Bibliothek," *LÄ*, 1:783–785.

———, "Die Bücherliste des Tempels von Edfu und Imhotep," *Göttinger Miszellen* 83 (1984): 85–89.

Westbrook, Raymond, "Codification and Canonization," in Edmond Lévy, ed., *La codification des lois dans l'Antiquité: Actes du Colloque de Strasbourg, 27–29 novembre 1997* (Paris: Boccard, 2000), 33–47.

Westenholz, Aage, "Old Akkadian School Texts: Some Goals of Sargonic Scribal Education," *AfO* 25 (1974–1977): 95–110.

Westenholz, Joan Goodnick, "Oral Tradition and Written Texts in the Cycle of Akkade," in Marianna E. Vogelzang and Herman L. J. Vanstiphout, eds., *Mesopotamian Epic Literature: Oral or Aural?* (Lewiston, NY: Edwin Mellen Press, 1992), 123–154.

Wilcke, Claus, *Wer las und schrieb in Babylonien und Assyrien: Überlegungen zur Literalität im Alten Zweistromland*, Bayerische Akademie der Wissenschaften, Phil.-Hist. Klasse, Sitzungsberichte Jahrgang 2000:6 (Munich: C. H. Beck, 2000).

Williams, Ronald J., "The Sage in Egyptian Literature," in John G. Gammie and Leo G. Perdue, eds., *The Sage in Israel and the Ancient Near East* (Winona Lake, IN: Eisenbrauns, 1990), 19–30.

———, "Scribal Training in Ancient Egypt," *JAOS* 92 (1972): 214–221.

Wilson, Robert R., *Prophet and Society in Ancient Israel* (Philadelphia: Fortress Press, 1980).

Wright, Benjamin G., III, "Putting the Puzzle Together: Some Suggestions concerning the Social Location of the Wisdom of Ben Sira," *SBL 1996 Seminar Papers*, Seminar Papers Series 35 (Atlanta: Scholars Press, 1996), 133–149.

Young, Ian M., "Israelite Literacy: Interpreting the Evidence," *VT* 48 (1998): 239–253, 408–422.

Zimmerli, Walther, "Vom Prophetenwort zum Prophetenbuch," *Theologische Literaturzeitung* 104 (1979): 481–496.

Index